GIANNI VATTIMO

GIANNI VATTIMO

PHILOSOPHER, COMMUNIST, CATHOLIC, NIHILIST

THOMAS JARED FARMER

Columbia University Press   *New York*

Columbia University Press
Publishers Since 1893
New York   Chichester, West Sussex

Copyright © 2026 Columbia University Press
All rights reserved

Library of Congress Cataloging-in-Publication Data
Names: Farmer, Thomas Jared author
Title: Gianni Vattimo : philosopher, communist, Catholic, nihilist /
Thomas Jared Farmer.
Description: New York : Columbia University Press, 2026. |
Includes bibliographical references and index.
Identifiers: LCCN 2025028036 (print) | LCCN 2025028037 (ebook) |
ISBN 9780231218917 hardback | ISBN 9780231218924 trade paperback |
ISBN 9780231562492 EPUB | ISBN 9780231564915 PDF
Subjects: LCSH: Vattimo, Gianni, 1936–2023 | Postmodernism |
Philosophy and religion | Nihilism (Philosophy) | Dialectic |
Philosophers—Italy—Biography | LCGFT: Biographies
Classification: LCC B3654.V384 F37 2026 (print) | LCC B3654.V384 (ebook)

Cover image: Thomas Jared Farmer

GPSR Authorized Representative: Easy Access System Europe,
Mustamäe tee 50, 10621 Tallinn, Estonia, gpsr.requests@easproject.com

*To Amy, Liam, and Rowan, whose love and
support make everything possible*

CONTENTS

Preface ix

Introduction 1

I PHILOSOPHY

1 Early Political Thought 39
2 Weak Thought 63

II RELIGION

3 Catholicism, Secularity, and the Age of the Spirit 113
4 Religion and the (Post)Secular World 135

III REFLECTION

5 Against Nihilism: Vattimo and His Critics 157
6 Final Reflections: New Pathways in Vattimian Thought 187

Epilogue 213

Chronology 223
Notes 237
Acknowledgments 307
Works by Vattimo 309
Bibliography 319
Index 349

PREFACE

On September 19, 2023, an intellectual giant in Italian thought, the philosopher Gianni Vattimo, passed away at the Rivoli Hospital in his native Turin. He was eighty-seven years old. Although Vattimo's work is not currently well known in the English-speaking world, he was for decades at the forefront of developments in both postmodern and postmetaphysical philosophy. Vattimo first made a name for himself within his home country as a translator of Hans-Georg Gadamer and later as an astute commentator on the works of Heidegger and Nietzsche. In the early 1980s, however, he gained wider notoriety with the publication (along with Pier Aldo Rovatti) of the edited volume *Il pensiero debole* (translated as *Weak Thought*). In Italy, this work served as a flashpoint in the so-called Crisis of Reason debates then raging between a primarily older generation of neo-Enlightenment scholars—represented by figures such as Carlo Augusto Viano—and a primarily younger group of scholars influenced by schools of thought such as existentialism, Marxism, and structuralism. Outside of Italy, the work influenced similar debates around the growing cultural influence of postmodernity.

In more recent decades, Vattimo became a central figure in continental philosophy's purported "return to religion." This shift in disposition with respect to the West's legacy of Christianity in particular has paralleled Vattimo's own surprising return to the Catholicism of his youth. This reconsideration is presented most clearly in his works *Credere di credere* (*Belief*, 1996), *Dopo la cristianità: Per un cristianesimo non religioso* (*After Christianity*, 2002), and *The Future of Religion* (written with Richard Rorty, 2005). In 1999, Vattimo was elected as a member of the European Parliament. Initially a member of the Democrats of the Left, he was elected for a second term in 2009, this time as a member of the Party of Italian Communists. At first, this transition from academic philosopher to politician may seem surprising, but it reflects Vattimo's lifelong engagement with politics—not merely as theory but as praxis. That said, during this time he also made significant contributions to political theory, especially with his book *Hermeneutic Communism* (written with Santiago Zabala, 2011). Against this backdrop, then, the present book is intended to serve as a critical presentation and assessment of Vattimo's contributions to the progressive shift away from modernity (with its focus on epistemological concerns) and toward postmodernity (with its focus on issues related to language and interpretation). In addition, it examines the cultural impact of this transition in the domains of religion and politics.

Although some critics may continue to claim that postmodernity amounts to a dangerous embrace of cultural and ethical relativism, Vattimo instead argued that the recognition of independent and ever-evolving "local rationalities" helps to stave off the sort of absolutism that too frequently translates into religious or political violence. If growing knowledge about the world now renders untenable the idea that there should (or even could) be a single, stable, universal, and timeless framework for understanding ourselves and the world, then the answer cannot be to retreat (now inauthentically) back into old patterns of thought and action. Furthermore, he maintained, if it is the case that reality resists univocity, then it seems that the way in which the term *truth* has been discussed at least since modernity must now either be revised or abandoned altogether. Herein lies the nature of the claim of so-called postmetaphysics and its relation to the history of hermeneutics (the science of interpretation).

Although Vattimo often leaned into the provocative characterizations of this "post-truth" reframing—choosing to describe himself, for example, as being a "nihilist" or speaking of the need to renounce the idea of "truth"—he did not actually advocate the sort of "anything goes" relativism that postmodernists are frequently accused of promoting. That is, nowhere does he claim that every conceivable position on a given issue is of equal value. Instead, his brand of philosophy, which he termed "weak thinking," is concerned primarily with taking a standpoint of provisionality and nonabsolutism. This is especially true when speaking of "highest values," or those values that could potentially motivate one to commit an act of violence in order to uphold their traditional status. Vattimo believed that while we cannot (and perhaps should not) do without deeply held values, we should at the same time allow them to be "weakened" by the knowledge of their sociohistorical origins, their cultural situatedness, and their ultimately transitory nature.

Nowhere, however, does this pragmatic fallibilism seem more contradictory than in relation to revealed religion, which leads one to question how Vattimo could have justified a return to Christianity. Yet it is precisely by undermining the reductive understanding of truth as mere correspondence that postmodernism, according to Vattimo at least, has opened a space for the return of religion to both social life and academic discourse. Following Lyotard's understanding of postmodernism, Vattimo argued that there are no longer any compelling philosophical reasons to discard belief in God or at least to reject religious worldviews as valid. Furthermore, he argued that by rejecting a clear modernist framing of religious beliefs, one is thereby free to recognize one's own religious preferences as meaningful, without compelling one either to proselytize or to condemn others for their own particular beliefs. In Vattimo's opinion, a fallibilist hermeneutic of religion leaves room for greater freedom and mutual acceptance while also offering a deeper depth to human experience.

Given the specific sociocultural form of religious tradition and language that dominates in the Western world, Vattimo acknowledged that his own Catholic beliefs, for example, were as much a matter of historical circumstance as of conscious choice. Even so, he saw no contradiction between the "universal" claim of Christianity and his own identification with it in this recognition of cultural influence because he ultimately regarded religion as being largely an expression of culture. In this context, he often quoted the words of Benedetto Croce that "we [in the West] cannot but call ourselves Christians." What Croce meant is that to be a Westerner is to be inseparable from the history of the church and the ongoing process of secularization. Vattimo even goes so far as to suggest that the West simply is secularized Christendom. To be clear, though, what Vattimo had in mind by such statements was not support for the kind of "cultural Christianity" now increasingly promoted by certain right-wing identitarians, which, while often denying doctrinaire belief in metaphysical Christianity, explicitly seeks to maintain the exclusionary framework of Western chauvinism. Instead, borrowing biblical imagery, Vattimo drew parallels between the process of secularization—which he characterized as the church's renunciation of temporal power and authority in order to fulfill its spiritual mission—and the *kenosis*, or "self-emptying," of Christ. That is, just as God set aside his majesty to approach his creation through his humanity, so the church should step away from the quest for authority, prestige, and power to better serve the cause of human liberation. If right-wing authoritarians want to hold onto

Christendom—weaponizing Christ as a symbol even while letting the person of Jesus of Nazareth fade into irrelevance—Vattimo instead wished to see once and for all the Constantinian bargain between church and empire come to an end.

For Vattimo, therefore, the ideal of Christian caritas (charity) must supersede our traditional ideal of truth because of our growing acknowledgment of the radical conditionality of much that passes for truth, a concern about the sorts of belief structures that ultimately motivate ideological violence, and the need for mutual understanding and human liberation. Ultimately, Vattimo's unique way of merging diverse intellectual currents and conceptions distinguishes his work from that of other contemporary philosophers and theologians, making it distinctive while at the same time situating it amid broader intellectual trends and developments.

GIANNI VATTIMO

GIANNI VATTIMO

INTRODUCTION

The relationship here between hermeneutics and facticity is not a relationship between the grasping of an object and the object grasped, in relation to which the former would simply have to measure itself. Rather, interpreting is itself a possible and distinctive how *of the character of being of facticity. Interpreting is a being which belongs to the being of factual life itself.*
 —Martin Heidegger, *Ontology—the Hermeneutics of Facticity*, 1923

When it is acknowledged that under the disguise of dealing with ultimate reality, philosophy has been occupied with the precious values embedded in social traditions, that it has sprung from a clash of social ends and from a conflict of inherited institutions with incompatible contemporary tendencies, it will be seen that the task of future philosophy is to clarify men's ideas as to the social and moral strifes of their own day. Its aim is to become so far as is humanly possible an organ for dealing with these conflicts.
 —John Dewey, *Reconstruction in Philosophy*, 1920

Though not as well known in the English-speaking world as many of his contemporaries, Gianni Vattimo was easily among the most significant and original thinkers to emerge in the second half of the twentieth century. For years, he was a central figure in the interrelated areas of postmodernity, hermeneutics, and postmetaphysical thought. In addition, in more recent decades he was at the forefront of philosophical discussions concerning the continued significance of religion for contemporary life.

Vattimo initially gained notoriety as an early translator of the work of Hans-Georg Gadamer and later as an important commentator on the works of Heidegger and Nietzsche. In the early 1980s, he developed his own distinctive philosophy termed *pensiero debole*, or "weak thought." In time, this approach would influence postmodern philosophers and theologians such as Jean-François Lyotard, John D. Caputo, and Richard Rorty. Indeed, over the years, Vattimo's unique contributions to philosophy, politics, and religious thought have been recognized by the likes of Karl-Otto Apel, Jacques Derrida, René Girard, Jean-Luc Nancy, Slavoj Žižek, Jack Miles, and Charles Taylor, to name but a few.

Despite being a controversial public figure—who described himself as a "nihilist," a "gay communist," and a Catholic—Vattimo nevertheless managed to serve two terms as a representative of Italy in the European Parliament and even to maintain an unlikely personal relationship with Pope Francis.[1] He was the recipient of numerous awards, including the Max Planck-Humboldt Award for Humanities and Social Sciences (1992), the Order of Merit of the Italian Republic (1996), and the Hannah Arendt Prize for Political Thinking (2002). Vattimo delivered the prestigious Cardinal Mercier Chair Lectures at Leuven (1998) and the Gifford Lectures at the University of Glasgow (2010). He was awarded numerous honorary degrees, including from the Universities of La Plata, Palermo, Madrid, Havana, and San Marcos of Lima. In 2016, an archive and center for Vattimo studies were established at Pompeu Fabra University in Barcelona, and plans for future critical editions of his works were announced.

VATTIMO'S EARLY YEARS

On January 4, 1936, Gianteresio ("Gianni") Vattimo was born at his family's home at 10 Via Germanasca in the working-class neighborhood of Borgo San Paolo in Turin, Italy. He was named "Gianteresio" after both his grandfather, Giovanni, and his grandmother, Teresa. His father, Raffaele Vattimo (b. 1885), had been a peasant from Cetraro, a coastal town in the southern Italian region of Calabria, who relocated to the North around 1910. After his arrival in Turin, Raffaele became a police officer and met Vattimo's mother, Rosa Richiero. The two eventually married, despite a fifteen-year age difference. Rosa (b. 1900) was from Pinerolo—a town about six miles (ten kilometers) southwest of Turin.

In the spring of 1937, Raffaele contracted pneumonia and died unexpectedly. Vattimo was only sixteen months old. Rosa, who had only an elementary-school education, became a seamstress to support the family. As a result of the hardship brought about by his humble origins and his father's early death, Vattimo and his older sister, Liliana (b. 1927), grew up in a state of what he would later refer to as "dignified poverty."[2] Despite this, Vattimo's earliest memories were of a close-knit community. He spent his days playing in the streets and storefronts of his neighborhood, surrounded by the familiar faces of local tradespeople, neighbors, shop owners, and near relations.

Even so, Vattimo's early youth was overshadowed by the gathering clouds of war. The Fascist regime had come to power in 1922 with the Blackshirts' March on Rome. Benito Mussolini had spent the subsequent decade consolidating his control over the country. In October 1935, just a few months before Vattimo was born, Italy invaded Ethiopia in an abortive attempt to establish an imperialist foothold in Africa. The ensuing defeat of Italy in the Second Italo-Ethiopian War, which concluded in February 1937, led to the country's increased economic dependence on its ally—Nazi Germany. Two years later, in May 1939, Italy would sign the so-called Pact of Steel (Patto d'Acciaio) with Hitler's government. World War II would begin in September of that same year with the Nazi invasion of Poland. Italy declared war on France and Great Britain the following June.

Vattimo was just four years old when Italy entered the war and nearly ten when it ended. In later life, he would discuss the traumatic effects of having lived through this tumultuous period in Italian history. He recalled, for example, citywide blackouts, the terrifying sound of air-raid sirens in the night, and once, when he was five years old, running for shelter from bombers overhead—fearful of tripping because he did not yet know how to tie his own shoelaces.

As the capital of the Piedmont region and a major industrial center, Turin was the target of frequent bombings by the Allies throughout the war. Thus, it happened that one night—while Vattimo and his family slept in a neighbor's bomb shelter—their home, along with much of their neighborhood, was completely destroyed in an aerial bombardment. Shortly thereafter, the family took refuge in the home of an uncle in Bricherasio, about twenty-five miles (forty kilometers) southwest of Turin, before finally being evacuated to Cetraro in the South. Vattimo later recalled that the two-day train journey to his late father's home region of Calabria was spent in a state of constant anxiety that the rail lines might be bombed as well.

Vattimo's family would spend the remainder of the war years displaced but in comparative peace and safety in the South. After moving between relatives several times, the family was eventually able to rent a small section of a villa in Cetraro. In time, Vattimo settled into a new normal. He returned to school, made friends with whom he wrote and performed theater pieces, played football, read books, and learned to talk politics with the local men who would gather outside a nearby pharmacy. He dreamed of becoming a writer. It was also during this period that Vattimo began attending church regularly—soon serving as an altar boy. Although he was raised religious, his home was not especially observant. Nevertheless, in a world riven by seemingly inscrutable forces, Vattimo was drawn to the stability and routine that the Catholic Church offered. Thus, by the time he was ten years old, Vattimo had already become a seriously committed Catholic.

Following the surrender of Germany, Vattimo's family returned to Turin in September 1945. As a consequence of their long sojourn, however, Vattimo no longer spoke anything but the Calabrese dialect, which marked him out as a *terrone* (a term that means "southerner" but when used pejoratively carries the negative connotations of "peasant" or "country bumpkin"). It did not matter that he was originally from Turin or that he was a precocious child who had skipped a grade and was "already playing the intellectual": To many of his young peers, Vattimo's strange rustic accent and conspicuous religiosity meant that he must be a yokel. Years later, he would note how his unfamiliar manner of speech "earned [him] a few beatings from [his] schoolmates."[3] Thus, from a young age Vattimo was often made to feel like an outsider.

In 1949, Vattimo began studies at the prestigious Liceo Classico e Linguistico Vincenzo Gioberti (Vincenzo Gioberti State Classical and Linguistic High School), where he was a student of the notable historian Annibale Bozzola.[4] It was also during this time that his local parish priest introduced him to the neo-Thomist philosopher Monsignor Pietro Caramello. At the time, Caramello was custodian of the Shroud of Turin—which until 1983 was owned by the royal house of Savoy. He had also edited several volumes of Aquinas's work for the publishing house Marietti. Caramello quickly became a spiritual mentor, friend, and something of a surrogate father to Vattimo, who, looking back, would credit him as being "maybe the person who did the most to bring me up." Vattimo would go on to relate: "From high school until the end of university, I went to confession with him twice a week. And we took trips to the mountains alone together more than once, to the Certosa di Pesio for example, weeks divided between spiritual exercises and study. . . . Intense years, years of ardent philosophical debate."[5]

In addition to these formative experiences, Vattimo attributed his early philosophical pursuits to his growing interest in the tradition of Christian humanism. As a young man, for example, he was strongly influenced by the writings of the French lay theologians Emmanuel Mounier and Jacques Maritain. As an expression of his fervent religious commitment, he joined the student group Azione Cattolica (Catholic Action) and eventually became the organization's diocesan representative. In 1954, Vattimo finished secondary school and thereafter began studies at the University of Turin. His working-class background and the environment of radical trade unionism active in the city at that time informed his developing political sympathies. However, these factors, coupled with a growing recognition and acceptance of his own homosexuality, also created tensions with his Catholic convictions. He noted, for example, "Above all, even then, I could not accept the idea of an immutable 'natural order' (in which, apart from anything else, there would have been no place for me). And I wrestled with the idea of 'natural theology,' which drove the Catholic Church straight into the arms of the right, whereas I was on the left. Catholic, but on the left."[6]

During his early university studies, Vattimo became friends with a fellow student, the future writer Umberto Eco (1932–2016). He and Eco soon began work together as journalists at RAI—Radiotelevisione

Italiana, a national public broadcasting company, where Vattimo worked on educational programming. Eco, of course, later became a noted medievalist, literary critic, novelist, and public figure—most known in the English-speaking world as the author of the historical-fiction book *Il nome della rosa* (*The Name of the Rose*, 1980) and the intellectual detective novel *Il pendolo di Foucault* (*Foucault's Pendulum*, 1988). In academic circles, Eco is perhaps equally well known for his political essay "Ur-Fascism" (1995), in which he explores and outlines the general features of fascist ideology. In 1975, he became professor of semiotics at the University of Bologna—and remained a life-long friend to Vattimo.[7]

After three years, Vattimo quit RAI and began teaching at the Casa di Carità Arti e Mestieri (House of Charity—Art and Tradecraft), a charitable vocational and trade school run by the Catholic Church.[8] There, he taught classes on culture, civics, and religion to other working-class students. He was eventually fired from this position, however, after he took students to participate in an anti-apartheid demonstration. Soon thereafter, he became a grade-school instructor at the Rosmini High School in Turin, teaching Latin, history, Italian, and geography.

VATTIMO'S TWO "MAESTROS"

Luigi Pareyson (1918-1991)

Around his second year as a student at the University of Turin, Vattimo (along with his friend the future literary critic Marziano Guglielminetti) began attending informal gatherings of Catholic students and faculty. These meetings were organized by Michele Pellegrino, who at the time taught early Christian literature at the university.[9] It was at one of these meetings that Vattimo first became acquainted with the existentialist philosopher Luigi Pareyson.

Like Vattimo, Pareyson was Piedmontese (having been born in Piasco, northwest of Cuneo). He had also been educated at Turin—later spending the majority of his career as a professor there. As a student, Pareyson had undertaken study-abroad trips to France and Germany over the summers of 1936 and 1937, where he met and befriended such figures as Karl Jaspers, Martin Heidegger, Gabriel Marcel, René Le Senne, and Louis Lavelle. His thesis, "La filosofia dell'esistenza e C. Jaspers" (The philosophy of existence and Karl Jaspers, completed in 1939 and published in 1940), was the first major treatment of existentialist philosophy written in Italian.

During the war, Pareyson had been arrested, briefly detained, and ultimately suspended from teaching because of his participation in the anti-Fascist Resistance movement. Vattimo once noted, "Pareyson enjoyed a considerable reputation which derived from the part he played with the partisans during the war . . . but in fact he never boasted about his role in any particular way. Pareyson was an atypical partisan in many ways: monarchist, legitimist, Catholic, all in all a bit of a 'rare bird.'"[10] After the fall of fascism, Pareyson was able to resume his career. Before taking a position at Turin in 1952, he briefly taught at the National University of Cuyo in Mendoza, Argentina, and at the University of Pavia in the northern Italian region of Lombardy.

Pareyson's work focused primarily on the themes of existentialism, Christian spirituality, and aesthetics. During this time, aesthetics had become a major concern in Italian thought in large part because of the work completed in that area by Benedetto Croce and Giovanni Gentile. Pareyson took this inherited concern and advanced an original philosophy of interpretation in his book *Estetica: Teoria della formatività* (Aesthetics: Theory of formativity, 1954), where he argued that artistic creation should be viewed as an exemplification of all human activity, which he characterized as a kind of struggling toward formation. Interpretation of any human activity then discloses to the observer not simply the final result of this struggle (i.e., the artistic product) but also the internal dimensions of drive and form that brought it to fruition. As Peter Carravetta has noted, "The key term in Pareyson is *Forma* in its dynamic, interacting sense. As such *Forma* is, at any one time, either *forma formante*—form as an enabling process which gives a specific shape to whatever it is dealing with—or *forma formata*—form as what something exhibits when at rest, what makes it recognizable as such. Pareyson anchors his vision in the heart of human existence, believing that humankind in its broadest sense is essentially a producer of forms."[11]

For Pareyson, "Truth" represents the great inexhaustible wellspring of human possibility, which is made manifest in the human ability to create and interpret the creations of others. In this regard, he viewed a completed work as a "form" (*formata*)—a kind of distillation of an ongoing process: a picture in time. Interpretation, conversely, represented a "forming" (*formante*)—a continuation of that process, its continual movement. The act of interpretation, therefore, is an existential activity, a praxis—not merely a rigid methodology or the categorization of definitively identifiable things.

In 1959, Vattimo completed his thesis under Pareyson's direction and received his *laurea* from the University of Turin. The work, "Il concetto di fare in Aristotele" (The concept of *poiesis* ["making/doing"] in Aristotle), was later revised and published in 1961. The choice to focus on Aristotle may be surprising at first glance, but it was a natural outgrowth of both Vattimo's Catholic context—which was always antimodernist and at the time still predominantly neo-Thomistic in character—and the influence of Pareyson's existential aesthetics. In particular, the decision to focus on the idea of ποίησις/*poiesis* (productive activity) in Aristotle clearly stemmed from questions raised by Pareyson's own approach. Similarly, Eco had just then recently graduated with his own thesis under Pareyson, examining aesthetics through the work of Aquinas—which would inform his own later understanding of semiotics.[12]

After graduating, Pareyson asked Vattimo to stay on at the university as his assistant. Vattimo would continue to work with him in one capacity or another until Pareyson's retirement from Turin in 1988.[13] This long period of support and mentorship would prove invaluable to Vattimo, not least of all because it would be through Pareyson that Vattimo discovered the work of Nietzsche and Heidegger. Reflecting on this time, Vattimo noted: "Our intellectual relationship was really a very intense one, we would sit down together every afternoon and he would read everything that I had written: my study of Heidegger developed in parallel with the development of certain fundamental theses of his own thought."[14] Thus, Pareyson, from this early period until his death in 1991, continued to be a central figure in Vattimo's life and thought.

Hans-Georg Gadamer (1900–2002)

In 1962, Vattimo received a prestigious scholarship from the Alexander von Humboldt Foundation to travel to the University of Heidelberg to study under Husserl's and Heidegger's former students, Hans-Georg Gadamer and Karl Löwith. In the first year, he lived primarily in Germany, returning to Turin only once a month. Significantly, it was during this period, removed for the first time from both his established social network and the strong links between Italian culture and Catholicism, that Vattimo, in his view, ceased being a practicing Catholic. Upon his initial arrival in Heidelberg, he had begun attending daily services at the nearby Church of the Holy Spirit. This practice, however, soon dwindled to Sundays only and then not at all.[15] Since he was a child, Vattimo had gone to Mass every morning. Indeed, this had been an important stabilizing routine during the tumultuous years of his early childhood. Here in Heidelberg, less than a day's drive from home, however, he might as well have been a world away culturally. Later, when discussing the impact of his time away from Italy, he stated, "I know that I stopped being [a Catholic] when I no longer read the Italian newspapers. My religious commitment was so much interwoven with my philosophical and political commitment that, when I lost contact with Italian politics, *boom*, it was all over."[16]

In his second year at Heidelberg, Vattimo published his first significant work, *Essere, storia, e linguaggio in Heidegger* (Being, history, and language in Heidegger, 1963). By that time, he had begun to work again primarily as Pareyson's assistant, staying in Turin and dutifully returning to Heidelberg to attend Gadamer's lectures and to pick up his stipend. In 1964, Vattimo completed his time in Germany and began lecturing at Turin, teaching courses on Nietzsche, Heidegger, Bloch, and Schleiermacher. He soon took over Pareyson's course in aesthetics as well. During this time, he remembered, "I worked like a beast. I had to work. I was a real proletarian."[17] In addition to his university lecturing obligations (which included holding office hours three afternoons a week), he also taught classes in the mornings at the Rosminian school, worked with Pareyson on the six-volume *Enciclopedia filosofica*, and somehow still managed to find time to write. In 1967, his book *Ipotesi su Nietzsche* (Hypothesis on Nietzsche) was released, and the following year he published *Schleiermacher, filosofo dell'interpretazione* (Schleiermacher: Philosopher of interpretation, 1968), for which he was appointed full professor of aesthetics. The physical stress induced by this breakneck work pace, however, would eventually take its toll on Vattimo's health. Around this time, he developed a persistent ulcer, for which he would eventually be forced to have surgery.

Vattimo had begun working on his Italian translation of Gadamer's magnum opus *Wahrheit und Methode* (*Truth and Method*, 1960) soon after his arrival in Germany in 1962. In the summer of 1969, he began returning to Gadamer's home in Heidelberg around once a week to discuss the work. Vattimo's translation, *Verità e metodo* (published in 1970), helped to introduce Gadamer's work to an Italian audience and thereby increase interest in hermeneutic philosophy in Italy more generally. The subsequent impact of Gadamer's thought on Vattimo's own work is also readily apparent. He once noted, for example, that "it was ... from Gadamer that I learned how every experience of truth is an interpretative experience.... An act of knowing is an affair that concerns both you and the object you are interpreting: the person of the other, the work you are reading. You yourself change as you interpret that thing, but the thing changes too, because a new interpretation is stuck onto it. This approach has led me to a vision of history that I've held to ever since."[18]

This emphasis is important to recognize because Gadamer's work departs from Heidegger in a number of meaningful ways. For example, Gadamer, despite explicitly claiming that he was following Heidegger through his famous *turn*, nevertheless characterized his philosophical hermeneutics as being phenomenological in character. Thus, he continued largely to accept the ontological framework established earlier in Heidegger's *Sein und Zeit* (*Being and Time*, 1927). In addition, he readily acknowledged his debt to Husserl (from whom Heidegger had broken away), building on the former's notions of "horizon" and "life-world."[19] Stylistically, Gadamer also attempted to emulate what he saw as the clarity and precision of Husserl—eschewing where possible the confusing Heideggerian neologisms and transposing Heidegger's concepts into a more palatable or accessible register. The character of *Truth and Method* and Gadamer's approach in general can perhaps best be summed up by a famous quote from Jürgen Habermas: "Heidegger was ... a radical thinker who dug a gorge about himself. I see the greatness of Gadamer's philosophic achievement in this, that he has bridged over this gorge. The image of the bridge, of course, brings along with it misleading connotations; it awakens the impression that here someone is furnished with a pedagogical crutch for the purpose of getting closer to an unreachable place. I do not intend it in this way. Hence, I would rather say that Gadamer urbanizes the Heideggerian province."[20]

In spite of what the title *Truth and Method* might suggest, Gadamer was not seeking to establish a methodological procedure from which one could be said to *derive* truth. Instead, he focused his attention on the relationship between interpretation and understanding (*Verstehen*). In the foreword to the second edition, Gadamer says, "My real concern was and is philosophic: not what we do or what we ought to do, but what happens to us over and above our wanting and doing."[21] More specifically, the book's underlying question concerns how understanding itself is possible.

Following Heidegger, Gadamer argued that understanding is not simply one activity performed by Dasein (that being for whom being is at issue), among others, but is instead its basic mode of being/existing in the world. Accepting this hermeneutic denotes Dasein's finite and historically conditioned experience of the world as it moves toward understanding. In this way, Heidegger and Gadamer universalized hermeneutics as a component of consciousness, the character of which is shaped by specific historical conditions. Furthermore, they argued that in becoming reflectively aware of this historical dimension of understanding, modern thinkers have ever since attempted to apply to it methodological direction (e.g., Schleiermacher and Dilthey).

There is yet a further implication of this concept beyond the mere recognition that belief structures and social institutions are the products of (often arbitrary) historical processes. Gadamer also meant that consciousness is embedded in a particular topos/place (τόπος) in space and time.²² This place serves as a vantage point from which certain dimensions of reality are visible, while others are obscured.²³ At first glance, this second claim may appear almost indistinguishable from the first, but upon closer inspection one can see that it makes a much bolder assertion—namely, that the past will always remain as such to the outside observer.

Here, we might recall the opening line from L. P. Hartley's novel *The Go-Between* (1953), where the author says, "The past is a foreign country: they do things differently there."²⁴ For Gadamer, no matter how much we improve our understanding of the past, it will always remain foreign to us. That is, the world *as it was through the lens of those who experienced it* in other times and places is ultimately unrecoverable. Both senses are captured in Gadamer's term *wirkungsgeschichtliches Bewußtsein*, "historically effected consciousness"—the conditions of which act upon us whether we are aware of them or not.²⁵

This is related to the process of "self-cultivation" (*Bildung*), according to which self-knowledge is achieved through dialogue, confrontation, or encounter with an "other." This process allows for a "fusion of horizons" (*Horizontverschmelzung*), wherein the distance between two conceptual spaces, although not erased, nevertheless finds points of juncture.²⁶ As Richard J. Bernstein has noted, "Gadamer sometimes characterizes himself as a Hegelian of the 'bad infinite,' and by this he means that there is no final *Aufhebung*. Experience is always open to further experience—without end. There is no finality in understanding and interpretation."²⁷ Vattimo would second this observation by referring to both Gadamer and himself as being "watered-down Hegelians."²⁸ In this way, Gadamer gave space for a recovery of the Western tradition (in particular antiquity) as a significant conversation partner, which is arguably central for understanding Vattimo's conception of the historical process as well as his later reembrace of Christianity. In strong contrast to Heidegger, who was prepared to consign virtually the whole of the Western tradition to the dustbin of history, Gadamer says:

> What man needs is not just the persistent posing of ultimate questions, but the sense of what is feasible, what is possible, what is correct, here and now. The philosopher, of all people, must, I think, be aware of the tension between what he claims to achieve and the reality in which he finds himself. The hermeneutic consciousness, which must be awakened and kept awake, recognizes that in the age of science philosophy's claim of superiority has something chimerical and unreal about it. But though the will of man is more than ever intensifying its criticism of what has gone before to the point of becoming a utopian or eschatological consciousness, the hermeneutic consciousness seeks to confront that will with something of the truth of remembrance: with what is still and ever again real.[29]

Before moving forward, we should briefly address the now common construal of Gadamer's work as being primarily a backward-looking, conservative hermeneutics of retrieval. This view is expressed somewhat sympathetically in Habermas's description of Gadamer as being a "bridge builder" and decidedly less sympathetically by John D. Caputo in the claim that "Gadamer's 'philosophical hermeneutics' is a reactionary gesture, an attempt to block off the radicalization of hermeneutics and to turn it back to the fold of metaphysics."[30] Indeed, similar dismissive assessments have been offered at times by others, such as Simon Critchley and even Richard Rorty. But what is the substance of these characterizations?

Perhaps no gulf seems as wide and unbridgeable as the chasm between the antimetaphysician Heidegger and the archmetaphysician Plato. Yet Gadamer referred to himself as being "a student of

Heidegger" who had "learned the craft of classical philology" and as a result considered himself to be both a Heideggerian and a Platonist.[31] What are we to make of this description? Did Gadamer's supposed "domestication" of Heidegger amount to a fundamental betrayal or misapprehension of Heidegger's postmetaphysical project—as Caputo and others would have us believe—or, as Habermas intimates, is there perhaps some other game afoot?

One can adopt at least two postures with respect to looking at the past. In what we might call the "traditionalist" outlook, one views the past as a storehouse of eternal, universal, and, indeed, "natural" truths.[32] Then there is the "historicist" view, which understands cultural developments as largely a play of unconscious forces and thus the products of particular events and their influences.[33] Caputo clearly views Gadamer as a self-conscious traditionalist, knowingly rejecting the "radical" implications of Heidegger; he claims that "Gadamer pursues a more *comforting* doctrine of the fusion of horizons, the wedding of the epochs, the perpetuation of the life of the tradition which sees in Heidegger only a philosophy of appropriation and which cuts off Heidegger's self-criticism in midstream."[34] Here, it appears to me, at least, that Caputo is simply being uncharitable to the point of distortion. Indeed, Caputo's book *Radical Hermeneutics* as a whole appears to have no real interest in presenting Gadamer's project except as a hapless foil to Caputo's preferred project of Derridean deconstruction.[35]

As David Tracy has noted, however, "There is no reason why Gadamerian hermeneutics should not be interpreted as both a hermeneutics of retrieval and a hermeneutics of suspicion, since it is constituted by two grounding principles: dialogical retrieval and *wirkungsgeschichtliches Bewußtsein*. As a dual hermeneutics, Gadamer's hermeneutics is, in principle, open to any other contemporary critical theory, in spite of Gadamer's own rather conservative tendencies."[36]

Likewise, Vattimo—whom no one could reasonably hold as betraying Heidegger from the right—always viewed Gadamer and Heidegger as being fundamentally two points on the same sliding axis. In this regard, he noted:

> Hermeneutics reveals its constitutive characteristics: those of ontology and *Sprachlichkeit*, linguisticality. In spite of all the emphasis that Heidegger places on language, especially in the later phase of his thought, he regards interpretation primarily from the point of view of the meaning of Being: in spite of all the emphasis that Gadamer places on ontology, interpretation is thought primarily from the point of view of language[;] . . . the intention here is not to return to Heidegger in a reversal of the Gadamerian urbanization. On the contrary, there is a decisive need to urbanize Heidegger's thought in many senses. . . . But such urbanization will be truly successful only if one does not forget the specifically Heideggerian ontological aspect of the discourse.[37]

The Groundwork for Weak Thought

In 1974, Vattimo succeeded Pareyson as chair of aesthetics at Turin. That same year he published his pivotal book *Il soggetto e la maschera* (*The Subject and the Mask*). This work is significant in Vattimo's development because it represents the high point of a perspective that he began developing around 1968 but would eventually reject in favor of weak thought. In 1978, he published the essay "*An-denken*: Il pensare e il fondamento" ("*An-denken*: Thinking and Foundation") in *Nuova corrente*. This work, which was later included in the book *La avventure della difference* (*The Adventure of Difference*, 1980), laid much of the conceptual groundwork for the development of his subsequent thought.

In 1979, Vattimo wrote the essay "Verso un'ontologia del declino" ("Towards an Ontology of Decline"), which two years later appeared in his book *Al di là del soggetto: Nietzsche, Heidegger, e l'emeneutica* (*Beyond the Subject: Nietzsche, Heidegger, and Hermeneutics*, 1981).[38] It is here that Vattimo first introduced the term *pensiero debole*, "weak thought." In 1983, Vattimo (along with Pier Aldo Rovatti) published an edited volume entitled *Il pensiero debole*. It was this book that popularized the idea of *weak* thinking and thereby sparked a debate in philosophical circles both inside and outside Italy. Vattimo stated later, "The concept of 'weak thought' is a product, in the first place, of a certain confluence between the existentialist and hermeneutic traditions . . . the idea that truth is essentially an experience of interpretation, and that human existence possesses an intrinsically hermeneutical character."[39]

We are always immersed in a context that gives us a certain preunderstanding of the world, and every subsequent interpretation is shaped by that context. We can no longer naively accept the traditional empiricist claim that we can simply access objects directly as if we were a blank slate. According to Vattimo, Heidegger's prominence as a theorist of both existential and hermeneutic thought is no coincidence because to view human existence outside the traditional metaphysical concept of "objectivity" is to recognize its inherently interpretative nature. In addition, weak thought emerges from the shift from neopositivist philosophy to linguistic philosophy. Building on the insights derived from Wittgenstein's later work, philosophy evolved into a form of analysis that acknowledges the diversity of our language games. From this viewpoint, avoiding philosophical errors means adhering to the specific rules of each language game. In this sense, weak thought arises from the understanding that in our actual experience of the world, we are always dealing with texts and words rather than with direct facts.

Perhaps even more than the general philosophical environment of the second half of the twentieth century, however, it was the influence of the political situation in Italy during the late 1960s and throughout the 1970s that ultimately proved decisive for Vattimo's development of the concept of weak thought. As Jon R. Snyder has observed, "Vattimo makes relatively few references to the work of other Italian philosophers past or present."[40] Yet Italian social and political conditions never seem to be very far from his mind. Whether it has been in his capacity as a representative of Italy in the European Parliament or through his numerous public talks, interviews, or articles written for popular publications (especially *La Stampa* and *L'Unità*), Vattimo always maintained a strong connection to the public life of his home country. Thus, it will be necessary to register here at least some brief comments on two interrelated social developments that provide the proper context for understanding the emergence of weak thought: the student protests of 1968 and the so-called Anni di Piombo (Years of Lead) that followed them in Italy.

A BRIEF ACCOUNT OF ITALY IN THE TWENTIETH CENTURY

Before the establishment of the First Republic in 1946, Italy had remained essentially a peasant-agricultural country with a predominantly rural population.[41] For example, as late as 1952 only a quarter of Italian homes had an indoor bathroom, while roughly half still lacked running water.[42] Italy's fortunes, however, would drastically change in the postwar years, especially after 1958, primarily because of increased integration into European markets. In 1949, Italy became a founding member of NATO, joined the United Nations in 1955, and (with the Treaty of Rome in 1957) helped to establish the European Economic Community—which was later absorbed into the European Union in 1993.

As an ally of the United States, Italy also benefited greatly from foreign aid through the Marshall Plan.[43] Under this arrangement, between 1948 and 1952 Italy received aid amounting to roughly $12 billion (or, an average 2.3 percent of its gross domestic product for five years).[44] More importantly, it reduced the "dollar gap" for imported goods, which helped to stabilize the economy.[45] Finally, trade allowed for the development of important sectors previously hampered by a lack of domestically available resources (such as energy and steel). Access to these sectors increased industrialization in northern manufacturing centers such as Milan, Genoa, and Turin, which in turn led to massive internal migration and increased urbanization.[46] These conditions, along with increased international tourism, worked in concert to give rise to the so-called economic miracle (*il boom economico*)—a sustained growth through the 1960s that in a relatively short period drastically raised standards of living throughout much of the country.

The official end of Mussolini's Fascist regime shortly before the end of World War II, to be sure, greatly affected the shape of the political situation for years to come. From its inception in 1944 until 1994, post-Fascist Italy was dominated by a single political party— the centrist and Catholic-influenced Democrazia Cristiana (DC, Christian Democracy Party). Even while frequently not holding an outright majority, the party consistently led a moderate coalition of center-left and center-right groups, with the main opposition initially coming from the far-left Partito Comunista Italiano (PCI, Italian Communist Party).[47] The Christian Democrats enjoyed wide support from more conservative regions in the south and northeastern regions of the country, while the PCI held sway among industrial workers in the densely populated metropolitan areas of the northwestern region. Despite being the largest party of its kind in the West at this time, the PCI (along with much smaller factions of far-right neofascists) long found itself effectively blocked from political power. The Christian Democrats (while later widely considered corrupt) were able effectively to remain in power largely because of fears among the liberal-conservative establishment and their U.S. backers that Communists could gain control of the country.

In 1968, violence and protest broke out in many locations across the globe. In Ireland, for example, civil rights activists marched in Derry, flouting a government ban on protests. They were met with violence by the Royal Ulster Constabulary, who beat them indiscriminately without provocation. This act of suppression became an important flashpoint in the lead-up to "The Troubles."[48] There were protests in Brazil and Pakistan against their respective military dictatorships.[49] In Egypt, the military suppressed antigovernment demonstrations by force. Elsewhere in Africa, there were notable (mostly student-led) protest movements in Morocco, Tunisia, Ethiopia, Tanzania, and the Congo. Protests in Mexico culminated in the Tlatelolco massacre, which saw government forces firing on demonstrators in Mexico City.[50] In Germany, England, and Japan, there were large-scale protests against U.S. involvement in the Vietnam War. There were student-led protests in Sweden against South African apartheid. Mass movements for peace, environmentalism, decolonization, gay rights, women's rights, sexual liberation, racial equity, and nuclear disarmament began or gained traction during this period—each meeting resistance, often violently, from opposing parties and establishment forces.[51]

In the United States, tensions over the conflict in Vietnam were at an all-time high. In March 1968, President Lyndon Johnson announced that he would not seek reelection. On April 4, Dr. Martin Luther King Jr. was assassinated in Memphis. On June 6, Robert Kennedy (brother of slain President John F. Kennedy) was assassinated in California as he ran for the Democratic nomination for president. In August, the Democratic National Convention was held in Chicago, where it was met with massive protests against both the Vietnam War and the Democrats' likely selection of pro-war Vice President Hubert Humphrey as their nominee. The selection of Humphrey would essentially leave both major political parties in the United States committed to continuing the unpopular conflict. In November, Republican nominee Richard M. Nixon defeated Humphry.

At the University of Paris at Nanterre, students began protesting against living conditions on campus and the broader social constraints they perceived in the country. Their protest quickly merged with political resistance to the conservative presidency of Charles de Gaulle and with general opposition to capitalism, consumerism, and American and French foreign policy. Arrests were made, and the campus was temporarily closed. In solidarity, students at the Sorbonne occupied a nearby amphitheater in protest. The Paris police responded with brutality to this provocation. A riot ensued, and hundreds were quickly arrested. In a matter of days, protests against police brutality expanded into a cultural revolt. As the journalist Eleanor Beardsley later stated in 2018, "The students' demands were diffuse—more philosophical than political."[52]

Sensing an opportunity, workers across the country used the moment to call a general strike in a demand for higher wages, better working conditions, and greater union representation. Around 10 million French workers walked off the job, bringing economic life to a standstill and threating to cause the collapse of the government. In May, President de Gaulle was forced to dissolve the National Assembly and call new elections. The French Communist Party, unwilling to seize control of the government by force, however, accepted the new elections as a compromise to avoid (a likely failed) revolution—an action for which the party's most radical Leninist-Maoist factions would never forgive it.

In Italy, the student movement likewise coincided with unrest among radical workers in places such as Milan. Nevertheless, unlike elsewhere, the demands of dissatisfied working-class Italians oftentimes quickly outpaced those of students (who were typically the children of more affluent bourgeois families) and even of the workers' own unions (which were forced then to catch up with their members).[53] A general strike was called in November, and a lockout of workers in December. Workers picketed, occupied areas, and even engaged in militant direct (or "wildcat") actions, such as sabotage and violence against bosses. A complicating factor in Italy, which was less pronounced elsewhere, was the presence of unofficial far-right fascist groups, which organized to respond to leftist students and workers with their own acts of political violence.

In Naples, radical students occupied a section of the city's university. In response, three fascist organizations took control of the faculty of law offices nearby. With police support, the fascists soon violently expelled the students from the offices. Fascists also firebombed a "house of students and workers" that had been established in an old hotel in the city. Similar actions occurred across the country as a cycle of increasing violence between leftist students/workers and government officials/right-wing paramilitary groups began to spin out of control. As Arthur Marwick has noted, "There was a deep sense that student agitation, then worker's agitation, was now giving way to haphazard terrorism."[54]

In March, as student protests were beginning in Paris, Vattimo was convalescing from ulcer surgery. To pass the time, he occupied himself by delving deeper into Marxist literature, and on March 13 he declared himself to be a Maoist. In effect, he was affirming himself to be a Marxist, albeit one who was opposed to the official PCI of the period—which radicals had begun to criticize for allegedly losing revolutionary fervor and instead settling into a moderate Soviet-backed dogmatism.[55]

It is perhaps here worth briefly explaining the significance of this transition in the political context of the time. In much the way that the memory of the February and October Revolutions in Russia will perhaps always be colored (for better or worse) by the historical knowledge of the Stalinist regime that would eventually succeed in their wake, it is perhaps difficult in hindsight to understand the widespread appeal of Maoism to liberationist and revolutionary movements of the 1960s. Much of this appeal, however, can be attributed to the favorable depiction of Mao in Edgar Snow's influential book *Red Star Over China*, published in 1937. Furthermore, at the time, Mao's emphasis on the agrarian peasantry serving as the vanguard of revolutionary Marxism—given the preindustrial condition of much of China during this period—had mass appeal as an "update" to orthodox Marxist doctrine, which gave pride of place to the most marginalized in the global struggle against capitalism.

This appeal also cannot be separated from the geopolitical situation of that moment, when opposition to U.S. involvement in the Vietnam War equated in many people's minds to support for the North Vietnamese and by extension for China. In addition, Mao's split in relations with the Soviet Union over the latter's bureaucratic structure and so-called revisionism found a receptive audience among those who were critical of the United States but also disillusioned with the leadership of the Soviet Union. Likewise, militant leftists supported the actions of the Cultural Revolution (1966–1976), which sought to undermine the entrenched social norms that, according to Mao and his supporters, perpetuated historical hierarchies and thus impeded the development of socialism.

The violence associated with many of these Maoist reforms was not widely known among Western leftists. Any negative reports of actual conditions were either (not unreasonably) dismissed as Western-capitalist propaganda or simply excused as regrettable but ultimately necessary means to an end. Over the next decade, as the crimes and death tolls associated with policies such as the

Great Leap Forward (1958–1962) became more readily known and considered factual, Western-leftist admiration for Mao waned heavily.⁵⁶ In any event, support for Mao in the West during the 1960s and early 1970s was arguably more defensible than many would consider it to be today.⁵⁷

For his part, Vattimo, in spite of his political conversion, did not immediately warm to the emerging student movement, stating later, "My stance as an *anticapitalist romantic* made me think: the capitalist world is a big rubbish heap, but these people here, these *well-bred students*, will never change anything, much less make the revolution."⁵⁸ Indeed, the student demands at Turin mostly concerned reorganizing the institutes into departments. Even so, leftist agitation by students in local factories and the distribution of political leaflets to workers would help to bring about a major shift in mood within the following year.

In what has since become known as the Autunno Caldo (Hot Autumn), waves of strikes began among dissatisfied workers in the North. The epicenter of this struggle was Vattimo's hometown of Turin, where Fiat workers began to organize themselves across unions to form workers' assemblies. Control thereby shifted away from official union leadership toward younger "unskilled" laborers (usually exploited transplants from the South). Strikes soon became endemic and expanded demands from better pay to health and safety issues, better union representation, greater rights for women, and so on. This shift is best captured by the workers' slogan "Vogliamo tutto"—We want everything!⁵⁹ They even challenged Fiat's owner, Gianni Agnelli, declaring, "Indochina [Vietnam] is in your factory!"⁶⁰

It was during this time that Vattimo began doing serious work in Nietzschean studies.⁶¹ The impact of the period's political events on Vattimo's thinking is little commented on and thus does not appear sufficiently appreciated in much of the secondary literature, but it simply cannot be overstated. Vattimo himself alludes to this fact by arguing,

> Italian interpretations of Nietzsche are characterized, in comparison to French ones, by a closer (and perhaps more "ideological") relationship with political events, since they took shape in the 1970s in very close contact with movements of the extreme left; and that for this reason they show a tendency not to settle for a merely critical-suspensive Nietzsche but strive to read him in a fuller sense, as the possible point of reference for a postmetaphysical philosophy. Both these characteristics, in my view, distinguish them fairly sharply from French interpretations, which, despite the undoubted political engagement ... of philosophers like Foucault and Deleuze, appear from this side of the Alps to have a lot more to do with artistic and literary experimentation, given their (quite obvious) links to the avant-garde.[62]

In the summer of 1972, Vattimo wrote *Il soggetto e la maschera*. The work attempts to read Nietzsche through a Heideggerian lens—Vattimo had published *Introduzione ad Heidegger* (Introduction to Heidegger) the year before.[63] While this reading, of itself, is perhaps not unique, the innovative element in Vattimo's approach was to view Nietzsche as a kind of libertarian-anarchist, even a "cryptocommunist prophet" for the "total revolution."[64] He meant that Marx, in spite of all of his insight and perspicacity, nevertheless continued to work within the constraints of a modernist metaphysical framework. By extension, the student movement suffered the same limitations. In discussions with Pareyson, Vattimo came to agree with the sentiment that "we [Heideggerians] are much more revolutionary than that lot [the students], all they want is to change a few university structures, we are people absolutely outside the organicity of this situation." Vattimo remarked later: "When Heidegger says that there is not principally man but Being, and we reply, Being thinks itself in us, well, that's Marx: There's no use exerting yourself trying to be different if society doesn't change. Marx imagines you can do it by taking the Winter Palace. Okay, but slow down. In order to take the Winter Palace, a quantity of conditions have to be realized, which it isn't that far-fetched to call Heidegger's Being. There needs to be a *great transformation*."[65]

Moving Marxism toward an acceptance of this Nietzschean-Heideggerian transformation as a condition of its realization was the intention of *The Subject and the Mask*, which was published in 1974. This reading of Nietzsche—which Vattimo would later acknowledge was too closely affected by "the spirit of '68"—argued that Marxist alienation can be equated with metaphysics in the Heideggerian sense. Thus, "the revolution, if it occurs, can succeed only by eliminating the persistent metaphysical residues that still weigh down the thought of Marx, a task to be accomplished with the help of Nietzsche's genealogical critique."[66] Nevertheless, Vattimo would eventually come to reject this formulation in at least two crucial respects.

The first came by way of realizing that the dialectical reconciliation of the subject and its essence proposed in Marx is not so easily convertible into the Heideggerian goal of overcoming metaphysics or the Nietzschean project of the Übermensch. The structure and teleology of the dialectic is still too shot through with metaphysical assumptions. Vattimo would eventually conclude that in order to be faithful to Nietzsche's postmetaphysical critique, he would have to follow the argument through to its logical terminus in nihilism. The second major departure was rejecting Heidegger's actual reading of Nietzsche and substituting in its place a more *Heideggerean* reading—which meant not taking seriously what Heidegger actually said about Nietzsche, "whom he sees merely as the last thinker of metaphysics." "My purpose," Vattimo said, "is to remain faithful to Heidegger even against the letter of his writings, recognizing that in order to really overcome metaphysics (Being as no more than presence, objectivity, and so on) we must follow Nietzsche into nihilism[;] . . . we must 'relinquish Being as the ground.'"[67] "One must say that the search begun in *Sein und Zeit* does not send us in the direction of going beyond nihilism, but rather of experiencing nihilism as the only possible path of ontology."[68]

In 1974, the Partito Radicale (Radical Party) successfully organized a political alliance to pass referendums on divorce and reproductive rights. That same year, the Fronte Unitario Omosessuale Rivoluzionario Italiano (Revolutionary Homosexual United Front, or "FUORI!"—the Italian word for "Out!") aligned itself with the Radical Party. In 1976, FUORI! wanted to run at least one homosexual candidate for every slate of that year's election. Party officials selected Vattimo without his knowledge and published his name as a candidate for FUORI in national newspapers without his consent. Although it had been an open secret among those who knew Vattimo that he lived with his partner, Gianpiero Cavaglià, he had not yet made his sexuality public. He later said, "They hadn't even asked me beforehand. They hadn't even told me afterward. I found out I was a candidate in the elections, and a homosexual candidate at that, from the papers. Perhaps if they had asked me first I wouldn't have accepted, but by now it was done. There it was in writing. It was official."[69]

Though he had never before run for office, this was not his first time participating in political action. In addition to his labor organizing and participation in strikes as a youth, for which he was asked to leave the Catholic lay organizations Azione Cattolica and the Fratelli delle Scuole Cristiane (Fratres Scholarum Christianarum), Vattimo also translated Irish Republic Army documents from English for a left-wing trade-union organization and as an assistant professor even found himself on the cover of *L'Unità* for his arrest while picketing outside a Fiat branch at Lingotto in Via Nizza.[70]

POST-'68 VIOLENCE AND THE ORIGINS OF WEAK THOUGHT

In 1978, at the height of political tensions in the country and despite his professed Maoism, Vattimo, along with another noted professor, Norberto Bobbio, was targeted by the Leninist guerilla group Brigate Rosse (Red Brigade) for the crime of being insufficiently radical. This was no idle threat. Vattimo was being targeted around the same time that the brigade kidnapped and murdered Aldo Moro, the former prime minister of Italy and a center-left Christian Democrat. From its beginning in the 1960s, the brigade engaged in acts of symbolic violence: beatings, robberies, kidnappings, and intimidation. In 1974, during a raid on the headquarters of the Italian neofascist party Movimento Sociale Italiano in Padua, brigade members killed two neofascists. On November 16, 1977, it assassinated the journalist Carlo Casalegno. In 1979 alone, there were more than two thousand separate terrorist incidents in Italy, many involving the Red Brigade. After Vattimo spent some time in hiding, however, tensions cooled enough for him to safely return to Turin.

His rejection of his earlier position in *The Subject and the Mask* was accompanied by his acceptance of ideas that would eventually grow into the concept of weak thought. According to Vattimo's close associate Santiago Zabala, "For Vattimo, the conceptual problem started when some of those arrested [for terrorism] wrote letters from prison (read to the philosopher by other students) that were, in his view, full of a 'metaphysical and violent rhetorical subjectivity' that he could accept neither morally nor philosophically. Vattimo realized at the time that his 'Nietzschean superman revolutionary

subject' had been misinterpreted and could not be identified with
the students' 'Leninist revolutionary subject.' Reading these 'metaphysical' letters made Vattimo realize that the ethical interpretation
of nihilism and of Heidegger's ontological difference created and
justified weak thought."[71]

In his book *Non essere Dio* (*Not Being God*, 2006), Vattimo spoke
in particular of one student possessed of "such revolutionary moralism" that Vattimo said to himself, "Is this supposed to be my new
Nietzschean overman?" "Take power? Look how that turns out . . .
give me a break!"[72] Richard Drake echoes this sentiment in his discussion of the legacy of terrorism during the Years of Lead when he
remarks, "The Red Brigades appealed to a core element in the Italian political tradition: *the religious faith of the extreme left in revolution*. This faith, going back to the French Revolution, has never
wanted for votaries in modern Italy. . . . The amazing destructiveness and staying power of the Red Brigades depended ultimately on
their success in gaining the support of astonishingly large numbers
of people who believed in revolution as something sacred."[73] Thus, as
Zabala has observed, "Weak thought came to life not out of fear of
terrorism but as a response to the terrorist interpretation of the Italian democratic left during the 1970s—as a recognition of the unacceptability of the Red Brigade's violence."[74] For his part, Vattimo
ultimately concluded that in politics "we should just obstruct the
development of the system; it's the only thing we can do. And [this]
contained a hint of the idea of weakening as a way of eluding power.
All powers, and at all levels. *Autonomia* appeared to me," he said, "as
a nonviolent form of anarchism."[75]

OVERVIEW

In part 1, "Philosophy," chapters 1 and 2 provide a detailed discussion of Vattimo's political and philosophical work, including an evaluation of concepts such as "weak thought," "truth," "*Verwindung*," "nihilism," and "hermeneutical communism." Such close analysis is necessary because Vattimo frequently used these and other familiar terms from the lexicon of recent philosophical thought in idiosyncratic ways. Failing to understand Vattimo's distinctive language will invariably lead to hopeless misunderstanding and mischaracterization.

In philosophical terms, Vattimo argued that the horizons of our understanding are historically and culturally conditioned. Thus, all claims to truth are necessarily mediated. For example, there cannot exist a Punctum Archimedis (Archimedian point, or "view from nowhere"), even in principle. For Vattimo, like Gadamer before him, to see is to see from a specific vantage point. The sort of questions we can ask and the corresponding shape of the answers we will find satisfying are thus constrained by our overall context. While education and experience can broaden the scope of our viewpoint—leading to a "fusion of horizons"—they cannot fundamentally alter the state of situatedness itself. Such a construal of understanding, however, has implications.

If the hope for grasping the fixed foundations of life and the world—the "really Real," the capital-T "Truth"—is fundamentally misplaced, then Vattimo (like Heidegger) reasoned that the traditional pursuit of metaphysics seems to have run aground. This is how such disparate expressions such as "the death of God," "the end of metaphysics," and "the linguistic turn" can essentially describe the same event. The wholesale rejection of the Platonic ideal of one overarching unified sense of the ideal state of being and of ever hoping to know that which lies *beyond phenomena* (or "mere appearance") becomes a moment within the shift in emphasis toward the conditions for interpretation. Rejecting any objective ground for privileging one symbolic system, paradigm, or way of orientating oneself in the world leads to a conclusion one can call the *death of God*—at least, a death of the "God of the philosophers," or God understood as an ontotheological "first principle," being the most radical symbolic expression of the ideal of objective measure.

This has led to a *weakening* of the foundations upon which the edifice of Western thought resides—that is, it amounts to a qualification of what this metaphysical framework can reasonably claim to be. These foundations can never really be destroyed. But they exist now most saliently as a historical reference point—a philosophical inheritance. We cannot, as it were, wipe the sleight clean and start from the beginning again. The world we find is always-already interpreted. We cannot, for example, read Aristotle without Aquinas, St. Paul without Augustine, Hegel without Christ. The West is incomprehensible without the legacy of Christianity and Greek philosophy. If the claims of these traditions now seem to be losing their grip on our collective consciousness, however, Vattimo contended, the answer cannot be simply a reactionary push to reaffirm the old order. Instead, the moment requires of us yet another reinterpretation of our shared symbols, a reinterpretation that will give renewed life to the present. Weak thought represents a *tempering* of our certainties, if not necessarily of our commitments to them. This recognition that we are inextricably bound to structures of belief—along with the recognition and acknowledgment of the ambivalence we often feel toward their strong exclusionary truth claims in light of postmodern orientation toward hermeneutics—informs every aspect of Vattimo's philosophy and return to religion.

Ultimately, the basis for a democratic order in which the competing play of interpretations is taken for granted is the mutual commitment to reduce violence. By "violence," Vattimo meant not merely physical coercion but also "the preemptory assertion of an ultimacy that, like the ultimate metaphysical foundation (or God of philosophers), breaks off dialogue and silences the interlocutor by refusing even to acknowledge the question 'why?'"[76] The need for alternative horizons is necessary because "truth" in this sense can never be fully sublated into a system. There will always be some aspect of truth that resists this integration—some dialectical remainder that preserves truth's dynamic character through its refusal of completion. If anything, in the moment of truth's resistance, the really crucial element of truth resides here, in this fragment, not in the system that seeks to absorb it. Thus, part 1 focuses on establishing an understanding of weak ontology as a condition of the social order that Vattimo envisioned.

The principle Vattimo works under consideration in this part include *Le avventure della differenza: Che cosa significa pensare dopo Nietzsche e Heidegger* (1980), *Al di là del soggetto: Nietzsche, Heidegger, e l'emeneutica* (1981), *Il pensiero debole* (edited with Pier Aldo Rovatti, 1983), *La fine della modernità: Nichilismo ed ermeneutica nella cultura post-moderna* (1985), *La società trasparente* (1989), *Oltre l'nterpretazione* (1994), *Nichilismo ed emancipazione: Etica, politica, diritto* (2003), *Addio alla verità* (2009), *Hermeneutic Communism: From Heidegger to Marx* (written with Santiago Zabala, 2011), *Della realtà* (2012), and *Essere e dintorni* (2018).

In part 2, "Religion," chapters 3 and 4 provide a detailed discussion of Vattimo's later work intersecting the areas of religion and theology, including an evaluation of his use of terms such as *kenosis, salvation history, secularization,* and *charity*. Vattimo frequently framed his philosophical arguments in the language of Christian theology. Again, one must remember that, for Vattimo, history and culture play decisive roles in shaping every aspect of our identities. One must recognize that in the end the West simply cannot break from its historic links to Christianity.

Indeed, in a radical sense for Vattimo, the West simply is *secularized* Christendom—that is, Christianity that has undergone the process of "weakening." "Secularization" is a concept with a very specific meaning for Vattimo. He characterized it as "a relation of provenance from a sacred core from which one has moved away, but which nevertheless remains active even in its 'fallen,' distorted version, reduced to pure worldly terms."[77] For this reason, he frequently invoked the title to an essay by Benedetto Croce, "Perchè non passiamo non dirci cristiani" ("Why We Cannot but Call Ourselves Christians") to tie many of the features of Western modernity—for example, equality, democracy, liberalism, subjectivity, and rationality—to the cultural inheritance of Christianity. Perhaps drawing on influence from another of his Heidelberg teachers, Karl Löwith, he contended that even the movement toward postmodernity itself should likewise be viewed as an event in salvation history (*Heilsgeschichte*).

Secularization is a return/recovery of religion in a weaker (and thus, in his terms, a more acceptable) form for a society that is at least nominally seeking pluralism and democracy. However, this recovery is not simply a return—in the sense of going back to a previous form of religiosity. Rather, it is like the preservation of a remnant, a stone recovered from wreckage that will in turn form the basis of a new edifice. In this, he believed, Christian society must repudiate its history of *universalism* (conceived of as the civilizing mission of imperialism and colonialism) and instead become "an authentic interlocutor in a cultural dialogue" by presenting itself as "a bearer of the idea of secularity for the sake of its own specific authenticity."[78] Being a first among equals necessarily undermines the notion of equality. This being the case, the universalism of Christianity should move away from the exclusive claim of possessing the absolute truth and instead toward the more radical universality of lived hospitality.

As a political practice and a religious ideal, Christianity should, where necessary, subordinate its claims to truth in favor of its commitments to charity (caritas). Vattimo gave a paraphrased quote from Aristotle's *Nicomachean Ethics* 1096a (cf. *Phaedo* 91b–c), "Plato is my friend, but truth is yet a greater friend [Amicus Plato sed magis mica veritas]," and compared it with a letter written by Dostoyevsky that says: "If someone proved to me that Christ is outside the truth and that in reality the truth were outside of Christ, then I should prefer to remain with Christ rather than with the truth."[79]

In keeping with the reimagining of Christian symbols and expressions, Vattimo adopted/appropriated the kenotic event as the paradigmatic representation of Christianity as weak ontology. The Incarnation does not affirm the rational order of the world. Indeed, it subverts it. For example, the last are first; kindness is owed to enemies; God has become man; and, indeed, power is made perfect in weakness (cf. 2 Cor. 12:9). In the Incarnation Vattimo perceived a radical inversion of the alterity found in the wholly transcendent and "world-denying omni-God" proclaimed in metaphysics. God's self-emptying reveals the dissolution of the violence of the sacred by the figure of the incarnated Christ, who redefines the sacred instead as radical inclusionary love.

In the end, truth, for Vattimo—the truth that matters for lived experience, anyway, that which relates to "value-rational action" (*Wertrational*)—is not a determination of the correspondence of sense impressions to mind-independent data. It is not incorrigible knowledge built upon an unshakable metaphysical foundation guaranteed by God as first principle. Rather, it emerges through the vulnerability of mystery, openness, and the commitment—in spite of the danger—to the love of our neighbor even amid the cloud of our own unknowing.

The principle Vattimo works under consideration in these chapters include *Credere di credere* (1996), *La religion: Seminaire de Capri* (edited with Derrida, 1996), *Dopo la cristianità: Per un cristianesimo non religioso* (2002), *The Future of Religion* (written with Rorty and edited by Zabala, 2005), *Verità o fede debole? Dialogo su cristianesimo e relativismo* (written with Girard, 2006), and *After the Death of God* (written with Caputo, 2007).

In part 3, "Reflection," chapters 5 and 6 serve as an overview and reflection on previous chapters. Here, I offer critical reflections on the contributions of Vattimo's project to postmetaphysical philosophy as measured against its own methodology and professed goals. Having done this, I evaluate (what are in my estimation, at least) the most salient criticisms of Vattimo's work. In particular, I examine the continued relevance of postmetaphysical hermeneutics in light of the recent return of metaphysical thinking in certain areas of theology and the philosophy of religion. Finally, in my concluding remarks I outline some of my own proposals for discussions in the future of Vattimian studies.

I
PHILOSOPHY

1

EARLY POLITICAL THOUGHT

The identification of theory and practice is a critical act, through which practice is demonstrated rational and necessary, and theory realistic and rational. This is why the problem of the identity of theory and practice is raised especially in the so-called transitional moments of history, that is, those moments in which the movement of transformation is at its most rapid.
—Antonio Gramsci, *The Prison Notebooks*, 1929–1935

In Soviet Marxism, historical materialism becomes one particular branch of the general scientific and philosophical system of Marxism which, codified into an ideology and interpreted by the officials of the Party, justifies policy and practice.... The dialectical process thus interpreted is no longer in a strict sense a historical process—it is rather that history is reified into a second nature.
—Herbert Marcuse, *Soviet Marxism: A Critical Analysis*, 1958

It is often noted that when beginning his lecture series on Aristotle, Heidegger did not provide the usual biographical sketch of the philosopher expected in any general introduction. Instead, he simply said, "The only thing of interest regarding the person of a philosopher is this: He was born on such and such a date, he worked, and he died."[1] By this, Heidegger meant that what matters in understanding a thinker is not the particular circumstances of their life but rather the work they leave behind. Although this approach is perhaps reasonable when considering Aristotle, it would be a wholly mistaken starting point for understanding Vattimo. Indeed, in an interview in 2009 Vattimo remarked, "When I look back over the past, I realize that my own biography has been very bound up with ideological matters. At the same time, my thought is a reflection of events: in some cases, I have simply echoed issues and problems that were part of the general environment around me, part of the air I was breathing every day. . . . My decision to study philosophy [for example] was largely a consequence of my religious commitment and my militant political attitude."[2]

Perhaps nowhere is the influence of circumstance more evident than in the development of Vattimo's most important contribution to postmetaphysical philosophy—namely, the concept of "weak thought." These first two chapters therefore focus specifically on the origin and shape of as well as the response to debolist thinking as it emerged in the late 1970s. In this chapter, I begin by exploring the background of philosophical currents in Italy at the time and tracing Vattimo's philosophical thought from its earliest period through to the development of his first critical philosophy as presented in his work *The Subject and the Mask* (1974). In the next chapter, I provide a detailed overview of weak thought along with some of the prominent criticisms made against it. Finally, in that same chapter, I end part 1 by exploring the political program for weak thought as presented most notably in Vattimo's work *Hermeneutic Communism* (2011, cowritten with Santiago Zabala).

ROMANTIC ANTICAPITALISM

Vattimo characterized his political position before 1969 as being one of "romantic anticapitalism."[3] It is here useful to remember that being anticapitalist in this context did not always mean identifying as a leftist. Though Vattimo would, of course, eventually move leftward politically, the overall thrust of his antimodernist, anticapitalist sentiment was not itself necessarily out of step with his early Italian Catholic milieu. For example, the official Catholic response concerning the rights and social conditions of the modern industrial worker during this period had been outlined much earlier in Pope Leo XIII's encyclical *Rerum novarum* (1891). In addition, Pius XI had later expanded upon these positions in his encyclical *Quadragesimo anno* (1931). Together, these two major works formed the basis for early Catholic social thought, which in the 1960s and 1970s stressed an "integralist" position that argued that Catholicism should be the basis for both civil law and public policy. With respect to class divisions, however, it stressed cooperation rather than conflict between workers and owners.[4] In essence, Catholic social thought attempted to delineate a distinctive "third way" for criticizing modern industrial society from a traditionalist (rather than liberal or Marxist/socialist) framework—one that severally recognized the destructive and dehumanizing effects of both capitalist exploitation and Communist collectivization.

To better accommodate this integralist position, the ecclesiastical hierarchy had sought among other things to establish separate Catholic trade unions under the church's auspices. In Catholic-majority countries such as Italy, these unions functioned as one way in which the church attempted to reassert itself as a central participant in the social life of an increasingly secularized world.[5] In addition, ostensibly apolitical parachurch organizations such as Catholic Action associations (like the one in which Vattimo was active during his high-school years) were originally conceived of by Pope Pius X as a means of combating modernism at nearly every cultural level. For example, they not only encouraged Catholic trade unionism but also organizations such as male confraternities (along with axillary movements for women and youth), sports associations, educational groups, trade guilds, and peasant leagues.[6]

Therefore, rejection of modern liberal capitalism was already as much a component of Vattimo's early thought as was his Catholicism (in fact, the former emerged out of the latter). What eventually changed was the nature and direction of this criticism. In many respects, this shift is unsurprising. The integralist position on modernity was often ambiguous—seeking both to accommodate changes to modern life and to hold onto ancient lifeways (many of them more social than religious). Already by the 1920s, many progressive Catholics had increasingly come to view integralism as an inadequate attempt to retain an essentially "premodern" perspective—one far too quixotic and backward looking to address the actual needs or concerns of contemporary life.[7] Furthermore, at a political level, perhaps nowhere else in Italy was less amenable to Catholic unionism's goal of *cooperation* with the forces of concentrated capital than was Vattimo's own hometown of Turin. The city had been the very crucible in which the Italian Marxist movement had been forged.[8] Indeed, Antonio Gramsci once even referred to Turin as "Italy's Petrograd."[9]

The militant unionism prevalent in Turin had already attracted Vattimo's attention even when he was a high schooler (eventually prompting his expulsion from Azione Cattolica). Thus, after entering university studies, he quickly became dissatisfied with the more conservative neo-Scholastic philosophy of his professor and spiritual adviser, Monsignor Pietro Caramello and began to gravitate instead (at least academically) toward the more left-leaning Pareyson.[10] In spite of his growing leftist political sympathies, however,

Vattimo was not yet ready to commit himself fully to the Marxist program, which he at that time associated with the official PCI. In this regard, he later stated, "Like many left-wing Catholics at that time, I read Emmanuel Mounier and Jacques Maritain, looking for a way out of the jaws of the trap formed by liberal capitalism and the bureaucratized communism of the Soviet Union. In short, I didn't want to be identified either as a liberal or a Marxist. And—like Maritain—I was especially interested in criticizing the dogmas of modernity."[11]

Thus, one of the principal reasons for his rejection of Marxism during this early period was, of course, theological. That is, in spite of Marx's liberative politics, Vattimo felt that historical materialism nevertheless still retained a fundamentally modernist framework—one that was simply too inimical to the possibility of God talk to properly reconcile with Catholicism. Thus, after completing his degree at Turin, he began to search for a contemporary (i.e., non-Thomistic) philosophy that was antimodernist in character and thereby more compatible with his then still fervent Christianity.[12] Although he was initially interested in the heterodox Marxism of Ernst Bloch and Theodor Adorno, he was eventually persuaded by Pareyson that Nietzsche's antimodernist work—in spite of its open hostility toward Christianity—would nevertheless prove more fruitful ground for research. Therefore, Vattimo began serious study of Nietzsche in the summer of 1960. The following year, as fate would have it, the first volume of Heidegger's *Nietzsche* was released in Germany. This, along with Heidegger's "Über den Humanismus" (Letter on humanism, 1946), which Vattimo also read around this same time, gave a new postmetaphysical shape to his antimodernist sympathies.[13] Thus, almost from the beginning, Vattimo's interest in Nietzsche became intertwined with his reading of Heidegger.

BACKGROUND TO COMMUNISM IN ITALY

The Partito Socialista Italiano (PSI, Italian Socialist Party)—not to be confused with the later Partito Comunista Italiano, or PCI—was founded as a social-democratic party in Genoa in 1892. Prior to the establishment of the PCI, the PSI served as the big-tent party for the Italian Left, which included trade unionists, social democrats, Marxists, and anarchists alike. After the end of World War I, an economic downturn and deteriorating labor conditions increased tensions in the country between leftists and reactionary forces from the right-wing social and political establishment. In 1919 and 1920— the so-called Biennio Rosso, or Two Red Years—the PSI was able to capitalize on growing worker unrest in order to expand its political base. Nevertheless, workers' councils, industrial strikes, and peasant revolts were correspondingly met with increasing violence from unofficial right-wing Squadrismo militias (the precursors to Mussolini's "Blackshirts").[14] Internal divisions within the PSI eventually caused a split in January 1921, resulting in the establishment of the Italian Communist Party.

In failing to capture the growing momentum for social revolution in the years between 1890 and 1922, the Left was unable to secure their gains or prevent the eventual coup by Benito Mussolini and the Partito Nazionale Fascista (National Fascist Party) in 1922. That year, with the backing of powerful landowners and industrialists, Mussolini organized his armed March on Rome (October 28–29), which compelled the resignation of Prime Minister Luigi Facta. Wishing to prevent a civil war, King Vittorio Emanuele (Victor Emmanuel III) quickly capitulated to this intimidation tactic and named Mussolini prime minister on October 30.

As president of the Consiglio dei Ministri (Council of Ministers), however, Mussolini was still theoretically subject to a vote of no confidence by Parliament. But through the use of coordinated violence and intimidation, he was eventually able to suppress political opposition to the point that on December 24, 1925, he was able to declare himself "head of government." This decree meant that his decisions and position as leader were now subject to intervention by the king alone, not Parliament. In the course of five years after seizing power, therefore, the new Fascist government was able to ban all other political parties—in the process establishing Italy as a one-party state with Mussolini as its legal dictator (or *duce*).

As one might expect, during the nearly twenty-one-year-long era of Fascist rule, the PCI was banned and its leadership, including Antonio Gramsci, Amadeo Bordiga, Umberto Terracini, Mauro Scoccimarro, and others, were imprisoned.[15] Indeed, the only significant PCI leader to escape imprisonment during this time was Palmiro Togliatti, who, as fate would have it, had been at the meeting of the Third Communist International (Comintern) in Moscow during the arrests. As a result, Togliatti became the PCI's de facto general secretary but was forced to remain in exile in the Soviet Union during the party's clandestine years. He would ultimately remain head of the Italian Communist Party for nearly forty years.

The absence of official Communist Party leadership during most of the war years meant several things: as leader in exile, Togliatti came to rely increasingly on Soviet support for the PCI's continued claim to legitimacy at home; this dependence on the Soviet regime meant that the PCI was severely handicapped in its ability to act independently; and, most significantly, the everyday business of organization and resistance to the Fascist government passed out of the hands of the top-down leadership and into the hands of ordinary workers. Together, these conditions led to a diffusion of leadership among the Italian Left during the Resistenza. As David P. Palazzo has noted, "Workers assumed the lead in the Resistance by forming agitation committees, workers' councils, and internal commissions, and in direct action through strikes, work stoppages, and sabotage.

As workers assumed this lead role—beginning with the strikes of March 1943—the allies expressed concerns about workers' power and its possible effect on reconstruction and the postwar order."[16]

In 1943, with the tide of World War II changing, the king finally deposed Mussolini, dissolved the Fascist Party, and changed official allegiance to the Allies. The long-standing and decisive role of Communists (and of the Left more generally) in the anti-Fascist resistance, however, meant that their wishes could not simply be ignored by the king's government—that is, if he hoped to avoid internal revolt and drive German forces out of substantial portions of the country that at the time were still controlled by Mussolini's rival government in the Nazi-backed Republic of Salò. In 1944, Togliatti returned from exile and helped to negotiate a compromise between the various anti-Fascist resistance groups and the king's government. This compromise, referred to as the Svolta di Salerno (Salerno Turn), meant that Communists and other anti-Fascists would agree to continue to fight against the Fascists, this time on the side of the king's government. This also meant that, at least until the close of the war, the partisans on the left would have to table their demands for a change in governmental structure.[17]

With the eventual dissolution of the monarchy and the establishment of the First Republic, however, the official Italian Communist Party chose to move closer to the political center. To gain new respectability, it disavowed armed revolution in favor of democratic proceduralism. As a means of accomplishing this goal, Togliatti agreed both to disband and to disarm the PCI's paramilitary wing (the Garibaldi Brigades), so the PCI was able to enter the Parliament of the new republican government as the largest Communist Party in the West.[18] Indeed, Togliatti himself served successively as deputy prime minister and justice minister in the early tripartite administration.

This state of affairs would soon change, however, with pressure from the U.S. government. Following its adoption of the Truman Doctrine in foreign affairs, the United States used the leverage it had created through the Marshall Plan's significant foreign aid to force the governments of Italy and France to exclude Communists from their leadership positions. In the words of Henry Kissinger, "The strong role [U.S.] allies play in defending Western interests in many regions of the globe . . . could not be expected from a nation where Communists share in government power."[19] Thus, the move to exclude the far left was accomplished in Italy by Prime Minister Alcide De Gespari's efforts to form a governing minority composed of his own Christian Democracy Party (DC) and a collection of monarchists and elements of the center left. This arrangement would hold fast for decades, giving the Christian Democrats a near monopoly on leadership in ruling coalitions in Italian politics well into the 1990s.[20]

After the close of World War II, the PSI also reemerged, this time as a primarily center-left party. This being the case, it frequently chose to join in coalition with the DC as well as the smaller Partito Socialista Democratico Italiano (Italian Democratic Socialist Party) and the Partito Repubblicano Italiano (Italian Republican Party) rather than joining with the modified yet still more radical PCI. This meant, in effect, that for most of the country's history a centrist coalition (usually under DC leadership) has held sway in the country. The increasing moderation of the PCI in these years may have resulted in wider support for the Communists among average Italians than it otherwise would have received. Even so, the party's pragmatic positioning routinely failed to translate into much real political power, while also having the effect of alienating more radical leftists. By the late 1970s, as far as most people could tell, there was little light separating the PCI's and the DC's politics—a reality that raised suspicions among factions on both the far left and far right of the political spectrum. For example, in an article written for the *Washington Post* dated May 18, 1978, the journalist Ronald Koven remarked:

> In many ways, the Italian Communists and Christian Democrats are closer to each other than to any of the other existing Italian parties. They are both interclass parties with what one Western diplomat called "remarkably similar social profiles." The Communist party is as much a middleclass [sic] party of teachers, professionals and small shopkeepers as workers. The Communists are fond of saying that a majority of their members are practicing Catholics, and there are professing Catholics right up to the Party's top reaches. "Both parties represent churches," said a diplomat. "It's as easy for them to hold a dialogue as, say, the Anglicans and the Greek Orthodox. They understand each other's approach and language." In their conversations, top Italian Communists demonstrate an obsession with Catholicism. They refer to it constantly[,] draw[ing] [an]alogies between themselves and the Church. The Italian Communist Party's willingness to put up with the . . . contradictions of its militants who are both Communist and Catholic "makes us different from almost all the other Communist parties in the world," said a Communist member of the Parliament. Long gone are the days when the church threatened such heresy with excommunication.[21]

In 1976, the Christian Democrats' monopoly on power appeared to be under threat for the first time, in part because of changing socioeconomic conditions. For example, the reforms of Vatican II were then beginning to reshape the adversarial relationship between church and state. In addition, the global economy was suffering from an international oil crisis, the effects of the "Nixon Shock," and the subsequent collapse of the Bretton Woods system.[22] A historic compromise (*compromesso storico*) was therefore brokered between the DC and the PCI to establish a mutually beneficial governing coalition. The Christian Democrats saw this arrangement as a necessary means to hold onto political control of the country, while the Communists (then under the leadership of Enrico Berlinguer) saw the opportunity to gain for themselves some real political power for the first time in roughly two decades.

In this regard, it may be easy for those on the left to criticize the PCI for supposedly betraying its radical roots and compromising its principles in exchange for political gains. Such a position is, of course, a matter of perspective. It is worth remembering, however, that following the *conventio ad excludendum* established under the guidance of the United States, the PCI had languished on the opposition bench since the premiership of De Gasperi. Furthermore, regardless as to whether one agrees with Berlinguer's decision to align himself with the majority, he also appears to have been, at least in part, motivated by events that had recently taken place across the Atlantic.[23] On September 11, 1973, President Salvador Allende of Chile—the first democratically elected Marxist leader of a Latin American nation—was deposed in a U.S.-backed coup d'état. Allende died by suicide during the coordinated military raid on the Presidential Palace in the capital city, Santiago. The military takeover of Chile by the head of its army, Augusto Pinochet—made possible with assistance from the CIA—seems to have convinced Berlinguer that the process of moderation and collaboration with establishment forces for the purpose of progressive change represented a safer strategy for Italian Communists than the alternative of open confrontation with the political right and their powerful international sponsors.

Though the historic compromise was initially presented as a power-sharing agreement in the spirit of national solidarity, in effect it represented little more than the "cooptation and neutralization of the PCI by the DC."[24] Despite initial efforts by Berlinguer and DC leader Aldo Moro, the agreement quickly became unpopular, particularly among those on the radical left, who, like Vattimo, dismissed the PCI as no longer being a significant player in the international socialist cause. The historic compromise ultimately came to a violent end. On March 16, 1978, members of the Red Brigade abducted Moro in Rome and in the process murdered three police officers and two members of Moro's security detail. Moro was held prisoner for fifty-five days before finally being executed by his captors. He was found shot to death in the trunk of a car on May 9, 1978. Though suspicions linger surrounding the motivations behind the assassination, the practical effect was the collapse of the historic compromise and the resurgence of the anti-Communist wing of the DC in the elections of 1980.

Autonomy, the New Left, and the Revolutionary Subject

Beginning in earnest in 1961, subjectivity (or, at least, its increased fragmentation) reemerged as a major theme in Italian philosophy.[25] A contributing factor to this development was arguably a lecture delivered by Jean-Paul Sartre at the Gramsci Institute of Rome in December that year.[26] The previous year Sartre had published his book *Critique de la raison dialectique* (*Critique of Dialectical Reason*), which reflected a new emphasis in his work on the individual's confrontation with the collective structures of society. Sartre, at this later stage, seems to have viewed the individual as a "universal singular"—one that embodied and reflected the sociohistorical conditions of its respective context(s). Following Heidegger, he maintained that "facticity," or that which is given, conditions "beings-in-themselves." For Sartre, however, the subject becomes "being-for-itself" only through the choice to pursue some goal or "life project" (*le project fondamental*). Nevertheless, such a deliberate pursuit depends not merely on the individual's choice but also on the "situation" or the particular conditions presented in the world as we find it.[27] Here, Sartre seems to acknowledge the decisive role of embodiment and material conditions, while also seeking to preserve room for his earlier emphasis on individual choice. This stands in contrast with Louis Althusser, who claimed that subjectivity lacks any real essence and merely emerges from the fact of social structures. In this regard, Althusser once stated, "History is a process without a subject."[28]

Given the emergence of structuralism and the growing recognition of the importance of social context during this period, then, Sartre's talk may seem rather unremarkable—at least in terms of breaking new philosophical ground. Nevertheless, the problem as presented by Sartre gained traction in the Italian context (as elsewhere) in large part because of wider debates then going on concerning the substance and continued validity of so-called Orthodox Marxism.[29] Many at the time felt that Marx needed to be updated or rethought—that is, if the Left were going to maintain relevance in light of the changed social conditions going into the 1960s. This conviction gave birth to the so-called New Left, which would see a shift away from traditional Marxist thought—with its supposed "rigid laborism"—and toward a wider critique of imperialism, mass culture, conventional social norms, and political economy.[30] In this regard, "the appeal of Sartre's theory is that it seems to give each individual a responsibility that can be realized immediately by that individual, whose action is said to further the revolution. He interprets *revolution* 'not as a movement for the overthrow of one power by another' but rather as 'a long movement of liberation *from* power.'"[31]

Sartre, given his emphasis on the individual, came to believe that institutions of all kinds (including the Communist Party) impeded rather than advanced the cause of freedom. Unlike the "vulgar materialists" who saw the party as an objective expression of the "conscious will" of the proletariat class, Sartre argued that consciousness is not merely "class consciousness" or the awareness of some set of material circumstances. Consciousness is instead necessarily "self-consciousness." In seizing hold of one's freedom, the individual *constructs* its subjectivity—the life project thus becomes an act of self-emancipation.[32]

Sartre would also draw into question the Hegelian view of history advanced by Marx's orthodox followers. Whereas, for example, Lukács had viewed history as "an already closed totality, of a totality of possibles awaiting actualization," according to Michel Kail and Raoul Kirchmayr, Sartre instead insisted that such a view ultimately robbed the subject of agency and allowed "subjectivity to intervene only insofar as it stoically acquiesces to the . . . necessity that a philosophy of history has already set in place, prior to subjectivity entering the stage."[33] Indeed, how could one even speak of the "conscious will" of the proletariat if the existence of freedom is nothing more that submission to the predetermined force of the ineluctable progress of history?

Sartre instead felt that revolutionary subjectivity has to be more than class consciousness in the individual.[34] This position does not so much contradict Marx as broaden the scope of what is entailed in the idea of "emancipation." So, for example, Marx believed that the working class, in effect, constructed itself as a "revolutionary subject" by becoming conscious of the struggles and class disparities it endures.[35] This notion of "becoming conscious," however, leaves wide latitude for interpretation concerning the development of revolutionary subjectivity. We will return to this point shortly in the discussion of Vattimo's work *The Subject and the Mask*.

As mentioned already, many on the Italian left, given the diminishing returns in influence purchased at the cost of their compromise with the ruling establishment, already by the 1960s had ceased to view the PCI as an avenue for significant or lasting change. The results of this realization, however, were parsed out in different directions. On one side, the New Left largely abandoned traditional labor issues, emphasizing, instead, personal identity and cultural issues. On the other, some disaffected leftists sought to reemphasize labor concerns, albeit apart from their historical connections to either unions or party. This gave rise to so-called *operaismo*, or "workerism." Running headlong in the opposite direction from the New Left, this viewpoint instead apotheosized working-class struggle—especially industrial factory work—as the privileged site for any would-be proletarian revolution.[36] Nevertheless, what both approaches shared was an increased independence from the established Communist Party. This turn of events, however, should not be all that surprising. Leftist workers in Italy had already more or less operated independently from the party's centralized authority structure throughout the war years. This fact, coupled with the increasing postwar dissatisfaction with the PCI, eventually evolved into the Potere Operaio (Workers' Power) movement—which was active primarily between 1967 and 1973.

Negri and Workerism

The Paduan social theorist Antonio ("Toni") Negri (1933–2023) served as a leader of one of the major wings of the Autonomia Operaia (Autonomous Workers) movement and was arguably its most significant intellectual spokesperson.[37] Negri was from the agriculturally rich northeastern region of Veneto. His mother, Aldina Malvezzi, had been a schoolteacher. His father, Nerio Negri, was a

Bolognese union leader and one of the founding members of the PCI. Nerio Negri died when Toni was just three years old as a result of the mistreatment he received while imprisoned by the Fascists. Despite the hardships of his youth, Negri went on to receive his doctorate in philosophy from the University of Padua in 1956.[38] For the next two years, he received a scholarship to study under Federico Chabod (1901–1960) at the Benedetto Croce Istituto Italiano per Gli Studi Storici (Benedetto Croce Institute for Historical Studies) in Naples. In 1959, he was appointed as professor of *dottrina dello stato* (state theory) at the University of Padua.[39]

In 1963, Negri moved to Venice, where he began giving militant speeches at pro-union rallies. He soon participated in the creation of grassroots committees organized for the purpose of fomenting industrial strikes. In 1970, he relocated to the more politically significant Milan, where he began to organize at the largest car factory in the city, Alfa Romero. It was here in 1971–1972 that he and fellow organizers launched Autonomia Operaia.[40]

In time, the movement became influenced by situationism and adopted many of its tactics.[41] Under the influence of anarchism (left libertarianism), autonomism grew into a distinct school of Marxist thought characterized by its opposition to centralized or top-down authoritarian leadership. Instead, it placed emphasis on self-directed worker action and mass movement (as opposed to the revolutionary vanguardism proposed by Lenin).[42] In terms of its contributions to theory, autonomy opposed the then still dominant deterministic reading of Marx advanced by orthodox Marxism's marriage with the scientific positivism that had risen to prominence in the latter-half of the nineteenth century.[43] According to the sociologist Teodor Shanin, this deterministic construal of Marx owes more to the subsequent interpretations of his works by Friedrich Engels, Karl Kautsky, Georgi Plekhanov, and other orthodox Marxists than it does to Marx himself.[44]

More significantly, autonomism inverted the traditional relationship between labor and capital. This important reconceptualization was advanced in the pages of the political journal *Quaderni rossi* (Red notebooks), to which Negri and other important theorists of the movement contributed. For example, according to Mario Tronti (1931–2023), labor should not be thought of as the reactive pole in class struggle. He argued that historically as labor advanced toward greater autonomy, capital continually reacted to those advances in order to maintain its continued capacity to exploit workers. Likewise, Raniero Panzieri (1921–1964) argued that the tendency toward increased mechanization extends not merely from the capitalists' desire to increase productivity and thereby profits but also from their need to shield those profits from the demands of labor. "Tronti was keen to reiterate the fact that the key commodity which lay at the heart of the capitalist system lay in their [the working class's] hands: capital has no 'active life' without labour power. 'The simplest of revolutionary truths,' he stated, was that 'capital cannot destroy the working class: [but] the working class can destroy capital.'"[45] According to Lucio Castellano and coauthors,

> Autonomy was formed in opposition to the Communist Party project of "compromise," in response to the crisis and failure of the revolutionary groups, and as a step beyond the factory-centered perspective, in order to interact conflictually with the restructuring of production that was taking place. Above all, however, Autonomy expressed the new subjectivity of the movement, the richness of its differences, and its radical separation from formal politics and mechanisms of representation. It did not seek any "political outlet" or solution, but looked rather toward the concrete and articulated exercise of power on the social terrain.[46]

With this in mind, Steve Wright has characterized autonomism as being "ideologically heterogeneous, territorially dispersed, organizationally fluid, [and] politically marginalized."⁴⁷ Even so, as a distinct idea it sought to act outside of traditional political structures and forms of organization. It instead focused on small-scale direct and spontaneous action by individuals and autonomous collectives.

These various workers' movements together, with their emphasis on direct action outside the sanctions of official channels, in turn inadvertently helped to give rise to left-wing terrorist organizations such as the Red Brigade and Prima Linea (Front Line). Between 1974 and 1976, "autoreduction" efforts (such as rent strikes, mass callouts, collective shoplifting, occupation of public spaces, refusals to work, etc.) took hold in major Italian cities. Demonstrations and violent clashes with police escalated tensions, leading to a vicious cycle of increased militarization and increased radicalization. Even so, what had initially developed organically as more or less defensive actions among militant workers facing state-sanctioned violence at the hands of the police eventually evolved into preplanned or unprovoked acts of performative violence—increasingly as an expression of *self-identity*. According to Castellano and colleagues, such acts represented for their practitioners "a positive affirmation of a new and powerful productive subject, born out of the decline of the centrality of the factory and exposed to the full pressure of the economic crisis."⁴⁸

Given Negri's public influence on the wider workers' movement at the time, he was initially implicated in the notorious kidnapping and murder of Moro.⁴⁹ Even though he was not a member of the Red Brigade and had not taken part in the planning or execution of Moro, he was eventually arrested for his supposed "moral" complicity in the assassination. In what became a controversial and highly politicized trial, Negri was ultimately convicted and jailed for what amounted to sedition (i.e., "constitution of armed group and subversive association"). After being temporarily released from prison in

1983, he escaped further punishment by fleeing to France—where he remained in exile until his sentence was expiated in 1997.[50]

While still in France in 1978—at the invitation of Louis Althusser—Negri gave an influential series of lectures on Marx's *Grundrisse* at the École normale supérieure in Paris, which would eventually form the basis of his work *Marx oltre Marx* (*Marx Beyond Marx*, 1979). Here, Negri argued that the power of capital now extends beyond the realm of mere production to impress culture into its service. Thus, in the "social factory" of wider society, the same mechanics function to manipulate and control "social labor" and "social capital." At root, he argued, class struggle is a power relation—between the bosses and the workers—that has become structured over time by particular command functions (i.e., the organized institutional forms that dictate the distribution of profit). These institutional forms, furthermore, structure our subjectivity (whether as bosses or workers) and the hegemony of capital maintained by the power of the state means that there is no longer anything outside the system.

The respective behaviors of both types of subjectivity arise from the interplay between the psychological needs and desires of their members, conditioned as they are by the parameters fixed by this seemingly inescapable institutional structure. In late capitalism, therefore, there is no longer "use-value" (utility) in the classical Marxist sense. Instead, the world is constituted wholly by "exchange-value." Commodification, in other words, has subsumed all other forms of value. As Andrea Righi notes,

> In Marx's theory, the law of value is grounded in the definition of labor qua unit of time, that is, the *labor time necessary* to produce a commodity. This is the moment of exploitation of the worker as well as his or her only means of survival. It is here that the worker can

make demands and bargain for better conditions by increasing the value of his socially necessary labor time. In a reformist perspective, this is all he or she might attain. In the context of the Movement, this lever undermined the system as a whole. Following *workerism*, the Movement contended that the wage gave lie to the proper exchange between labor-power and the capitalist, and that the supremacy of the working class in the transformation of society demonstrated the fact that socially necessary labor was simply the result of political struggle. So the law of value was ultimately determined by class conflict more than by abstract economic calculations (i.e., the supply and demand model).[51]

Negri contended that the recognition of the capacity of proletarian demands to determine social transformation can, even in defeat of the proletariat, lead to the birth of a new revolutionary subjectivity with the ability to see the protean potential even in this moment of capitalist hegemony.

THE SUBJECT AND THE MASK

This framework represents the political/theoretical environment in which Vattimo completed his early philosophical work.[52] Indeed, Vattimo would be influenced in various respects by the emergence of both the New Left and autonomism. He first encountered the changing winds of Italian Marxism in the student movement that began in Italy in late November 1967, when protestors occupied the Palazzo Campana—then seat of the humanities at the University of Turin.[53] In spite of his initial ambivalence toward the protests, Vattimo, as already mentioned, had something of a conversion experience to revolutionary Marxism the following spring through his reading of Herbert Marcuse's works *Eros and Civilization* (1955) and

Soviet Marxism: A Critical Analysis (1958).⁵⁴ Marcuse, a central influence on the New Left, had once stated, "Certainly today, every Marxist, who is not a communist of strict obedience, is a Maoist."⁵⁵ Thus, it was in this general ("nondoctrinaire Marxist") sense that Vattimo also declared himself at this time to be a Maoist.

Between 1968 and 1972, having recently abandoned Catholicism and now filled with the radical political fervor of the period, Vattimo labored to develop a philosophy that would describe his own conception of "revolutionary subjectivity" by stitching together Nietzsche, Heidegger, and Marx into a single coherent program for the total emancipation of the individual. The result of this work was the book *Il soggetto e la maschera: Nietzsche e il problema della liberazione*, written over the course of twenty days in the Alps in the summer of 1972. Here, Vattimo drew a link among Heidegger's "history of being," Nietzsche's critique of metaphysics, and Marx's notion of "alienation" (*Entfremdung*).⁵⁶

Heidegger had, of course, envisioned a return to an authentic experience of Being, while Nietzsche had seen a vision of the overcoming of humanity. In a parallel fashion, Marx had imagined the ultimate dissolution of prevailing class antagonisms and a return to an *authentic* and creative mode of human labor—beyond the estrangements born of capitalist production. Though these pursuits and ends are (historically speaking) not reducible one to another, Vattimo nevertheless believed at the time that a "total revolution" of human life necessitated some dimensions of all three. Echoing the criticisms expressed by Sartre and Marcuse, however, Vattimo contended that so-called Communist countries had failed (or betrayed) Marx's revolutionary message—thus necessitating a reexamination of Marxist principles.

In *The Subject and the Mask*, therefore, Vattimo argued that if "really existing socialism" had actually been achieved in the Soviet bloc, then workers would fully control all facets of the labor process.

He observed that, instead, the same top-down productive rational that obtained in bourgeois-capitalist societies remained present in the East. Nevertheless, he argued that this was ultimately unsurprising because to the extent to which Marxism retains a modernist framework, it remains bound to the same metaphysical and rationalistic schema as capitalism. This is precisely why Vattimo thought that Nietzsche and Heidegger were of decisive importance for the rethinking of Marxism. For example, if we concede for the moment that the two main avenues for liberation that emerged in late modernity have been socialism (freedom from social hierarchy and class-based oppression) and psychoanalysis (freedom from the weight of repressed emotions and experiences), then, from a Nietzschean-Heideggerian perspective, this still leaves unaddressed the oppressive force of metaphysics.[57]

In *The Birth of Tragedy* (1872), Nietzsche saw the creative tension between Apollonian and Dionysian drives as pivotal for a healthy experience of the human condition. He felt that the highest creative interaction of this relationship had existed in the age of Greek tragedy (exemplified by Aeschylus and Sophocles). This creative lifeway, he felt, was stultified, however, by the eventual domination of Apollonianism in Western thought (as represented by Euripides and Socrates). For Nietzsche, the breakdown of this primal dichotomy, therefore, also represents in symbolic form the unbalanced course of modernity. He felt that the ultimate relationship between rationality and reality (most clearly espoused in Hegel) constitutes nothing more than a mere appearance—or, as Vattimo would term it, a "mask."[58] In this regard, Vattimo states, "Nietzsche's so-called *irrationalism* thus reveals itself for what it really is—namely, the revolt of Dionysian creativity that has now matured in humankind against all forms of external and internalized oppression, that still oppose its free development."[59] As Stefano G. Azzarà has noted,

The Dionysian recovery from submission to reason is presented by Vattimo as the rebellion against all social domination and any individual subjection. At the same time, the "perpetuating decision" has become an entirely political decision, an appeal to a genuine "revolution" that—starting from the release of the symbolic sphere (but also of instincts and desire)—lets us escape all intensive colonization by capital or state and then find a wholly new world. The repoliticization in this new reading of Nietzsche is radical. For the first time [Nietzsche] was likened now, in an explicit and politically significant way, to Marx and, along with him, was elected as prophet of that total revolution that the modern communist movement has not yet been able to achieve in the West and that had completely failed in the socialist camp.[60]

The Subject and the Mask, which Vattimo hoped would serve as a kind of manifesto for the libertarian left, represented the basic framework of his thinking until roughly 1978. Not long after the book's publication, however, he began to question his own contentions regarding the notion of revolutionary subjectivity. Indeed, he soon came to believe that the traditional conception of the revolutionary ideal was too metaphysically structured and therefore needed also to undergo the process of "demythization."[61] Furthermore, he came to regret the sometimes strident rhetoric with which he had expressed himself in the work, feeling that it could inadvertently inspire violent action—for example, in passages such as the following:

> When Nietzsche spoke of "philosophizing with a hammer" and posed the problem of the education of the new humanity, he showed that he was well aware that the violence from which metaphysics was born and that it itself represents has not completely disappeared, and

indeed *requires a "violent" decision that eliminates it completely*, establishing the real conditions of a world and a thought that are no longer metaphysical. . . . A different, adequate humanity must truly mature from these new conditions. The entire moral-metaphysical structure which is still *de facto* dominant in our ethical, social and intellectual world is however opposed to such a new situation.[62]

The Red Brigade's ensuing violence as well as Vattimo's own interactions with former students who had become terrorists eventually convinced Vattimo that the liberated Nietzschean subject that he had earlier envisioned could not be reconciled with the image of the Leninist "professional revolutionary."[63] Far from being liberated from metaphysics, such revolutionary subjects had turned out to be enamored of their own moral superiority to the point of self-delusion.[64] "Instead of trying to form a Leninist advance guard of the revolution, we wished to create autonomous and anarchistic communities which would escape and transcend the prevailing logic of power. Hence our ambition to live without relation to institutions of power at all: as if subjectivity itself was inevitably bound up with subjection, as if we only became subjects by subjecting ourselves to the structures of power. . . . The true revolution would be an inner revolution which would involve a dismantling of subjectivity," Vattimo would explain in a later interview.[65]

2

WEAK THOUGHT

Real truth was what we knew without being aware of it, and without thinking or believing that we knew. Everything was relative, and we have believed everything to be absolute.
—Giacomo Leopardi, *Zibaldone*, 1821

Hardness and strength are death's companions. Pliancy and weakness are expressions of the freshness of being.
—Andrei Tarkovsky, *Stalker*, 1979

THE EARLY STAGES

During the brief transitional phase between the philosophy of *The Subject and the Mask* (1974) and the publication of *Weak Thought* (1983), Vattimo published two significant books, each containing essays he had written over the course of the late 1970s. The first of these works, *Le avventure della differenza: Che cosa significa pensare dopo Nietzsche e Heidegger* (*The Adventure of Difference: Philosophy After Nietzsche and Heidegger*, 1980), is a somewhat "heterogeneous" collection that examines the growing prevalence of Nietzsche and

Heidegger in the philosophy of the time. The essays in this volume are loosely organized around the leitmotif of "difference," which Vattimo characterized as the disintegration of an overarching metaphysical unity and an "ungrounding" of presence. Here, as Peter Carravetta has noted, one can observe the early seeds of weak thinking, particularly in the essays "Nietzsche and Difference," "The Will to Power as Art," and, perhaps most clearly, *An-denken*: Thinking and the Foundation."[1] For example, in the latter essay, drawing explicitly on the later Wittgenstein's parallels to Heidegger, Vattimo argued, "The game is a game only by virtue of the fact of its having *rules*. The legitimacy of these rules is not founded on anything other than the fact that they are given. There is no 'game of games,' nor any fundamental ontology. We must forget about Being as foundation, remaining quite unnostalgically within the 'games' there are, taking on once and for all the task of promoting the multiple techniques of reason."[2]

Furthermore, Vattimo insisted that every attempt to sublate this dialectical *difference* into some final harmony must be resisted because, he maintained, the conditions of alienation can never be fully resolved—especially not by some fleeting political program. Vattimo's rejection of any idea of ultimate totality, of course, brings us back to similar developments in the works of other figures. Consider, for example, Nietzsche's concept of the "Übermensch," Gadamer's self-description as being a "Hegelian of the 'bad infinite,'" Derrida's idea of "play" and his rejection of a "transcendental signified," and even Adorno's concept of "negative dialectics."[3] All these positions in some respects see in the compulsion to harmonize or dissolve difference the need, as it were, to displace or even devour the Other. Herein lies Vattimo's charge, going back at least as far as *The Subject and the Mask*, that the "metaphysical" desire for an ultimate singularity, unity, and totality in the end leads to domination and violence—a point to which he continually referred thereafter.[4]

This being the case, the manner in which Vattimo himself conceived of weak thought as providing an actual *response* to such violence remains to be clarified.[5] His contention in this regard, which he expressed in greater clarity in subsequent works, essentially boils down to the conviction that once we collectively reach a state of realized nihilism—that is, the realization that other claims to truth are as potentially valid as our own—we will no longer have any ideology for which to crusade, no underlying cause that could conceivably set aflame the pyres either for would-be murderers or for martyrs. Even if this realization does not ultimately end all violence, it seems that Vattimo wanted to prevent the apologists of such violence from finding safe haven in transcendent principles. In later chapters, we will examine the ultimate tenability of such a proposal.

The second significant book from this transitional phase, *Al di là del soggetto: Nietzsche, Heidegger, e l'emeneutica* (*Beyond the Subject: Nietzsche, Heidegger, and Hermeneutics*, 1981), focuses on establishing a reconfigured notion of subjectivity. Here, Vattimo argues that in the age of the "decline of Being," we must move beyond the modernist notion of subjectivity as foundation—that is, as a stable structure capable of grounding experience in the world as somehow objectively given. This "degrounding" (*sfondante*) of the subject substitutes "reflection" (conceived of foundationally as a mirroring of the world or the transcendent) for *An-Denken* (conceived of as an ongoing act of retracing and renegotiation within the historically conditioned givenness of an inherited tradition, or *Überlieferung*). This characterization gets at the hermeneutical shape of the connection Vattimo continually drew between Nietzsche and Heidegger.

Though these two works were published in 1980 and 1981, respectively, it should be noted that the majority of the essays they contain were written prior to 1979. This is important if one wishes to follow this development in Vattimo's thought chronologically because it was in 1979 that he first indicated the break with his earlier philosophy in the preface to the second edition of *The Subject and the Mask*.⁶ That same year Vattimo also wrote two significant essays in which he first began using the term *pensiero debole*, "weak thought." It is useful to think of these two essays together, as a result of their overlap in content and proximity in time, as establishing the true point of departure for weak thought. I therefore discuss both of these essays in turn.

As a bit of background, it should be noted that postwar Italian philosophy had generally reacted to the irrationalism of the Fascist years by attempting to buttress what was perceived as the cracking walls in the edifice of rationality. This is perhaps best captured by the call made by figures such as Nicola Abbagnano and Norberto Bobbio for a "new Enlightenment."⁷ This search for a new systematic basis on which to establish reasoned foundations also likely contributed to the rapid growth in interest in structuralism and semiotics in Italy during the 1950s and 1960s. The import of post-structuralist ideas (primarily from France) during the late 1960s and early 1970s, however, led to a veritable philosophical crisis in Italian thought.⁸

As a result of this crisis, earlier in 1979 Aldo Gargani had edited an influential work in Italy entitled *Crisi della ragione* (The crisis of reason). The essays in this volume dealt with the then emerging problem of postmodernity and its critique of reason, univocal meaning, and the idea of a unified subject.⁹ One of the contributors to the work, Carlo Augusto Viano defended in his essay "La ragione, l'abbondanza e la credenza" (Reason, abundance, and belief) the legacy of modernity and instead warned *against* what he referred to as the weakening of reason.¹⁰

Inspired by this turn of phrase, Vattimo borrowed Viano's originally derisive expression while discussing his own understanding of

Heidegger's ontology and its relation to metaphysics.[11] The first use of the term *pensiero debole* thus appears in the essay "Verso un'ontologia del declino" ("Towards an Ontology of Decline"), which was later included in *Beyond the Subject* (1981). In order to properly contextualize the following discussion of Vattimo's position in this essay, it may be helpful to offer here some preliminary comments on Heidegger's understanding of ontology.

HEIDEGGER AND THE METAPHYSICS OF PRESENCE

Heidegger had argued in *Sein und Zeit* (Being and Time, 1927) that everything that occurs does so within the superstructure of time. Thus, he argued, Dasein's mode of life is necessarily conditioned and manifests itself temporally. Heidegger felt that at a fundamental level we orient ourselves in relation to time both as something "objectively there" (i.e., given outside of ourselves) and "subjectively there" (i.e., given within conscious experience). In terms of the various horizons that bind Being in its essential finitude, none is more universal than time.[12] Thus, "to be" in the world means also "to be" within time.[13]

This is important because Heidegger argued that the ordinary, "vulgar" conception of objective time as a linear-horizontal structure means that most people view time as merely a series of successive "nows." For example, under such a view, the *present* is the "actual" or "current-now," the *past* is the "no-longer-now" and the *future* is the "not-yet-now." One side effect of this episodic conception of time, however, is that it confers on the present alone the status of the real. Heidegger argued that such a view is mistaken. According to him, for example, it is not as if the past is no longer *present*—that is, abiding or persisting in the "current-now." Indeed, in a sense, he could say with Faulkner: "The past is never dead. It's not even past."¹⁴ Instead, the "present" exists in a durative sense as the cumulative force and effect of the past (*Gewesenheit*, the "having-been").¹⁵

Furthermore, for Heidegger, Dasein projects its being into the future such that the being of the present is fundamentally shaped by the future in the form of dread, hope, expectation, and so on—with the meaning of Dasein's existence finding ultimate expression under what the Romantic poet Shelley called "the gigantic shadows which futurity casts upon the present."¹⁶ Ultimately, Heidegger conceives of the three *Ekstases* of time (past, present, future) as a single unified structure.¹⁷

It might be expected, then, that this "in-between-ness" of existence, caught as it is betwixt the seemingly determinative poles of birth and death, should have led Heidegger to a despairing sense of fatalism or resignation. To the contrary, though, he viewed the present, above all, as the space wherein *action* becomes possible. Thus, he maintained that when Dasein *chooses* to *seize hold* of "the moment of vision" (*Augenblick*) and act decisively, this "time" becomes the space for creation or transformation.¹⁸ In doing so, Dasein accepts its "fate/destiny" (*Schicksal/Geschick*)—not in the sense of resignation in the face of some predetermined outcome but rather in the sense of rising with resoluteness (*Entschlossenheit*) to meet the occasion (come what may). Again, what is being faced up to, in this sense, is the cumulative effects of the past and the future bringing themselves to bear on those beings existing in the present.

Why is this examination of the nature of time significant for the current discussion? Well, it has to do with the idea of Being as *being present*—in both senses of the English term *present* ("occurring now" and "abiding with"). Following St. Augustine and Boethius, Christian theology has tended to view finite time in relation to the infinite (the "eternal present/presence") of God.¹⁹ Inasmuch as the present alone is conceived of as *real*, the "really real" of metaphysics must ipso facto be eternally present. In this regard, consider, for example, the words of Aquinas:

> Now God knows all contingent things not only as they are in their causes, but also as each one of them is actually in itself. And although contingent things become actual successively, nevertheless God knows contingent things not successively, as they are in their own being, as we do but simultaneously. The reason is because His knowledge is measured by eternity, as is also His being; and eternity being simultaneously whole comprises all time.... Hence all things that are in time are present to God from eternity, not only because He has the types of things present within Him, as some say; but because His glance is carried from eternity over all things as they are in their presentiality. Hence it is manifest that contingent things are infallibly known by God, inasmuch as they are subject to the divine sight in their presentiality; yet they are future contingent things in relation to their own causes.[20]

Heidegger argued that Being (*Sein*) constantly "gives," "sends," or "communicates" itself (*es gibt*) to each "here-being" (*Dasein*). What is actually "given" to all things/beings (*Seiendes*) in this ongoing process of existence, however, is *an allotted time* in which each briefly passes out of potentiality and into actuality (or presence)—before eventually returning to a primal state of nothingness (*das Nichts*). Crucially, for Heidegger, this potentiality is not a definite state—that is, a kind of waiting room wherein resides objects of "precreation." Instead, to the extent to which one can extrapolate a general notion of "Being" from Heidegger, he seems to conceive of *Being* as a term for the concrete unfolding of existing things communicating their existence to each other across time and related to each other in respect to this material continuum of communication (or givenness).

I say "extrapolate" because it is expressly not his intention to provide such a general claim about "Being as such."

Unlike traditional metaphysics, Heidegger does not view "Being" (or for that matter "the Nothing") as any sort of transcendental thing, substrata, or universal oneness, or *pleroma*, from which particulars emerge and/or to which they return. Rather, Being, as we encounter it, is always the "Being of beings," which is distinct from both "beings" and "Being as such" (conceived of as a separate discrete *transcendent* object or entity). The constant threat of *das Nichts* that hangs over existence like the sword of Damocles, therefore, is not some sort of folding back into an underlying fabric of Being—like a single drop returning to an ocean—but is instead the inevitability of every being's ultimate annihilation.[21]

It would be tempting to categorize this notion as nothing more than a species of nominalism, but that would not be quite right—at least not in a clear-cut way. Nominalism (indeed, as the term suggests) maintains that "Being as such" is just a name that possesses no underlying reality. Heidegger argues instead that Being does not have separate reality from the Being of beings, but this does not mean that it does not exist in some generalizable (or even univocal) way.[22] The "forgetting of being" is the forgetting of the fundamental difference by focusing on "what exists" (beings) instead of "that it exists" (the Being of beings). For Heidegger, Being is not an absolute, as it were, outside of space and time. Rather, he conceived of it as what Vattimo refers to as an "ontology of actuality"—that is, of the chain of beings that have actually existed, are currently existing, or will exist. Thus, all potentiality exists immanently within this constant unfolding.[23] For example, at a lecture delivered in Freiburg in 1941, Heidegger argued,

> We lay claim to being everywhere, wherever and whenever we experience beings, deal with them and interrogate them, or merely leave

them alone. We need being because we need it in all relations to beings. In this constant and multiple use, Being is in a certain way expended. And yet we cannot say that Being is used up in this expenditure. Being remains constantly available to us. Would we wish to maintain, however, that this use of being, which we constantly rely upon, leaves Being so untouched? Is not Being at least consumed in use? Does not the indifference of the "is," which occurs in all saying, attest to the wornness of what we thus name? Being is certainly not grasped, but it is nevertheless worn-out and thus also "empty" and "common." Being is the most worn-out. Being stands everywhere and at each moment in our understanding as what is most self-understood. It is thus the most worn-out coin with which we constantly pay for every relation to beings, with-out which payment no relation to beings as beings would be allotted us.[24]

Heidegger felt that Dasein was unique among beings insofar as it is aware of its own finitude—that is, the realization that its existence, viewed as a totality from beginning to end, fills a particular slot in space–time. This is what he means by Dasein "dwelling" or "residing" within Being. Part of the problem with metaphysics, from this perspective, is that it reifies this abstract ontological process—forgetting its origination in Being as *the point of unveiling* from which entities come into presence. Through the process of remembering this forgotten origin, he claimed, one undermines the privileging of the horizon of presence. Furthermore, Heidegger argued, this prevents any one metaphysical framework from ever being able to credibly claim exclusivity for itself. That is, none can pretend at being an absolute foundation because all metaphysical formulations that take hold in any given epoch of human history refer equally to a moment of origination in the "sending" or "giving" of Being (*Geschick*).

The conditions of each epoch arise from the nature of this sending—they imprint themselves as the realizable horizons of each era. Heidegger contended, however, that in running through the history of these distinct epochs of metaphysics one can discern the growth of this forgetfulness culminating in the contemporary era of technoscience, where talk of Being is abandoned altogether. For Heidegger, this is the final winding down and ultimate terminus of this form of metaphysics (that is, the form achieved in positivism). As Richard Kearney has observed,

> Phenomenologically considered, Being is no longer reducible to a simple presence—whether this be the idealist notion of a subject present to itself, or the realist notion of an object given to us in its real presence. Heidegger maintains that phenomenology enables us to consider the Being of man as a possibility rather than a simple, substantified presence. Phenomenology reveals that we are beings who exist beyond our present selves, that we are always extending ourselves along ever-expanding temporal horizons. We discover ourselves to be beings in time, beings continually moving beyond the actual givens of the present towards the future and the past: those dimensions of ourselves which we possess only as absences, as *possibilities*. Phenomenology is therefore the first philosophy which permits us to "overcome" the traditional hegemony of presence, fundamental to all metaphysics.[25]

THE ONTOLOGY OF DECLINE

Now, having established the basic contours of Heidegger's argument, we can return to Vattimo's essay "Towards an Ontology of Decline." Here, Vattimo characterized Heidegger's position as being an "ontology of decline." By this, he meant that the history of being is the history of this *inevitable* reduction of the concept of Being. Accordingly, he maintained that the different epochs/dispensations of the interpretation of Being have been the "dialectical preparation for [their] own overcoming in the direction of a recalling thinking [pensiero rammemorante]."[26] This is significant because Vattimo's interpretation of Heidegger differs from that of interpreters who see in Heidegger "the thinker who—though in somewhat problematic and purely preparatory fashion—foresees a return of being, or to being, on the basis of a broadly defined religious perspective."[27] Rather, Vattimo contended that this failure to see metaphysics as now finally having exhausted itself stems from this continual tendency (even among many Heideggerians) to view "Being" in terms of something separate from "beings"—a kind of fountainhead or foundation from which beings emerge. For example, he claims that this tendency appears even in Pareyson, noting that "Pareyson had continued to speak of the well-spring of truth, something which appeared to me to be a residual metaphysics, a sort of nostalgia for an ultimate ground or origin, although Pareyson always rejected this criticism. In my eyes, it seemed as if he wanted to rediscover some foundation, which was no longer of course an Aristotelian kind of God, but one who had triumphed over nothingness by creating the world."[28]

Vattimo argued instead that Heidegger viewed Being as existing only through the "event" (*Ereignis,* or "coming into view") of beings—the observable conditions that allow us to interpret a given era. Thus, the "giving" or "sending" of Being follows the rhythms of generations that come into and out of presence as a historical reality. But Being itself is not an object apart from this *presencing.* Now, as a result of the recognition of this decline, we realize that "being is *nothing,* but *happens.*"[29] In this regard, Vattimo claimed,

> Already in *Sein und Zeit,* being is "let go as foundation." Instead of being as capable of functioning as *Grund,* what we glimpse—especially with regard to the centrality of the existential analytic and the

elucidation of the nexus with time—is Being as constitutively no longer capable of founding anything: therefore being as weak and disempowered (*un essere debole e depotenziato*). The sense of being which *Sein und Zeit* searches for and to some degree find themselves already pointed, in a movement that leads them not to a stable base, but to a further and permanent dislocation wherein they are dispossessed and deprived of any center. The situation described by Nietzsche . . . as characteristic of nihilism, namely, that beginning with Copernicus "man rolls away from the center toward an X," is also that of Heidegger's *Dasein*. Much like the post-Copernican human being, *Dasein* is not the founding center, nor does it inhabit, possess, or coincide with this center. In the radical unfolding which it has in *Sein und Zeit*, the search for the sense of being shows progressively that this sense is given to human beings only as direction toward dispossession and degrounding (*spossessamento e sfondamento*). Therefore, even against Heidegger's texts, we must say that the search begun in *Sein und Zeit* does not lead us toward the overcoming of nihilism, but rather toward the experience of nihilism as the sole possible path for ontology.[30]

A second essay from 1979, entitled "Dialettica, differenza, pensiero debole" (Dialectics, Difference, Weak Thought"), builds on the first and warrants further attention. This work would ultimately serve as the principal essay in Vattimo and Rovatti's seminal book *Il pensiero debole* (*Weak Thought*, 1983).[31] Indeed, Vattimo's subsequent work on the topic can largely be thought of as elaborating on the basic framework he sketches out here.

Vattimo begins by attempting to separate weak thought from the standard conceits of a metaphysically construed approach to philosophy. Even with respect to logic, the ordinary practice of critical thought operates on the belief that for any particular evidentiary claim or set of claims to count as proof (and thus be considered "true"), they must be situatable within a wider nexus of previously accepted statements corroborating some observable set of data. For a claim or set of claims to be *justified*, then, means that they are broadly congruent or interpretable within an admissible hermeneutical framework. According to Vattimo, however, what is considered to be an "admissible" hermeneutical framework at any given time is, of course, subject to similar vicissitudes. In this way, grounding the *truth* of any given case at any given time depends on that particular claim's ability to, as it were, "borrow" some of the credibility of previously justified positions. Furthermore, in theory, one should be able to follow this same procedure all the way down until every valid statement eventually resolves itself into a set of self-evident axioms. Contrariwise, the further one ventures down such sequences, the more tenuous their relationships to one another become, and, thus, the more unstable the cumulative force of their justification appears.

Even so, within a traditional framework, the metaphysical attempt to construct a rational sequence of logical inferences typically moves in one of two directions. We may, for example, attempt to establish first principles and proceed discursively away from some shared point of origin. Alternatively, we could begin with the notion of incompleteness and proceed by attempting to fill in missing data points until a complete picture of the whole emerges. Vattimo, however, rejected what he viewed as the ultimate untenability (*insostenibilità*) of both projects because, for him, all that can be meaningfully said about Being as such is that it consists in "trans-mission, in forwarding [*invio*]: *Überlieferung* and *Ge-schick*." Furthermore, under such a view, the transmission of Being is always communicated as a particular "historical cultural happening." In this regard, he noted, "The world plays itself out in horizons constructed by a series of echoes, linguistic resonances, and messages coming from the past and from others (others alongside us as well as other cultures). . . . True Being never is but sets itself on the path and sends itself [si mette in strada e si manda], it trans-mits itself. Thus, Vattimo rejected the idea that there can exist some transhistorical *epoché* or suspension of the conditions of experience. Instead, he argued that the manifestation of Being is always "historically qualified and culturally dense." Against the Aristotelean-Avicennean-Thomistic tradition, therefore, Vattimo argued that Being is not some transcendent or stable substance undergirding reality. Rather, Being qua Being is, in its very essence, immanent and ephemeral. On this point, he said: "That which constitutes the objectness of objects is not their standing across from us in resistant stability (*gegen-stand*) but their be-falling [*Ereignis*], that is, their consisting thanks solely to an openness constituted by the anticipatory resolve upon death.... To recall Being means to recall such transitoriness [*caducità*]. Thinking the truth does not mean 'grounding,' as even Kantian metaphysics maintains. It means rather revealing the waning and mortality which are properly what make up Being, thus effecting a break-through or *de-grounding* [*sfondamento*]."[32]

Similarly, Vattimo rejected the shape of the metaphysical tradition that flows out of Hegel and through Marxist thought. Hegel had famously concluded in the preface to his work *Grundlinien der Philosophie des Rechts* (*Elements of the Philosophy of Right*, 1820), that "when philosophy paints its grey in grey, a shape of life has grown old, and it cannot be rejuvenated, but only recognized"—in other words, that "the owl of Minerva begins its flight only with the onset of dusk."[33] That is to say, for Hegel, truth is a totality, a completeness, an end—one whose successive phases and final shape can be adequately understood only retrospectively. Understanding, therefore, consists in adopting a perspective on *the particular* from the vantage point of *the whole*.[34] By contrast, Vattimo concludes that there is no meaningful sense in which such a holistic vantage point can even be said to exist (much less be accessible).[35]

This fallibilistic position separates Vattimo not only from Hegel and his followers but also from religious thinkers such as Karl Barth and Paul Ricoeur, who, in spite of their skepticism concerning human capacities, nevertheless can also be said to retain the ideal of totality.[36] But, perhaps more interestingly, Vattimo's perspective is also set at variance with major influences on his work, such as Adorno, Bloch, and Benjamin, because, as he contended, each of these thinkers responds to the problem of alienation through some process of dialectical reappropriation (or a kind of folding difference back into the whole).[37] Furthermore, for each of the aforementioned thinkers, this reintegration into the whole takes on, in varying degrees, an eschatological, even messianic, shape.[38]

For Vattimo, however, such an apparent teleological justification—whereby alienation furthers the ultimate culmination of a final integration (in some utopian, if not explicitly religious, eschaton)—makes their solution "deeply complicitous with the alienation it intends to combat."[39] He was concerned that this sort of reappropriation of otherness, to the extent to which it retains the stable/strong structures of a metaphysics of presence, will always retain the selfsame logic of domination. Emancipation, Vattimo contended, is not achieved through sublimation—as, for example, when former slaves become the masters—but rather when the logic of mastery itself is discarded. To the extent that the remnant of alterity is merely recuperated by metaphysics (by simply taking command of its "armamentarium of strong categories"), it ceases to be an Other at all.

Instead of speaking of an eventual "overcoming" (*Überwindung*) or "sublimation" (*Aufhebung*) achieved through the "declining" effects of difference mediated through the dialectical process, which can still be characterized as progress (however circuitous) toward some ultimate end, Vattimo maintained that we should think of this process as merely an ongoing act of "declination/distortion"

(*Verwindung*) and "recovery" (*rimettersi*).⁴⁰ He meant this in the sense of a "recovery from," "entrusting oneself to," or "sending on," in relation to the tradition handed down by metaphysics. As an example, Vattimo cites Nietzsche's announcement of the "death of God" not as a metaphysical pronouncement on the (non)existence of God but instead as the "true realization [*presa d'atto*] of an 'event.'" He states:

> Heidegger's *Verwindung* is the most radical effort to think Being in terms of a "taking account of" [*presa d'atto*] which is at once a "taking leave of," for it neither conceives Being as a stable structure nor registers and accepts it as the logical outcome of a process. *Verwindung* is the mode in which thought thinks the truth of Being as *Uber-lieferung* and *Ge-schick*. In this respect it is synonymous with *An-denken*, the other more current term with which the later Heidegger designates postmetaphysical thought. This is thought which recalls Being: it never renders Being present but always recalls it as already "gone." We must let go of Being as foundation. One has access to Being not through presence but only through recollection, for Being cannot be defined as that which is but only that which has passed on [*si tramanda*].⁴¹

Since weak thought recognizes that all thinking is historically conditioned and that any attempt to construct a new "truer" set of metaphysical categories is both unnecessary and ultimately undesirable, it accepts the history of Western philosophy simply as the tradition that has eventuated in its own postmetaphysical thought.⁴² Notably, for Heidegger, the West (Abendland—or, the "Land of Twilight") represents not only a geographical designation but also an ontological one. That is, it represents the "land of the setting of Being" (*tramanto dell'essere*). This makes the Western metaphysical tradition *the* "history of Being." In other words, according to

Vattimo, "This means that beyond metaphysics, there is no other history of being. Thus, the West is not that land where being sets, whereas elsewhere it shines (used to shine, will shine again) high in the noontime sun. The West is the land of being precisely insofar as it is also, inextricably, the land of the setting of being."[43]

With this in mind, Vattimo concludes that any question of the "appropriateness" of these particular metaphysical categories quite misses the point. These are the categories we have received from the tradition with which we in the West invariably operate. Even so, he argues that we can now use them in a postmetaphysical way because "*Verwindung* frees metaphysical categories from precisely what made them metaphysical: the presumption of gaining access to an *ontos on*. Once this presumption is dispelled these categories become 'valid' as moments, as a heritage evoking the *pietas* due to the traces of what has lived."[44]

This is not meant as a legitimation of such structures as normative but merely as an acknowledgment of their effect on the present shape of the discourse. If we disabuse ourselves of our realist/metaphysical prejudice, Vattimo argued, we can see that truth is not a matter of logic or metaphysics but instead a matter of rhetoric (in the classical sense). For example, he states, "Truth is the product of interpretation not because through its process one attains a direct grasp of truth (for example, where interpretation is taken as deciphering, unmasking, and so on), but because it is only in the process of interpretation, in the Aristotelian sense of *hermeneia*, expression, formulation, that truth is constituted."[45]

NIHILISM AND THE END OF MODERNITY

Apart from his unexpected reengagement with Christianity (which began seriously in 1992 with the publication of *Religion* with

Derrida), Vattimo's work remained largely consistent in outlook and focus after the initial publication of *Il pensiero debole* in 1983. As a result, this section devotes less attention to the specific circumstances of particular works and instead moves more freely between his subsequent writings in order to examine the themes and topics most relevant to understanding weak thought as a philosophical project. These important elements include principally discussions of nihilism, truth, and the destiny of modernity.

Vattimo followed the by now familiar narrative that during the period of early modernity, the broadly realist framework that had been in place since antiquity became inextricably bound with epistemological concerns and the practices of the emerging natural sciences. Among other things, this entanglement led to the development of a self-conscious project of "enlightenment" (*Aufklärung*), which Kant famously characterized as "man's emergence from his own self-incurred immaturity (*Unmündigkeit*)."[46] As a result, modernist thinkers came to view the process of enlightenment in terms of a quest to uncover the *secrets* of the universe and thereby to *master nature* in order to improve the quality of human existence through the vehicle of technological innovation.[47] "The idea of 'overcoming,'" states Vattimo, "which is so important in all modern philosophy, understands the course of thought as being a progressive development in which the new is identified with value through the mediation of the recovery and appropriation of the foundation-origin. However, precisely the notion of foundation, and of thought both as foundation and means of access to a foundation, is radically interrogated by Nietzsche and Heidegger."[48]

The events of the "death of God" and the corresponding mythization of the "real world" are just the inevitable terminus of the logic of modernity's project of *Entmythologisierung*, "disenchantment" and/or "demythologization." Advocates of the Enlightenment in particular had sought to dispel fantasy and faith from our collective consciousness and in their stead to enthrone reason, objectivity, and certainty—literally so in the case of the Culte de la Raison. Vattimo concluded, however, that it was always inevitable that the enlightenment project of *Entmythologisierung*, "demythization," which had so unceremoniously reduced all other modes of being in the world to "mere interpretations," would eventually turn its scrutinizing gaze inward and, at the last, reveal itself to likewise be *nothing but an interpretation*.[49] As Max Horkheimer and Theodor Adorno note in *Dialectic of Enlightenment* (1947), "Mythology itself set in motion the endless process of enlightenment by which, with ineluctable necessity, every definite theoretical view is subjected to the annihilating criticism that it is *only a belief*, until even the concepts of mind, truth, and, indeed, enlightenment itself have been reduced to animistic magic."[50] Similarly, Vattimo states that "even scientific rationality, which has for many centuries been of definitive value for European culture, is ultimately a myth, a shared belief on the basis of which our culture is organized[;] . . . the idea that the history of Western reason is the history of an exodus from myth, an *Entmythologisierung*, is a myth as well, an undemonstrated and indemonstrable article of faith."[51]

For Vattimo, this is the meaning of the *post* in *postmodern*—not in the sense of having moved beyond modernity but instead of having completed the project of modernity—and having accomplished its prime directive, thereby having nowhere else to go. Put another way, *post* is not to be thought of as a progressive "overcoming/going beyond" (*Überwindung*) of the modern but instead, again, as a "distortion" or "twisting" (*Verwindung*) in which the methods of modernist criticism reveal the ultimate vacuity of its own professed goals. In effect, modernity has been "hoist with its own petard!" In a moment reminiscent of the revelations of the "man behind the curtain" trope from *Das Testament des Dr. Mabuse* (1933) and *The Wizard of Oz* (1939), the postmodern condition resides here, in the last analysis, as the disclosure of the grounding principle of "reality" as a mere projection of ideology.

Vattimo argued that this realization of the mythic nature of modernity's project of "disenchantment" (*Entzauberung*) represents an inflection point best captured by Nietzsche in the famous chapter from *Twilight of the Idols* entitled "How the Real World at Last Became a Myth."[52] That is, according to Vattimo, in Nietzsche's thought the character of the understanding is such that it can never reach the ideal of disinterested reason. It is too much shaped by its own finitude and "thrownness" (*Geworfenheit*) in the world. The realization of the intellect's inability to, as it were, get outside of itself—that is, outside the ambit of the interpretive enterprise—ultimately has a radicalizing and relativizing effect.

As one can see with Nietzsche's philosophical development, modernist criticism birthed contemporary hermeneutical philosophy, which in turn realized the interpretive character of its own modernist assumptions—which included assumptions not only about the fantastical character of much popular religion but also about the ultimately *mythic* nature of scientific discourse. This, of course, does not remove the usefulness or functionality of science (anymore perhaps than it does popular religion), but it does undermine the pretense that science (or any interpretive enterprise for that matter) grasps the "really Real," apart from any and all interpretive frameworks.[53] Indeed, once one rejects the bifurcation of the world into "reality" and "appearance," then one sees that it is, as it were, interpretation all the way down, or, to paraphrase Hegel, "The *real* is interpretation, and *interpretation* is what is real." In the end, for Vattimo, hermeneutics is inherently nihilistic because once everything is exposed as nothing more than a play of interpretations, what is left to be done? It would perhaps be easy to despair of such a picture. Vattimo, however, sees in this conception of the world an opportunity for greater emancipation.

While Vattimo may have criticized "Reason," he was not necessarily criticizing what we might call "reasonableness." Instead, following Heidegger, he was criticizing what Max Weber termed "instrumental rationality" (*Zweckrationalität*)—the calculations of the positivist and the technocrat. Likewise, when Vattimo rather extravagantly called for us to abandon "Truth," he had something more circumspect in mind. What Vattimo wished us to be liberated from is the notion of truth qua totality, truth as system building, truth as metaphysics. The goal of nihilism—as he conceived it at least—is not to *destroy* logic or rationality but rather to reveal that it amounts to nothing more or less than a kind of rhetoric (or a system of persuasion).[54] It is a Wittgensteinian game—namely, one sort of useful rule-governed activity in which we participate for specific and defined ends.

PARADIGM AND PROCEDURE: TRUTH AS A FORM OF RHETORIC AND ART

It is important to keep in mind that this is not a description of an epistemological position relative to questions about, say, mind-independent objects or the like. Indeed, on such questions Vattimo seemed pragmatically content to leave correspondence (*adaequatio intellectus et rei*) as an *adequate enough description* of our relations to things. Crucially, for Vattimo, this is not because such a view is *true* independent of the observer or their context (as in *ens et verum convertuntur*). Instead, he argued, we can recognize such a relation of things as *true* only insofar as we recognize the operation of a historically given framework that has determined for the contemporary observer the parameters of what constitutes an *adequate enough description of a thing*.[55]

In this regard, he said, "To be sure, there is no sense in purely and simply denying the world a 'unitary reality,' in a kind of reprise of naïve empirical idealism. It makes more sense to recognize that what we call the 'reality of the world' is the 'context' for the multiplicity of 'fablings.'"[56] For Vattimo, then, "truth" is what we call the *product* of an accepted or agreed-upon procedure. It is the interpretive model or procedure that gives a claim the warrant or license to be considered "true." Disagreements about what amounts to the truth stem, more often than not, from disagreements about which procedures are operative in a given case and whether their respective parameters have been adequately met or not.[57] This applies to scientific claims as much as to artistic ones. The difference is just that in the former case the parameters are more definitively circumscribed by the nature of its subject—providing the illusion that the differences in method between the humanities and the sciences are in kind and not merely in degree.

The philosophers of science of today also talk about the fact that a single phenomenon (a kettle of water that boils at 100 degrees Celsius) is not somehow *better* known whenever science is able to generalize it in a formula. By generating formulas, science in some way transcends the single phenomenon and places it inside a complete artificial system. The thermometer is not useful because it allows me to better know the boiling of the water; it serves me only to generalize this discourse in a wider sphere. In other words, abstraction is not intended to penetrate into the phenomenon and find its true essence. The essence we reach is only the general structure of a certain world of phenomena that becomes truth in some way that has nothing to do with individuality.[58]

In the final analysis, this repudiation of positivism (as representing the most crystalline form of Western metaphysics) really amounts to the vehement rejection of the idea that all claims to truth can fall under (or be forced under) the rule of a single procedure or paradigm (e.g., natural science). For instance, when confronted with the lies of a politician seeking to go to war, Vattimo once said, "We cannot swallow the lies[;] . . . naturally, these moral principles appear 'true' to us, but not in the 'metaphysical' sense of the term 'true,' not because they correspond descriptively to some objective datum. What does it mean to oppose war because all men are brothers? Is human brotherhood really a datum to which we ought to conform because it is a fact?"[59]

The goal of postmetaphysics, in this regard, is to undermine the "myth of transparency" concerning our viewing of the world as being in any regard presuppositionless. Following Thomas Kuhn, Vattimo maintained that the critical distance that serves as the goal of science should involve science's ever-present critical awareness of its own inherently limited and tendentious nature. This is not to say that its own internal rules and rationales are not useful or appropriate, only that they are not absolute or infallible. Here, one can perhaps compare Vattimo's position with that of Gadamer, who said, "When we say 'to know' [*erkennen*] we mean 'to recognize' [*wiedererkennen*], that is, to pick something out [*herauserkennen*] of the stream of images flowing past as being identical."[60] For both Gadamer and Vattimo, paradigms are, of course, not arbitrary. Rather, they are forms of realization, which "come to stand" (*Zum-Stehen-Kommen*) as bearers of meaning for those who seek answers according to their specified parameters.[61] As Gaetano Chiurazzi has observed,

> The interpretative character is [in Vattimo] tightly anchored to an experience of truth. What transforms is truth, and interpretation is not the creative act hovering over the nothingness of nonsense, but rather the transformative rearticulation of meaning (*senso*). The cited definition in fact presupposes that 1) there is truth, 2) one has experience of truth, 3) such experience is of an interpretative kind, and 4)

hermeneutics is a theory not of truth but of the experience of truth. If one wants to speak of nihilism, this does not consist so much in some metaphysical thesis perhaps expressed in the claim that "truth does not exist," but rather in the experience one has thereof.[62]

In keeping with Nietzsche, this invective against the modernist dominance of what we might call the "Apollonian spirit" is really a call for a counterbalance. Like Nietzsche and Heidegger before him, Vattimo found this desired balance in the practice of art and the figure of the artist. For example, Vattimo argued that "the model of active nihilism ... is not the 'blond beast' of the Nazis, but neither is he the philosopher aware of the historicity of every *Weltanschauung*, the transcendental psychologist of the Diltheyan type. The model most constantly referred to by Nietzsche ... is the artist, whom he calls tragic or Dionysian."[63] For Vattimo, the work of art is a grand metaphor for the rendezvous between the Apollonian and the Dionysian—not as an integration or sublation of these two separate and primal forces but rather as a *moment of contact* (an "event") channeled or brought together through the activity of the artist. In his view, Nietzsche's "will to power" does not represent the artist's *domination* over the materials of their construction through the imposition of a form. Instead, formation by the artist is a means by which the artist as an *interpreter* of experience can affect a rearticulation of meaning by asserting themselves "over and against the apparent negativity of existence."[64]

As Andrzej Zawadzki has noted, Vattimo sees "a critical and emancipatory meaning of art in Nietzsche's thought ... as that sphere of human activity which is most capable of undermining the ruling symbolic order, the appointed canons of sense, the socially sanctioned divisions into true and false, the established systems of communication, norms of rationality, etc., on which social organization is based."[65] Hearkening back to Pareyson's aesthetics, the "form"—a structure that captures a moment of expression (like a photo of two dancers)—is always merely an instantiation of a dynamic movement that continues beyond such momentary snapshots. In Nietzschean fashion, then, for Vattimo truth is not some set of inert data (however complete); it is instead an animate force that requires participation for it to function. As Vattimo's student Santiago Zabala explains, quoting Gadamer, "'Interpretation is an insertion [*Einlegen*] of meaning and not a discovery [*Finden*] of it.' But this meaning does not belong only to the interpreter; it also has an important intersubjective dimension because it grounds a communal experience, that is, a 'claim to truth.'"[66]

CRITICISM OF WEAK THOUGHT

From the beginning, weak thought generated controversy and often acrid responses from critics. For example, Carlo Augusto Viano (who had inadvertently lent weak thought its name) was among the first to simply dismiss Vattimo's work as amounting to little more than an inconsequential irrationalism.[67] A more critical engagement with weak thought, however, quickly appeared in the work of the philosopher of history Paolo Rossi (Florence), who criticized it as, ironically enough, offering a one-sided and reductionist account of modernity and the history of science.[68] Certainly, for his part, Rossi offers a more complete and nuanced image of the course of scientific development than the simple narrative concerning technology proffered by both Heidegger and Vattimo. But, in some respects, his argument appears as little more than shadowboxing. Even if one grants the validity of such criticism (and there seems little reason not to do so), this of itself does not appear to significantly undermine any of the core assumptions related to what we might call "debolist thinking."[69] That is, Rossi ultimately fails to demonstrate the presence of any instances of decidedly irreconcilable internal incoherence in the position itself.

Some Latin American thinkers, in particular Enrique Dussel (1934–2023), leveled valid criticism against early expressions of weak thought.[70] For Dussel, praxis is the ultimate litmus test for any aspiring theory of emancipation. As a result, he offered his concerns about what he viewed as the abstract and Eurocentric nature of weak thought and, thus, his doubts about its ultimate usefulness or applicability for those most in need of liberation (namely, the poor of the Global South). For example, in his essay "Un diálogo con Gianni Vattimo: De la postmodernidad a la transmodernidad" (A dialogue with Gianni Vattimo: From postmodernity to transmodernity, 2007), Dussel wrote: "Nihilism is a twilight experience of the West, of Europe, of Modernity. It has been posed to Vattimo then, 'What meaning does this have for a Hindu beggar muddied by the rising waters of the Ganges, for a member of a Bantu tribe from the Sub-Sahara who dies of thirst, for the millions of semi-peasant Chinese, or for hundreds of thousands of marginal poor in Mexico, from suburban neighborhoods like Nezahualcoyotl or Tlalnepantla (which are as populous as Turin)?'"[71]

There is much in weak thought with which Dussel was in agreement. Nevertheless, he argued at the time that Vattimo—like other philosophers from Europe and the United States in general—suffered from an insufficient appreciation of the role of the dialectical process between the center and periphery in the construction of modernity itself. That is, the "centrality" of European hegemony, since its inception, has relied on the existence of such a "periphery."

> There is no Modernity without "modernized" civilization or without the "barbarian." But this hidden, forgotten, unnoticed relationship also covers what I have called the "Myth of Modernity": the justification of irrational violence against the periphery in the name of the

civilizing process—placing the perpetrators (conquerors, merchants, colonial empires, "superior" culture) as innocents and the victimized as guilty. Among the violence that Vattimo (Nietzsche or Heidegger) attributes to the modern strategic-instrumental *ratio* does not include the one by which it annihilates the non-European cultures of the planet, reducing the vast majority of humanity to being a colonial world, dominated and excluded. Vattimo is not opposed to these proposals, but it is positively necessary to go further beyond his critique, unfold it, deepen it, give it a global meaning. In that case, the "barbarians" excluded although affected, can benefit from a "weakening" of the dominating, nihilistic reason, but this . . . is not enough.[72]

As Dussel admitted, such criticism does not so much undermine weak thought as recognize certain blind spots or deficiencies in its approach.[73] As with Rossi's criticism, however, these points can be acknowledged without destroying the underlying framework of weak thought. If anything, they point to areas in which theorists or practitioners of debolist thinking can deepen or move beyond Vattimo's work and personal idiosyncrasies. Indeed, as we will see in the discussion of *Hermeneutic Communism*, Vattimo seemed to have taken such criticism to heart and responded accordingly.

In contrast to this largely "friendly-fire," it is worth briefly examining the more substantial criticisms of weak thought that have emerged from the work of the so-called neorealists or speculative realists, such as Graham Harman, Tom Sparrow, Quentin Meillassoux, and Maurizio Ferraris, Vattimo's former student.[74] A full account of the neorealist critique of weak thought—and postmodernity in general—would, of course, require a monograph of its own. In this limited space, therefore, I instead focus attention on two criticisms that I think have the potential to significantly impact the framework of weak thought. The first of these criticisms stems from phenomenology's claim to *bypass* the traditional debate over the status of realism. For example, phenomenology has from its inception treated the traditional realism/antirealism debate as amounting to little more than a "pseudoproblem." It claimed instead that "the mind was always already outside itself in intending objects, or Dasein was always already thrown into a world, even though this world and its objects were said to exist only as correlates of human beings."[75]

In so doing, phenomenology hoped to plot a distinct "third way," thereby simply passing through the horns of the dilemma. Graham Harman, for his part, argues that such a position amounts to a confusion or an obfuscation—and that its maintenance derives from either a lack of courage or a lack of candor on the part of phenomenologists.[76] As far as he is concerned, one must seize hold of one of the horns of the dilemma and decide for a realist or antirealist position. If this is so, then, he maintains, weak thought obviously represents an antirealist position—and thus is tainted by what he and other neorealists consider to be the unscientific blight of postmodernity. Ferraris explains further,

> The ironic theory of weak thought . . . reproposed in more than one case the characteristics of a long period of Italian philosophy: suspicion toward science and technology, traditionalism, idealism. That is, suspicion toward realism (and the idea of progress in philosophy), always seen as a penalizing mistake with respect to the flights of thought. The ideal enemy of weak thought, then, was not the declared one (namely, dogmatism) but rather Enlightenment, that is, the claim of reasoning with one's own mind. . . . De Maistre described the protestants' [sic] spirit as: "a spirit of cavil, envious to death of being in the right—quite natural, indeed, in every dissenter, but in Catholics wholly inexplicable." In retrospect, weak thought shows the reappearance of the Catholic polemic against the *esprits forts* [strong spirits], against those who bring forward the absurd claim of being right.[77]

For Ferraris, weak thought has less in common with a "theory" than with an ironic detachment from any theory—in the vein of Duchamp's critique of academic art. On this point, Vattimo might have been inclined to agree, though their respective perceptions as to the implications of such an admission would no doubt have differed.[78] While one can criticize Ferraris and other neorealists for attempting to pigeonhole weak thought into accepting a framework but without (in any final sense at least) addressing the original or underlying causes of its skepticism, one can also likewise fairly maintain that weak thought's implied relativism ultimately does negatively affect its ability to advance its own ends without the potential of falling into a vicious cycle of self-negation.

The second notable criticism comes specifically from Ferraris concerning what he sees as the failure of postmodernity to make good on its claim that the relativizing effects of nihilism will ultimately translate into less violence or ideology. For example, in a debate with Vattimo for the Italian newspaper *La Repubblica* on August 19, 2011, Ferraris stated:

> The last few years have taught me, it seems to me, a bitter truth. And that is, that the primacy of interpretations over facts, the overcoming of the myth of objectivity, did not have the emancipatory results that illustrious postmodern philosophers like Richard Rorty or yourself imagined. That is, what you announced thirty-five years ago in your beautiful lectures on Nietzsche and the "fabling" of the "real world" did not happen: the liberation from the constraints of a too monolithic, compact, peremptory reality, a multiplication and deconstruction of perspectives, which seemed to reproduce, in the social world, the multiplication and radical liberalization (we believed at the time) of television channels. The real world has certainly become a fantasy; indeed, it has become a reality show. Unfortunately, this is a fact, although we both wish it was an interpretation.[79]

Against what is arguably the central motivating claim of weak thought, then, Ferraris contends in his *Manifesto of New Realism* that "you can have truth without violence and violence without truth, and that consequently the abandonment of truth does not lead to the abandonment of violence and universal peace but only to superstition."[80] This is a crucial point that I will return to in chapter 5.

PENTAPARTITO AND THE RISE OF BERLUSCONI

Before we look at *Hermeneutic Communism*, it is worth briefly exploring the political environment in Italy after the collapse of the historic compromise, which will provide the context for understanding both Vattimo's later political writings and his successful entry into electoral politics. Even for a politically active thinker such as Vattimo, the transition from academic philosophy to governance is rarely attempted, much less achieved. His move was at least in part motivated, however, by the extraordinary circumstances facing the country beginning in the early 1990s.

Throughout the 1980s, Vattimo busied himself with writing, teaching, lecturing abroad, and serving as editor of the Italian Philosophical Yearbooks, a series on contemporary debates in philosophy published by Laterza. In 1992, the publisher expanded the series to offer a European Philosophical Yearbook—this time, with Vattimo and Derrida as coeditors. What Vattimo could not have known at the time, however, was that this year would ultimately prove to be portentous not merely for himself but for Italy as well. In what was a defining personal tragedy, Vattimo lost his longtime partner Gianpiero Cavaglià shortly after Christmas in 1992. Cavaglià passed away due to complications from AIDS, a condition he had battled since 1986. He was only forty-three years old at the time of his death.

As reflected in moving passages from Vattimo's autobiography, Cavaglià's passing affected him deeply and cast a long shadow over his own reflections in his subsequent years. Vattimo coped, at least in part, by not slowing down.

On the public political front, the first rumblings of the coming earthquake that would soon remake the landscape of Italian politics were just becoming perceptible. In February, the prominent Milanese socialist leader Mario Chiesa was arrested on suspicions of bribery and corruption. This was the first arrest in a series of investigations that would ultimately come to be known as the Mani Pulite (Clean Hands) Affair.

As already mentioned, since its reestablishment the PSI had positioned itself to the right of the PCI, even as the PCI continued to moderate itself in hopes of achieving greater electoral representation. As the two traditional parties of the historic Italian left, however, both groups were forced to cannibalize the same base of support. As both parties continued their rightward drift during this period, the PSI, under the leadership of Bettino Craxi, began to make overtures to propertied-class interests by taking more business-friendly positions on policies of liberalization, privatization, and territorial sovereignty. Craxi's break with the Left's historic ties to labor foreshadowed the later "third way" liberal politics now most often associated with Bill Clinton and Tony Blair. His political positioning, however, allowed the PSI—never a serious electoral rival to the DC or even to the PCI—to make serious gains after the collapse of the "historic compromise" and thereby to command an important negotiating position in later ruling coalitions.

After 1980, the party system realigned again, this time establishing a durable ruling coalition known thereafter as the Pentapartito—consisting of the DC, the PSI, the Italian Democratic Socialist Party, the Partito Liberale Italiano (Italian Liberal Party), and the Italian Republican Party. In 1992, however, the prominent position played by the PSI in this coalition was threatened by the corruption revelations about Mario Chiesa. As a result, Craxi was quick to condemn Chiesa as unreflective of the PSI. This narrative of a lone bad actor quickly unraveled, however.

Feeling abandoned by the PSI after his arrest and after having spent five weeks in prison, Chiesa confessed and began implicating others. It soon became clear that corruption, bribery, extortion, racketeering, and self-dealing were systematic and endemic not only in the PSI but also in every major political party in Italy. For its part, the PCI was able to escape scrutiny both because it had been excluded from participation in the ruling coalition and because it had already officially dissolved itself in 1991 amid the ongoing collapse of the Soviet Union. At the time of the scandal, the PCI was in the middle of reestablishing itself as the Partito Democratico della Sinistra (Democratic Party of the Left).

Chiesa's allegations set off a chain reaction of investigations that quickly embroiled the entire political establishment in scandal. These investigations eventually revealed what Martin Rhodes has referred to as a "cross-party cartel" involved in, among other things, price fixing and the selling of contracts in collusion with powerful members of the private sector.[81] The estimated cost to the Italian public of this cartel—now frequently referred to as "Tangentopoli," or "Bribesville"—was somewhere in the range of tens of billions of lire. Craxi was forced to resign from the PSI leadership in December (he eventually fled to Tunisia to avoid arrest), which was followed in time by the forced resignations of Giorgio La Malfa, leader of the Republican Party; Renato Altissimo, leader of the Liberal Party; and Carlo Vizzini, leader of the Social Democrat Party. These resignations came amid a wave of arrests and high-profile suicides of politicians implicated in crimes.

Over the next two years, turmoil caused by these events and the subsequent trials associated with them undermined general confidence in the five major governing parties to the point that there was widespread expectation that the general election of 1994 would deliver the first major victory for the Democratic Party of the Left. This expectation, however, was upended when the Italian media tycoon and former associate of Craxi, Silvio Berlusconi, announced the formation of a new anti-Communist party, Forza Italia! (Forward Italy!), as well as his own bid to become prime minister. Through a populist-style media blitz and overtures made to the far right, Berlusconi was able to use the fear of a Communist-led government in order to consolidate a winning coalition. In northern Italy, Forza Italia aligned itself with Polo delle Libertà (Poll of Freedoms), a regional association of parties including the Lega Nord (Northern League), the Centro Cristiano Democratico (Christian Democratic Center), and the Unione di Centro (Union of the Center). In central Italy and the southern regions, Forza Italia aligned itself with the Polo del Buon Governo (Pole of Good Government), a separate regional association composed of the Christian Democratic Center, the Union of the Center, the neofascist Alleanza Nazionale (National Alliance), and the Polo Liberal Democratico (Liberal Democratic Pole). Berlusconi won a decisive victory to lead what was then Italy's most conservative government since the end of World War II.

At the dawn of the Italian Republic, leftists had been able to boast of having the largest Communist Party in the West. From the late 1940s through the 1970s, left-wing forces had commanded significant social influence (if only rarely official power). But by the 1980s the rightward turn in Italian politics, the growing influence of popular media (much of it owned by Berlusconi), and the spread of consumer culture all began to take hold in the country—a trend that largely extends to the present. As a result, in more recent years the once vibrant tradition of the Italian Left has all but disappeared. According to Santiago Zabala, "One of the reasons Vattimo sought to become a European deputy in 1999 and again in 2009 was that he believed his 'hermeneutic political project' could be more easily developed in the European Union than in Italian national politics."[82] This has become even more apparent since the 2022 Italian general election victories of Giorgia Meloni and her right-wing populist party, the Fratelli d'Italia (Brothers of Italy Party). Indeed, the strength of that party in recent Italian politics was demonstrated once again in the 2024 European elections, which saw a more widespread swing to the right in several European countries.

HERMENEUTIC COMMUNISM

The final section of this brief overview of Vattimo's philosophical work concerns his book *Hermeneutic Communism: From Heidegger to Marx* (2011), cowritten with Santiago Zabala and published in English.[83] It is significant that Vattimo and Zabala worked on this volume between 2004 and 2010 because this timeframe is crucial for understanding the work. That is, it covers a period of several sociopolitical developments that contributed to the shape of its content. In the West, these developments included the U.S.-led invasion of Iraq (in which Italy, under Berlusconi, participated until he was replaced as prime minister by Romano Prodi in 2006) as well as the series of deadly troop surges in Afghanistan ordered by President Barak Obama of the United States. In the Global South, by contrast, this period saw the ascendency of a series of left-wing populist and anti-imperialist governments with the elections of Hugo Chávez in Venezuela, Luiz Inácio "Lula" da Silva in Brazil, and Evo Morales in Bolivia. It was also during this time that Vattimo completed his first term serving as a representative of Italy in the European Parliament (1999–2004) and the beginning of his second term with his reelection in 2009. Thus, *Hermeneutic Communism* was written largely against the backdrop of the George W. Bush administration's international war on terror, tensions between East and West, as well as then hopeful signs of progressive social developments stirring in several Latin American countries.[84]

The first thing we can note about the content of this work concerns its title. Anyone familiar with the history of Marxism should be struck immediately by the curiosity of the qualifier *hermeneutic* before *communism*. Famously, in contradistinction to so-called utopian socialists such as Henri de Saint-Simon and Charles Fourier, Marx and Engels viewed their position as a form of "scientific" socialism.[85] That is, they argued that historical materialism rested on a firm foundation of empirical observation and deductive rationality. As we have seen, however, Vattimo long argued that such a modernist framework for Marxism should be discarded. Furthermore, in response to Marx's famous comment that "the philosophers have only interpreted the world, in various ways; the point, however, is to change it,"[86] Vattimo and Zabala argued that there is an appreciable difference between *interpreting* the world and merely *describing* it. "Unlike a description, for which reality must be imposed, interpretation instead must make a new contribution to reality."[87]

As what can perhaps best be described as the "political project of weak thought," hermeneutic communism retains several elements of the socialist tradition that align it with the veins of left libertarianism (anarchism), autonomism, situationism, and third-world socialism that we have discussed thus far. For example, from the left-libertarian tradition, hermeneutic communism rejects top-down hierarchical leadership structures. This is part of the reason why Vattimo and Zabala did not look back to the Soviet era or to contemporary China when they were searching for models for their emancipatory political project. Instead, they looked to the democratically elected Communist governments in South America—which, whatever these governments' shortcomings, relied on mass movements and attempted to make reforms to address the plight of the poorest elements of society.

One can see not only connections to third-worldist movements in Vattimo and Zabala's writings but also clear parallels and resonances with liberation theology's "preferential option for the poor."[88] On this point, Vattimo and Zabala make a (perhaps obvious) connection between weak thought and the "weak" elements in society—what Frantz Fanon called "the wretched of the earth" and Giorgio Agamben describes as *homo sacer*. As we have seen, for Vattimo, preserved in the *es gibt* of Being is what he describes as that remnant unassimilated into metaphysics, or "what Derrida calls 'the margins of philosophy' and Benjamin 'the tradition of the oppressed.' It is in this forgotten, defeated, and different history that one can find the victims of the politics of descriptions—and probably also an emancipation from it."[89] This, again, is the reason for the focus on Latin America (or the third world more generally): in a world fully integrated into globalized neoliberal capitalism, Latin America constitutes a pocket of ongoing resistance.[90]

Finally, like the situationist attempts at "culture jamming" and deeper progressive legacies of civil disobedience and nonconformism, Vattimo and Zabala sought alternative means by which to realize their vision for a society beyond neoliberal capitalism. Unlike Negri and other contemporary Marxists (such as Alain Badiou), Vattimo and Zabala saw nothing to be gained from militant revolution. They instead claimed that global integration presents new possibilities for resistance beyond armed struggle. On this point, they conclude *Hermeneutic Communism* with the following sentiment: "Forms of passive resistance, such as boycotts, strikes, and other manifestations against oppressive institutions, may be effective, but only if actual masses of citizens take part, as in Latin America. These mass movements might avoid falling back again into the practico-inert, which is the natural consequence of those revolutions entrusted to small and inevitably violent avant-garde intellectuals, that is, those who have only *described* the world in various ways. The moment now has arrived to *interpret* the world."[91]

In 2017, in collaboration with Vattimo and Zabala, Springer International published a collection of critical essays on hermeneutic communism edited by Silvia Mazzini (Institute for Doctoral Studies in the Visual Arts) and Owen Glyn-Williams (DePaul). For this collection, entitled *Making Communism Hermeneutical: Reading Vattimo and Zabala*, the editors invited scholars from around the world to consider the impact of Vattimo and Zabala's work. It includes contributions from respected thinkers from Italy, the United States, the United Kingdom, Canada, Australia, Ireland, Columbia, France, Portugal, Hong Kong, Hungary, Chile, Germany, and Argentina. Though the essays in this volume are largely appreciative of the aims of *Hermeneutic Communism*, they do offer several salient criticisms that are worth mentioning here, and the editors gave Vattimo and Zabala the space to respond to each of the essays. Although, as one might expect, a full engagement with the various arguments presented in the work is beyond the scope of our present purpose, I would here like to examine some of the positions staked out in three of the contributing essays.

In "The End of Metaphysics, the Uses and Abuses of Philosophy, and Understanding Just a Little Better," Eduardo Mendieta (Penn) treats *Hermeneutic Communism* as a kind of manifesto and thereby evaluates its merits in relation to the affective rhetorical functions that, he argues, manifestos serve for practical politics. That is, he maintains, "Manifestos are ... credos or confessions of faith and thus operate as exhortations and a call to action based on the mobilization of moral suasion and power."[92] For example, he cites the moral force implicit in other notable manifestos, including *The Communist Manifesto* (1848), *The First Declaration of the Lacandon Jungle*

(1994), *The Declaration of the Occupation of New York City* (2011), and Horkheimer and Adorno's abandoned project *Towards a New Manifesto* (1956, finally published in 2011).[93] In each case, Mendieta argues, such proclamations not only provide a litany of grievances or a matter-of-fact program of political action but also function to shape political consciousness through moral reasoning and seek to empower subjects to take agency over the lived conditions of the world and thereby transform them.

Nevertheless, Mendieta expresses some concern regarding the limitations of such work. In particular, he (following Rorty) argues that philosophy should not be taking a guiding role in any political program. In this regard, he cites Rorty's frequently used phrase "Take care of freedom and truth will take care of itself."[94] By invoking this phrase, he is referring to Rorty's skepticism toward the idea that the force of politics should require the clarification of ontological or metaphysical categories. Phrasing this concern differently, we might ask, "Does Vattimo and Zabala's emphasis on hermeneutical philosophy serve to needlessly reinscribe metaphysics back into the practical work of democracy, where it can only obfuscate actual material concerns?" In response, Vattimo and Zabala point out that for Rorty himself philosophy and hermeneutics were not coextensive.[95] Thus, although Mendieta cites Rorty's postmetaphysical pragmatism, he does not seem to recognize the degree to which it overlaps with the role of hermeneutics in Vattimo and Zabala's conception of the political. Indeed, as has been demonstrated, if one is attentive to the specific construal of terms such as *philosophy*, *hermeneutics*, *truth*, and *metaphysics* in Vattimo's wider oeuvre, such criticisms largely appear misplaced.

Similarly, in their essay "Politics, Hermeneutics, and Truth," Jeff Malpas (University of Tasmania) and Nick Malpas (University of Sydney) argue that politics cannot do without the prescriptive *force* of truth, but their criticism appears to turn on a metaphysical reading of truth incommensurate with Vattimo and Zabala's argument. They say, for instance, that there is a clear contradiction between holding at one and the same time the beliefs that truth is "a reflection of a given objective order" and that truth is "'an imposition' (of 'the existing paradigm') by the strong on the weak."[96] Granted, Vattimo and Zabala are oftentimes much less clear on this point than they otherwise could be, but the apparent contradiction arguably arises less from internal conceptual inconsistency than from the various and often imprecise ways in which we use the term *truth*.

"Truth," as a commonplace description of something *objectively given*, amounts to the generalizable narratives concerning aspects of the world as we currently understand and agree them to be (independent of our perceptions of them). The strength or force of our shared understanding, however, varies depending on the specific objects or operations under consideration. Even so, many aspects of this givenness are sufficient enough to render them, for all intents and purposes at least, *practically* indubitable. Again, on my reading, Vattimo and Zabala—following in the venerable tradition of phenomenology—are not particularly interested in contesting the ontological nature of those dimensions of "reality" that can be said to *command belief* at a sensorial level. By contrast, few dimensions of politics (should) enjoy such incontrovertibility. Instead, the degree to which we wish to call something "true" and utilize the implicit force of that designation within political arguments serves a rhetorical, not merely a descriptive, function.

I mean that calling something "true" in general typically functions rhetorically as a shorthand reflecting confidence in the defensibility of a claim relative to the means by which a claim is verified. If people make contradictory truth claims, such disagreements might arise from differences over whether a particular assertion meets some specific shared criteria or differences over which criteria themselves are operative in a given case. For example, if I say, "It is true that the MMR (measles, mumps, rubella) vaccine does not cause autism," the use of the word *true* in this instance *stands in* for a much broader set of rationales—all of which may be perfectly defensible, but few of which will be, in principle, incontestable.

In a real sense, we know this—which is why the word *true* can stand as a shorthand—at least for those who share a similar set of assumptions about how beliefs themselves are justified. If I say, "It is true that the MMR vaccine does not cause autism," I likely mean something along the lines of "When thoroughly tested in duplicatable studies over a long period of time in multiple observed settings, there has been no discernable empirical link discovered between receiving an MMR vaccine and increased instances of autism." Furthermore, implicit in this description are multiple other connected assumptions about the nature of evidence and its verification, all of which are bound together. We know that these claims are contestable but also maintain that they are defensible because they meet standards that we think are operative relative to the sort of claims we are making in this instance. It would of course be more precise to say that by the generally accepted standards of empirical science, this claim is highly defensible based on the best available evidence to date. But the concision dictated by ordinary speech means that we default to simply calling this claim "true" as a practically settled matter.

What about political claims that carry within them the same sort of bound-up sets of internally reinforced rationales that can be deployed as commonsense statements of truth? For example, someone might say, "States have a right to protect their borders," in response to the migrant crisis, or "Communism has failed everywhere it has been tried," in relation to proposals for even moderate social reforms. Taken as a self-evident maxim, such truth claims tend to function more as thought-terminating clichés.

If two people hold contrary positions on a topic yet maintain as operative the same basic criteria for determining the truth of their claims, then all that is necessary to establish that one claim overrides another is to determine which claim is best supported by the currently available body of evidence. In this way, we can say that the implicit force of the accepted criteria exerts sufficient pressure on both parties to recognize the more substantial assertion as having the greater claim to "truth" (however provisional it may ultimately be). If, however, the disagreement stems from a lack of mutually held principles for determining the validity of claims, then evidence alone will be insufficient to arrive at an agreement. Understanding that separate sets of rules or language games exist as parameters for different discourses—sometimes on overlapping topics—and adjudicating how those sets of rules relate to one another require hermeneutics.

To return to the point advanced by Malpas and Malpas, it is admittedly confusing (even equivocal) to say without qualification both that *truth* has *force* as a reflection of a given objective order and that *truth* serves as a term for the *forced* imposition of an existing paradigm by the strong on the weak. But is it necessarily contradictory? That arguably depends on if we are willing to recognize the validity of both senses of the terms *truth* and *force* relative to their use in different (but related) discourses. I think this confusion results primarily from a lack of clarity over which sense of the words *truth* and *force* is being utilized in a particular instance. If there are, for example, two competing claims, they are judged by the same set of criteria, and claim A meets the agreed-upon standards for warranted assertability more sufficiently than claim B, then we can say that, mutatis mutandis, any reasonable subject would be *forced* to accept claim A over claim B. The imperatival force implied in the logic of rules is, I think, clearly not the same as physical coercion—even if the former can be used to justify the latter.

This distinction is important because while Malpas and Malpas assert that beliefs can be imposed, they want to emphasize that such an imposition does not make them "true" in the sense of their possessing the logical force that stems from the brute givenness of a certain set of sensorial experiences. Again, however, this argument is made against a position that Vattimo and Zabala do not appear to be making. Instead, Vattimo and Zabala are discussing those beliefs that have indeed been imposed by forms of coercion and continue to support structures of power in society—some of which have, through the process of historical accretion, perhaps taken on the valence of objective or transcendent truth. This state of affairs requires not so much wholesale rejection of such beliefs as a reevaluation.

This being the case, one might well ask, "Why not simply call such imposed or coerced beliefs 'mere appearances' or 'falsehoods,' then?" and "Why attack the notion of truth if one is not actually advocating for relativism?" I think these questions make a fair point. As I see it, however, the reason for Vattimo and Zabala's refusal to utilize the common appearance/reality distinction is that they would argue that the ordinary ways in which we speak of truth are too laden with metaphysical preconceptions. For the necessary reevaluation to take place, we must disrupt our preconceptions and timeworn patterns of thought.

It is fair to say that the confusion oftentimes generated over Vattimo's professed nihilism (and what that entails) may be viewed as counterproductive to his actual aims. We cannot here parse the long philosophical history of the nature of assent—or its relation to logic, cognition, and rhetoric—but Vattimo and Zabala's goal is clearly not some attempt to readjudicate the nature of claims regarding perceptual experience. Their argument regarding truth is instead firmly centered around politics and in this respect aims to replace the transhistorical/foundationalist/metaphysical conception of absolute truth with the countervailing notion of truth as self-consciously provisional and arrived at via conversation and consensus. This is why Vattimo and Zabala state in their response to Malpas and Malpas, "As a central concept of our philosophical tradition (together with Being), truth should not be overcome in the sense of '*überwunden*' (defeating, forgetting or removing), but rather in the sense of '*verwindung*,' that is, twisting or weakening in a productive manner."[97]

Finally, in his essay "Nietzsche the Communist? A Genealogy of Interpretation," Robert T. Valgenti (Lebanon Valley College) centers his critique on two interrelated aspects of Vattimo and Zabala's argument. First, Valgenti highlights that the middle figure in the movement from Heidegger back to Marx in Vattimo and Zabala's argument is Nietzsche. He argues that even while pressing Nietzsche into the service of their postmetaphysical position, Vattimo and Zabala fail to properly engage with Nietzsche's pointed rejection of both Christianity and left-wing political movements (i.e., socialism, communism, anarchism): "If there is a problematic (yet perhaps only seeming) contradiction at the core of the argument put forward by Gianni Vattimo and Santiago Zabala in *Hermeneutic Communism*, it centers upon the Christian-socialist principles of emancipation and community that motivate the authors' political and philosophical program, ones that appear to ignore the powerful critique of such principles put forward by one of their primary philosophical touchstones, Friedrich Nietzsche."[98]

Valgenti contends that the authors' stated "preference for an integral transformation/distortion/twisting (*Verwindung*) of late-capitalism and democracy rather than its simple overcoming (*Überwindung*)" is out of step with Nietzsche's conception of "an *Übermensch*, an anti-Christ, an anti-nihilist, or anyone else who might restore strength and vitality to the human figure."[99] Nietzsche's critique of Christianity and left-wing social movements was that they were based on resentment, which leads socialists, he argued, to denigrate society and seek revenge against their social betters, whereas Christians instead project their consolatory vengeance into an imagined future (the Final Judgment). Both, he felt, lack a powerful causal impulse, or élan vital, to borrow a term from Bergson.

For Nietzsche, revolutions are always destructive because they are born out of insipidness, lack, weakness, so that the ends for which they seek cannot but be perverse. Nietzsche rejected the dialectical process of Socrates/Plato through Christianity to Hegel as being the logic of plebian struggle (a "slave morality"): that is, the refusal to see the necessity of difference and hierarchy and thus the refusal to likewise see beauty, superior strength, and greatness. The ideal of the Übermensch is the Machiavellian prince, a self-asserting figure like Cesare Borgia, not a life-denying character like Christ or Parsifal.[100] Nietzsche's antimetaphysics conceives of the "will to truth" as a product of this resentment, perhaps also with all its implied violence. This being the case, Valgenti asks, by grounding their ideas in community and emancipation, have Vattimo and Zabala given in to a "metaphysical temptation"? His response: "It is not altogether clear from their work if the essentializing structures of framed democracies and global capitalism will undergo the same sort of weakening such that they are neither overcome nor destroyed but rather metabolized and incorporated into a new awareness of our global responsibilities."[101]

Valgenti contrasts this approach of recovery and emancipation with what he sees as the more thoroughgoing call for a radical upheaval of society advanced in Vattimo's earlier works, in particular *The Subject and the Mask*. Through Vattimo's embrace of weak thought, Valgenti says, his political project "takes a decidedly pacifist turn" and "exchanges the demand for liberation for an increasing focus on the reduction of violence." Drawing on the Second Treatise of Nietzsche's *Genealogy of Morals* (1887), Valgenti argues that the Christian and the anarchist have a shared history based on resentment. Each, therefore, has "transformed the positive ideals of liberation and community into the most abstract and totalizing terrors."[102] The remedy for this from within the Nietzschean frame, he contends, is the notion of the "sovereign individual" who can attain individual liberation and shared community without being imposed on from the outside.

Valgenti asks pointedly, "Do Vattimo and Zabala really interpret (rather than blindly accept or condemn) the patrimony of positive and negative guiding principles inherited from the history of Christianity, socialism, and capitalism—one that cannot be completely overcome, and that for good reasons, should not be entirely tossed out? What in the end keeps the authors' interpretation of the world from being just another violent (and expedient) imposition upon it, just another symptom of resentment?"[103] This concern appears to be borne out by the Latin American examples provided by Vattimo and Zabala, who close *Hermeneutic Communism* with a discussion of the importance of President Hugo Chávez (1954–2013) of Venezuela in fostering the "pink tide" that revitalized communism in areas of Central and South America in the early years of the twenty-first century.

For Vattimo and Zabala, Venezuela under Chávez as well as other South American democracies represent(ed) "an example, not necessarily an exemplar," of the alternative economic and political formations that are possible outside the sphere of Western neoliberal hegemony. Even so, Chávez was accused of undermining democracy by gradually centralizing too much power in the hands of the executive, threatening the independence of the judiciary through his intimidation and imprisonment of Judge María Lourdes Afiuni, and committing various human rights violations.[104] Valgenti refers to this section of *Hermeneutic Communism* as the "most philosophically problematic moment of the book":

[Vattimo and Zabala] tell us that "we should stop considering as scandalous the idea that a revolution can occur without a previous authorization by the citizens as expressed in a referendum; after all, no modern constitution was ever born 'democratically'..." (*HC* [*Hermeneutic Communism*], 136). And while the South American governments in question "have not yet betrayed parliamentary democracy," they have a right to violate those rules because, citing Mao, "revolution is not a dinner party" but "an act of violence by which one class overthrows another" (*HC*, 136–7). Having now entertained (or even endorsed) the violence they spent the previous 130 pages condemning, the authors conclude with what many could (and I suspect will) view as four pages of hermeneutic equivocation. On the one hand, regarding the issue of whether or not hermeneutic communism justifies a violent revolution, the authors seem to suggest that this might be an unavoidable and unfortunate consequence of the violence that already permeates the order of framed democracies; on the other hand, the authors insist that mass movements of passive resistance offer the surest confirmation that a hermeneutic communism does not take up the arms of its oppressors or fall back into Sartre's "practico-inert" (*HC*, 140). Everything depends, in the end, on how we interpret the world at this crucial moment—the very sort of emergency that the authors contend the world today lacks.[105]

These are serious challenges. If among the core tenets of your philosophical/political program are democracy and a commitment to the reduction of violence, then support for the former governments of Chávez in Venezuela and Fidel Castro in Cuba would for many readers seriously undermine confidence in those commitments. No doubt, one could retort that supporters of supposedly pro-democracy policies by Western powers in the Global South are in no position to criticize the use of violence for political ends.

Regardless of how valid such a countercritique may be, engaging in this sort of whataboutism doesn't actually address the underlying criticism.

In response, Vattimo and Zabala clarify that weak thought—along with its accompanying commitment to the reduction of violence—does not represent a "pacifist turn" in Vattimo's thought. Instead, they state,

> the "series of political and personal events" at the origins of "weak thought" are not only a response to the violence of the Red Brigades, but also [an effort] to overcome the dichotomy [between] violence/pacifism in favor of the defense, rights, and liberation of the weak. . . . In sum, the call to "reduce violence" comes after accepting the end of metaphysics, that is, the possibility of another metaphysics. This acceptance does not imply resignation, passivity and "pacifism," but rather productive interpretations against the impositions and conservations propagated by the bearers of power.[106]

Though they do not say so, this position appears in keeping with the view on violence advanced by Noam Chomsky, who has stated: "I think you can give many cases in which resistance to oppression, terror and violence is justified, I am not a pure pacifist. . . . However, I think it carries a very heavy burden of proof and the burden of proof is always on those who choose violence. Sometimes the burden can be met in my opinion, but it's a heavy burden."[107] Recognizing that resistance against oppression often entails violence, even if only defensive, is not the same as advocating armed resistance as a plank in your political program. Furthermore, that such a position follows from a Nietzschean-inspired position vis-à-vis metaphysics does not mandate that the position should remain loyal to Nietzsche's own personal political commitments. Indeed, the liberation of the individual in Nietzsche has very little to do with politics in the first place.[108] That Vattimo and Zabala ultimately choose to depart from Nietzsche in certain respects in favor of a Christian-socialist frame appears immaterial to the question regarding the effectiveness of hermeneutic communism as a political program.

II

RELIGION

3

CATHOLICISM, SECULARITY, AND THE AGE OF THE SPIRIT

These concepts of "God" arise strictly from metaphysics, according to the sole demand of onto-theo-logy[;] . . . if the thought that wants to "deconstruct" the ontology of metaphysics attempts to reach "a more divine god," this quest belongs still and always to the meditation of Being, whose theology [sic] touches beings—without relation to the theology touched by faith.
—Jean-Luc Marion, *God Without Being*, 1991

No one can comprehend the uncreated God with his knowledge; but each one, in a different way, can grasp him fully through love. Truly this is the unending miracle of love: that one loving person, through his love, can embrace God, whose being fills and transcends the entire creation.
—*The Cloud of Unknowing*, fourteenth century

Some have interpreted Vattimo's use of religious language and imagery as representing Christianity, as it were, transposed into the key of weak thought.[1] Still others, perhaps less charitably, have viewed this interest with suspicion—characterizing it as Vattimo's procrustean attempt to force the venerable traditions of the Catholic Church into a delimited Nietzschean-Heideggerian box.[2]

For his part, Vattimo seemed instead to view his explicit reengagement with religion in his final years as representing merely a recognition, acknowledgment, and exploration of the fact that his idea of weak thought has always had an unmistakably Christian character. For our purposes, I argue in the present chapter that an important component in drawing out the religious dimensions of weak thought concerns how Vattimo connects the process of the "weakening/decline of strong structures" to the idea of "secularity."

Vattimo described "secularization" and its connection to weak thought as the "keystone" to his religious argument.[3] Therefore, in this chapter I begin by discussing the relevant distinctions between two modes of understanding the concept of secularity. I then situate Vattimo's particular construal of secularity within the wider "return to religion" that has emerged in continental philosophy in recent decades. Next, I offer a brief excursus examining the historical process of secularization in Italy and corresponding developments in contemporary Catholic thought. This brief detour provides the background and context that, I maintain, is necessary for thinking about (Catholic) Christianity and secularity in appropriately "Vattimian" terms. Finally, with this structure in mind, I discuss Vattimo's own return to religion as well as his understanding of "salvation history," "kenosis," and "charity" and relate how these concepts feature specifically within the scope of weak thought.

SECULARITY AND THE "RETURN" OF RELIGION

As figures such as Charles Taylor, Akeel Bilgrami, and José Casanova have demonstrated, secularity is an ambiguous concept.[4] In common usage, the term *secularity* is often meant to denote the separation from religion or, indeed, the retreat of religion into the private sphere during the modern period (where it is meant to play no further guiding role in public life). But this modern notion is not the only or even the original sense of the word.[5] As Ingolf U. Dalferth has noted, "On the one hand [secularity] can mean that which is not religious, while on the other hand it can mean that which is not divine. The non-secular, from which the secular is being differentiated, means on the one hand the religious, and on the other hand the divine. The two contrasts are not the same, but define different ideas of secularity."[6] In the original sense of the word, therefore, there is no obvious or necessary conflict between the sacred and the secular. Indeed, they can be thought of—along with the ideas "transcendence" and "immanence"—less as distinct realities than as different vantage points. "Transcendence is the plan of salvation that counterposes itself, drags along events, or judges them from a point of view different from that of mere events. But 'distinct' does not mean that it is situated 'on high,' or somewhere else."[7]

The End of the "End of Ideology"

The commonly held narrative surrounding the ultimate course of Western modernity obviously follows this first mode of understanding the secular—namely, that it somehow represents a steady progression from the supposed superstition of religion to the rationality of science. This being the case, such a construal would seem to forever preclude the return of theological themes into the "respectable" circles of academic discourse. Nevertheless, Vattimo's reconnection with religious themes did not occur in a vacuum. Beginning primarily in the 1990s, there emerged a surprisingly renewed interest in theological themes and topics among many philosophers and cultural theorists (in particular those influenced by the phenomenological tradition).⁸ At present, we can say that even if theological considerations have not regained their previous position at the proverbial head of the table, for now at least, it seems, they are no longer confined to some irrelevant position in the academy's vestibule.⁹

Much of the credit for this "return of religion" as an object of serious study and consideration in the humanities is arguably owed to the engagement with religion found in the influential works of Jewish thinkers such as Walter Benjamin, Jacques Derrida, and Emmanuel Levinas.¹⁰ But a necessary condition for this reassessment also has to do with the development of specific themes and intellectual movements discussed in previous chapters as well as with many of the broader sociopolitical trends of recent decades. To cite just one example, this return is arguably inseparable from the steady collapse of general confidence in the modern idea that history follows some progressive trajectory toward a satisfactorily culminating "end of ideology."¹¹

In 1992, Francis Fukuyama had, of course, popularized the thesis that with the collapse of the Soviet Union and Soviet-backed regimes in the late 1980s and early 1990s, the world would somehow see a (figurative) "end of history." That is, with the collapse of the West's only major geopolitical rival, there could emerge a final sublation of previously antagonistic forms of social life into a single integrated system dominated by modern liberal-democratic (Western-style) nation-states.¹² Similarly, Nils Gilman spoke in his book *Mandarins of the Future* (2003) of this hope for a technocratic social world in which ideologies are no longer necessary as "an age in which science trumps politics."¹³ Over time, however, such positions have ultimately proved to be no less chimerical than any fantasy ever conjured by religion.¹⁴ In this regard, however, as we have already seen, science cannot trump ideology because science itself is irreducibly laden with both theories and specific values.

For Vattimo, secularity primarily entails the second mode of Dalferth's explication of the term—that is, a reorientation toward the sacred, albeit a reorientation that is, at least in part, facilitated by the declining sociopolitical significance of conventional religiosity.[15] In a certain sense, "secularization" is yet another name or aspect of the same ongoing process that has been variously described under the rubrics of hermeneutics, the "linguistic turn," postmetaphysics, postmodernity, the "death of God," nihilism, weak thought, and the ontology of decline. Yet there is another sense in which secularization is distinct from these other dimensions insofar as it is an irreducibly "Christian" process. In this regard, Vattimo claims that "secularization, the departure from the sacred characteristics of Western modernity, is an occurrence within the history of Western religiosity."[16] Furthermore, "to embrace the destiny of modernity and of the West means mainly to recognize the profoundly Christian meaning of secularization."[17] Here, one can see surprising parallels with a similar sentiment offered by the Peruvian liberation theologian Gustavo Gutiérrez, who once stated: "Secularization . . . is a process which not only coincides perfectly with a Christian vision of man, of history, and of the cosmos; it also favors a more complete fulfillment of the Christian life insofar as it offers man the possibility of being more fully human. . . . [Even so,] secularization poses a serious challenge to the Christian community. In the future it [the community] will have to live and celebrate its faith in a *nonreligious* world, which the faith itself has helped to create."[18]

Secularization is the result of an internal tendency that Vattimo has described favorably as the "self-consuming dynamic within Christianity."[19] Yet, he maintains, this purgation—this refining fire—is not consuming more and more idols on the way to the realization of some *ultimate metaphysical truth*. Instead, if Christianity and thus the Catholic Church is to have a future, it must (be)come a nondogmatic religion of charity—that is, a faith centered exclusively on an ever more purified love of God and neighbor. "By saying this," Vattimo asserts, "I am not putting forth the usual message of tolerance. Instead, I am speaking of the ideal development of human society, hence the progressive reduction of all rigid categories that lead to opposition, including those of property, blood, family, along with the excesses of absolutism."[20]

Joachim di Fiore and the Age of the Spirit

In his book *Dopo la cristianità* (*After Christianity*, 2002), Vattimo utilizes the tripartite division of history offered by Joachim di Fiore (c. 1135–1202) as a useful model for thinking about this conception of "salvation history" as, in part, the church's steady divestment from worldly power.[21] Fiore's scheme divides history into three successive epochs, each named for a different person of the Trinity. According to Fiore, the Age of the Father (the period under the Jewish law) was characterized by the believer's fear and awe before the majesty of the divine. The Age of the Son (the period of Christ's appearing to the present) is characterized by the believer's faith in Jesus as the hope of ultimate salvation. Finally, the Age of the Spirit (the eschatological future) is to be characterized by the believer's freedom and the true embodiment of Christian charity—where the "spirit of the law" (τὸ πνεῦμα τῆς διαθήκης) takes precedent over the "letter of the law" (τὸ γράμμα τῆς διαθήκης) (2 Cor. 3:6).

In the first stage, he argues, God was viewed as something akin to a *mysterium tremendum et fascinans*. Human beings, correspondingly, related to God as slaves. In the second stage, God is instead viewed as the loving Father, and human beings relate to him as his beloved children. In the final stage, however, God is to be viewed as "life-giving spirit"—as love incarnate. In this way, we can be said to have transitioned from being mere servants of God to instead being friends of God (John 15:15; Jas. 2:23).[22]

To be sure, this process of secularization—or moving toward the Age of the Spirit by means of divesting from the sense of certainty and security that accompanies power—has not always been voluntary or led by internal forces within the church. More often than not, the church's leadership has been vehemently opposed to such changes. Even so, Vattimo sees something like the hand of providence guiding the process.[23] He states that "a particularly striking example, for those who are familiar with Italian history, is the destruction of the Pope's temporal power in the nineteenth century; this was interpreted at first as a sacrilege worthy of excommunication, but later acknowledged, at least by shrewder religious minds as a 'liberation' of the proper Christian core of the Church and the affirmation of its authentic image and was implicitly accepted by the ecclesiastical hierarchy."[24]

HISTORICAL BACKGROUND TO CONTEMPORARY CATHOLICISM

With this description of Fiore's history in mind, I would like to turn our attention briefly to the process of secularization in Italy in order to see what parallels we can draw between events in Vattimo's home country and his proposed process of weakening. This excursus will serve at least two purposes. First, it will provide a concrete example for exploring this abstract process of secularization. Second, it will provide some useful historical background for understanding important changes in both Italy and contemporary Catholicism. Indeed, the histories of secularization and the church are often so inexorably intertwined as to be practically indistinguishable.

Church and State: Catholicism in Italy

The first thing to know is that the power dynamics created by the pope's presence in Rome meant that Westphalian-style sovereignty was always going to be difficult to achieve in Italy. Furthermore, it meant that in Italy, even more so than elsewhere in Europe, there has historically been very little light separating politics from religion. The dual nature of the bishop of Rome's office—as both *summus pontifex* of the international Christian faith as well as regional prince of the Stati della Chiesa (Papal States)—has traditionally divided loyalties and historically made papal support for the cause of Italian nationalization always an unlikely prospect. Indeed, writers as early as Dante and Machiavelli had recognized that the very presence of the Papal States constituted an internal wedge issue within Italy that would invariably inhibit its consolidation.[25] Furthermore, by the mid-nineteenth century the ecclesiastical hierarchy recognized that the growing determination among nationalist liberals and revolutionaries to set clear boundaries between church and state represented an unambiguous threat to the historical prerogatives of the papacy.[26]

The example of what such reforms might entail had been set by the royal house of Savoy in the leading Italian state of Piedmont-Sardinia, which between 1850 and 1852 enacted a number of liberal reforms meant to modernize the state and establish more secular control for the ruling class. Though such efforts stopped far short of democracy, they did manage to pass a number of important ecclesiastical reforms, including legislation denying the right of sanctuary to individuals on church property, removing the church's official censorship authority, limiting the jurisdiction of ecclesiastical courts to "religious matters," curtailing the ability of ecclesiastical bodies to acquire property, establishing freedom of worship for Jews and Protestants, and drastically reducing the number of contemplative and mendicant orders.[27]

Unsurprisingly, these efforts enraged Pope Pius IX, who in 1864 notoriously responded by issuing the encyclical *Quanta cura*, which included a "Syllabus of Errors" that bitterly condemned eighty propositions, which he separated into ten distinct categories of casuistry. In effect, the work rejected any suggestion that the Holy See should moderate its position on the Roman pontiff's absolute sovereignty over the Papal States or accept the validity of contemporary ideas such as modernism, liberalism, secularism, rationalism, socialism, democracy, higher (biblical) criticism, freedom of the press, and freedom of conscience and religion. Similarly, political events in Italy also contributed to Pius's ultimate decision to convoke the First Vatican Council (1869–1870), which aimed to curtail the expansion of modernity and reinforce (the sharply declining) papal authority.[28]

Nevertheless, in some respects the pope had already lost this battle. After the Napoleonic Wars (1803–1815), the tides had already begun to shift in favor of the nationalists, leading to the Risorgimento (unification of Italy) and the eventual establishment of the Kingdom of Italy.[29] In spite of growing nationalist sentiments, the papacy was initially able to maintain most of its territorial holdings in central Italy with unlikely military support from the French emperor, Napoleon III. By 1861, however, many of the regions previously under papal control (some since the eighth century) had been absorbed into the new kingdom headed by Victor Emmanuel II.

The decisive moment in the mounting tension between king and pope came when at the start of the Franco-Prussian War (1870–1871) Louis-Napoléon recalled the last remaining garrison of French soldiers from Rome. These soldiers had been stationed in the Lazio (Latium) region to protect papal sovereignty over the city.[30] With their departure, the region was left exposed. When subsequent negotiations over the Vatican's integration into Italy held between the king's government (led by Prime Minister Cavour, the chief minister of Piedmont-Sardinia) and Pope Pius IX quickly broke down, Rome was annexed by force. In 1871, the capital of Italy was thereby moved from its previous location in Florence to the "Eternal City."

With the humiliating loss of all temporal power outside of St. Peter's Basilica and its immediate environs, the intransigent pope retaliated by excommunicating the Italian king and declaring himself to be a political prisoner confined to the Vatican.[31] Thus, as an act of defiance, Pius IX and his papal successors chose to remain exclusively within the walled confines of the Vatican until 1929—refusing to accept the legitimacy of the king's claim to Rome.[32] Despite the pope's refusal to accept the reality of the situation, the "liberal revolution" radically changed the context for how the church would operate in Italy thereafter. Among other things, Rome's absorption into the Italian state would influence papal attempts for generations to reclaim temporal authority and reestablish the papacy's previous societal position (especially in Italy). For example, as I have already noted, with traditional orders now largely curtailed, the hierarchy instead sought to exercise authority over the growing number of parochial and parachurch organizations that were then emerging amid an unexpected revival of European Catholicism in the second-half of the nineteenth century.

Yet despite the significant impact these liberal reforms had on the church's finances and organizational structure, at the time they had surprisingly little effect on the cultural life of average Italians. The society as a whole (when compared with, say, French society of the same period) remained for the most part socially conservative, patriarchal, conventionally moral, and staunchly Catholic. One area in which these reforms did begin to affect average Italians concerned the increasingly precarious position of the poor. Indeed, over time these changes helped to open a space for the development of unconventionally radical politics even amid an otherwise largely conservative society.

For example, one unforeseen consequence of the church's forced divestment of its landholdings was its impact on the living conditions of the peasantry. The redistribution of these lands most often meant their purchase by established (i.e., bourgeois) property owners, who then uprooted or renegotiated terms for their poorer leaseholders. While this process aided the rapid industrialization and capitalization of agriculture, it correspondingly swelled the ranks of the working poor (hourly and day laborers). In addition, this increase in precarity emerged at the same time that traditional avenues for assistance (i.e., Catholic charities and orders) were being shuddered for political or economic reasons, which contributed to the widespread internal migration of traditional agricultural labor in the South to newly industrialized factories in the rapidly urbanizing North. Thus, this state of affairs indirectly affected the conditions that eventually gave rise to the radical labor movement and the receptiveness to communism that began to emerge among disaffected Italians in the early decades of the twentieth century.[33]

Neo-Scholasticism: Traditionalism versus Modernity

In 1198, Pope Innocent III sent a letter to Prefect Acerbus and the nobles of Tuscany in which he claimed that just as God had set in the firmament one "great light" to govern the day and another "lesser light" to govern the night, so too had he appointed two types of rulers on the earth—the lesser to govern the bodies of men and the greater to govern their souls.[34] In this analogy, Innocent left little ambiguity as to which of the lights represented the bishop of Rome. Furthermore, at the time such a grand claim of papal authority was not without warrant. For example, in 1214, following a dispute with Innocent over the appointment of bishops, King John of England was forced to write a contrite letter to the pontiff in which he said, "All men should obey [Christ's] Vicar on earth, so that, as every knee is bowed to Jesus . . . so all men should obey His Vicar and strive that there may be one fold and one shepherd. All secular kings for the sake of God so venerate this Vicar, that unless they seek to serve him devotedly they doubt if they are reigning properly."[35]

Needless to say, by the time of the pontificate of Pius IX (1846–1878), such widely recognized claims of the pope's "fullness of power" (*plenitudo potestatis*) had long since become a thing of the past. In effect, the embattled pontificate of Pius IX represented the last dying embers of the old imperial church. As a result, those who would follow after him in the seat of St. Peter would have to contend with and adapt to this new reality. Indeed, this fact was recognized by Pius's immediate successor, Leo XIII (1878–1903). As James Hennesey writes, "Leo XIII did not dream of military victory. . . . He knew that his world was not that of the past. . . . What he wanted was to realize ultramontane goals unrealized under Pius IX by intellectualizing the combat with modernity, by providing a theoretical underpinning for his policies. He would not come to terms with modern values; rather, he would restore in the world *an objective and immutable order*, with the church as its most effective guardian. Renewal of Thomistic philosophy was the tool essential to his purpose."[36]

During this period, as part of the church's concern over the growing dominance of higher criticism and liberal theology (particularly in Germany and France), there had already been an increased interest in reviving medieval Scholastic thought as a means of combating the perceived spread of pluralism and subjectivism into Catholic theology.[37] In Italy in particular, this effort had been spearheaded by figures such as Gaetano Sanseverino, Giovanni Maria Cornoldi, and Giuseppe Pecci (older brother to Leo XIII). To this end, in 1879 Pope Leo issued the encyclical *Æterni Patris*, which elevated the thought of the medieval Italian San Tommaso d'Aquino (St. Thomas Aquinas) to official status, thereby ensuring that his would be the single unified system of theology employed in Catholic seminaries.[38]

> [Pope Leo] looked out at Europe and beyond and observed the breakdown of the Church's temporal authority, the growth of Modernist philosophy and secularism, and the need of the Church to address a host of complex questions regarding the Church and political sovereignty, industrialism and the economy, and other matters of personal and social ethics. To address these issues effectively, the Pope saw a decisive advantage in being able to ground the Church's teaching in a stable, authentic, and united philosophy. In other words, any reformation of the modern political, economic, and moral order required as its prerequisite the restoration of theology's intellectual integrity and unity.[39]

Thus, what neo-Scholastics of the period found so attractive in the thought of Aquinas in particular was not just that it harkened back to a pre-Reformation period—a period in which there was a (theoretically) unified Christendom under the auspices of a powerful pope—but also the stable sense of timelessness, unity, and totality they perceived in the Thomistic system. As Gerald A. McCool, SJ, notes,

> *Æterni Patris* . . . expressed the serene conviction of the nineteenth-century neo-Thomists that scholastic philosophy was a single metaphysical system, common to all the scholastic doctors, and that scholastic philosophy could gather up, preserve, and represent the essence of the patristic thought which it had superseded. Like every Aristotelian science, *scholastic philosophy was independent of history. It was unaffected by the personality and the cultural milieu of individual thinkers. Differences in time, historical outlook, and cultural expression were*

accidental. The encyclical saw no essential difference between the scholasticism of St. Thomas and St. Bonaventure and perceived no appreciable diversity between their philosophies and the philosophies of baroque scholastics like Cardinal Cajetan and Pope Sixtus V.[40]

As a result, neo-Scholasticism would remain a major intellectual trend, particularly in Europe, until the time of the Second Vatican Council (1962–1965).[41]

The Catholic Church's philosophical reaction to modernity reached its climax with a series of actions taken by Leo's successor, Pope Pius X. In 1907, the pontiff issued the antimodernist decree *Lamentabili sane exitu*, which condemned a series of propositions on perceived errors in biblical exegesis and interpretation. He followed this decree later in the same year with the encyclical *Pascendi Dominici gregis*—often referred to by its subtitle, *On the Doctrines of the Modernists*—which indirectly (but unmistakably) attacked the biblical criticism and philosophical approach of Catholic thinkers such as Louis Duchesne, Maurice Blondel, Édouard Le Roy, George Tyrrell, and Alfred Loisy.[42] After 1910, Pius even required all those with teaching authority in the church, from clergy to professors, to swear the Oath Against Modernism (a requirement not rescinded by the Congregation for the Doctrine of the Faith until 1967). The normativity of Thomism for the Catholic Church was further reinforced by the first codification of canon law, *Codex Iuris Canonici*, completed in 1917 (and remaining in force until its supersession in 1983).

By the first decades of the twentieth century, however, the interpretation of this *unified* system had begun to fracture into competing schools of Thomistic interpretation. The most influential approach to neo-Thomism prior to Vatican II was arguably best represented by figures such as Réginald Garrigou-Lagrange and Jacques Maritain (other important figures were Étienne Gilson and Cornelio Fabro). Despite their individual differences from one another, these thinkers affirmed a traditionally "realist" starting point for Thomistic thought. It was in this regard, therefore, that the most important rival to their approach came to be known as "transcendental Thomism." This approach is most often associated with Pierre Rousselot and Joseph Maréchal. In turn, their works would also later greatly influence figures such as Henri de Lubac, Karl Rahner, and Bernard Lonergan.

Against the more traditionally minded "realists," these "transcendental" thinkers did not begin, as it were, by asking questions about "reality" as such; rather, they began by considering the phenomenological conditions necessary for "asking" in the first place. That is, they felt that if we can be said to have a presumption about things, then the proper starting place for any inquiry is with the "presumption," not with the "things." As a result, critics have sometimes accused the transcendentalists of erroneously "read[ing] Thomas with the eyes of German idealists."[43]

La Nouvelle Théologie

In spite of neo-Scholasticism's increasing institutional codification during this period, beginning primarily in the 1930s thinkers associated with the so-called *nouvelle théologie* movement began to challenge its theological hegemony in Catholic thought. Interestingly, one can draw many parallels between this movement and similar developments occurring around the same time among Protestant thinkers such as Karl Barth and Rudolf Bultmann. For example, one can see points of similarity concerning their respective emphases on divine revelation, "existentialist" themes, and the necessity of critical engagement with the language of scripture. Against the ideal of "timelessness" espoused by the neo-Scholastics, there was among *nouvelle* thinkers instead a recognition of the hermeneutical situatedness of the individual and the historically conditioned shape in which each person hears and responds to the voice of divine revelation. Unlike corresponding shifts in Protestantism, however, *nouvelle théologie* was arguably less a reaction to the challenge of higher criticism than it was an attempt to retrieve the "multiple senses of scripture" that its proponents argued were prevalent during the Patristic Period (c. 100–451). The primary thinkers generally grouped together under this broad category of "new theology" included Karl Rahner (a former student of Heidegger), Henri de Lubac, Henri Bouillard, Pierre Teilhard de Chardin, Hans Urs von Balthasar, Hans Küng, Marie-Dominique Chenu, Yves Congar, Edward Schillebeeckx, and Joseph Ratzinger (Pope Benedict XVI).[44]

In 1946, the neo-Thomist Garrigou-Lagrange famously criticized these developments as representing nothing more than a surreptitious return to liberal modernism.[45] Garrigou-Lagrange took issue in particular with Bouillard's emphasis on the human role in conversion as well as his conviction that the eternal truths of faith should be expressed in contemporary philosophical terminology in order to aid modern readers in understanding. Like Rudolf Bultmann, Bouillard contended that while God's truths were eternal and universally applicable, the manner in which they are expressed is not. Garrigou-Lagrange, however, was concerned that accepting the position that the church's traditions concerning the divine were "time and culture specific" would invariably undermine their claim to represent transcendent truth.

Garrigou-Lagrange's argument can be viewed in broad terms as the institutional response toward the "new theology" at the time. The last major institutional reaction to modernism from the ecclesiastical hierarchy prior to Vatican II came in the form of an encyclical by Pope Pius XII, *Humani generis* (promulgated in 1950), which attacked trends in the church among certain unnamed dissenting theologians. As Gerard Loughlin notes, "The final concern of

Humani Generis was that people should attend to what the church taught and, when all other justification was lacking, simply submit to its authority and assent to its teaching. The encyclical asserts its own status as that of the ordinary teaching authority of the church, which is to say of Christ himself."[46]

Aggiornamento: Pope John XXIII and Vatican II

As the Argentinian theologian José Míguez Bonino once noted,

> The Church, unprepared for a culture in which it would have to gain its place in society through direct persuasion and influence, naturally sought support in those groups and parties which offered the possibility of extending the traditional forms of influence; it became both dependent on and allied with the conservative parties made up of the rich landowners and the old . . . aristocracy. It became estranged both from the peasant and emergent workers' classes (who clung to their traditional folk-Catholicism coupled with a profound mistrust and hostility toward the hierarchic Church) and from the intelligentsia who embraced the new philosophical and political ideas.[47]

Nevertheless, in spite of more than half a century of the church's official animus toward the modern world, the winds of fate began to shift quite drastically in 1958. Following the death of Pius XII, Angelo Giuseppe Roncalli was elected as his successor to the throne of St. Peter—taking the regnal name John XXIII. Roncalli, then serving in semiretirement as patriarch of Venice, had been elevated to the papal office largely because he was the least objectionable option.[48] With his famously cheerful disposition, he had over the years amassed few enemies among the Roman Curia, and many felt that he would represent a welcome change in tone from the combative posture and "siege mentality" that the church leadership had assumed over the previous century. Furthermore, most observers expected that as someone who was seventy-six years old at the time and not then known for taking controversial positions, Roncalli would have a relatively short and uneventful time in office. These expectations were shattered, however, when Pope John made the surprise announcement in January 1959 of his intention to convene an ecumenical council.

Unlike previous councils, Vatican II initially had no clearly defined purpose beyond "updating" (*aggiornamento*) the church. To determine the agenda, therefore, the pope created a commission tasked with facilitating a large-scale consultation with the Curia, the bishops, and even faculties of theology from Catholic universities. In short, these consultations resulted in thousands of suggestions that were then organized into a series of schemas. During the meetings, these schemas were discussed and voted on by commissions headed by the bishops (in consultation with theological advisers). Notably, *nouvelle théologie* figures such as Rahner, de Lubac, Küng, Chenu, Congar, Schillebeeckx, and Ratzinger served as theological advisers (or *periti*) to the bishops (the so-called council fathers) who had actual voting authority, and they thereby exercised influence on the shape of the council's final documents.[49] The work of the council continued even after the death of Pope John in 1963 and the election of his successor, Giovanni Battista Montini, as Pope Paul VI. In the end, Vatican II was in preparation from 1959 1962 and in session on and off between 1962 and 1965.

Although it would obviously be impossible (and far too tangential) to summarize here all that the Second Vatican Council achieved, in the decades that have followed it two of its agreed-upon documents have remained central for any proper understanding of contemporary Catholicism. The first was the *Lumen gentium*, the Dogmatic Constitution of the Church, promulgated in 1964. Here, the council broke with the position previously advanced by Pius XII in his encyclical *Mystici corporis Christi* (1943), in which he restricted the ascription of the "Body of Christ" exclusively to the "One Holy, Catholic, and Apostolic, *Roman* Church." As Cardinal Avery Dulles later noted, "Relying on the sacramental model, the Council was able to declare that while the Church of Christ, considered as a society 'subsisted' in the Roman Catholic communion, this did not exclude the presence of ecclesial elements elsewhere."[50] This, of course, opened the way for a more open and ecumenical dialogue with non-Catholic Christians and members of other faiths.[51]

Vatican II's second major contribution was *Gaudium et spes*, the Pastoral Constitution on the Church in the Modern World, promulgated 1965, which set forth an examination of the role of the church in the world outside of Christianity. This work argues for the inherent dignity of humanity, the communal nature of existence, and the need to acknowledge human rights. As a result, it calls for the church to be an agent of unity. In stark contrast with the church's positions during the prior century, *Gaudium et spes* proclaims:

> Christ, to be sure, gave His Church no proper mission in the political, economic or social order. The purpose which He set before her is a religious one. But out of this religious mission itself come a function, a light and an energy which can serve to structure and consolidate the human community according to the divine law. As a matter of fact, when circumstances of time and place produce the need, she can and indeed should initiate activities on behalf of all men, especially those designed for the needy, such as the works of mercy and similar undertakings. The Church recognizes that worthy elements are found in today's social movements, especially an evolution toward unity, a process of wholesome socialization and of association in civic and economic realms. The promotion of unity belongs to the innermost nature of the Church, for she is, "thanks to her relationship with

Christ, a sacramental sign and an instrument of intimate union with God, and of the unity of the whole human race." Thus, she shows the world that an authentic union, social and external, results from a union of minds and hearts, namely from that faith and charity by which her own unity is unbreakably rooted in the Holy Spirit. *For the force which the Church can inject into the modern society of man consists in that faith and charity put into vital practice, not in any external dominion exercised by merely human means.*[52]

In spite of the church's profound institutional shift in disposition enacted during the late 1960s, the practical effects of Vatican II for the church (both inside and outside of Italy) have been decidedly mixed. On the one hand, by making pragmatic changes and shifting the church's approach toward the modern world, Vatican II made the liturgy more accessible to average Catholics; expanded the leadership role of the laity; validated the concepts of democracy, human rights, and the freedom of conscience; and opened a dialogue with non-Christians and members of other Christian confessions. In addition, it has empowered progressive elements in the church to go further than the council ever did, speak more candidly about other pressing issues, including priestly celibacy, contraception, bioethics, environmentalism, gay rights, and the role of women in the church, as well as, more recently, discuss the harmful legacies of clergy sexual abuse and the church's historical role in European colonialism and imperialism.

On the other hand, many Catholics felt that the changes initiated by Vatican II went too far too fast, sparking a long-standing conservative backlash that continues to divide the church to this day. The papacies of John Paul II and Benedict XVI, although not explicitly breaking with Vatican II, clearly reflected this more conservative appraisal of the meaning of the council for the role of the church in the world.[53] The elevation of Pope Francis in 2013 in some respects realigned the official leadership of the church more closely with the reforming spirit of Vatican II, though most of the changes made under his leadership were in emphasis and style rather than in doctrine. The recent selection of Francis's close associate, Robert Francis Prevost, to head the church looks likely to continue this long-term shift toward secularization. In addition, Cardinal Prevost's selection of the papal name "Leo XIV," explicitly echoing Leo XIII and his concerns for laborers, is a telling indication of the new pope's intended direction.

4

RELIGION AND THE (POST)SECULAR WORLD

The church does not exist for its own sake; it exists for the other, for the liberating redemption of the world in solidarity.
—Anselm K. Min, *The Solidarity of Others in a Divided World*, 2004

Every religion is originally a "worldview" or "comprehensive doctrine" in the sense that it claims authority to structure a form of life in its entirety. A religion must relinquish this claim within a secularized society marked by a pluralism of worldviews.
—Jürgen Habermas, *Between Naturalism and Religion*, 2009

VATTIMO'S RETURN TO RELIGION

As the reader will recall, Vattimo quietly walked away from his own Catholic faith during his Heidelberg days (1962–1963).[1] Though he made no public spectacle of his apostasy at the time, it is clear from his writings that as a "cradle Catholic" and daily communicant since early childhood, he viewed his break with the church as among the most significant events of his adult life. It is for this reason that Vattimo described his subsequent return to

Christianity as "the ultimate and most scandalous chapter of my history."[2] This unlikely turn of events first began in 1985, when Vattimo's former student, the art historian and film critic Marco Vallora, who was at the time working as an editorial consultant at Einaudi Press, asked Vattimo to review the recent Italian translation of René Girard's influential book *Des choses cachées depuis la fondation du monde* (*Things Hidden Since the Foundation of the World*, 1978).

The impact of this work on Vattimo was both immediate and decisive. He stated later that "[Girard's book served to open] the way to a conception of the postmodern as a kind of radicalization of secularization, as the end of metaphysics, the end of this entire victim structure."[3] That is, there were key elements in Girard that, Vattimo felt, not only fit comfortably within his wider conception of weak thinking but also helped to fill out that image in new and distinct ways.

Before outlining elements of Girard's thought (and Vattimo's appropriation of them), however, I think it will be instructive to mention what arguably laid the conceptual groundwork for Vattimo's initial receptiveness to Girard's position. Without such context, it would perhaps not be immediately clear why Vattimo should have found elements of Girard's argument either useful or persuasive in the first place. Arguably, the best place to begin is with a lecture Heidegger gave in 1938, "Die Zeit des Weltbildes" ("The Age of the World Picture," published in his essay collection *Holzwege* in 1950). Here, Heidegger argues that modernity conceives of the world as a representation or a picture. In this way, our relation to the world as subjects viewing an external object becomes a matter of "world-viewing." Even so, Heidegger felt that modernity's tendency toward reduction and univocity would lead invariably to conflicts between "competing" worldviews or pictures of the world. Important for Vattimo, however, is the fact that implicit in this framework is the seeming impossibility of ever representing as privileged any single unified worldview over another.

This hermeneutical framework found in Heidegger also becomes crucial for the second key element in understanding the philosophical background for Vattimo's eventual return to religion—namely, his acceptance of Jean-François Lyotard's conception of postmodernity. Lyotard had characterized his much-discussed general "incredulity towards grand narratives" as being a consequence of the "truth condition of science being turned back against itself," resulting in "a process of delegitimation fueled by the demand for legitimation itself."[4] In this way, an unforeseen consequence of the hollowing-out of modernist claims was that it appeared to leave open a backdoor for the return to religion (even if the religion returned to is now in a "weakened" form—that is, as one story among others, with no legitimate claim to master status). In this regard, Vattimo has stated: "The 'end of modernity,' or in any case its crisis, has . . . been accompanied by the dissolution of the main philosophical theories that claimed to have done away with religion: positivist scientism, Hegelian and then Marxist historicism. Today there are no longer strong, plausible philosophical reasons to be atheist, or at any rate to dismiss religion."[5] Moreover, ironically, "postmodernity, as envisaged by Lyotard, like the dissolution of metaphysics in Heidegger, has reopened the space for religious discourse: if the grand narratives are finished, the possibility of speaking of God is also reborn, in the sense that religious discourse can no longer be contradicted by the results of science, or interpreted simply as a primitive phase in the evolution of humanity. In this connection, my discovery of René Girard was decisive."[6]

SACRED VIOLENCE: RENÉ GIRARD AND THE MYTH OF VICTIMIZATION

Vattimo states in his autobiography that it was Girard who "re-Christianized" him, albeit in his own way, stating, "It was with him that I began to think that it might be possible to bind weakening, secularization, and Christianity closely together."[7] Indeed, elsewhere Vattimo has even stated that "reading Girard's work was as decisive for me as it was to read some of the works of Heidegger, which left a profound mark on me in a different period of my life, and not just in intellectual terms but existential and personal ones too."[8] What then, we might ask, is Girard's position, and how does it relate to weak thought?

In *Things Hidden Since the Foundation of the World*, written as Girard's dialogue with two psychiatrists, Guy Lefort and Jean-Michel Oughourlian, Girard argues that individual choice and conceptions of value exist within a wider economy of "mimetic desire."[9] That is to say, we want things primarily because others also want them. In other words, Girard thought that as one person or group begins to desire some particular thing, others (whether as a result of biology or social conditioning) likewise begin to mirror that same desire. Apart from the satisfaction of basic needs, however, the ostensible objects of desire can be altogether arbitrary. Indeed, the value of most objects is purely instrumental. As a consequence of our having learned how to desire from observing the desires of others, he believed that we all are ensured to want the same (or at the very least similar) things. This would arguably not be an issue, of course, if the desired resources or objects in question were plentiful and renewable—only for those objects whose scarcity is perhaps their sole claim to value. Unfortunately, most objects of desire exist under conditions of scarcity. There are, after all, only so many Fabergé eggs or paintings by da Vinci or Cézanne in the world—or, for that matter, royal titles or luxury villas on the French Riviera. As a result, the value of such objects increases relative to supply—as does the likelihood of conflict between competing parties over access to them.

Girard sees this tendency toward a triangulation of desire (or what we might simply call "envy") as the root cause of all social hostility and violence. Furthermore, when the unresolved animosity between competing parties reaches a certain level, such that it threatens a veritable bellum omnium contra omnes, Girard maintains that the only effective way to resolve the conflict and thereby preserve social bonds is to find a common enemy—that is, a mutually agreed-upon third party on whom to deflect collective opprobrium. He refers to this party as the "scapegoat"; within a "victimage mechanism," this ritual victim is sacrificed (literally or metaphorically) to act as a pressure valve for a society experiencing internal tensions. According to Girard, in traditional societies this important communal function was institutionalized in ritualistic civic and religious practices. Thus, the sacrificial victim dies so that the society might live (cf. John 11:50).

The title of Girard's work, *Things Hidden Since the Foundations of the World*, is, of course, derived from Jewish and Christian scripture (Ps. 78:2; Matt. 13:35). Indeed, it was here that Girard for the first time applied his earlier proposed theory of mimetic desire explicitly to the biblical narrative. In doing so, he argued that the Gospels, far from being yet another example of the scapegoat mechanism, instead deconstruct it. That is, the story of Jesus subverts ingrained social expectations concerning the nature and relationship of the sacrificial victim.

Girard maintained that earlier myth had traditionally functioned to sacralize official violence and persecution.[10] This was done in an attempt to contain and direct the violence and persecution by demonstrating the ultimate guilt and thus the rightful condemnation of the victim.[11] In this way, as Vattimo explains, "the scapegoat is invested with sacred attributes and made into a cultic object, while still retaining the status of sacrificial victim."[12] Such actions, Girard argued, are preserved in attestations of Greek *pharmakós* (φαρμακός) rituals as well as in the eponymous biblical image of the "scapegoat" (לַעֲזָאזֵל, Lev. 16).[13] Paradigmatic literary examples of this principle are also provided in Sophocles's *Oedipus* and in the character Encolpius from Petronius's *Satyricon*.[14] As a result, Girard boldly asserts that "religion is organized around a more or less violent disavowal of human violence." Following this essentially anthropological claim, however, Girard also immediately offers his own equally broad and assertive theological conviction that "the religion which comes from man amounts to [violence], as opposed to the religion which comes from God."[15]

In his estimation, Christianity represents a revolutionary dismantling of this logical framework of violence and victimization. To be sure, Girard argues that an inversion of expectations regarding guilt and punishment is intimated in several places earlier in the Hebrew Bible (e.g., Abel, Joseph, Job, Isaiah's "suffering servant," etc.), but these examples do not go far enough in actually *overturning* the victimage mechanism. By contrast, Christianity breaks from this pattern through its explicit identification of the divine with the victim of such sacrificial violence—God himself becomes the victim of religious violence! Through this inversion, Girard argues, the systemic violence against the "Other," orchestrated and sanctioned by the "powers that be," is thereby unmasked or "revealed" in the Gospel narrative. As a result, the Gospels serve as a critique *from below* of the prevailing socioreligious order. Intimately connected to the proclamation of God's revelation in Christ, then, is a subversive hermeneutics of suspicion leveled against those who would wield or sanction violence and persecution in the name of some prevailing social order (particularly against the marginalized; cf. Matt. 25:31–46). Girard claims:

> Because it reproduces the founding event of all rituals, the Passion is connected with every ritual on the entire planet. There is not an incident in it that cannot be found in countless instances: the preliminary trial, the derisive crowd, the grotesque honors accorded to the victim, and the particular role played by chance, in the form of casting lots, which here affects not the choice of the victim but the way in which his clothing is disposed of. The final feature is the degrading punishment that takes place outside the holy city in order not to contaminate it.[16]

For there to be an effective, sacralizing act of transference, it is necessary that the victim inherit all the violence from which the community has been exonerated. It is because the victim genuinely passes as guilty that the transference does not come to the fore as such. This bit of conjuring brings about the happy result for which the lynching mob is profoundly grateful: the victim bears the weight of the incompatible and contradictory meanings that, juxtaposed, create sacredness. For the Gospel text to be mythic in our sense, it would have to take no account of the arbitrary and unjust character of the violence done to Jesus. In fact, the opposite is the case: the Passion is presented as a blatant piece of injustice. Though later theological development rationalized the Passion in sacrificial terms, the New Testament authors could never bring themselves to treat those responsible for Jesus's execution as guiltless or as having acted justly, even if they conceived of the actions of those responsible as having fulfilled God's providential plan of salvation. Likewise, nowhere is Jesus presented as having deserved the treatment he received at the hands of the political and religious authorities.[17]

GIRARD AND CHRISTIANITY: SOME METHODOLOGICAL CONCERNS

Before we go any further, I would like to briefly highlight what I take to be at least one potentially troubling aspect of Girard's approach in order to effectively outline where I believe Vattimo differs from Girard in key respects: namely, Girard's position that Christianity is *alone* among the world's faith systems in representing the nonviolent "religion which comes from God," as opposed to the inherently violent "religion which comes from man." From a strictly anthropological perspective, this assertion appears to give undue priority to Christianity over other symbolic systems.[18] As a result, the somewhat liminal space Girard's argument occupies between anthropological theory and confessional theological statement leads, in my estimation at least, to methodological confusion concerning the actual nature and extent of his claims.

That is, in presenting as disinterested observation his position that Christianity is superior to other religions vis-à-vis sacrifice and violence, Girard seems to give license to a now widely discredited tendency from a previous era of academic discourse regarding the origins and meaning of religion.[19] The methodological predilection to which I am referring was the tendency among early European and American scholars of religion to frame Christianity as constituting either the culmination of a progressive development away from "primitive superstitions" or as a sui generis break from all other so-called natural religions. This is troubling not merely because Girard seems not to have recognized this framing as a bias but more importantly—in light of Christianity's now unavoidable historical associations with western Europe—because such a position invariably smacks of ethnocentrism.[20]

This methodological disposition in favor of Western Christianity is obviously not restricted to Girard. To be sure, it goes back to the earliest period of academic studies in religion. For example, similarly negative comparisons between Christianity and other faith traditions can be observed in Hegel's distinction between "determinate religions" and "consummate/absolute religion," Schleiermacher's "natural religions" versus "positive/true religion," and F. Max Müller's "natural religions" versus "theosophical religion."[21] This trend also continued through writers in the so-called History of Religions School (Religionsgeschichtliche Schule). In each case, human societies (and thus their respective religious traditions) are viewed as existing on a singular linear trajectory from barbarism to civilization—with European Christian society generally taken as the most advanced stage on this journey. This same tendency was, of course, later carried forward by figures such as E. B. Tyler, James George Frazer, and Sigmund Freud—this time with scientific rationalism or demythologization being the culmination of this progressive movement away from supposedly "primitive" thought patterns.[22] If history has taught us anything, however, it is that such claims should be approached with more than a tincture of suspicion.[23] *Viatores, cave! Hic sunt dracones.*

The desire to present the natural preference one might have for one's own tradition (in this case Western Christianity) as being somehow *objective* (or grounded in a *scientifically* verifiable way) when compared to others' preference for other belief systems has, to say the very least, some rather unsavory implications. Certainly, the idea of religious progress has been more than incidentally implicated in the long history of Western cultural imperialism. Indeed, as Tomoko Masuzawa has noted in *The Invention of World Religions* (2005),

> The eighteenth- and nineteenth-century discourse on religion [was] ... dominated by an array of abstract speculative theories about the origin of religion and the subsequent stages of its development. By

common accord, scholars today opine that these bygone theories of religious evolution were concocted largely on the basis of the unwarranted assumption of European hegemony, that is, on the basis of a monolithic universalist notion of history as a singular civilizing process, of which modern Europe was the triumphant vanguard and all other civilizations and non-European societies merely markers of various interim phases already surpassed by the people of European descent. It may be reasonably suggested that it was the European interest in the future of religion—or the future beyond religion, as the case may be—that motivated much of the nineteenth-century search for the origin of religion, which were presumed to be equivalent, more or less, to the ones observable in the lives of contemporary savages, lives on the brink of disappearance.[24]

According to this mode of thinking, societies organized differently than our own Western one must represent underdeveloped stages in social evolution; and, this being the case, it appears morally incumbent upon societies that have reached this final stage of development to act as beneficent tutors to "backward" Indigenous cultures. Indeed, a necessary component of the so-called white man's burden to civilize the world was viewing its other inhabitants as, in the words of Rudyard Kipling, "half-devil, half-child"—unwilling or unable to take the necessary steps toward their own *betterment*.[25] Furthermore, one should not discount the role of religious justifications in the advancement of such beliefs.

It should go without saying that it is not my intention to suggest that Girard himself in any way harbored such sympathies. Even so, it should be easy enough to see how his argument could lend itself to such a position. Furthermore, for Vattimo, this is no incidental problem because a central pillar of weak thought is that the path of such exclusionary thinking terminates inexorably in metaphysically motivated violence.

VATTIMO'S WEAKENING OF GIRARD'S MYTH OF VICTIMIZATION

At first glance, then, there appears to be a basic tension (or even contradiction) between Vattimo's acceptance of Girard's progressive Christocentric model and his own persistent defenses of hermeneutical nihilism. In what way did Vattimo utilize Girard's argument? What's more, in doing so, did he not risk opening himself up to similar criticisms or, indeed, to undermining many of the fundamental claims of weak thought? First, let's look at some of the notable similarities between their respective positions. Vattimo, we can say, was in basic agreement with Girard regarding the existence of mimetic desire and its leading to the establishment of a "victimary mechanism" in society. Furthermore, Vattimo also appears to have accepted Girard's framing of Christianity as being a radical and distinct break from "natural religion." Finally, Vattimo was even willing to attribute this difference, in some respects at least, to divine agency. For example, Vattimo states:

> [Jesus] was nailed to the cross because he repudiated the victimary mechanism. This is such a shattering novelty that it could only have come from "outside." I would even hazard that the proof that Jesus is God is precisely the fact that it could only have come from a nonhuman wisdom, this radically new news. This is not a proof of the existence of God, of course, or the divinity of Jesus, but for me it's a beautiful thing. Almost too beautiful to be true. I am unable reasonably to disavow it. Therefore, in recent years I have increasingly considered myself a Christian philosopher.... It remains the case that as a Christian I think that history has a salvific meaning: there is a history of salvation, in well-marked stages.[26]

Despite these similarities, it seems to me that the crucial distinction between Girard and Vattimo concerns the respective interpretive frameworks within which these same beliefs find their locus and meaning. That is, Girard was still operating within a traditional metaphysical framework, which aimed at *uncovering* and *describing* a set of *facts* about the desires and the motivations that lead to violence. Thus, his largely structuralist approach to religion sought to establish a universal paradigm by which one could evaluate and *explain* "every ritual on the entire planet." This framework—although not crudely reducing religious language to a set of cognitivist propositions—nevertheless demands that arguments appear from an impossibly objective and disinterested position. Thus, such a construal will not allow Girard, for example, to acknowledge the subjective preference for Christianity that he obviously holds. Thus, in order to justify (rather than just admit) his biased position, he must perform the hat trick of trying to create a criterion according to which Christianity is demonstrably superior to other faith traditions without seeming bigoted or "unscientific."

In contrast, Vattimo's weak framework does not engender the same sort of demand for "objective-looking" justifications for such a preference.[27] To describe Vattimo's position in Wittgensteinian terms, it simply accepts the mutual irreducibility of other language games. In the same way it would make little sense to speak of the supposed "superiority" of one language over another (e.g., Tamil over Urdu or Mandarin over French), so too does such a compulsion to order and rank symbolic systems reflect—at least from a hermeneutical perspective—something akin to a category mistake in understanding what is at play in religion.[28] Of course, that is not to say that religions never make specific claims or that those claims are never empirically verifiable; it is merely to say that religions, as dynamic symbolic systems, are closer to languages than to the objects described by language.[29] They are not merely a set of discrete propositions but have a greater "family resemblance" to methodologies, dispositions, and worldviews—they are the nexus of shared symbols and sacred history common to a given faith. Here, we could reference R. M. Hare's concept of *bliks* or John Wisdom's original "invisible gardener" argument.[30] In both cases, the examples provided by Hare and Wisdom represent clear and definite vantage points, but ones that are not forced to make the same sort of pretense of objectivity as Girard.

One brief analogy before moving on: it seems to me that there is a marked difference between someone cheering on a sports team because the team in question happens to hail from that same person's hometown versus someone trying to *objectively demonstrate* the inherent superiority of their hometown team. The first instance seems to be a harmless and perfectly understandable preference akin to familial sympathies (though obviously to a lesser extent).[31] The second instance, however, seems, at best, quixotic. While the first person may continue to claim that theirs is "the best team in the world," if pressed they would likely admit that their opinion is not a rational one based on empirical standards (e.g., weighing individual player statistics or the number of games won in a given season). Instead, it is a disposition emergent from other considerations. All this is to say that preference is not necessarily a question of superiority. The difference between the two hypothetical sports fans in their respective attempts at justifying the "greatness" of their teams, we might say, then, is that one is "rational," whereas the other is "reasonable."

As a result of this hermeneutical framework, Vattimo did not concern himself too much with the topic of religion per se but instead with the intersection of religion and politics. That is, his concerns and claims were much more circumscribed and pragmatic, having to do specifically with Western Christianity (and, in its secularized form, modernity). In a crucial sense, for Vattimo, his choice to speak from within the tradition of Western Christianity is not because Christianity or the West is superior in any sort of objective or demonstrable way but, rather, because it is the tradition (the language, symbols, and history of interpretation) that has been transmitted to those of us in the West. It is this ongoing dialogue with our tradition(s) that invariably gives recognizable form to our collective conceptions of the divine. This inherited context in which we construct meaning is what Israel Scheffler has referred to as our "symbolic world," and we are as much enmeshed in it as in the physical world.[32]

This is the case even if we consciously attempt to reject it. To feel compelled to reject something means that it is, in some sense at least, still operative and that we are thereby irrevocably shaped by it—there remains, as it were, a Derridean "trace."[33] This is why Vattimo so frequently pointed to the title of Croce's essay "Why We Cannot but Call Ourselves Christians." It is also why he was so fond of the popular ironic saying "Thank God, I am an atheist," which he argued, is another way of saying that it is only because of a particular historically conditioned construal of the divine that took shape in Western thought, leading to modernity, secularization, and the dissolution of a particular notion of the "transcendental signified," that it is even meaningful that someone can describe themselves as being an "atheist."[34] In other words,

> This means that to profess faith in Christianity is first of all to profess faith in the inevitability of a certain textual tradition that has been passed down to me. Take away the Bible, and I would not be what I am. Perhaps I would be something or someone else, but it would be useless for me to think that I could just as easily be a native of the Amazon. It is true that I could be, but how does that help me to understand who I actually am? If I reflect on my existence, I must realize that without the text of the Bible I would be bereft of the very instruments I have in order to think and to talk.[35]

VIOLENCE, SACRIFICE, AND SUBSTITUTIONARY ATONEMENT

The differences in interpretive framework between Vattimo and Girard, we can observe, manifest themselves in their respective understandings of Christianity.[36] For example, one can consider their separate understandings of the significance of the central Catholic ritual of the Mass. Girard, for instance, argued that the institution of the Mass (the celebration and re-presentation of Christ's sacrifice) is a symbolic enactment of the final divine gesture that exposed the victim mechanism in operation at the heart of our conception of sacrifice. Furthermore, he argued, its continued practice provides the same sort of "pressure-valve" function that sacrifice once satisfied in earlier societies. Thus, for Girard, the celebration of the Eucharist is necessary to prevent the return of social violence. Vattimo, however, rejected the idea that the Eucharist serves such a social function and went further by questioning Girard's assumption that "without recourse to the symbolism of sacrifice, we can only perpetuate the cycle of violence, rather than eliminating it."[37]

Vattimo argued instead that the Gospels represent a complete repudiation of what Walter Wink has referred to as "the myth of redemptive violence."[38] For Vattimo, that is, "Jesus Christ comes to renounce, not fulfill, the sacrality and the necessity of the victim. . . . He comes and declares to everyone that it's not true that we have to offer sacrifice to God. On the contrary, God calls us friends."[39] In this way, he opposes the notion of substitutionary atonement.[40] For Vattimo, God did not send Jesus to die for our sins. Jesus came instead to offer the liberating message of divine love. This message, simple as it is, was so revolutionary and threatening to "the powers that be" that *he had to die*. That is, Christ's death might not have been necessary, but it was always in some sense inevitable.[41] Even so, the Gospels portray Jesus as fully aware of the deadly implications of his actions (Matt. 16:21–28, 17:22–23, 20:17–19, 26:1–2; Mark 8:31–33, 9:30–32; Luke 9:22–27; John 12:23–24) yet also resolute that, come what may, he would compromise neither his message nor his example (Mark 14:36; Matt. 26:39; 42; Luke 22:42). As Richard Rohr says, "[Jesus] did not come to change God's mind about us. *It did not need changing.* Jesus came to change our minds about God—and about ourselves—and about where goodness and evil really lie."⁴²

KENOSIS: THE WEAKNESS OF GOD

Shortly before his execution at the hands of the Nazis in 1945, the German Lutheran pastor and political dissident Dietrich Bonhoeffer wrote in a letter from prison:

> God lets himself be pushed out of the world on to the cross. He is weak and powerless in the world, and that is precisely the way, the only way, in which he is with us and helps us. Matt. 8.17 makes it quite clear that Christ helps us, not by virtue of his omnipotence, but by virtue of his weakness and suffering. . . . Only the suffering God can help. . . . That is a reversal of what the religious man expects from God. Man is summoned to share in God's sufferings at the hands of a godless world.⁴³

Elsewhere Bonhoeffer had stated earlier, "If Jesus Christ is to be described as God, we may not speak of this divine being, nor of his omnipotence, nor his omniscience; but we must speak of this weak man among sinners, of his manger and his cross. If we are to deal with the deity of Jesus, we must speak of his weakness."⁴⁴

Vattimo interprets the incarnation in similarly *weak* terms. That is, in contrast with figures such as Barth, Levinas, and Derrida who stressed the radical alterity and transcendence of the divine, Vattimo (along with Bonhoeffer) emphasized the importance of God's willful shedding of his majesty as representing the movement of the divine toward his creation motivated by love.[45] In this way, Vattimo saw in Christ's kenosis (κένωσις, "self-emptying")—his taking on flesh—not only an apt metaphor for the dissolution of (metaphysical) Being (Phil. 2:5–11) but also what he has referred to as "the nihilistic recovery" of the core of the Christian message.[46] Vattimo stated that, in his view, "God is not the content of a proposition; he is a person who walked among us and left us an example of charity." He explained, "This is why theology as such, a purely scientific theology, which spends time unraveling this or that topic without worrying about what is happening [in the world] does not convince me. . . . I can speak of God only in so far as I meet him in everyday life. . . . This is theology."[47]

In Vattimo's estimation, this kenotic image of God seen in the incarnation of Christ is "the only great paradox and scandal of Christian revelation" because of the kerygma's inherent resistance to recuperation by *the powers that be*.[48] There is nothing exceptional about the image of a high God robed in resplendent glory or, indeed, in finding its analogue in earthly rulers (who insist upon such rights and privileges for themselves). A God, however, who finds his proper place among *"the least of these,"* one who chooses to endure a life of relative squalor and in the end to suffer the pain and humiliation of a brutal and ignominious death for no other purpose than for the love of his creation—undermines the very logic upon which the present order of the world is founded (cf. 1 Cor. 1:27; Matt. 20:16, 25–28). According to Vattimo, everything else can be debated. Everything else is adiaphora. In the final measure, "the essence of revelation is reduced to charity, while all the rest is left to the non-finality of diverse historical experiences, even of mythologies that at the time appeared to be 'binding' to particular historical humanities."[49]

"UBI CARITAS ET AMOR, DEUS IBI EST"

Despite the long-term movement of secularization, Vattimo does argue that there is an end point to the process. That is, it reaches its terminus and resolves itself in charity. For example, citing St. Paul's First Letter to the Corinthians, Vattimo argues that in the great expanses of time, "even faith and hope will end at one point or another," but love—not the contemplation of the truth of first principles—endures forever.[50] The specifically Christian character of this notion should therefore be readily apparent, though it need not be emphasized. Arguably, the same principle (though less coded by explicitly religious terminology) can be observed in what is often referred to in philosophy as the "principle of charity."[51] That is, when interpreting the thoughts and intentions of others, we should be generous and maximally optimize our understanding for agreement. When others see the world differently from us, appealing to a body of evidence or general principle will be of little use if the disagreement is the result of a different worldview (or set of concepts for organizing belief). Then the misunderstanding is less a matter of error than an issue of translation. For speakers of different languages to be able to effectively communicate, there has to be a desire to understand one another (based on a shared respect and concern each for the other). Love/respect and understanding go hand in hand.

Vattimo claims, "The death of the 'moral' God marks the end of the possibility of preferring truth to friendship, because this death means that there is no 'objective' or ontological truth, etc., which can claim to be anything other than simply the expression of a friendship, or of a wish for power, or of a subjective relationship."[52] Rather than seeing the *end* of objective metaphysical truth in cataclysmic terms, however, Vattimo emphasizes that Aquinas's definition of truth, "veritas qua adaequatio rei et intellectus"—while indeed important in certain respects—has in the most important areas of life always been secondary to charity. That is, considerations of objectivity are secondary to interpersonal give-and-take, to the patient resolve to live in mutuality with others. As an example, Vattimo refers to the relationship one might have with an aged relative. He says that there is perhaps no use in trying to convince them to fully see the world as you do, but it would be silly to think that grandchildren should value their grandparents simply because they happen to agree with them or that they should not commit to being in their grandparents' lives simply because they do not agree. In the end, for Vattimo,

> the idea of "secularization" is not so much a description of some linear and objective development of history as a proposed interpretation of the historical process that is to be preferred over others. I believe that I can detect certain moments of the European past to which I am sympathetic precisely because they were secularizing in character and effect, but certainly not because they inevitably reflect a supposedly necessary historical process. Secularization, in short, is not the same as what was once defined as "progress." The entire opening section of my text [*The Transparent Society*] was a critique of such a linear historicist conception: history as a story of a progressive "weakening" must be taken as an interpretation, not as a supposedly objective description.[53]

Vattimo viewed the "weakening" of metaphysics as largely coextensive with the Christian concepts of secularization and "salvation history." He viewed kenosis—Christ's incarnation—as a metaphor and example of this process, whereby charity (self-giving love, respect, and the desire for understanding) supersedes metaphysics and the latter's understanding of "veritas qua adaequatio rei et intellectus." For Vattimo, truth is not an eternal ideal form that exists outside of ourselves. Truth is not a mirror we hold up to "external" reality. Instead, as St. Augustine reminds us, "Interiore homine habitat veritas" (Truth lives in the inner human).[54] Regarding his continued personal commitment to Christianity, Vattimo stated, "I hold firm that Jesus came from God because the things he says are really of divine origin, that is, they are the most divine I have found in my life.... I believe in the divinity of Jesus Christ above all because of what he has said to me."[55]

III

REFLECTION

5

AGAINST NIHILISM

Vattimo and His Critics

The true world—we have abolished . . . [and with it] we have also abolished the apparent one.
—Friedrich Nietzsche, *Twilight of the Idols*, 1889

WEAK THOUGHT AS PRACTICAL PHILOSOPHY

There is a sense in which one can say that Gadamer rehabilitated classical Greek philosophy in relation to post-Heideggerian hermeneutics.[1] A central aspect of this focus, though, concerned a renewal of interest in so-called practical philosophy.[2] According to Gadamer, there is an internal relation between "understanding" (*nous*/νοῦς) and "praxis" (πρᾶξις). For instance, the form of critical judgment or informed intuition exercised in the application/enactment of reason—the one that, for example, leads a person to choose between competing conceptual schemes or to determine the extent to which a general principle is applicable in a given situation—is what Aristotle referred to as "phronesis" (φρόνησις, "prudence," "sagacity," or "practical wisdom").[3]

This intellectual virtue is intimately connected with *prohairesis* (προαίρεσις, "character," "will," "intention," "volition") and relates to the act of giving or withholding assent. Aristotle contrasted phronesis with other forms of knowledge, such as *epistēmē* (ἐπιστήμη, "empirical/scientific knowledge"), *téchnē* (τέχνη, "knowledge related to a skill," "technique," or "craft"), and *theōría* (θεωρία, "abstract/theoretical knowledge," "contemplation"). All these forms were viewed as distinct components of the more general notion of *sophía* (σοφία, "intelligence," or "wisdom").[4] In this vein, Gadamer says,

> In my own eyes, the great merit of Aristotle was that he anticipated the impasse of our scientific culture by his description of the structure of practical reason as distinct from theoretical knowledge and technical skill. By philosophical arguments he refuted the claim of the professional lawmakers whose function at that time corresponded to the role of the expert in the modern scientific society. Of course, I do not mean to equate the modern expert with the professional sophist. In his own field he is a faithful and reliable investigator, and in general he is well aware of the particularity of his methodical assumptions and realizes that the results of his investigation have a limited relevance. Nevertheless, the problem of our society is that the longing of the citizenry for orientation and normative patterns invests the expert with an exaggerated authority. Modern society expects him to provide a substitute for past moral and political orientations. Consequently, the concept of "praxis" which was developed in the last two centuries is an awful deformation of what practice really is. In all the debates of the last century practice was understood as application of science to technical tasks. That is a very inadequate notion. It degrades practical reason to technical control. In fact, reason as guiding our practical behavior is much more than technical control. Praxis is not restricted to the special area of technical craftsmanship. It is a universal form of human life which embraces, yet goes beyond, the technical choice of the best means for a pre-given end. Aristotle's concept of prudence includes, as a matter of fact, the concrete determination of the end. It

is a misunderstanding to suppose that prudence is restricted to the finding of the means.[5]

Although I am not presently aware of any instance of Vattimo discussing weak thought as a form of phronesis or practical philosophy—apart from his occasional allusions to similar ideas in contemporary pragmatism—I think that this connection is important for understanding the main thrust of his approach to philosophy: namely, that philosophy is primarily an edifying activity, one whose goals should be more social than scholastic. In this regard, I think it is useful to conceive of weak thought (and at least some of postmodernity more broadly) as representing a reemphasis on an approach to philosophy frequently neglected by modern thinkers, who tended to focus more heavily instead on epistemic, technical, and theoretical dimensions of thought.[6]

Although Vattimo did not place great emphasis on the study of ethics as such, praxis (the lived application of philosophy) runs like a red thread through both his life and his body of work.[7] It can be seen from his early pro-union activism to his time in elected office, from his early writings on Aristotle to his more recent discussions of the need for the development of a hermeneutic communism. As I hope to demonstrate in the next section, therefore, at least some of his disputes with critics arguably stem less from particular differences than from this more basic disagreement over the ultimate purpose, goals, and orientation of philosophy itself.

ADDRESSING OBJECTIONS

In keeping with the admittedly artificial distinction I have thus far maintained between Vattimo's philosophical and religious views in my presentation of his work, let's address first those objections that do not concern (at least in any specific or direct manner) the Christian character of his thought.

Philosophical Objections

First, in the interest of transparency, let me begin by saying that I accept as valid Richard Rorty's assertion that "one's standards for philosophical success are dependent upon one's subsequent philosophical views."[8] Furthermore, I agree that a significant portion of disagreements turn on differences of outlook and interpretation rather than on actual matters of fact. As I stated at the outset, therefore, I believe the fairest way to proceed when evaluating a philosophical theory is to try, as best one can, to measure it against its own professed assumptions and standards in order to determine its internal coherence.[9] To answer the question, then, regarding the self-consistency of Vattimo's position, let's now finally return to the specific criticisms advanced by neorealists such as Graham Harman, Tom Sparrow, and Maurizio Ferraris.

THE END OF PHENOMENOLOGY AND THE RETURN TO REALISM

The first such criticism I alluded to earlier in this work concerned the phenomenological tradition itself (and, by extension, would also include hermeneutics, as previously described): the neorealist rejection of the claim that phenomenology somehow bypasses the problem of choosing between realism and idealism. For example, Sparrow claims that

> ever since Heidegger the project of realizing phenomenology as a rigorous science complete with a worked-out method of investigation has been abandoned. . . . Phenomenology forsakes metaphysical realism

in favor of a timid "realism" of phenomena that is nothing more than a modified version of idealism, Kantianism by another name. It is commonplace . . . for phenomenologists to pay homage to realism, but not without qualifying their allegiance with scare quotes. What they call the "real" or "realism" is what is given in "concrete" lived experience. To speak of concrete experience, then, amounts to speaking about the real as it appears to a human observer, not as the real is in itself.[10]

How Sparrow can be so confident in asserting the qualities of things *outside* of "concrete lived experience" or in speaking about experience *outside* the scope of the "human observer" is never adequately addressed. Remember that for Husserl and for the traditions that come out of phenomenology, "Just as we cannot investigate objects outside the way they present themselves to consciousness, we cannot investigate consciousness as uncoupled from its relations to objects"—hence, the hermeneutical claim that all experience is, in fact, mediated.[11] In attempting to reduce phenomenology to nothing more than an underhanded idealism, however, neorealists not only refuse to take phenomenologists on their own terms but also risk rehashing centuries worth of epistemological debates that phenomenology and hermeneutics had sought to ignore or bury.

At the end of the day, though, it is difficult to establish where mere semantics end and real disagreement begins in some of these characterizations. For instance, it would seem from Sparrow's comment that postmodernists such as Vattimo are not, in fact, "antirealist" but rather insufficiently realist to the neorealists' liking. Given the background covered here already (coupled with the general thrust of post-Kantian thought), it is perhaps not difficult to see why the implications of Sparrow's comment—namely, that one can somehow simply *see reality* as it exists "in itself" apart from the constraints of our specifically embodied animality and sociohistorical setting—appears, from the hermeneutical standpoint at least, rather naive. In contradistinction to Sparrow, consider the following quote from Bertrand Russell (who was no postmodernist):

> The greater part of what would commonly pass as knowledge is more or less probable opinion. In regard to probable opinion, we can derive great assistance from *coherence*, which we rejected as the *definition* of truth, but may often use as a *criterion*. A body of individually probable opinions, if they are mutually coherent, become more probable than any one of them would be individually. It is in this way that many scientific hypotheses acquire their probability. They fit into a coherent system of probable opinions, and thus become more probable than they would be in isolation. . . . Thus the mere organization of probable opinion will never, by itself, transform it into indubitable knowledge.[12]

In a similar fashion to Sparrow, Ferraris has stated that "reality possesses a structural (and structured) link that not only resists conceptual schemes and perceptive apparatuses (and unamendability consists of this resistance) but precedes them. For this reason, the concept of 'external world' is to be understood primarily in the sense of 'external to our conceptual schemes and perceptive apparatuses.' Such a world exists; otherwise all our knowledge would be indistinguishable from a dream."[13]

As I believe I have shown, however, Vattimo does not, in fact, reject the idea that a physical world *exists* apart from our perceptions of it, merely that our understanding of this world is inescapably constrained by our perceptions. Again, this is a point on which a realist such as Russell would have agreed. Furthermore, our perceptions of this reality are what matter to us in the long run. Thus, differences in our perceptions of reality are *experientially* indistinguishable from differences in reality.

For example, are we really going to say that a human being and a fruit fly experience this shared world in the same (or even in substantially similar) ways?[14] If not, then, what are we even saying when we insist on the affirmation of the bare existence of the world—just that we and other sentient beings share the same domain of external stimuli? If we are being honest, this claim of itself seems rather meager, and the phenomenologist should, again, be willing to grant it (with some qualification). At a deeper level, though, I feel compelled to ask, "What matter is it really if the fruit fly and I are pressed upon by the same external stimuli if we experience them in fundamentally different and mutually unintelligible ways?"[15] That is, after we grant the bare existence of a shared external world, is there a greater "realist" point to be made? As John Locke said, "No man's knowledge here can go beyond his experience," and our experience is always unavoidably human.[16] In the end, the advantage of phenomenology has been its acknowledgment that we can constructively treat the observable world *as* "real for us"—and largely disregard as unanswerable questions concerning the manner of its existence apart from our perceptions or conceptual schemes.

In this sense, Vattimo's position is better understood as a "qualified" or "critical realism," one that simply refuses to equate the "observable world" with the "real world." It is not as though our *shared plane of existence* is an illusion; it is merely that our field of vision is necessarily limited and conditioned—making talk of the "real world," apart from recognition of such conditions, inherently misleading. Although it may seem tedious and pedantic to note the subtle difference between "talk of the *real world*" and the "real world" as such, the difference is not insignificant, even if by now it is a dead horse well past further beating.[17] In response to calls for a return to realism, then, Vattimo once remarked, "One cannot speak of Being except by participating in it and being an active moment of its history. . . . A truly 'realistic' ontology that does not ignore the fact that it is itself a moment of the Being about which (or in which) it speaks is a hermeneutic ontology."[18]

THE ENLIGHTENMENT AND ITS DISCONTENTS
In contrast to his claims about phenomenology, Ferraris's critiques of both the intellectual lineage and what he sees as the unfulfilled promises of postmodernity are arguably more incisive. For example, he maintains that whereas the Enlightenment tied human emancipation to knowledge, postmodernity instead ties knowledge to domination and power. The latter, however, he argues, obscures the traditional alliance between "throne and altar," which despite each jockeying for domination over the other, have nevertheless historically served to defend and legitimize one another. Furthermore, the truly awful implication of such a picture, he contends, is that if knowledge and repressive power are seen as inseparable from one another, then human emancipation becomes predicated on the rejection of knowledge and rationality.

In contrast to the negative picture of the Enlightenment painted by postmodernists, Ferraris argues, modernity sought to break the hold of such power by its very appeals to unassailable universal principles, which could not themselves be subordinated to the whims of popes or kings. "E pur si muove!" In this, Ferraris, like Abbagnano, Bobbio, and Viano before him, maintains that there is no sense in pretending that society has not progressed or that the Enlightenment did not represent a positive social change in this direction. By criticizing the Enlightenment, he argues, weak thought, like all postmodern thought, in effect throws out the proverbial baby with the bathwater. That is, rather than focusing its skeptical ire on dogmatism, postmodernity instead undermines itself by attacking "Reason" tout court.

For myself, at least, I think that Ferraris's comments here, on balance, are not without some merit. That is, when the dominant narrative of Western thought was a relatively uncritical valorization of Enlightenment values, such postmodern criticism represented a much needed counterweight—one that was meant to cast light on the contradictions, mistakes, blind spots, and unintended consequences of the central ideas and figures in this narrative.[19] In more recent times, however, at least in many areas of the humanities, a primarily negative picture of the Enlightenment has emerged to replace this older rose-tinted image. Over time, however, this narrative counterweight itself has now become a largely unchallenged orthodoxy. Nevertheless, rather than calling for, say, a dialectical sublimation—whereby these postmodern criticisms themselves are integrated into a more nuanced but ultimately still positive appreciation of modernity—Ferraris instead seems intent on simply returning to an older uncritical admiration of the Enlightenment.

In broader terms, though, Ferraris's primary concern about postmodernity seems to be that it removes gates and gatekeepers from their privileged and guiding role in the process of determining truth in society. The image he creates is one of cynical opportunists on the religious and political right exploiting the now eroded confidence in truth created by postmodern theorists in order to weasel their way out of any and all justified criticism they may otherwise face for failing to adhere to recognized standards for establishing defensible claims.[20] In his estimation, the supposed "democratization" of the "marketplace of ideas" has really meant little more than the unchecked proliferation of dangerous ideologies among the cynical and the credulous.

What Ferraris sees as the recuperation of relativism by the political and religious right, then, is ultimately made possible only by the presence of confused or defective "intellectuals" on the political left—who, he believes, either harbor furtive right-leaning tendencies[21] or are simply cowed into submission by an oppressive atmosphere of "political correctness."[22] In such an atmosphere, he laments, all opinions, even obviously ridiculous ones, *must be* countenanced in the public square in the name of a puerile conception of tolerance.[23] Ferraris, however, is not the only one to make such claims.

In his book *Post-Truth* (2018), the philosopher of science Lee McIntyre attempts to summarize postmodern views on truth in the following way: "Having power allows us to control what is true, not the other way around. If there are many perspectives, then insisting that we accept any particular one is a form of fascism." Perhaps, sensing the inadequacy of his own description—while also not wishing to elaborate further—he notes, "Some will complain that the account just given is not sufficiently detailed or nuanced to do postmodernism justice. Others may object to my thesis that postmodernist thought is in any way a precursor to post-truth." Undaunted by these seemingly fair and reasonable objections, he goes on to claim,

> I am confident that further study of postmodernist texts would help to undercut the claim that its ideas may legitimately support right-wing ideology. But *I am equally sure* that postmodernists have contributed to this situation by *retreating within the subtlety of their ideas*, then being shocked when they are used for purposes outside what they would approve. *It is true that the right-wing folks who borrow from postmodernist thought do not seem very interested in its nuance. If they need a tool, they will use a boning knife as a hammer.* Indeed, thirty years ago conservatives were similarly uninterested in the subtleties of postmodernist thought when they were attacking it as a sign of degeneracy on the left![24]

In this regard, McIntyre has in mind examples such as an interview in 2017 where Kellyanne Conway, U.S. counselor to the president, defended a factually false claim made by then White House press secretary Sean Spicer by labeling his inaccurate statements not lies but "alternative facts."[25] One could likewise refer to the Orwellian "doublespeak" of Rudy Giuliani, former New York city mayor and personal attorney to the U.S. president, when he declared in an interview on national television in 2018 that "Truth isn't Truth."[26] At risk of pointing out the obvious, however, it must be said that nowhere in the exercise of such transparent attempts at deception did Spicer, Conway, or Giuliani ever reference the works of Foucault, Derrida, or Deleuze to justify their claims. Nor did postmodernists on the political left leap to defend these speakers' right to say such things by appealing to the nonexistence of truth.[27] More directly in the Italian context, Alessia Ricciardi has even seemingly laid responsibility for the resurgence of the Italian Right at the feet of Vattimo, stating, "Ideologically, weak thought represents a way of thinking that has never resisted—and in fact has facilitated—Berlusconi's ascent to power by encouraging passive receptivity toward popular opinion."[28]

Clearly, there is something deeply unserious about blaming postmodernity for the apparent increase in many people's willingness to embrace brazen falsehoods—particularly in our recent civic discourse. Indeed, the charge is something akin to blaming a meteorologist for the ravages of a hurricane. Even McIntyre admits that a further study of postmodern texts would no doubt undercut his claim that "its ideas may legitimately support right-wing ideology," albeit before simply proceeding to blame right-wing post-truth politics on postmodernity, anyway—regardless of the presence of evidence to the contrary. In this casting of blame, there is something poignantly ironic.

One should earnestly consider the plausibility of the claim that a handful of postmodern university professors are primarily to blame for the epistemic parameters of our current geopolitical discourse. Upon even the briefest of reflections, though, this factor hardly seems to be among the most compelling of potential causes. Consider, for example, that since at least the mid-1970s society has struggled with the increasingly destabilizing effects of globalization and the financialization of the world economy.[29] And let us not forget the epochal changes brought about by the invention of the personal computer, the internet, cellular phones, and social media. This rapid proliferation of information technologies and the digitalization of communications that has come in their wake have together amounted to a revolution in culture on par with the invention of Gutenberg's printing press—all within living memory.

As Michael Hardt and Antonio Negri have argued, "The computer and communication revolution of production has transformed laboring practices in such a way that they all tend toward the model of information and communication technologies. Interactive and cybernetic machines become a new prosthesis integrated into our bodies and minds and a lens through which to redefine our bodies and minds themselves. The anthropology of cyberspace is really the recognition of the new human condition."[30] This "new condition" is the result of the specific ways such technology redraws the parameters in which we operate—expanding and delimiting certain pathways of thought and action. As Marshall McLuhan reminds us, "The medium is the message because it is the medium that shapes and controls the scale and form of human association and action."[31] The manifold changes to the ways that we collect and disseminate information in society means that programmers at Google, Facebook, and Twitter arguably have had much more impact on the generalized willingness to accept misinformation than has the work of Rorty, Lyotard, or Vattimo.[32] Given the seismic shifts in culture in recent decades, then, I honestly find the priority that is so frequently given to postmodern *theories* in describing these changes, rather than to the events themselves, more than a bit baffling.[33]

All that said, the sort of "confirmation bias" and "motivated reasoning" that allow people to disregard evidence when politically or emotionally expedient is no more justified by postmodernism—with its calls for good-faith efforts at open dialogue with other worldviews—than by more traditional appeals to "truth." Nowhere, for example, does Vattimo advocate for the sort of uncritical relativism that would make Spicer's, Conway's, or Giuliani's efforts somehow indistinguishable from evidence-based claims to the contrary. No matter the framework, truth and knowledge of any kind cannot be meaningfully sought by those in whom there is a total lack of honest self-scrutiny or desire to understand.

"POST-TRUTH" POLITICS AND THE "RETURN TO ORDER"

In his appeals to science not merely as a method or process but as an institution, Ferraris seems concerned that if one were somehow to remove all authoritative bodies from the deliberative process, then there would be no guarantee that people would prefer "evidence-based" solutions over merely emotive ones. In effect, he is troubled that there is no *guarantee* that people will see the world as he sees it. To this end, he argues:

> Deobjectification, while formulated with emancipative intentions, turns into the delegitimation of human knowledge and into the reference to a transcendent foundation. So, on the one hand, postmodern philosophers adhere to skepticism and have no ultimate reasons to justify Copernicus's superiority with respect to Ptolemy or Pasteur's with respect to Asclepius, because these are, anyhow, confrontations between conceptual schemes, as there is no "outside" reality. On the other hand—beyond the equivalence of things in the world and overcoming the inanity of learned quarrels—there opens up space for transcendence. Underlining "how deep the self-doubt of the modern age, of science and of technology goes today," the former pope [Benedict XVI] easily recovers the prestige that the Church had lost when its worldview was contested by science.[34]

First, I would like to point out that in Ferraris's statement that postmodern philosophers have "no ultimate reasons to justify" their preference of one conceptual scheme over another, the word *ultimate* is doing a lot of conceptual work. That is, although it is technically correct to say that there are no reasons that could be considered "ultimate" or "final" for a figure such as Thomas Kuhn, that does not preclude the possibility of there still being coherent, rational, pragmatic, or defensible reasons to prefer one system over others. This possibility would include the emergence of a consensus that one scheme more satisfactorily accounts for presently available evidence than others. That sense of satisfaction itself, as Vattimo and others would point out, is rule governed.

To the extent that there are "nonnegotiables" in a given discourse, it is merely a recognition that there are specific claims that structure a language, without which that discourse cannot function, but they are rules that govern language and inference, not necessarily reality apart from the human experience of it. To use a classic example, consider again that there is no noncircular way to justify something such as induction, but this lack of "ultimate" justification does not stop us from using science, nor indeed should it.[35] Likewise, it is impossible to establish how far classical laws of logic—such as the law of identity, the law of noncontradiction, and the principle of excluded middle—can distinguish "discourse" from "reality."

Furthermore, one might well respond to Ferraris by pointing out that blind faith in institutions (even scientific ones) does not guarantee truth. Even if we recognize rightly that most scientists are intellectually honest and committed to the truth as they understand it, they, no less than priests, are human beings and, as such, can have motivations beyond a merely impartial interest in the facts. Ferraris's arguments in support of what he seems to view as the inviolability of the scientific process therefore rely perhaps too heavily on an overidealized confidence in the pure motives and superior judgment of scientists and technocrats. Indeed, in practical terms, his arguments seem to share little *functional* difference from similar arguments in support of reassuring trust in the church's pure motivations and authoritative decrees.

In effect, what Ferraris and others of a like mind call for in the face of the steady erasure of old confidences is essentially a "return to order" based on popular faith in science rather than on religion but whose enforcement remains similarly institutional and exclusive in character.[36] That is, in order to avoid what they view as an interminable democratic process of interpretation, they make an implicit appeal to a sense of sovereignty in their realist conceptions of institutional authority.[37] Consider the following example: In 2016, as a response to the Brexit campaign in the United Kingdom and the rise of Donald Trump in the United States, the journalist James Traub published an article in the global-affairs magazine *Foreign Policy* that he entitled "It's Time for the Elites to Rise Up Against the Ignorant Masses." In the article, Traub argues that "maybe we have become so inclined to celebrate the authenticity of all personal conviction that it is now *elitist* to believe in reason, expertise, and the lessons of history. If so, the party of accepting reality must be prepared to take on the party of denying reality, and its enablers among those who know better. If that is the coming realignment, *we should embrace it*."[38]

While we can say that this statement alone does not necessarily capture an antidemocratic sentiment, it does reflect a judgment in line with new realism that if democracy is seen as being in tension with the "experts," then it is the democratic process that must be jettisoned. "Amicus [democratia], sed magis amica veritas." In response to Traub and the new realists, however, I would say that it is not elitist to be more experienced or better informed on a particular topic than others. Nevertheless, it is quite elitist to state or imply that the "ignorant masses" should ideally not participate in the political process lest they needlessly hamper the "superior judgments" of their social and intellectual "betters." In this regard, I would instead agree with the Russian anarchist Mikhail Bakunin, who once argued:

> Does it follow [from my anarchism] that I reject *all* authority? Far from me such a thought. In the matter of boots, I refer to the authority of the bootmaker; concerning houses, canals, or railroads, I consult that of the architect or engineer. For such or such special knowledge I apply to such or such a *savant*. But I allow neither the bootmaker nor the architect nor the *savant* to impose his authority upon me. I listen to them freely and with all the respect merited by their intelligence, their character, their knowledge, reserving always my incontestable right of criticism and censure. I do not content myself with consulting a single authority in any special branch; I consult several; I compare their opinions, and choose that which seems to me the soundest. But I recognize no infallible authority, even in special questions; consequently, whatever respect I may have for the honesty and the sincerity of such or such an individual, I have no absolute faith in any person. Such a faith would be fatal to my reason, to my liberty, and even to the success of my undertakings; it would immediately transform me into a stupid slave, an instrument of the will and interests of others.[39]

In contrast to claims by Ferraris and other new realists, Vattimo and most other postmodern thinkers do not reject the authority of scientific institutions tout court. Instead, their position tends to be more in line with Bakunin's argument: namely, that "for science as well as for industry, [there exists] the necessity of the division and association of labor. I receive and I give—such is human life. Each directs and is directed in turn. Therefore, there is no fixed and constant authority, but a continual exchange of mutual, temporary, and, above all, voluntary authority and subordination."[40]

Likewise, in advocating for nihilism, Vattimo is not calling for a kind of arbitrary relativism. Instead, what he has in mind is something more akin to what C. S. Peirce referred to as "fallibilism" and John Dewey as "warranted assertability." His position, therefore, upon deeper reflection (and in spite of some of his own book titles, such as *A Farewell to Truth*), is less provocative than it might first appear. To illustrate this point, consider that a particular hermeneutical perspective, like any (language) game, might accept that its rules are not "ultimate" or "absolute" but not that those rules are therefore arbitrary or that following them is irrational. It is not irrational to follow the rules of a specific game in order to achieve some specific end—even while simultaneously recognizing that this is precisely what one is doing. For example, one does not adhere to the rules of football because one believes that they reflect an immutable ordering of the world but because one wishes to score enough points to win the match. To the contrary, the (ir)rational thing to do would be to pretend as though one is *not* engaged in such a (language) game and thereby to carry on as if the narrow rules and parameters of one's own enterprise are somehow fixed, eternal, and all-encompassing.[41] In this regard, Vattimo has stated: "I myself have never known a relativist, just as I have never known anyone who said, 'All theories, including mine, have equal value.' I don't really see relativism as a mistaken theory because it isn't a theory. If anything, it is a doctrine of society, but in society, for reasons of charity, we have to allow different points of view, and in general I stake out this position: let's not say that we will reach agreement once we have found the truth. Let's say we have found the truth when we have reached agreement."[42]

Once one gets past the specific shape of Vattimo's language, one can see that this position is not so terribly unconventional. To say that one believes, as a principle of social organization, that all "sincerely held beliefs" deserve a public hearing and reasonable accommodation does not mean that one has to abandon one's convictions (unless and only to the extent that such convictions lead one to impose their will on or suppress the sincerely held beliefs of others). Thus, Vattimo viewed interpretation—and the shared consensus regarding the truth that emerges from interpretation—as ideally being a collective democratic process. What we think of as "objective Truth" is determined by consensus, not by authority, and should be maintained by persuasion, not by force. For such a defused system to work, however, it would require us to bolster democratic values, which encourage the cultivation of a more informed and compassionate populace—not merely to turn control of society over to a specialized class of intellectual and cultural elites empowered to make decisions on behalf of the "ignorant masses."[43]

WEAK THOUGHT AND THE REDUCTION OF VIOLENCE

The final and arguably most substantial criticism of weak thought offered by Ferraris is his contention that despite Vattimo's claims, "the abandonment of truth does not [actually] lead to the abandonment of violence." To this end, Ferraris argues that the objections that weak thought makes against truth and violence are only objections to violence, not to truth as such. Therefore, he contends, its objection to truth is based on a mere confusion.

Unfortunately, Ferraris's *Manifesto* never actually defines what he means by the term *violence*.[44] Although he may assume that the term's common or everyday usage is sufficient for any and all understandings of its semantic limits, he would be mistaken. This is why it is standard practice in philosophy to define one's terms—especially if and to what extent they diverge from common usage—lest we misrepresent a thinker's position through equivocation. This point is not incidental because it would seem that the issue of weak thought's internal coherence, in this case at least, hinges on how we define the terms *truth* and *violence*.

If by *truth* Ferraris means "the correspondence between mental concepts and objective reality naively construed," and if by *violence* he means "physical force or intimidation," then he is certainly correct to note that the denial or acceptance of something such as Newton's gravitation constant or the Zeroth law of thermodynamics arguably has little bearing on the amount of physical force exercised in a given society in order to achieve a particular end. Is this really what Vattimo was referring to, though? That is, does Ferraris think that Vattimo was really suggesting that a general recognition of any broadly scientific claims amounts to physical coercion? No. Obviously he was not. Clearly, Vattimo had something else in mind by the use of such terms. We know this because Vattimo said so. Despite how Ferraris frames his argument, I suspect he is also aware of this.

We have already explored in considerable detail Vattimo's construal of capital-T "Truth" as it relates to metaphysics. So there is no need to define it again or to point out the ways in which this definition differs from Ferraris's. If we bother to look, though, we can see that Vattimo did, in fact, also give a very specific definition of his idea of violence as it relates to philosophy: "Violence can only be defined as the silencing of questions.... Put it this way: given the dissolution of metaphysics, it seems to me that the only supreme principle to be propounded, both in ethics and in law, is the reduction of violence.... The notion of primeval evidence... of a moment in which I have reached bedrock, of a foundation at which no questions can or need be asked—that state, in which questions are lacking, is not the end product of violence, but its origin."[45] This suppression of dissent can, of course, be accomplished through physical coercion, but it need not be.[46] So, in contrast to Ferraris, Vattimo argued that there is an ineluctable connection between the desire to arrive at a final uncontestable "theory of everything" and the impulse to suppress dissent (by force or intimidation if necessary). This is a more circumscribed construal of violence, and to the extent that our conceptions of truth retain this metaphysical character, he argued, they will likewise continue to encourage the ideological intolerance that leads to this kind of violence. This claim, by my lights at least, appears perfectly defensible and consistent from within Vattimo's overall position.

Apart from questions regarding weak thought's own self-consistency, though, we can additionally ask about its practical effects—that is, the consequences of its implementation. In other words, we might wish to ask the question "Does weak thought actually lead to a reduction in violence (of any kind)?" To this end, Ferraris has stated, "The last few years have taught me . . . that the primacy of interpretations over facts, the overcoming of the myth of objectivity, did not have the *emancipatory results* that illustrious postmodern philosophers like Richard Rorty or [Vattimo] imagined."[47]

This seems to me to be a rather peculiar response, though. Setting aside for a moment the difficulties one would have in isolating and measuring the effects of weak thought (or of any other ideology, for that matter) relative to other factors to determine its statistical impact on trends in social violence of the kind Ferraris has in mind, this notion, from my perspective at least, immediately encounters an even more basic problem.[48] Ferraris's criticism seems to implicitly assume that postmodern principles advanced by Rorty, Vattimo, and others have already been widely disseminated, accepted, and implemented in some fashion at a general societal level. As a result, Ferraris thinks that the continued (if not increased) presence of violence in society has definitively demonstrated such approaches to be ineffective.

I am not convinced that that is the case. As James K. A. Smith once quipped, "The news of Modernity's death has been greatly exaggerated."⁴⁹ Certainly, there has been an observable decline in confidence in institutions and traditional narratives in recent decades, but, as I believe I have shown, this has very little to do with postmodern *theory*. Theory, after all, is largely the attempt to trace the intellectual history of such large-scale societal attitudes, to diagnose them, and (sometimes) to propose remedies for their perceived maladies. Most of these attempts and proposals, for better or worse, however, will forever remain within the isolated confines of academia. The suggestion, therefore, that theories in the humanities are somehow the secret drivers of culture and politics, if true, would certainly be a case of the tail wagging the dog. Furthermore, as already mentioned, from the perspective of a thinker like Vattimo, such conceptions fundamentally misunderstand the proper role of philosophy in society.

Religious Objections

FREDERIEK DEPOORTERE

In his work *Christ in Postmodern Philosophy* (2008), the Belgian theologian Frederiek Depoortere offers a comparative analysis of the religious thought of Vattimo, Girard, and Slavoj Žižek. Though the description of Vattimo's religious thought in this work is more than serviceable, the criticisms that Depoortere offers in response appear to have emerged from a rather superficial engagement with Vattimo's thought. It is not useful or necessary to offer a point-by-point response to his work in this regard, but I will discuss some of his objections as illustrative of this point. For example, he argues that Vattimo's position is not "truly free of metaphysics" insofar as it treats disparate conceptions of philosophy under the reductive and all-encompassing category of "metaphysics."⁵⁰ As I think it has been exhaustively pointed out by now, however, Vattimo does not see the "end" in the "end of metaphysics" (or the "end of modernity" for that matter) as an actual cessation of anything except perhaps confidence in our schemes as being anything other than our own *perspectives*.[51]

An acceptance of the ultimate inescapability of our tendency toward formulating metaphysical schemes is the very reason why *Verwindung*, "distortion," is such a central concept in Vattimo's work. It is *because* metaphysics cannot be escaped that it must be weakened. It is because we are bound to interpret that our interpretations cannot reasonably be seen as absolute. As Friederike Rass has rightly noted in this regard, "On the one hand, metaphysics forms the necessary prerequisite for every interpretation; on the other hand, the goal of the interpretation is the twisting of metaphysics."[52] To fail to grasp this point is to miss a central component of Vattimo's overall argument.

Other, similar questions from Depoortere likewise seem to miss the mark. For example, he asks, "If [Vattimo] does not claim to offer a *true, objective description of reality*, how can [his criticisms of other positions] ever be justified?" Likewise, "How can [Vattimo] know that metaphysics will never come back again?"[53] These sorts of comments appear merely to be instances of ignoratio elenchi. Such criticisms suggest that Depoortere takes issue with Vattimo for somehow failing to provide what Vattimo himself argues cannot be given—namely, final answers. If Vattimo argues that no *final* answers can be meaningfully admitted in interpretive discourses (lest they cease to be discourses at all), it seems odd that someone would criticize such a position *on the grounds that* it fails to satisfactorily provide a final objective description of the world by which one can measure all other possible descriptions.

Echoing earlier criticisms by Peter Jonkers, Depoortere goes on to argue that Vattimo's use of charity as a limit on the relativizing effects of secularization and nihilism represents a wholly *arbitrary* choice on Vattimo's part.⁵⁴ To my mind, however, this is a bit like saying that John Stuart Mill's "harm principle" is a totally arbitrary limit on the notion of freedom or that Karl Popper's "paradox of tolerance" is a totally arbitrary limit on society's tolerance of belief.⁵⁵ That is, to describe these choices as *arbitrary* suggests that no thought went into them, that they serve no purpose, that they are incoherent, or that any other principle might just as well have been chosen. Is this really the case, though? Or, contrariwise, are they all examples of pragmatic regulative principles that function to create or allow a space for discourse to continue? In arguing that charity sets the parameters of "play" (in a Derridean sense) between mutually exclusive worldviews, is Vattimo transgressing his arguments concerning final metaphysical claims, or is he merely acknowledging that if dialogue between divergent positions is to be had at all, charity is required as a condition of the possibility of meaningful exchange? In conversation with the theologian Carmelo Dotolo, Vattimo addressed this concern. He asked rhetorically, "But what might it mean to deconstruct charity? Perhaps to ask why I 'must' love my neighbor? It is a question which lacks a satisfactory answer. . . . I mean that for charity, logical-verifiable motivations are not valid, but only pragmatic-existential motivations. . . . [T]here is a communitarian constitution of our existence . . . it is a preconceptual, pre-theoretical, datum. That is why it is impossible to deconstruct."⁵⁶ In other words, to ask why one should be charitable to others is to ignore, in effect, the motivations for dialoging with them in the first place. In this regard, once again, Depoortere's criticism seems rather thin.

Admittedly, there is perhaps an obvious tension between holding a worldview and claiming its ultimate provisionality. Nevertheless, is this tension really so difficult to maintain in practice? It seems to me that traditional discourses around, say, scientific knowledge function in a similar manner by noting that conceptions are *always* subject to emendation as new evidence presents itself. The crucial difference in weak thought, as opposed to science, however, is that the latter more explicitly extends this provisionality to the discourses themselves, so that these changes are not construed as an ever-greater fine-tuning that moves inexorably closer to objective truth but are instead viewed as the constant state of rhetorical flux occurring within broader (yet ever-shifting) paradigms of meaning.

Again, consider the analogy of games. One plays a game and recognizes that the rules are basically fixed yet not immutable. It is this predictable fixity that sets expectations and allows for "play." Even so, we recognize that most games do in fact change over time. Though opposing sides may compete against one another, in principle they have to agree on some basic rules—otherwise, they are not actually engaged with one another in the same game but are instead merely doing separate activities in close proximity. Even with the acceptance of a shared framework of rules by competing sides, however, these rules themselves frequently evolve over time. As initially unforeseen difficulties arise in the actual playing of the game, the rules themselves may from time to time need to be adjusted or amended accordingly so that the game may continue to be played.

Noting this feature of games is not surreptitiously subscribing to a metaphysical belief in a transcendent "game of all games" so much as merely acknowledging that if games are either so rigid that they cannot change (even to account for emergent contradictions) or so malleable that the rules can change on a whim to suit its players' immediate desires, they would quickly break down and become unplayable. This being the case, weak thought places an almost obsessive emphasis on the state of provisionality lest any single position calcify into rigid dogma. In turn, this recognition of the provisionality of one's own position is meant to foster the sort of self-reflection and intellectual humility required to create bonds of mutuality across ideological or religious divides. All in the service of play.

THOMAS G. GUARINO

I think Thomas G. Guarino's book *Vattimo and Theology* (2009) represents a significant contribution to the study of weak thought. Though I do not agree with all of his points, it is in many respects a model for how to engage in constructive disagreement. Guarino offers many insightful critiques of weak thought but largely manages to avoid the bristly and polemical tone one finds in sections of Depoortere's book and throughout Ferraris's work.

In engaging with Vattimo, Guarino instead takes as his preferred method the classical Christian approach of "despoiling the Egyptians," which seeks to find in the work of others those elements most useful to one's own understanding (regardless of whether the position under consideration is well disposed to one's own or not).[57] This approach isn't mere syncretism but rather an openness to engagement with other worldviews (based in confidence, not doubt, of one's own position). It sees that every position possesses some measure of truth and that a generous orthodoxy should seek out such truths no matter their provenance. In the words of St. Augustine, "Domini sui esse intellegat, ubicumque invenerit veritatem" (Wherever one finds the truth, it belongs to God).[58]

In my view, the most important of Guarino's criticisms of weak thought concerns its relationship to Christianity. For Vattimo, the embrace of the Other in genuinely equal terms requires rendering as "nonessential" any and all doctrinal positions that could potentially lead to the sort of strong claims that would terminate in philosophical (or physical) violence. As Vattimo saw it, this means that one need only repudiate one's beliefs to the extent that those beliefs separate us from God and neighbor—or, more specifically, separate us from the God who is found only in the embrace of our neighbor.

It appears to me, then, that Vattimo thought that by making this argument, he had, first, preserved the Christian perspective by successfully foregrounding the one necessary and universal hermeneutical key Jesus offered for assessing all religious claims—namely, Does it lead one closer to or farther away from the love of God and neighbor? Second, from an interreligious perspective, this appeal to the "golden rule" is also a principle that presumably non-Christians of all faiths can likewise affirm.[59] Finally, this minimalist set of commitments allows one, at least in theory, to continue to accept (at the level of personal conviction) some traditional doctrinal beliefs, provided that they do not lead one to contravene charity. Guarino questions to what extent the distinctive characteristics of a given faith tradition can survive after such a procedure. For his part, Vattimo appeared satisfied merely by the fact that such separate identities would still exist as a trace, memory, or set of distinct histories. Herein lies the religious suspicion among critics such as Guarino that Vattimo is, in effect, asking us to exchange a robust historical Christianity for a comparatively paltry, nondescript, and ultimately ineffectual philosophical substitute. If, for example, G. K. Chesterton is right that "every heresy has been an effort to narrow the Church," then Christian suspicion is perhaps not without warrant.[60]

As a result, both Guarino and Depoortere express concern regarding this stipulation of charity's priority over truth. In this regard, each maintains that the Christianity that would emerge from such a procedure would be so departicularized as to have effectively been eroded away to nothing. From a religious perspective, I think that this is a substantial criticism worth considering because in some respects this reduced Christianity does indeed appear to be the destiny of the secularization, universalization, and decline that

Vattimo had in mind. That is, at least at a social level, Vattimo saw it as the only real way to put into practice the Christian ideal of charity and hospitality in a pluralistic world. To continue to define ourselves by what separates us instead of what unites us is a recipe for continued conflict. Guarino, in contrast, sees this as a fool's bargain. What he thinks lies on the other side of this procedure is not a harmony of difference but instead a soulless gray uniformity. In such a world, difference—at least real difference—appears inadmissible.

In a similar fashion, Depoortere has argued that in Vattimo's thought "the religious tradition is merely adapted, dissolved even. This seems to indicate," he says, "that Vattimo's weak thought is not really hospitable to Christianity but rather reduces it to itself."[61] In response, I feel compelled to point out that this characterization presumes, of course, that weak thought is a philosophy in conflict and competition with Christianity, a presumption it is crucial to note that Vattimo did not seem to share. Vattimo instead appears to have believed that weak thought is simply Christianity boiled down to its essence—that is, the love of God and neighbor. In this regard, I think that it is honestly strange that Vattimo did not make greater use of Jesus's words concerning the "greatest commandment" in Matthew's Gospel: "'You shall love the Lord your God with all your heart, and with all your soul, and with all your mind.' This is the greatest and first commandment. And a second is like it: 'You shall love your neighbor as yourself.' On these two commandments hang all the law and the prophets'" (Matt. 22:36–40). Instead, to illustrate this same point Vattimo often referred to the word of St. Augustine: "Dilige, et quod vis fac" (Love [others], and do what you want).[62] The "sticky wicket," however, is of course in trying to determine what that love of neighbor looks like in actual practice (particularly in dialogue with others who see the world in a radically different way).

AN ATHENIAN IN JERUSALEM: THE RELATIONSHIP BETWEEN FAITH AND REASON

By way of summary, it seems to me that the overriding issue regarding the religious (specifically Christian) critique of weak thought concerns the ambiguous relationship it has with respect to religion. This problem, though, is not exclusive to weak thought. Indeed, the contested borders between philosophy and theology have been a major point of contention in the West since at least the Patristic period.[63] That is, since Tertullian famously asked, "Quid ergo Athenis et Hierosolymis? Quid academiæ et ecclesiæ?" (What indeed has Athens to do with Jerusalem? What concord is there between the Academy and the Church?). Indeed, Tertullian's assertion that "We [Christians] want no curious disputation after possessing Christ Jesus, no inquisition after enjoying the gospel. . . . [T]here is nothing which we ought to believe besides" would fit just as comfortably in a work by Luther or Barth.[64]

For a "revealed religion" such as Christianity, there is always going to exist a tension concerning the manner in which it can be integrated with (or subsumed under) any philosophical system, whether Stoic, Platonic, Aristotelean, or Vattimian. How exactly one adjudicates this relationship does not depend so much on the particular system in question as on the orienting assumption about whether the relationship between philosophy and theology should construe them as coextensive or parallel activities. That is, one can see philosophy and theology as either being distinct ways of mapping essentially the same terrain or being engaged in fundamentally different pursuits. In addition, in either case these relationships can be framed as existing in conflict/competition or collaboration with one another. For example, with respect to classical theology, Tertullian viewed religion and philosophy as making coextensive yet irreconcilable claims. By contrast, figures such as Justin Martyr and Clement of Alexandria viewed Christianity as essentially a form of philosophy.⁶⁵ Likewise, Augustine and Aquinas viewed philosophy and theology as parallel yet complementary activities.⁶⁶ With this in mind, I suggest that the most important concerns of religious critics such as Depoortere and Guarino should likewise extend to theological appropriation of any philosophical system, not merely that of weak thought.

6

FINAL REFLECTIONS

New Pathways in Vattimian Thought

Have we helped out neighbor, given even from our surplus, loved the least among us? This is the only criteria, the only crisis, the only test.
—Jean-Luc Marion, *Prolegomena to Charity*, 1986

Every commitment inspired by the Church's social doctrine is "derived from charity, which according to the teaching of Jesus is the synthesis of the entire Law (cf. Matt 22:36–40)." This means acknowledging that "love, overflowing with small gestures of mutual care, is also civic and political, and it makes itself felt in every action that seeks to build a better world."
—Pope Francis, *Fratelli tutti*, 2020

In this concluding chapter, I would like to offer some suggestions for areas of exploration for future Vattimian studies. They include recommendations for engaging fields of research where there has so far been little to no direct encounter with weak thought. I present these suggestions here as inchoate ideas with the hope that others (and I) will be able to develop them further in the future.

PHILOSOPHY

Weak Thought and the Law

In the interest of brevity, we can think of traditional Western legal philosophy in broad terms as being roughly divisible between an older "natural-law theory" and the more dominant modernist theory of "legal positivism." Natural-law theory contends that there exist in nature some set of principles that are timeless, universally valid, and knowable through reason. It is this set of principles, therefore, the theory maintains, that should form the normative standards for right (legal) behavior in any given society. Christian natural-law theory, furthermore, identifies this set of principles with the general revelation of God's law available to all humans, which is separate from the "special revelation" of Christ necessary for salvation.[1]

Natural-law theory itself can be traced to antiquity in the works of Aristotle, Cicero, Ulpian, and others. It received further development from the medieval period onward through the works of Thomas Aquinas, Francisco de Vitoria (c. 1483–1546), Francisco Suárez (1548–1617), Hugo Grotius (1583–1645), and others. Its assumptions also undergirded the reasoning of much of the medieval canon law of the Roman Catholic Church. Conversely, the notion that there exists a natural order to the cosmos dictated by a coherent internal logic knowable through the human faculty of reason was also incidentally a foundational assumption of modernity in general and of the Enlightenment in particular. Thus, natural law played a guiding role in the thought of Renaissance humanists, Protestant reformers, as well as Enlightenment-era Lumières and revolutionaries.[2] During the nineteenth century, however, for a whole host of reasons mostly having to do with the ambiguity of its application in specific legal cases, natural-law theory almost entirely fell out of favor in practical jurisprudence in favor of legal positivism.[3]

Legal positivism argues instead that laws do not depend on ideals. The "fact" of a law depends rather on its enforceability, which in turn relies on the supervening realities of the state apparatus in question. Whether a law adheres to some set of foundational moral precepts or not is peripheral to the work of judges, lawyers, and officers of the law tasked with its actual day-to-day interpretation, implementation, and enforcement. A law is determined by what it says and how it can be reasonably interpreted. With the movement toward codification—that is, basing laws on written statutes and constitutions, which occurred after the enactment of the French Civil Code (or Code Napoléon) in 1804—this formal proceduralism acted to constrain the perceived ambiguities and arbitrariness of previous systems.[4] Many felt that judges previously had too wide a latitude to base their findings on potentially idiosyncratic readings of local customs, ancient codes, or personal moral feelings colored by the guise of natural law. By contrast, legal positivism enjoyed a functional advantage because it more clearly limited the scope of the law to what is written on the page.

This approach can be traced to Thomas Hobbes (1588–1679), David Hume (1711–1776), Jeremy Bentham (1747–1832), and other like figures. Even so, the most important representatives of this school of thought are arguably John Austin (1790–1859), Oliver Wendell Holmes Jr. (1841–1935), Hans Kelsen (1881–1973), H. L. A. Hart (1907–1992), and Joseph Raz (1939–2022).[5] Nevertheless, the atrocities of World War II, including the legal status of the Nazi regime's antisemitic actions, drew into question the soundness of an approach to the law that had no basis in morality or social justice. As a result, Gustav Radbruch (1878–1949) and others began to argue for a theory of human rights grounded in natural law as a failsafe against the possibility of legal despotism. Other contemporary advocates for a return to some form of natural-law theory include Germain Grisez (1929–2018), John Finnis (b. 1940), and Robert P. George (b. 1955).

In his book *Nichilismo ed emancipazione: Etica, politica, diritto* (*Nihilism and Emancipation: Ethics, Politics, and Law*, 2003), Vattimo argued that, as with other domains of knowledge, legal reasoning (even when exercised with methodological rigor) derives its justification ultimately from norms, rules, and decisions previously taken, not on pure facts alone. As Ana Messuti has noted, "There is a close connection between justice as administration and philosophy as hermeneutics, because both are lacking a metaphysical foundation. Just as democracy is no more than the application of a certain voting procedure, justice for Vattimo is the administration of, or the procedure for, the application of laws."⁶ Understanding the rational of some statute or precedent, therefore, requires a disassembly of that statue or precedent's history and cultural context. "Law," Vattimo contended, "does justice only by means of interpretive acts, the application of given laws by judges in dialogue with lawyers, public prosecutors, and various legal experts. The problematic of the relationship between justice and law goes back to the problematic of beginning, and interpretation operates on this problematic, either nakedly revealing its profound lack of foundation (which can in the last analysis provoke a shift to the place of mysticism) or filling the gap by rhetorical expedients, ad hoc adjustments, what [Pier Giuseppe] Monateri . . . calls fabulations."⁷

As elsewhere, in *Nihilism and Emancipation* Vattimo was skeptical of natural-law theory and contended that a focus on the historical basis of any interpretive act will disabuse one of any notion that decisions are made in an objective way that faithfully mirrors a real world external to our present contexts. He asks, therefore, "What becomes of our notions of justice and law when we take seriously the idea that metaphysics is without foundations?" Vattimo concludes that interpretation of the law that successfully produces consensus around specific applications is a model of good rhetorical discourse. The lack of ultimate foundations we find in a recognition of the nihilism of legal reasoning need not result in an abandonment of the process of building consensus, which forms a real basis for law as an acceptable standard for social behavior. He goes on to argue, however:

> The increasing complexity of state forms has enormously accentuated the distance between the law and justice. Juridical formalism does not, in practice, really appear to be taking account of the "reality" of facts, the truth of the "rights" claimed by individuals and groups, of new rights, those, for example, demanded by the "new subjects" who are pressing for recognition in everyday life, and its procedural mechanisms for ensuring fairness seem to proceed so slowly that they provoke impatience in those who are thirsting for justice. Such impatience is another reason for interpretation to assume a more active role. In a democracy it must be seen for what it concretely is, no longer hiding behind the sacrality of the judge and his (in principle) unquestionable impartiality, and precisely because it is no longer clouded in a sacral aura, it is also called upon to heed the concrete demands, the voices that are rising from the world of new needs.[8]

Unlike other postmodern critical approaches to the law, which assume an outsider (etic) perspective on the legal system, Vattimo (as a legislator in the European Parliament) actually had an insider (emic) perspective on democratic proceduralism. This means that his approach arguably bears closest resemblance in both style and substance to the interpretivist legal hermeneutics of Emilio Betti (1890–1968), John Rawls (1921–2002), Ronald Dworkin (1931–2013), and other thinkers like them than it does to the more abstract considerations of the law given by Nietzsche, Foucault, Lyotard, Derrida, and Rorty—none of whom ever studied or practiced law.[9] Though

Vattimo directed little of his academic work to the area of juridical philosophy, his position as a minister of the European Parliament makes Vattimo a unique representative within critical legal thought on the application of postmodern concepts to the law. This is a vantage point, therefore, well worth considering from both a legal and a philosophical perspective.

RELIGION

In Anglophone philosophy, interest in the religious dimensions of Vattimo's thought have so far been restricted largely to the area of so-called radical theology. This term and its associated movement originated with the "death of God" theologies of the 1960s (especially those of William Hamilton, Paul van Buren, and Thomas J. J. Altizer).[10] Even so, the contemporary intellectual inheritors of this earlier movement share some overlapping beliefs with postliberal narrative theology yet differentiate themselves from the latter by being ostensibly nonconfessional or even anticonfessional (in some cases eschewing the notion of revelation altogether).[11] By far the most visible intellectual figure currently associated with radical theology of this kind is John D. Caputo.[12] In many respects, this connection is unsurprising. For example, Vattimo would approvingly cite Bonhoeffer's statement "Einen Gott, den 'es gibt,' gibt es nicht" (There is no God that "exists"; literally, "A God that exists does not exist"), noting that the truth of Christianity is not some Tarskian proposition.[13] Instead, as Vattimo once noted, "I know full well that, from the early centuries, biblical hermeneutics was familiar with the doctrine of the different levels of the meaning of Scripture: literal, moral, allegorical, and anagogic.... Certainly, every believer knows that Jesus is seated neither to the right nor to the left of the Father [literally] and is horrified by the suggestion that we calculate the point in space where we might find the body of the Virgin Mary."[14]

These comments are perfectly in keeping with most conscientious orthodox readings of scripture. Even still, on this point, Vattimo would press further than many (more theologically conservative) Christians would be willing to follow:

> Deciding which meaning to give to a certain passage of the Bible is always reserved by the Church hierarchy.... But, if we assume that Jesus seated on the right of the Father and Mary ascended into heaven are "poetic metaphors," could we not also think that the resurrection and the incarnation are propositions of the same type? There is no empirical proof for either. It is the Catholic Church that literally prohibits us to think this way.... Only those who hold power are really interested in truth as the objective description of things and matters of fact. This too I do not "demonstrate" apodictically. I suggest only that we ask ourselves who it is that rejects, and has always rejected as an aberration, the thesis that there is no objective truth but only interpretations, which are never unbiased.[15]

Although the term *radical theology* is often used in a more general sense to describe a loose confederation of distinct thinkers (including Vattimo) who are linked together by their shared interest in contemporary postmodern/postmetaphysical continental thought and their commitments to a postsecular recuperation of religious language, radical theology as a "school of thought" should perhaps more accurately be restricted to describing the specific work of Caputo and associated thinkers such as Jeffrey Robbins, Clayton Crockett, and Peter Rollins, each of whom has embraced the label.[16] In the United States, with the recent fracturing of the already diffuse Emergent Church movement, radical theology has also come to serve as something of an intellectual home (or waystation) for many post-Evangelicals as they continue to deconstruct their faith.[17] This has granted a higher degree of visibility for radical theology outside of the strict confines of the academy than one might otherwise expect—particularly with respect to the work of Caputo and Rollins, both of whom have become popular seminar speakers.

Though it is not difficult to see the appeal of weak thought for radical theology, I think it would be a mistake to conflate the two or to blur too greatly the lines between their respective approaches.[18] In what follows, therefore, I propose thinking of Vattimo's work along different theological lines. The first approach looks at parallels between weak thought and liberation theology. The second approach builds on this connection to explore (or, in many cases, to propose for the first time) links between weak thought and the related areas of feminist, Black, intersectional, and queer theologies. Finally, moving beyond the internal discussion within Western theology, the third approach looks at potential avenues for constructing interreligious dialogue in Vattimian terms with faith traditions other than Christianity.

Weak Thought and Liberation Theology

One potentially fruitful area of discussion, which is sometimes alluded to in Vattimian studies but as yet has not produced any substantial literature, concerns the parallels between weak thought and liberation theology.[19] I think that in many respects, even if only at the periphery, weak thought fits more comfortably within this religious framework than it does with the postconfessional Derridean a/theism of Caputo and other self-styled "radical theologians."[20] I think that this is especially true in light of Vattimo's comments on the state of the church since the election of Pope Francis to the throne of St. Peter. Before detailing these comments, however, I think that it would be useful first to briefly describe the relationship between liberation theology and the Vatican before and after the election of Francis.

According to Gerd-Rainer Horn, there were two major interrelated movements of left-wing Catholicism during the twentieth century. The first occurred between 1924 and 1959—that is, between the establishment of the working-class lay-Catholic organization the Young Christian Workers (Kristene Arbeidersjeugd/Jeunesse ouvrière chrétienne) and the launch of Vatican II.[21] Young Christian Workers had been established in Belgium by Joseph-Léon Cardinal Cardijn but quickly spread to other countries. Unlike many other Catholic organizations for youth at the time, it was self-governed by its own members and (at least initially) focused primarily on the social concerns of the working class. Such Catholic organizations were meant as an alternative to socialism/communism but often enough resulted in Catholic youths developing left-wing, pro-labor sympathies.

The culmination of this first-wave of "liberationist" thinking was Vatican II, which, as we have already seen, represented a brief moment of ascendency for Catholic progressivism. This widescale institutional reform was the result of decades of work by lay Catholics operating mostly behind the scenes to effect change. More astonishing still, it was accomplished during a time in which the church hierarchy seemed resolutely against socialism/communism. Indeed, until John XXIII (1958–1963), the church hierarchy had been deeply affected by its struggles against and competition with communism and left-wing social movements.[22] According to a report by British special envoy to the Holy See in 1922, Count de Salis, "Everything in the Vatican is dominated by the Pope's [Pius XII] fear of Russian Communism, that the Soviets may reach Western Europe."[23]

After the death of Paul VI in 1978, this emphasis on fighting communism would again return in force during the pontificate of John Paul II (1978–2005).[24]

The second and more visible movement of liberationist thought emerged as Indigenous concerns in the Global South began to be filtered through the lens of a post–Vatican II theological framework. The crucial event in this regard was the Second Episcopal Conference of Latin America held in Medellín, Columbia, in the momentous year 1968. The earlier development of Catholic social teaching's "preferential option for the poor" and the institution of alternative organizational forms ("base communities," *comunidades eclesiales de base*) had laid the groundwork for the more formal development of what would eventually be viewed as liberation theology proper.[25]

Inarguably the most important founder of this theological trend was the Peruvian Dominican priest and philosopher Gustavo Gutiérrez. In order to connect his thought with the previously discussed movements of lay Catholicism in Europe and the developments of Vatican II, however, it is worth mentioning that among Gutiérrez's most important theological influences, he cites Chenu, Congar, de Lubac, de Chardin, Schillebeeckx, Metz, Rahner, and others like them.

The primary difference between European left-wing Catholicism and the liberationist movements of the Global South concerned the differences in social circumstances between Europe, on the one hand, and Latin America, Asia, and Africa, on the other. As Deane William Ferm has noted, though, "Both proponents and critics of liberation theology stress the importance of Vatican II and its convener, Pope John XXIII. [For instance] Gustavo Gutiérrez... has said that the Medellín conference would not have been possible without Vatican II and Pope John XXIII."[26] This is not to say, of course, that liberation theology—which is associated primarily with Latin America—is somehow secretly a European invention. It is merely to note that there are historical congruities between these two instances. While the experiences of ordinary Christians living in desperate poverty in Peru, Guatemala, El Salvador, Nicaragua, and other places like them were certainly the catalyst for the development of liberationist thought, the language that the movement ultimately came to adapt in order to describe such experiences is a language also shared by other left-wing Catholics, who only decades earlier had been struggling for workers' rights in recently industrialized European countries such as Germany, France, and Italy.[27]

A full accounting of the church's responses to liberation theology is obviously far beyond the scope of the present discussion. With that in mind, I limit the following comments merely to developing an image of the changed institutional attitudes toward liberationist thought and left-wing social movements, which emerged during Francis's papacy.

In 1984, in his capacity as prelate of the Congregation for the Doctrine of the Faith, Ratzinger (later Pope Benedict XVI) issued *Instructions on Certain Aspects of the "Theology of Liberation,"* which did not so much reject the positions advanced by liberationist thought as take issue with its applications. In effect, the main concerns laid out are that liberation theologians have rendered the spiritual salvation of Christians secondary to their physical liberation from oppressive social forces and, as a result, have become too embroiled in politics (particularly of a Marxist variety). Two years later, the congregation followed this statement with a similar work, *Instruction on Christian Freedom and Liberation.*

Although there was no formal discontinuity between Francis and previous popes on the matter of liberation theology—indeed, Francis never publicly self-identified with the movement—his actions were nevertheless telling.[28] In 2015, for instance, Gutiérrez was invited by the Holy See to give a presentation at the Twentieth General Assembly of Caritas Internationalis at the Vatican, an invitation that would have been unimaginable just a few years earlier.²⁹ Francis also oversaw the beatification of Father Rutilio Grande and Archbishop Óscar Romero, liberationist martyrs assassinated by CIA-trained death squads for their criticism of the U.S.-backed right-wing military junta in El Salvador. Likewise, he furthered the canonization process of the Brazilian bishop Dom Helder Câmara and the beatification of the Argentinian bishop Enrique Angelelli. He reinstated controversial figures such as Father Miguel d'Escoto Brockmann and Father Ernesto Cardenal, both of whom had been suspended by John Paul II for their roles in the Sandinista government of Nicaragua. In 2015, Francis even graciously accepted a gift given to him by President Evo Morales of Bolivia, a socialist, provocatively depicting a crucifix carved into a sickle and hammer—though Francis did not consider himself to be a Marxist.³⁰

In terms of his own thought, it is instructive not only to look at such oblique gestures (which can obviously be construed as little more than good diplomacy) but also to consider Francis's written works. One such important work is the final draft of the general meeting of the Conference of Latin American Bishops in Aparecida in 2007, where he served as head of the editing committee. Then functioning in his role as archbishop of Buenos Aires, Jorge Mario Bergoglio and the other members of the committee chose to use the document to "[reassert] central concerns of liberation theology." For example, "they reintroduced the see-judge-act scheme from Medellín and Puebla, reaffirmed the preferential option for the poor, restated the importance of the base communities (CEBs), and confirmed the core issue from liberation theology of an integral liberation (conversion of persons and transformation of structures in the society). What is more, Aparecida broke the telling silence in the 1992 documents from Santo Domingo about the martyrs that had not yet been canonized but who still were considered saints in the Latin American church."³¹ The so-called Aparecida Document has also served as an early reference point for later works that defined Francis's papacy: *Evangelii gaudium* (2013), *Lumen fidei* (2013), *Laudato si'* (2015), *Amoris lætitia* (2016), and *Fratelli tutti* (2020).

It is worth asking at this point what all this has to do with weak thought and the future of Vattimian studies? Well, first, Vattimo was quite candid concerning his admiration of Francis (whom he had met prior to Francis's papal election and with whom he shared mutual friends).³² For example, he stated on several occasions that with Francis as pope, he "no longer feels embarrassed to be a Christian." He even noted that he had been reproached by some "for believing more in Pope Francis than in the Eternal Father." In response, Vattimo said, "The God who is given as a word addressed to me and to my neighbor is the only thing I can believe, to which I can turn and to which I can pray among other things." Even so, he also noted, "A pope is a pope. You cannot think he is going to be anything else." Despite the structural limits that the institution of the church necessarily imposes on anyone in such a position, it is not incidental to church culture how its leadership engages with the world outside the Vatican. "How the pope presents himself represents how he is felt and lived by the faithful, so he is not just an outward appearance."³³

On January 31, 2022, Vattimo spoke with Debora Tonelli and Antonio Cecere about Francis's encyclical *Fratelli tutti* in a dialogue organized jointly by Georgetown University, Civiltà Cattolica, and Filosofia in Movimento. In the conversation—which has since been published in a volume edited by Tonelli entitled *Fratelli tutti? Credenti e non credenti in dialogo con Papa Francesco* (*Fratelli tutti?* Believers and nonbelievers in dialogue with Pope Francis)—Vattimo reflected on what Tonelli refers to as the pope's "decentered" and "inclusive" message.³⁴ The encyclical *Fratelli tutti* and Francis's Abu Dhabi Document present a practical and pastoral approach to the church. They address the problems of cultural conflict, political violence, migration, human rights, environmental destruction, and our culture of waste.[35]

Vattimo stated in his own comments at the time, "One of the things I would still like to do is to write a book on the Church under Francis; to make a 'Franciscan theology' I would like to say, which includes a whole series of things that identify the 'Other' as a subject of charity . . . a 'Franciscan theology,' *in quotation marks*, would be a theology of charity and not of structure, not one of objective structures and principles."[36] Unlike the pontificates of John Paul II and Benedict XVI, which were frequently mired in contentious debates over church teachings—particularly in matters of sexual ethics—Francis instead chose to de-emphasize such "line drawing" in favor of fostering a Christianity characterized by "[an] open mind [and a] faithful heart."[37] In keeping with liberation, then, Francis's theology was not an academic theology *of* the people but a practical theology *for* the people. This is why Vattimo, in his discussion of *Fratelli tutti* claimed, "The interest of Pope Francis is to found an authentic communism, a true communism."[38]

In one of his final works, *Essere e dintorni* (*Being and Its Surroundings*, 2018), Vattimo argued that today, because of the hegemony of globalized capitalism in the post-Soviet world, it no longer seems possible to imagine a Communist International (Comintern) that could serve as a focal point to unify and direct the struggles of the world's most marginalized. Provocatively, he claimed, "The only place we can look to find it is the Catholic Church of Pope Francis. . . . In the current state of the global class war, the only possibility of building a counterforce that offers some hope is the 'religious' kind."[39] This focus on Europe and Christianity, he argued, was based on the reality of the present structure of global power and spheres of influence. Despite the rise of China and India as major players on the world stage, imperialism and concentrated capital continue to emanate from the West, where the long shadow of Christianity continues to shape symbolic concepts and values.

As Vattimo acknowledged, the legacy of Christianity vis-à-vis temporal powers has a fraught history. In art, for example, one can see this tension reflected in the imperial iconography of "Christ Pantocrator" and "Christ Militant" versus the images of the suffering or murdered Christ one finds in the harrowing crucifixion and entombment panels of Matthias Grünewald's *Isenheim Altarpiece* (c. 1512–1515) or in the grotesque depiction of Hans Holbein the Younger's *The Body of the Dead Christ in the Tomb* (c. 1520–1522).[40] Part of this Janus-faced legacy has to do with the exigencies of history. Christianity began its life as a marginalized and persecuted sect of Judaism within occupied Roman Palestine. By roughly the middle of the second century, however, it had fractured into numerous competing factions, each becoming noticeably distinguishable from its Jewish roots. During both early phases, nascent Christianity(ies) were at odds with Rome until the Battle of the Milvian Bridge.[41]

The success of the majoritarian orthodox faction and its later official favor by the Roman state after Constantine meant that the church eventually inherited the civil function of religion previously exercised by the Roman *mos maiorum*. There is a reason why, for example, one of the pope's traditional titles is *pontifex maximus*. Furthermore, with the decline of Western power during the period of late antiquity, the church gradually assumed from the collapsing state not only the role of representative but also protector of social norms and what remained of public institutions. This is how and why the Roman Catholic Church took on the mantel of imperial power. This is also why Vattimo argued that the process of secularization—stemming from the Protestant Reformation through to the Enlightenment—has served to reorient the church back toward its original emancipatory religious function.

As Vattimo pointed out, many will no doubt find it paradoxical that one would attempt to locate an emancipatory project in an ancient institution headed by an exclusively male monocratic authority figure. In response, he argued, "In our late modernity, the function of conserving and maintaining social order has passed almost completely to science and technology. It is here, and certainly not in an ever-weakening 'ecclesiastical authority,' that the capitalist order has its most effective and loyal allies."[42] Vattimo cited comments that Francis made to a group of Argentinian youth on his first international trip as pope to Rio de Janeiro, Brazil, in July 2013, where he told attendants, "I want the Church to go out to the streets," admonishing them to "Hacer lío," meaning "Make some noise," "Wreak havoc," or, to borrow a famous phrase from the late U.S. congressman John Lewis, "Get in good trouble." Vattimo thought that the church should constitute the unassimilable element that always stands outside any totalizing system—the anarchic element that is necessary for permanent revolution.

> There is a sense in which the communism I am talking about in reference to the Church of Pope Francis has a "spectral" aspect: it does not think of itself as a party that wants to govern, for reasons of "realism" (it makes no sense today to think of revolution as a violent takeover of power, since the forces of capitalist self-preservation are too strong) and because it wants to avoid relapsing into the practical-inert, which seems to be the fate of "successful" revolutions. The communism I have in mind can only take the form of a shadow that accompanies and torments (*hanter, hantise* is the French term to keep in mind: it pursues, hounds, disturbs . . .) the established order and the prevailing power structure.[43]

Furthermore, this is a vision of Christianity, he argued, that sees all conversion as internal conversion. It represents a form of ecumenism that does not seek to *make the world Christian*. Instead, it seeks to make the Christian a better Christian, the Buddhist a better Buddhist, the Muslim a better Muslim, and so on. Spirituality is a form of intimacy that opens one's ears to hear. Fidelity to a tradition does not mean a slavish adherence to the literal words of a text but instead means returning to it as to a wellspring from which one draws water (cf. John 6:68). This vision, also, of course, calls to mind Gadamer's notions of *Bildung* and *Horizontverschmelzung*—conversations with the traditions of the past that hold the capacity to change us now in the present. With all of this in mind, it is perhaps little wonder that Vattimo has said, "I myself no longer make any big difference between philosophy and religion."[44]

Weak Thought and Doing Theology from the Margins

FEMINIST THEOLOGY

In her book *Kenosis and Feminist Theology: The Challenge of Gianni Vattimo* (1998), Marta Frascati-Lochhead argues that weak thought can be employed in the task of overcoming the "violence of patriarchal thought," while also offering feminist theology a means of moving beyond its essentialist metaphysical categories. Frascati-Lochhead maintains that feminist thinkers such as Elizabeth Schüssler Fiorenza, Rosemary Radford Ruether, and Mary Daly accepted the historical conditionality of knowledge yet also remained ensconced within a traditional metaphysical framework arguing that "the feminist perspective is truer to reality than the patriarchal perspectives it is called to replace."[45]

Meanwhile, Frascati-Lochhead comments, thinkers such as Susan Brooks Thistlethwaite, Rebecca S. Chopp, and Morny Joy—although largely accepting the postmodern critique of essentialist categories—nevertheless still refused to accept the critique's nihilist implications for fear of creating an intellectual permission structure for the powerful to simply impose their own oppressive vision of women's roles. Weak thought, by contrast, is able to accept the nihilism of postmodernity, while seeking to oppose both unfettered relativism and violence. Frascati-Lochhead concludes: "From the perspective suggested by Vattimo, feminism, like any other movement at the end of modernity, reacts in ambiguous ways to the self-dissolution of metaphysical thought. On the one hand, it does accept its own historical specificity, partiality, limited validity, and even—sometimes—mortality. On the other hand, it tries to reestablish, out of a certain fear of its own dissolution, some kind of validity or permanence that seems to be the temporally conditioned expression of a basic truth."[46]

BLACK THEOLOGY

In important ways, Black liberation theology (or simply "Black theology")—as exemplified in the work of James H. Cone, among others—potentially offers a compelling conversation partner to weak thought. Drawing inspiration from figures such as Martin Luther King Jr. and Malcolm X as well as from the leaders of the Black Power movement—such as Kwame Ture (Stokely Carmichael), Ron Karenga, and members of the Black Panther Party—Black theology attempts to reconcile Christianity with Black Power and the latter's cultural critique of "whiteness." In so doing, it confronts many of the same challenges faced by the political and religious dimensions of weak thought vis-à-vis the role of violence in the face of sustained and systemic oppression.

Although I am currently unaware of any direct engagement in the secondary literature exploring weak thought from the perspective of Black theology or vice versa, I think that there are several obvious points of convergence as well as potential areas of disagreement and critique that run in both directions. This is particularly true with respect to the work of Cone, whose theology is at times expressly militant. For example, in his second major work, *A Black Theology of Liberation* (1970), he states: "As the oppressed now recognize their situation in the light of God's revelation, they know that they should have killed their oppressors instead of trying to 'love' them."[47]

While, for Cone, God's love is certainly central to any theology that claims to be Christian, God's love is not to be confused with some generalized sentimentality. It cannot be divorced, therefore, from God's sense of justice and rectitude. This being the case, theology is not a neutral undertaking. Indeed, as the German liberation theologian Dorothee Sölle once said, "In the face of suffering you are either with the victim or [with] the executioner—there is no other option."[48] With this in mind, Cone argued, "The God of the oppressed takes sides with the black community. God is not color-blind in the black–white struggle, but has made an unqualified identification with blacks."[49]

In this way, Black theology often speaks of its perspective in a manner that represents it as being a truer reality than the picture presented by the theological legacy of white enslavers. Here, mutatis mutandis, we might recall Vattimo's critique of the militancy of the Red Brigade and wonder about the trajectory of revolutionary moralism in such a position. Nevertheless, like Dussel's early critique of weak thought as being too Eurocentric and academically focused, those wishing to engage with Black theology from the perspective of weak thought would have to contend with Cone's numerous assertions that white theologians are in no moral position to dictate the manner in which the oppressed struggle for their own freedom. Specifically, though, Cone was speaking primarily of white liberal theologians in the United States who demurred at the often-strident rhetoric of his work. Whiteness and Blackness, he argued, are social (as much as, if not more so, than cultural) conditions. Rejecting whiteness, for both white and Black individuals, then, means having an unqualified commitment to the Black community (as Nat Turner or John Brown did). Those interested in justice must become Black as God is Black.[50]

> Black theology believes that it is not only appropriate but necessary to begin the doctrine of God with an insistence on God's blackness. . . . The blackness of God, and everything implied by it in a racist society, is the heart of the black theology doctrine of God. There is no place in black theology for a colorless God in a society where human beings suffer precisely because of their color. . . . Either God is identified with the oppressed to the point that their experience becomes God's experience, or God is a God of racism.[51]

Again, one can see parallels here between weak thought/hermeneutic communism and Black theology's liberative goals. The primary barrier to engagement would appear at the outset in deciding whether the work of someone such as Vattimo has standing to speak among those engaged in the continued struggle for Black liberation. I think that there are potential arguments on both sides, but this should be read as a suggestion because I am likewise not in a position to decide that point.

INTERSECTIONAL THEOLOGY

The term *intersectionality* was coined by the Columbia law professor Kimberlé Crenshaw in 1989 to describe the various ways in which "multiple forms of inequality or disadvantage sometimes compound themselves and create obstacles that often are not understood among conventional ways of thinking."[52] For example, the various ways the U.S. legal system discriminates against women and is disproportionately weaponized against people of color and the poor means that a poor Black woman living in the United States exists at the intersections of several lanes of marginality. Though this terminology is relatively recent, the reality underlying it has long since been recognized by those who exist at the margins. With respect to theology, for example, one can consider the work of a thinker such as Delores S. Williams, who explored such intersectional dimensions in her notable article "Womanist Theology: Black Women's Voices" (1987) and more fully in her book *Sisters in the Wilderness: The Challenge of Womanist God-Talk* (1993). In these works, Williams seeks to dialogue with (and critique) both Black and feminist theologies for the ways in which they exclude Black women or reduce them to one aspect of their identities instead of viewing them holistically.

Although there is certainly valid criticism of what is oftentimes derisively dismissed as "identity politics," a strictly class-based understanding of political oppression, as Crenshaw and others have correctly pointed out, fails to fully account for the ways in which even class discrimination is compounded by and unequally divided along lines of race/ethnicity, religion, gender, and sexual identity. Furthermore, regarding Christian theology, the explicit identification of Christ with "the least of these" (Matt. 25:31–46) demands attentiveness on the part of theologians to the various ways in which elements of a person's identity prevent the social recognition of their innate value. It is my contention that intersectional theology in conversation with weak thought could potentially offer a unique perspective on engaging with the various problems that arise from discussions of identity and its role in the perpetuation of systemically oppressive social structures.

QUEER THEOLOGY

The origins of queer theology can be traced to the Argentinian contextual theologian Marcella Althaus-Reid's work *Indecent Theology: Theological Perversions in Sex, Gender, and Politics* (2000). Like Cone's work, Althaus-Reid's work was uncompromising and controversial in its self-conscious radicality. Like Williams' work, Althaus-Reid critiqued the ways in which liberationist thought too often neglects discrimination *within* marginal communities (particularly over sexual and gender difference). As a means of expressing Christ's kenotic embodiment and identification with the "Other," she provocatively advocated for the use of sexual and even "indecent" language to describe God—for example, speaking of "God the Faggot" or discussing the vulva of Our Lady of Guadalupe. Like a literary equivalent to Andres Serrano's famous image *Piss Christ* (1987), such expressions were *intended* to shock, inflame, and provoke.[53] Her goal, however, was to force an examination within the church of the various ways in which normative views of the body arise from certain social conventions and serve certain social functions.[54]

Alternatively, one could consider the work of the Episcopal priest and theologian Patrick S. Cheng. Rather than "queering" the Christian tradition in the forceful and incendiary manner of Althaus-Reid, Cheng's work—as reflected in his books *Radical Love: An Introduction to Queer Theology* (2011), *From Sin to Amazing Grace: Discovering the Queer Christ* (2012), and *Rainbow Theology: Bridging Race, Sexuality, and Spirit* (2013)—instead considers the "queerness as otherness" already reflected in the Gospel. In the same way that Christ's radical identification with the suffering of the oppressed means that in a racist society "God is Black," so, too, does it mean that in a homophobic society "God is queer." God takes on these aspects always and to the extent that these qualities of personhood are used as a justification for denying people their dignity and rights.

Despite advocating politically for gay rights and marriage equality, Vattimo only rarely discussed the implications of weak thought for sexual or gender difference.[55] This is surprising because he cites a recognition of his own sexual difference as a major catalyst for rejecting the predominant natural-law theory of the Catholic Church and its implications for a certain kind of normativity existing in nature and morality. In my view, a point of contact between weak thought and queer theory in general and queer theology specifically stems from Gadamer and Vattimo's construal of their position(s) as being a kind of corrupted Hegelianism—one that embraces the "bad infinite" of perpetual change without a final sublation. This position parallels Vattimo's insistence that the faithful church should serve as the unassimilable anarchic element in society, always insisting on justice and liberation. In this way, one can think of Jesus's words in Matthew 22:36–40 as providing the hermeneutic principle that should guide the perpetual development of the church. In the words of Karl Barth, "Ecclesia semper reformanda est" (The church must continually be reformed), which means that just as the faithful church must always challenge social structures that marginalize and oppress, the church must also always be challenged from within from the perspective of love/charity. "'Teacher, which is the great commandment in the law?' And [Jesus] said to him, 'You shall love the Lord your God with all your heart, and with all your soul, and with all your mind.' This is the great and first commandment. And a second is like it, 'You shall love your neighbor as yourself.' On these two commandments hang all the law and the prophets.'"

Weak Thought and Eastern Philosophy

On September 30, 2022, a conference was held at the Universitat Pompeu Fabra in Barcelona on the topic "Vattimo and Chinese Thought." This event was sponsored in conjunction with the University of Warwick and the Duke Kunshan Humanities Research Center. It included papers by Massimiliano Lacertosa (Warwick), Graham Parkes (Vienna), Robin R. Wang (Loyola Marymount), Liangjian Liu (East China Normal University), James Miller (Duke Kunshan University), Erica Onnis (RWTH Aachen University/

Turin), Mario Wenning (Loyola University Andalusia), Ming Xie (Toronto), and Santiago Zabala. This is the first (and, to date, only) conference exploring the connections between Eastern philosophy and weak thought.

The conference papers (which have not yet been published as of June 2025) primarily explored the relationship between weak thought and Daoism. For example, Lacertosa's paper examined the possibility of drawing parallels between weakness and the principle of *wuwei* (無為, "nonobstructive action"). In both cases, weakness is not perceived as inaction or passivity but rather as a nonviolent counterforce that subverts the very idea of power as commonly conceived. In his essay, Graham Parkes draws upon the Heideggerian/Vattimian critique of technology and *Zweckrationalität* (instrumental rationality) to see similarities with Daoist notions of living in harmony with the creative and sustaining rhythms of existence. Likewise, Erica Onnis's paper compares the interpretive play of hermeneutics with the idea of "formless form," which traditionally draws inspiration from the properties of water (strength, malleability, etc.).

Apart from Daoism, one can see broad similarities with Confucianism and its focus on cultivating the virtues of *ren* (仁), a "benevolent disposition towards humanity"), *yi* (義, "Justice/Righteousness"), *li* (禮, "ritual/propriety/ceremony"), *zhi* (智, "wisdom"), and *xin* (信, "honesty/sincerity"), each with the goal of establishing a just and orderly society against the backdrop of ever-present change. In his paper, Liangjian Liu, therefore, attempts to put into conversation Vattimo and Zabala's hermeneutic communism with both Confucianism and the legacy of Chinese communism. This paper is additionally unique insofar as it expands the discussion of Vattimo's philosophy into weak thought's broader connections to communism as well as to the potential for more dialogue between weak thought and the Confucian tradition.[56]

Other potential parallels with Eastern thought not explored during this conference but possibly proving worth considering in time are weak thought's links to Indian philosophy. For example, in Jainism there is an emphasis on praxis and principles such as *ahiṃsā* (अहिंसा, "nonviolence") and *aparigraha* (अपरिगर्ह, "nonattachment" or "greedlessness") as the necessary path to *mokṣa* (मोक्ष, "liberation"). Notably, this connection was important in the civil disobedience campaigns of Gandhi, which he characterized as *satyagraha* (सत्यागर्ह, "holding firmly to what is true"). In addition to this emphasis on nonviolence, perhaps most intriguingly for weak thought's connection to Jainism is the latter's notion of *anekāntavāda* (अनेकान्तवाद, "many-sidedness," "open-mindedness," or "nonabsolutism"). This idea reflects a similarly hermeneutical and contextual understanding of truth and likewise emphasizes dialogue and mutual understanding.[57] At this stage, however, these avenues of future exploration are little more than suggestions.

In John Berger's novel *G*, the eponymous character G[iovanni] declares, "Never again will a single story be told as though it were the only one."[58] This perhaps best sums up the trajectory of Western thought away from its habit of narrow and rigid system building through a process of weakening and decline. As a result of changes in philosophy over the course of the twentieth century, there has been a gradual shift away from traditional Western emphases on logic, epistemology, and metaphysical foundationalism. In their place, however, has grown a renewed interest in philosophy and religion, not as rigidly systematized bodies of doctrine but rather as lived praxes that manifest themselves through the cultivation of open dialogue and mutuality—in a word, *charity*.

At a time of increased social divisions over conflicting understandings of what constitutes "facts" and "reality," when conspiracy theories spread on social media and dominate the headlines—in this time that has come to be characterized, rightly or wrongly, in much popular media as an era of "post-truth"—the philosopher who called for us to "bid farewell to Truth" is arguably more relevant now than ever. However, this is not (as some might charge) because he has caused or advocated for the kind of chaos and "crisis of meaning" with which we are at the present moment contending. Instead, it is because he attempted to show that whereas facts may exist apart from our lived experience of them, "truth" is inseparable from the values of human communities. As I hope that I have demonstrated over the course of this volume, the work of Gianni Vattimo occupies an important and unique place in ongoing discussions regarding the importance of language and its interpretation for the practices of philosophy, religion, law, politics, and culture.

EPILOGUE

ma non eran da ciò le proprie penne:
se non che la mia mente fu percossa
da un fulgore in che sua voglia venne.
A l'alta fantasia qui mancò possa;
ma già volgeva il mio disio e 'l velle,
sì come rota ch'igualmente è mossa,
l'amor che move il sole e l'altre stelle.
—DANTE, *Paradiso*, canto 33

"Are you happy?" you ask me . . .
I could tell you about moments when I've been happy. But I didn't
know that I was. Life is the dream of these moments of intensity. That
have befallen. Constellations that freeze. For an instant. Flashes.
Traces. Fragments.
—GIANNI VATTIMO, *Not Being God*, 2006

The last few weeks of Vattimo's life were spent in the nephrology ward at the Rivoli Hospital in Turin. During that time, many of his lifelong friends, his few remaining relatives, and his erstwhile assistant turned life partner, Simone Caminada, had come to his bedside for what they knew was soon to be the end.¹ By this time, Vattimo was sleeping more and more and beginning to have difficulty recognizing visitors. It was clear to everyone that the flame that had burned so brightly for so long was beginning to fade. Finally, a little after 9:00 p.m. on September 19, 2023, Gianni Vattimo, a giant of Italian philosophy and one of the most original thinkers of the past century, passed away quietly in his sleep. He was eighty-seven years old.² At his own request, the epitaph "Ero debole" (I was weak) was posted on social media shortly thereafter.

COURT CASES

The majority of this present volume was completed prior to Vattimo's passing. That being the case, I had not initially planned to discuss what were at the time ongoing and messy legal issues surrounding his relationship with Caminada. Unfortunately, Vattimo's final years were plagued both by declining health as well as by a fractious public battle over his private life choices. Vattimo's personal life had become a matter of public concern when in 2018 his physician and a group of his close friends filed a formal complaint against his then thirty-five-year-old Brazilian partner.³ The complaint alleged that Caminada was taking advantage of the eighty-two-year-old Vattimo's increasingly vulnerable state in order to seize control of his assets. This serious allegation of elder abuse led to a series of lengthy legal battles in which the increasingly frail yet still lucid Vattimo attempted to defend Caminada and his own right to make decisions for himself regarding his finances and personal affairs.

For his part, Caminada countered the allegations by claiming that he was, in fact, the one who was attempting to protect Vattimo by sending away ungrateful hangers-on, who had for too long unduly benefited from the philosopher's largesse. Caminada and his lawyer, Corrada Giammarinaro, furthermore suggested on more than one occasion that the magistrate's office was motivated to pursue the case by latent feelings of classism and homophobia.[4] The prosecutors in the case, Dionigi Tibone and Giulia Rizzo, responded: "We would like to say that we reject the accusation that the prosecutor's office had a classist attitude or that it took into account the sexual inclinations of the parties involved.... We have only evaluated behaviors that we believe constituted a crime."[5]

From the outside, it is difficult to determine with any certainty who was right in this instance. Was this, as Caminada and Vattimo himself maintained, a case of paternalistic magistrates overstepping their bounds and in the process violating Vattimo's privacy as well as his freedom to love whom he wished and make decisions for himself? Or was this a case in which the court acted appropriately to shield a vulnerable person from criminally exploitative behavior that, for whatever reason, the person was unwilling or unable to rightly recognize as abuse. Regardless of who should be characterized as the perpetrator, it is difficult not to see Vattimo in either case as the victim.

In 2006, when Vattimo was seventy years old, he published the collaborative autobiography *Not Being God* with the writer and journalist Piergiorgio Paterlini. Paterlini related in his closing remarks to the work,

> [Vattimo] is totally incapable of not being generous almost to the point of heedlessness. Then too, he wants a family.... He always pays, with everyone, however many guests there are. And he could reel off an endless list of persons to whom he regularly gives a little money at the end of every month. Generosity. An atavistic sense of guilt for a financial comfort he could never have imagined, and which

he takes so little for granted that he fears: "If I go on like this I'll wind up on the sidewalk and then they'll have to support me." And that ironic knowing bittersweet smile of his flickers once again: he knows they wouldn't.[6]

Likewise, Irene Famà, writing for *La Stampa* shortly after Vattimo's death, noted that "Gianni Vattimo was a generous man. He liked to think of himself this way and, indeed, everyone who had the opportunity to know him—friends, acquaintances, and those in need—would agree. It's true that many have also taken advantage of that altruism. Vattimo probably knew it, but he always turned a blind eye. He would say, 'I lead a good life and like to help others.'"[7]

These quotes perhaps offer a window into aspects of Vattimo's personality useful for understanding the context of this wretched situation. They convey, for instance, his well-known munificence—and the way it related not only to his concern for others but also to his own ever-present desire to be loved. One gets a sense of how his charitableness toward others and his (sometimes transgressive) playfulness seemed to buoy him against a lifetime filled with personal tragedies and of how his humble upbringing and the feelings of being an outsider gifted him arguably the rarest of qualities for an academic—the ability not to take himself too seriously.[8] Still, the unbidden companion to this irrepressible impishness was an abiding sense of profound loss. Indeed, Vattimo remarked in 2006, "I've outlived those dearest to me, outlived my family. For the first time, I'm alone. And I've become an expert in a very special literary genre, the obituary."[9]

Apart from the deaths of his father (whom he lamented that he barely knew), his mother, his sister (Liliana), beloved aunts, as well as his partners Gianpiero Cavaglià and Sergio Mamino, Vattimo also mourned the family he always wanted but never felt he really had. He once stated, "I've always desired a family. Always ... I ardently wanted to have a normal family. And I miss not having had one, not having one even now. I would be happier today if I had one. I wanted a wife, children, a mother-in-law," adding with tongue in cheek, "And with any luck, a house in Morocco where I could have boys.... Complicated, having a heterosexual family and being homosexual. Yes. Sure. Expensive above all."[10] Although some readers may bristle at the explicit heteronormativity in Vattimo's idyllic description of conventionality (and no less so than at the implied infidelity), others still, no doubt, will recognize in this description not a confession of queer self-hatred so much as the expression of a universal desire for mutual love, comfort, security, belonging, and acceptance for who one is—things frequently denied to homosexual men (particularly those of Vattimo's generation). In his final years, Vattimo suffered from Parkinson's disease, which impaired his mobility. As his health began slowly to decline, it was arguably these personal qualities and unfulfilled desires that made him susceptible to potential manipulation.

Vattimo and Caminada had first met in 2010 when Vattimo was still a minister of the European Parliament. Caminada was initially hired as a chauffeur but soon became Vattimo's assistant, household manager, and, later, life partner—eventually moving into an apartment adjacent to Vattimo's flat on Via Po. Investigators accused Caminada of using his position and relationship with Vattimo to induce him over time to make injurious financial decisions, requesting payments to Caminada's mother and other "unjustified" expenses amounting to €60,000 (U.S.$63,583.80), pressuring Vattimo to take out a €415,000 (U.S.$439,754.75) life insurance policy with Caminada named as a 40 percent beneficiary, as well as compelling Vattimo to draft a will first naming Caminada as partial heir (dated July 16, 2018) and later as sole heir (dated September 22, 2018). As evidence of malfeasance, the judge in the case cited wiretap recordings that revealed that while Caminada was publicly affectionate toward

Vattimo, in private he created a toxic environment of calculated coldness to get his way. Contrariwise, Vattimo testified that he was within his capacities to manage his own estate, that Caminada's financial decisions were made with his consultation and consent, and that the transfers in question were acts of generosity. Vattimo went further and accused the prosecutor's office of "persecution."[11]

The case dragged on for several years, with the court on a number of occasions appointing custodians to manage Vattimo's affairs over his objections. On the day Caminada was scheduled to give his defense argument in the case, he and Vattimo filed paperwork to obtain a civil union (same-sex marriage is not yet legal in Italy), which was to be celebrated in the municipality of Vimercate in the province of Monza. However, the prosecutor's office in Turin was notified by the civil service that they had received the paperwork required for the union. In light of the circumstances of the case, the civil service decided to suspend the request. Vattimo, who had long fought for the rights of LGBTQ+ people to get married in Italy, was ultimately denied that right for himself.

Ironically, in 2010 Vattimo did get married, but to a woman. Before he became involved with Caminada, he wed Martine Tedeschi, the daughter of one of his longtime friends. The two were never romantically involved. Instead, she later recalled in an interview:

> One day, he told me that he didn't want his assets to be lost and, having no one to leave them to, he proposed that we get married, but that we should each continue to live our own lives. I thought he was joking. Then, after the umpteenth renewal of the proposal, I asked him, "Are you serious?" To keep the news from getting around, we got married in France, in Roquebrune-Cap-Martin, where he had a house. Only close friends were with us. After that, everything went on as before. At least until Simone arrived. . . . The explanation I gave myself [for the proposal] is that he thought of me because among his

friends' children I'm the only one who isn't married, who doesn't have a house and to whom no one has left anything.

The two divorced in 2022 so that Vattimo could pursue a civil partnership with Caminada.[12]

In February 2023, Caminada was found guilty of "circumvention of an incapacitated person," sentenced to two years in prison, and given a €900 (U.S.$953.75) fine. The prosecutors had initially requested a four-year prison sentence.[13] Despite Caminada's conviction, Vattimo never distanced himself from his assistant. Instead, during the trial he testified on his behalf, saying, "I have never doubted him. . . . I will not walk away from him."[14] Caminada continued to attend to him until his death.

Vattimo's funeral was held at 10:00 a.m. on September 23, 2023, at the Real Chiesa di San Lorenzo in the central Piazza Castello in Turin. The small Baroque-style church was unable to contain the crowd of friends, family, colleagues, former students, and supporters who gathered to pay their final respects. The mayor of Turin, Stefano Lo Russo, sat in the front row with the city's councilors, Jacopo Rosatelli and Andrea Tronzano. Lo Russo spoke of Vattimo as "a man who was, without a doubt, a fundamental cultural point of reference for entire generations in Italy." In his funeral homily, the Catholic philosopher and rector at San Lorenzo Giovanni Ferretti noted: "Gianni once said that, 'Charity cannot be secularized, in the sense that charity is the insurmountable limit for the process of secularization itself. It goes beyond history; it makes us live beyond death." At the end of the service, one former student raised her voice to say, "Grazie, maestro!" (Thank you, teacher!). The gesture was met with a slow emotional applause with others soon joining in the same chant.[15] Finally, Vattimo's body was laid to rest next to Giampiero Cavaglià and Sergio Mamino at the Cimitero Monumentale in Turin.

Toward the end of July 2024, a judge invalidated the inheritance requests of Vattimo's two wills of 2018 after determining that Caminada, based on the nature of his conviction, was no longer an eligible beneficiary. Instead, two of Vattimo's surviving first cousins initially agreed to take over his estate as his legitimate heirs, though aspects of the estate continue to remain unresolved. The final judicial step for Caminada, however, concerned the execution of the court's judgment. In the end, his prison sentence was commuted. Instead, along with his disinheritance and fine, he was given probation and required to complete three years and ten days of community service.[16]

FINAL THINGS

No, I have no fear of death. My own death has almost no importance to me. The really scandalous death you have to bear isn't your own, it's that of others close to you.... The uncompletedness of their lives[, it scandalizes me].... I am simply unable to imagine that death is the end of everything.

—Gianni Vattimo, *Not Being God*

At the beginning of the present volume, I noted that Heidegger did not start his lectures on Aristotle by dwelling on aspects of the great philosopher's life. He instead argued that the legacy of a thinker is the body of work they leave behind. In this respect and by any measure, Gianni Vattimo leaves behind an impressive corpus—the fruit of a vigorously creative mind and a rigorously productive work ethic. That said, I will have to respectfully disagree with Heidegger. For myself, at least, I don't think that a philosopher's work should be measured solely by the number of erudite volumes they produce.

Rather, I would argue that the real legacy of any thinker is their commitment to engaging with and understanding those questions that affect our shared existence. In the end, even if one disagreed with many of his positions or life choices, Vattimo was a thinker committed to exploring and pursuing those principles that, however imperfectly we embody them, distinguish our lives as being truly human—namely, justice and charity. He found these values in the ideals aspired to by both Christianity and socialism and in the fitful progress of the historical church. To the extent to which these principles are true, he would argue, it is because they inhere in us. Their history abides in us, and, conversely, we exist as we are only because of that history.

CHRONOLOGY

1846   Pope Gregory XVI dies. Giovanni Ferretti elected papal successor and takes the regnal name Pius IX.
1850   Ecclesial reforms begin in the Italian state of Piedmont-Sardinia.
1864   Pope Pius IX issues the encyclical *Quanta cura*.
1861   The Savoyard dynasty establishes the new Kingdom of Italy under King Victor Emmanuel II.
1869   Pope Pius IX convenes the First Vatican Council.
1870   Vatican I adopts the Apostolic Constitution on Faith, *Dei Filius*. Annexation of Lazio and Rome by the Kingdom of Italy. End of the Papal States. Indefinite interruption of the proceedings of Vatican I.
1871   Rome becomes capital of Italy. Pope Pius IX refuses to leave the Vatican.
1878   King Victor Emmanuel II dies and is succeeded by his son, Umberto I. Pope Pius IX dies. Vincenzo Pecci elected papal successor and takes the regnal name Leo XIII.
1879   Pope Leo XIII issues the encyclical *Æterni Patris*.
1889   Friedrich Nietzsche suffers a mental breakdown in Turin.
1900   Hans-Georg Gadamer is born in Marburg. Nietzsche dies in Weimar.

1903   Pope Leo XIII dies. Giuseppe Sarto elected papal successor and takes the regnal name Pius X.
1907   Pope Pius X issues the decree *Lamentabili sane exitu* and the encyclical *Pascendi Dominici gregis*.
1908   Nietzsche's *Ecce Homo* (written in 1888) is first published.
1914   Archduke Franz Ferdinand, heir to the Austro-Hungarian throne, is assassinated while visiting Sarajevo, setting in motion the events that would lead to the start of World War I. Pope Pius X dies. Giacomo della Chiesa elected papal successor and takes the regnal name Benedict XV.
1916   Ferdinand de Saussure's University of Geneva lectures of 1906 and 1911 are published posthumously as *Cours de linguistique générale* (*Course in General Linguistics*).
1918   The armistice is signed at Le Francport on November 11, effectively ending World War I.
1919   The Treaty of Versailles is signed, officially ending the war between Germany and the Allied Powers. The so-called Biennio Rosso (Two Red Years) begin in Italy with domination by left-wing political movements.
1900   King Umberto I is assassinated by the Italian American anarchist Gaetano Bresci. He is succeeded by his son, Victor Emmanuel III.
1922   In Italy, a faction of approximately thirty thousand Fascist Blackshirts gather in Rome to demand the resignation of liberal prime minister Luigi Facta and the appointment of a new Fascist government. King Victor Emmanuel III asks Benito Mussolini to form a new government. Pope Benedict XV dies. Achille Ratti elected papal successor and takes the regnal name Pius XI. Wittgenstein publishes a translation of *Logisch-Philosophische Abhandlung* in English with the assistance of C. K. Ogden (and Frank P. Ramsey). G. E. Moore suggests the title of the English

edition appear as the Latin *Tractatus Logico-Philosophicus* after the style of Spinoza's work *Tractatus Theologico-Politicus* (1670).

1923　Martin Heidegger becomes professor at Marburg.

1925　The problems of foundational mathematics (Frege and Russell) and language (Wittgenstein) begin to be discussed among the members of the Vienna Circle.

1927　Heidegger publishes *Sein und Zeit* (*Being and Time*).

1928　Heidegger leaves Marburg to accept the professorship at Freiburg following the forced retirement of Husserl.

1929　In Italy, the Lateran Pacts are ratified, ending the "prisoner in the Vatican" stand-off between Italy and the Holy See.

1931　The work "La dottrina del fascismo" ("The Doctrine of Fascism"), written by Benito Mussolini in collaboration with Giovanni Gentile in 1927, is first published.

1933　Heidegger elected rector at Freiburg and joins the Nazi Party.

1935　Walter Benjamin publishes "Das Kunstwerk im Zeitalter seiner technischen Reproduzierbarkei" ("The Work of Art in the Age of Mechanical Reproduction").

1936　Gianteresio ("Gianni") Vattimo is born at home in the neighborhood of Borgo San Paolo of Turin, Piedmont, Italy.

1939　Pope Pius XI dies. Eugenio Pacelli elected papal successor and takes the regnal name Pius XII.

1940　Benjamin publishes "Über den Begriff der Geschichte" ("Theses on the Philosophy of History"). He commits suicide in Spain rather than be deported to Nazi-occupied France. Italy joins the war on the side of Germany.

1943　King Victor Emmanuel III of Italy replaces Mussolini as prime minister with Marshal Pietro Badoglio. Mussolini is subsequently arrested. The Fascist Party is soon dissolved, and Italy changes allegiances in the war, joining the Allies to fight Germany. Two months after Mussolini is deposed, German troops overtake his captors and install him as head of the Salò Republic, a German puppet state in northern Italy under Nazi occupation.

1944 Prime Minister Pietro Badoglio is replaced by Ivanoe Bonomi, who had previously served as prime minister in 1921–1922, before Luigi Facta.

1945 In April, Allied forces advance on northern Italy. Sensing the impending end of the Nazi-supported Salò Republic, Benito Mussolini and his mistress attempt to flee to Spain via Switzerland. They are captured and identified by a group of Italian Communist resistance fighters. They are summarily shot the next day near Giulino di Mezzegra. Mussolini's corpse, along with the bodies of other dead Fascists are mutilated and displayed hanging from a gas-station sign in Milan before being buried in an unmarked grave. Ferruccio Parri replaces Ivanoe Bonomi as prime minister, briefly serving from June through December. Before the end of the year, he is replaced, on December 10, by Alcide De Gasperi.

1946 King Victor Emmanuel III abdicates the throne in favor of his son, Umberto II, before fleeing to Alexandria, Egypt. Umberto II serves as king from May through June. A referendum passes to abolish the monarchy and declare Italy a republic.

1947 Horkheimer and Adorno publish *Dialektik der Aufklärung: Philosophische Fragmente* (*Dialectic of Enlightenment: Philosophical Fragments*). Horkheimer publishes *Eclipse of Reason*.

1948 Antonio Gramsci's prison notebooks are published posthumously. Enrico De Nicola becomes the first president of the Republic of Italy. Before the end of the year, he will be replaced by Luigi Einaudi.

1953 Giuseppe Pella replaces Alcide De Gasperi as prime minister. Wittgenstein's *Philosophische Untersuchungen* (*Philosophical Investigations*) is published posthumously.

1954 Vattimo finishes high school and begins studies at the University of Turin. Around this time, he and others are asked to leave Azione Cattolica (Catholic Action) over their progressive political views. He also becomes friends with the writer Umberto Eco. Vattimo comes under the influence of the work of Emmanuel Mounier. He and Eco begin work as journalists at Radiotelevisione Italiana (RAI), a national public broadcasting company. Heidegger's work "Die Frage nach der Technik" ("The Question Concerning Technology") is published posthumously. Amintore Fanfani briefly succeeds Giuseppe Pella as prime minister. He is quickly replaced by Mario Scelba.

1955 Antonio Segni succeeds Mario Scelba as prime minister. Giovanni Gronchi succeeds Luigi Einaldi as president.

1957 Vattimo quits his job at RAI. His friend and spiritual adviser Monsignor Pietro Caramello finds him a job as a teacher in the Casa di Carità Arti e Mestieri, a charitable vocational and trade school.

1958 Pope Pius XII dies. Angelo Roncalli elected papal successor and takes the regnal name John XXIII.

1959 Vattimo receives his *laurea* from the University of Turin, studying under the great existentialist philosopher Luigi Pareyson, who asks Vattimo to stay on at the university as his assistant. Later that year, Vattimo is arrested at a protest for picketing on behalf of metal workers.

1960 Gadamer publishes *Wahrheit und Methode* (*Truth and Method*).

1961	On November 28, Vattimo is invited to deliver a public lecture at the Biblioteca Filosofica of Turin. It forms the basis for the opening chapter of his first major published work, *Essere, storia, e linguaggio in Heidegger* (Being, history, and language in Heidegger).
1962	Antonio Segni succeeds Giovanni Gronchi to become president of Italy. Vattimo receives a scholarship from the Alexander von Humboldt Foundation to the University of Heidelberg to study under Gadamer and Karl Löwith. It is during this two-year fellowship that Vattimo, now removed from the strong links between Italian culture and Catholicism, ceases being a Catholic.
1963	Pope John XXIII dies. Giovanni Battista Montini elected papal successor and takes the regnal name Paul VI. Vattimo publishes *Essere, storia, e linguaggio in Heidegger*.
1964	Vattimo begins lecturing in aesthetics at Turin. In July, Gilles Deleuze invites Vattimo to the international conference on Nietzsche at Royaumont Abbey, located near Asnières-sur-Oise in Val-d'Oise, approximately nineteen miles (thirty kilometers) north of Paris. There, Vattimo meets Michel Foucault, Pierre Klossowski, Henri Birault, Gabriel Marcel, and others.
1967	Rorty publishes the edited volume *The Linguistic Turn: Essays in Philosophical Method*. Vattimo publishes *Ipotesi su Nietzsche* (Hypothesis on Nietzsche). Vattimo's fiancé ends their relationship under pressure from her father, who has become aware of Vattimo's homosexual affairs. Jacques Derrida publishes *De la grammatologie* (*Of Grammatology*) and *L'écriture et la différence* (*Writing and Difference*). Guy Debord publishes *La société du spectacle* (*The Society of the Spectacle*).

1968	In March, Vattimo becomes a Maoist after reading Marcuse while convalescing from an ulcer surgery. Later that year, in June, he begins a romance with Gianpiero Cavaglià, who becomes his longtime partner. He is promoted to full professor of aesthetics at Turin. He publishes *Schleiermacher, filosofo dell'interpretazione* (Schleiermacher, philosopher of interpretation).
1969	Vattimo completes his Italian translation of Gadamer's *Wahrheit und Methode* as *Verità e metodo*. He visits Budapest and meets Gyorgy Lukács.
1970	Vattimo's Italian translation of Gadamer's *Truth and Method* is published.
1971	Vattimo publishes *Introduzione ad Heidegger* (Introduction to Heidegger).
1972	Vattimo finishes work on *Il soggetto e la maschera* (*The Subject and the Mask*) while on a holiday in the Alps. It will be published in 1974. In September, he travels to the United States for the first time to serve as visiting professor for a semester at the State University of New York (SUNY, Albany).
1973	Vattimo returns to SUNY for the fall semester. He and Gianpiero travel by bus to an anti-Nixon protest in Washington, DC.
1974	Vattimo succeeds Pareyson as chair of aesthetics at Turin. He publishes *Il soggetto e la maschera*.
1976	Vattimo is publicly "outed" by the Italian Radical Party when it designates him as a candidate on its Homosexual List, spreading the news in the national newspapers, without his consent, for the elections of that year. Heidegger dies. Five days after his death, his famous interview "Nur noch ein Gott kann uns retten" ("Only a God Can Save Us") with *Der Spiegel* in 1966 is published.

1977 Around this time, Vattimo meets Sergio Mamino. Shortly thereafter, Sergio will begin to live with Vattimo and Gianpiero.

1978 Pope Paul VI dies. Albino Luciani is elected papal successor and takes the regnal name John Paul. Only thirty-three days after his elevation, however, Pope John Paul I dies. Karol Józef Wojtyła is elected papal successor and takes the regnal name John Paul II. Vattimo becomes dean of the Faculty of Turin. His life is threatened by the Red Brigade. He publishes the essay *"An-denken*: Il pensare e il fondamento" (*"An-denken*: Thinking and the Foundation"). It will soon be reprinted in his book *Le avventure della differenza* (*The Adventure of Difference*, 1980).

1979 Rorty publishes *Philosophy and the Mirror of Nature*. Vattimo writes the essay "Verso un'ontologia del decline" ("Toward an Ontology of Decline"), in which he first uses the term *pensiero debole*, "weak thought." Vattimo and Rorty meet for the first time at a conference on postmodern thought held at the University of Wisconsin Milwaukee. Rorty hears Vattimo speak and asks for a copy of his paper. In return, he gives Vattimo a copy of *Philosophy and the Mirror of Nature*. Jean-François Lyotard publishes *La condition postmoderne* (*The Postmodern Condition*).

1980 Vattimo publishes *Le avventure della differenza: Che cosa significa pensare dopo Nietzsche e Heidegger*. The English translation appears in 1993 as *The Adventure of Difference: Philosophy After Nietzsche and Heidegger*. Vattimo's mother dies.

1981 Vattimo publishes *Al di là del soggesto: Nietzsche, Heidegger, e l'emeneutica*. The English translation appears in 2019 as *Beyond the Subject: Nietzsche, Heidegger, and Hermeneutics*.

1983 Vattimo and Pier Aldo Rovatti publish the edited volume *Il pensiero debole*. The English translation appears in 2012 as *Weak Thought*. This book sparks a debate in philosophical circles both inside and outside Italy. Vattimo ends his time as the dean of the Faculty of Turin. Vattimo's sister, Liliana, dies.

1985 Vattimo publishes *La fine della modernitàe: Nichilismo ed ermeneutica nella cultura post-moderna*. The English translation appears in 1991 as *The End of Modernity: Nihilism and Hermeneutics in Post-Modern Culture*. He also publishes *Introduzione a Nietzsche*. The English translation appears in 2002 as *Nietzsche: An Introduction*. He also publishes *Poesia e ontologia* The English translation appears in 2008 as *Art's Claim to Truth*.

1986 Vattimo becomes editor of the Italian Philosophical Yearbooks, an annual series from the publisher Giuseppe Laterza on the most important and relevant themes of international philosophical debates. In February, Vattimo's partner, Gianpiero, tests positive for AIDS.

1988 Vattimo contributes two chapters to the volume *Recoding Metaphysics: The New Italian Philosophy*, edited by Giovanni Borradori.

1989 Vattimo publishes *La società trasparente*. The English translation appears in 1992 as *The Transparent Society*. He also publishes *Etica dell'interpretazione* (Ethics of interpretation).

1990 Vattimo publishes *Filosofia al presente* (Philosophy in the present).

1991 Vattimo's teacher Luigi Pareyson dies. Fredric Jameson publishes *Postmodernism, or, the Cultural Logic of Late Capitalism*.

1992	The publisher Giuseppe Laterza decides to expand the Italian Philosophical Yearbooks, of which Vattimo is editor, to include volumes on European thought. The new European Yearbook series is jointly edited by Derrida and Vattimo, with the editorial participation of Éditions du Seuil of France. Derrida and Vattimo decide that the first theme should be religion, and they organize a seminar in Capri, which includes contributions from the two organizers as well as from Gadamer, Eugenio Trias, and others. Vattimo is awarded the Max Planck-Humboldt Research Award for Humanities and Social Sciences. Shortly after Christmas, Vattimo's partner, Gianpiero, dies of complications from AIDS.
1994	Vattimo publishes *Oltre l'interpretazione*. The English translation appears in 1997 as *Beyond Interpretation: The Meaning of Hermeneutics for Philosophy*.
1995	Umberto Ecco publishes the essay "Ur-Fascism."
1996	Vattimo and Derrida edit the book *La religion*. It is the result of the European Yearbook series and the conference organized at Capri in 1992. The book is first published in French. The English translation appears in 1998 as *Religion*. Vattimo also publishes *Credere di credere*. The English translation appears in 1999 as *Belief*. He says later in his autobiography, *Non essere Dio* (*Not Being God*, 2006), that the work was a response to Massimo Cacciari. He, together with Edward Said, Umberto Eco, and others, is awarded the annual Italian Academy Lectureship by the Italian Academy for Advanced Studies in America at Columbia University. His lectures there will later result in his book *Dopo la cristianità* (*After Christianity*, 2002), which involves a specific philosophical request to recognize the possibility of and need for a "nonreligious Christianity."

1997 Vattimo becomes Grand Officer of Merit of the Italian Republic. He publishes *Tecnica ed esistenza: Una mappa filosofica del Novecento* (Technique and existence: A philosophical map of the twentieth century).

1999 Vattimo is elected to serve as a member of the European Parliament representing Democratici di Sinistra (Democrats of the Left). He is a member of the alliance Party of European Socialists.

2000 Vattimo publishes *Dialogo con Nietzsche*. The English translation appears in 2006 as *Dialogue with Nietzsche*. He also publishes *Vocazione e responsabilità del filosofo*. The English translation appears in 2010 as *The Responsibility of the Philosopher*.

2001 Vattimo contributes the chapter "The Christian Message and the Dissolution of Metaphysics" to *The Blackwell Companion to Postmodern Theology*, edited by Graham Ward.

2002 Vattimo publishes *After Christianity* in English through Columbia University Press. It appears in Italian as *Dopo la cristianità: Per un cristianesimo non religioso*. Vattimo is awarded the Hannah Arendt Prize for Political Thinking in Bremen. He delivers a lecture entitled "Globalization and the Relevance of Socialism."

2003 Before Easter, Vattimo's partner Sergio Mamino dies of complications from lung cancer while he and Vattimo are aboard a flight from New York to Amsterdam. Vattimo publishes *Nichilismo ed emancipazione: Etica, politica, diritto*. The English translation appears in 2004 as *Nihilism and Emancipation: Ethics, Politics, and Law*, for which Rorty provides the foreword. Vattimo also publishes the chapter "After Onto-Theology: Philosophy Between Science and Religion" in the volume *Religion After*

Metaphysics, edited by Mark A. Wrathall. Vattimo and Habermas are invited to give introductory speeches at the World Conference of Philosophy in Istanbul, Turkey.

2004 The session of the European Parliament ends, and Vattimo completes his first period in office. He publishes *Il socialismo ossia l'Europa* (Socialism or Europe).

2005 Pope John Paul II dies. Joseph Ratzinger elected papal successor and takes the regnal name Benedict XVI. Vattimo and Rorty together publish *The Future of Religion*. It appears in Italian the same year as *Il futuro della religione*. Rorty publishes *An Ethics for Today: Finding Common Ground Between Philosophy and Religion*, for which Vattimo provides the introduction.

2006 Vattimo retires from the University of Turin. He and René Girard publish *Verità o fede debole? Dialogo su cristianesimo e relativismo*. The English translation appears in 2010 as *Christianity, Truth, and Weakening Faith: A Dialogue*. The festschrift *Weakening Philosophy* is published to honor Vattimo. It includes contributions from, among others, Jack Miles, Charles Taylor, and Jean-Luc Nancy. He also publishes *Non essere Dio: Un'autobiografia a quattro mani* with Piergiorgio Paterlini. The English translation appears in 2009 as *Not Being God: A Collaborative Autobiography*.

2007 Vattimo publishes *Ecce comu: Come si diventa ciò che si era* (Ecce comu: How you rebecome what you were). He and John D. Caputo publish *After the Death of God*. Rorty dies of pancreatic cancer on June 8 in Palo Alto, California.

2008 Vattimo writes the foreword to Santiago Zabala's book *The Hermeneutic Nature of Analytic Philosophy: A Study of Ernst Tugendhat*.

2009 Vattimo publishes *Addio alla verità*. The English translation appears in 2011 as *A Farewell to Truth*. He is elected for

	a second time to the European Parliament, running for the anticorruption Italia dei Valori (Italy of Values) Party. He is part of the Alliance of Liberals and Democrats for Europe.
2010	In June, Vattimo delivers the Gifford Lectures at the University of Glasgow. His work *Introduzione all'estetica* (Introduction to aesthetics), originally published in 1977 as an introduction to the anthology *Estetica moderna*, is republished as a standalone text.
2011	Vattimo and Santiago Zabala publish in English *Hermeneutic Communism: From Heidegger to Marx*. The work is influenced by Vattimo's earlier book *Ecce comu* (2007) and Zabala's book *The Remains of Being: Hermeneutic Ontology After Metaphysics* (2009). Vattimo also publishes *Magnificat: Un'idea di montagna* (Magnificat: A monumental idea).
2012	Vattimo publishes *Della realtà*. The English translation appears in 2017 as *Of Reality: The Purposes of Philosophy*. The book is based on his Gifford Lectures and his Cardinal Mercier Chair lectures in Leuven.
2013	Pope Benedict XVI retires, becoming the first pope to abdicate the papal office since 1415. Jorge Mario Bergoglio elected papal successor and takes the regnal name Francis. He becomes the first pope from the Americas and the first Jesuit pope. Vattimo and Michael Marder publish the edited volume *Deconstructing Zionism: A Critique of Political Metaphysics*.
2014	Vattimo completes his second period in office with the end of the European Parliament session.
2015	Vattimo contributes the chapter "Anatheism, Nihilism, and Weak Thought" to the edited volume *Reimagining the Sacred: Richard Kearney Debates God*, edited by Richard Kearney and Jens Zimmerman

2016	The Center for Vattimo's Philosophy and Archives is inaugurated at the Universitat Pompeu Fabra in Barcelona, Spain.
2018	Vattimo publishes *Essere e dintorni*. The English translation appears in 2021 as *Being and Its Surroundings*.
2023	Vattimo dies on September 19 at the Rivoli Hospital in Turin.

NOTES

INTRODUCTION

1. See Santiago Zabala, "Why Did the Pope Phone the Philosopher?," *Aeon*, October 1, 2018, https://aeon.co/ideas/why-did-the-pope-phone-the-philosopher (quote); Ferruccio Pinotti, "Vattimo: 'Papa Francesco? È un amico. Oggi mi manca un figlio, adesso mi starebbe vicino,'" *Corriere della sera*, June 6, 2022, https://www.corriere.it/cronache/22_giugno_06/vattimo-papa-francesco-amico-oggi-mi-manca-figlio-adesso-mi-starebbe-vicino-d6270966-e271-11ec-9f19-f9603cda965c.shtml; Andrés Beltramo Álvarez, "El Papa llama a Vattimo, el filósofo del pensamiento débil," *La Stampa*, July 9, 2018, https://www.lastampa.it/vatican-insider/es/2018/07/09/news/el-papa-llama-a-vattimo-el-filosofo-del-pensamiento-debil-1.34030484/.
2. Gianni Vattimo and Piergiorgio Paterlini, *Not Being God: A Collaborative Autobiography*, trans. William McCuaig (Columbia University Press, 2009), 90.
3. Vattimo and Paterlini, *Not Being God*, 10–11.
4. Liceo Classico e Linguistico Vincenzo Gioberti, "In memoria di Gianni Vattimo," Ministero dell'Istruzione e del Merito, Italy, n.d., https://www.liceogioberti.edu.it/pagine/in-memoria-di-gianni-vattimo, accessed March 12, 2024.
5. Vattimo and Paterlini, *Not Being God*, 13.
6. Vattimo and Paterlini, *Not Being God*, 13.
7. Though Eco contributed to the original volume on weak thought edited by Vattimo and Rovatti, he did not consider himself a weak thinker. Instead,

much of his work on hermeneutics was concerned with the limits of valid interpretation. A useful volume in exploring this theme in Eco's work is his book *The Limits of Interpretation* (Indiana University Press, 1990), which is a collection of fifteen earlier essays written on the topic. Here he argues, for example, that there may exist numerous valid interpretations, but each interpretation must begin by acknowledging the literal sense of a passage. Any valid interpretation must be guided by an acknowledgment of this plain literal sense. In this regard, Eco largely takes for granted that such a literal sense exists in most instances, and thus he does not provide any substantial arguments for why preferring one set of conventions over others should constitute a valid starting point. Other significant related works by Eco in the areas of hermeneutics, semiotics, and the philosophy of language include *Opera aperta* (*The Open Work*, 1962), *Trattato di semiotica generale* (*A Theory of Semiotics*, 1975), and *Semiotica e filosofia del linguaggio* (*Semiotics and the Philosophy of Language*, 1984). See Istituto della Enciclopedia Italiana, "Umberto Eco," in *Lessico del XXI Secolo* (Istituto della Enciclopedia Italiana fondata da Giovanni Treccani S.p.A., 2012), https://www.treccani.it/enciclopedia/umberto-eco_(Lessico-del-XXI-Secolo)/.

8. Specifically, it was an interagency school run jointly by the Unione Catechisti del Santissimo Crocifisso (Catechistic Union of the Holiest Cross) and a suborder of the Fratelli delle Scuole Cristiane (Brothers of the Christian Schools). Vattimo and Paterlini, *Not Being God*, 48.

9. Pellegrino later served as archbishop of Turin and then cardinal-priest of the Chiesa del Santissimo Nome di Gesù, the mother church of the Jesuit Order.

10. Gianni Vattimo, "Gianni Vattimo—Philosophy as Ontology of Actuality: A Biographical-Theoretical Interview with Luca Savarino and Federico Vercellone," *Iris: European Journal of Philosophy and Public Debate* 1, no. 2 (October 2009): 313.

11. Peter Carravetta, "An Introduction to the Hermeneutics of Luigi Pareyson," *Differentia: Review of Italian Thought* 3–4, no. 22 (Spring–Autumn 1989): 219.

12. See Grit Fröhlich, "Culture and Invention—Umberto Eco and the Aesthetics of Luigi Pareyson," in *Umberto Eco in His Own Words*, ed. Torkild Thellefsen and Bent Sørensen (De Gruyter Mouton, 2017), 34–40.

13. See Gianni Vattimo, "Luigi Pareyson," in *Dizionario biografico degli Italiani*, vol. 81 (Istituto della Enciclopedia Italiana Fondata da Giovanni

Treccni, 2014), https://www.treccani.it/enciclopedia/luigi-pareyson_ (Dizionario-Biografico)/; see also Silvia Benso, "On Luigi Pareyson: A Master in Italian Hermeneutics," *Philosophy Today* 49, no. 4 (Winter 2005): 381–90; Silvia Benso, "Luigi Pareyson's Ontology of Freedom: Encounters with Martin Heidegger and F. W. J. Schelling," in *Open Borders: Encounters Between Italian Philosophy and Continental Thought*, ed. Silvia Benso and Antonio Calcagno (SUNY Press, 2021), 21–43; and Nicolás Abbagnano, *Historia de la filosofía*, vol. 4, book 2: *La filosofía contemporánea* (HORA, S.A., 1996), 582–87.

14. Vattimo, "Gianni Vattimo—Philosophy as Ontology of Actuality," 320.
15. In mentioning this period, Vattimo calls the church he attended the "Church of the Holy Spirit," but he is presumably referring to the Jesuitenkirche (officially the Pfarrkirche Heiliger Geist und St. Ignatius), not the nearby and more famous Heiliggeistkirche, which has been a Protestant church since the early twentieth century.
16. Vattimo and Paterlini, *Not Being God*, 27.
17. Vattimo and Paterlini, *Not Being God*, 30.
18. Vattimo and Paterlini, *Not Being God*, 103–4.
19. Hans-Georg Gadamer, "The Phenomenological Movement" (1963), and "The Science of the Life-World" (1969), in *Philosophical Hermeneutics*, trans. David E. Linge, paperback ed. (University of California Press, 1977), 130–81, 182–97.
20. Jürgen Habermas, *Philosophical-Political Profiles*, trans. Frederick G. Lawrence (MIT Press, 1983), 190.
21. Hans-Georg Gadamer, *Truth and Method*, 2nd ed., trans. rev. Joel Weinsheimer and Donald G. Marshall (Continuum, 2004), xxv–xxvi.
22. Gadamer, *Truth and Method*, 431.
23. See Thomas Nagel, *The View from Nowhere* (Oxford University Press, 1986).
24. L. P. Hartley, *The Go-Between* (1953; reprint, New York Review of Books, 2002), 17.
25. Gadamer, *Truth and Method*, 301.
26. Gadamer, *Truth and Method*, 367.
27. Richard J. Bernstein, "The Constellation of Hermeneutics, Critical Theory, and Deconstruction," in *The Cambridge Companion to Gadamer*, ed. Robert J. Dostal (Cambridge University Press, 2002), 276.
28. Vattimo and Paterlini, *Not Being God*, 157.
29. Gadamer, *Truth and Method*, xxxiv.

30. John D. Caputo, *Radical Hermeneutics: Repetition, Deconstruction, and the Hermeneutic Project* (Indiana University Press, 1987), 5.
31. See Walter Lammi, "Hans-Georg Gadamer's 'Correction' of Heidegger," *Journal of the History of Ideas* 52, no. 3 (July–September 1991): 487–507.
32. See, for example, Edmund Burke, *Reflections on the Revolution in France* (1790) and Joseph Comte De Maistre, *Les soirées de Saint-Pétersbourg* (1821). Narratives written from such a perspective tend to focus on the character and agency of providence, nations, and "great men" as the drivers of history. This has been true of historians from Carlyle to Spengler. Of course, viewing history as a resource for moral instruction is not inherently conservative. Instead, "traditionalism" can perhaps best be characterized as when such moral instruction becomes about preserving unaltered the dominant attitudes or prevailing social structures of a given era (in particular hierarchies of stratification and domination) by claiming that they are somehow commonsense truths revealed from time immemorial—departure from which, it is believed, can only lead to the degeneration, decline, or collapse of "civilization."
33. Under the influence of Marxism, this approach would eventually give rise to so-called histories from below, which attempt to account for the impact of events on ordinary people.
34. Caputo, *Radical Hermeneutics*, 5–6, my emphasis.
35. In contrast to his criticism of Gadamer, Caputo offers frequently effusive (and, frankly, uncritical) praise of Derrida. The same disparaging attitude toward Gadamer, however, cannot be ascribed to Derrida, who, despite whatever disagreements he might have had with Gadamer philosophically, nevertheless remained well disposed toward him. Indeed, both men expressed regret at not being able to find common ground when they famously met at the conference "Text and Interpretation" at the Sorbonne in 1981. Derrida spoke highly of Gadamer in his acceptance speech of the Adorno Prize in the city of Frankfurt in 2002 and wrote a eulogy for Gadamer upon the latter's passing that same year. See Jacques Derrida, "*Fichus*: Frankfurt Address," in *Paper Machine*, trans. Rachel Bowlby (Stanford University Press, 2005), 164–82; and Derrida, "Wie recht er hatte! Mein Cicerone Hans-Georg Gadamer," *Frankfurter Allgemeine Zeitung*, March 28, 2002. Richard Bernstein has attempted to reconstruct how the dialogue between Gadamer and Derrida might have gone if the two had been able to understand each other

better at the time they met. See Richard J. Bernstein, "The Conversation That Never Happened (Gadamer/Derrida)," *Review of Metaphysics* 61, no. 3 (March 2008): 577–603.

36. David Tracy, "The Dialogical Turn of Contemporary Thought," in *Selected Essays*, vol. 1: *Fragments: The Existential Situation of Our Time* (University of Chicago Press, 2020), 208.
37. Gianni Vattimo, *Beyond Interpretation: The Meaning of Hermeneutics for Philosophy*, trans. David Webb (Polity Press/Stanford University Press, 1997), 3.
38. See Gianni Vattimo, "Towards an Ontology of Decline," in *Beyond the Subject: Nietzsche, Heidegger, and Hermeneutics*, ed. and trans. Peter Carravetta (SUNY Press, 2019), 17–34. It was also translated earlier in *Recoding Metaphysics: The New Italian Philosophy*, ed. Giovanna Borradori, trans. Barbara Spackman (Northwestern University Press, 1988), 63–76.
39. Vattimo, "Gianni Vattimo—Philosophy as Ontology of Actuality," 331–32.
40. Jon R. Snyder, "Translator's Introduction," in Gianni Vattimo, *The End of Modernity: Nihilism and Hermeneutics in Postmodern Culture*, trans. Jon R. Snyder (Polity/Johns Hopkins University Press, 1988), x. Indeed, Vattimo himself stated: "For a variety of reasons, I don't think I can say that I have been particularly deeply influenced by my Italian colleagues: I have always enjoyed very cordial relations with philosophers such as Sini, Cacciari, and Severino, but I would hardly speak of any real 'theoretical' fellowship in this connection." Vattimo, "Gianni Vattimo—Philosophy as Ontology of Actuality," 333.
41. Harold James and Kevin H. O'Rourke, "Italy and the First Age of Globalization, 1861–1940," in *The Oxford Handbook of the Italian Economy Since Unification*, ed. Gianni Toniolo (Oxford University Press, 2013), 37–68. See also Giovanni Frederico and Paolo Malanima, "Progress, Decline, Growth: Product and Productivity in Italian Agriculture, 1000–2000," *Economic History Review* 57, no. 3 (2004): 437–64.
42. Richard Drake, "Italy in the 1960s: A Legacy of Terrorism and Liberation," in "Rethinking 1968: The United States and Western Europe," special issue, *South Central Review* 16, no. 4–17, no. 1 (Winter 1999–Spring 2000): 62.
43. In July 1943, King Victor Emmanuel III of Italy dismissed Benito Mussolini as head of the government and had the former *duce* arrested. Mussolini was

soon freed, however, by members of the Waffen-SS and was installed as nominal head of a short-lived Nazi puppet government, the Republic of Salò, in rivalry to the official government in Italy, which was now led by Pietro Badoglio. Both governments claimed sovereignty over the Piedmont region. After Mussolini's arrest, however, the Italian government would no longer prosecute the war on the Axis side and quickly made overtures to the Allies, which allowed it to secure better terms after the war.

44. Nicola Bianchi and Michela Giorcelli, "Reconstruction Aid, Public Infrastructure, and Economic Development: The Case of the Marshall Plan in Italy," *Journal of Economic History*, working paper, n.d.

45. Gianni Toniolo, "An Overview of Italy's Economic Growth," in *The Oxford Handbook of the Italian Economy Since Unification*, ed. Toniolo, 3–36.

46. Paul Ginsborg, *A History of Contemporary Italy: Society and Politics, 1943–1988* (Palgrave Macmillan, 2003).

47. Mark Donovan, "Democrazia Cristiana: Party of Government," in *Christian Democracy in Europe: A Comparative Perspective*, ed. David Hanley (Pinter, 1996), 71–86.

48. Simon Prince, *Northern Ireland's '68: Civil Rights, Global Revolt, and the Origins of the Troubles* (Irish Academic Press, 2018), chap. 6.

49. See Victoria Langland, *Speaking of Flowers: Student Movements and the Making and Remembering of 1968 in Military Brazil* (Duke University Press, 2013); Tariq Ali, *Uprising in Pakistan: How to Bring Down a Dictatorship* (Verso, 2018); George Katsiaficas, *The Global Imagination of 1968: Revolution and Counterrevolution* (PM Press, 2018).

50. See Susana Draper, *1968 Mexico: Constellations of Freedom and Democracy* (Duke University Press, 2018); and Elaine Carey, "Mexico's 1968 Olympic Dream," in *Protests in the Streets: 1968 Across the Globe*, ed. Elaine Carey (Hackett, 2016), 91–119.

51. Chen Jian et al., eds., *The Routledge Handbook of the Global Sixties: Between Protest and Nation Building* (Routledge, 2018).

52. Eleanor Beardsley, "In France, the Protests of May 1968 Reverberate Today—and Still Divide the French," NPR, May 29, 2018, https://www.npr.org/sections/parallels/2018/05/29/613671633/in-france-the-protests-of-may-1968-reverberate-today-and-still-divide-the-french.

53. Following the first major conflict between students and police at the University of Rome in Via di Valle Giulia, Pier Paolo Pasolini famously wrote

verses in his poem "Il PCI ai Giovani" where he pointed out the irony of the class dynamics of a situation in which affluent university students were agitating for socialism against police, who were themselves mostly the children of working-class parents.

54. Arthur Marwick, *The Sixties: Cultural Revolution in Britain, France, Italy, and the United States, c. 1958–c. 1974* (Bloomsbury Reader, 2012), part 3, chap. 12, sec. 4.

55. Stefano G. Azzarà, "Left-Wing Nietzscheanism in Italy: Gianni Vattimo," *Rethinking Marxism* 30, no. 2 (2018): 275–76.

56. A similar reckoning with the legacy of Stalin had occurred following the speech given by Soviet leader Nikita Khrushchev in February 1956, "On the Cult of Personality and Its Consequences," which condemned many of the actions of the previous Stalinist regime. Although the economists Amartya Sen and Jean Drèze have demonstrated that Chinese rural policies also potentially saved millions of lives, any fair assessment of Mao's legacy has to account for his government's role in the Great Chinese Famine. See Drèze and Sen, eds., *The Political Economy of Hunger: Selected Essays*, 3 vols. (Clarendon Press, 1991).

57. See Quinn Slobodian, "The Meanings of Western Maoism in the Global 1960s," in *The Routledge Handbook of the Global Sixties*, ed. Jian et al., 67–78; and Julia Lovell, *Maoism: A Global History* (Penguin Random House, 2019). Cf. Vattimo and Paterlini, *Not Being God*, 52.

58. Vattimo and Paterlini, *Not Being God*, 61, original emphasis.

59. Nicola Pizzolato, "'I Terroni in Città': Revisiting Southern Migrants' Militancy in Turin's 'Hot Autumn,'" *Contemporary European History* 21, no. 4 (November 2012): 619–34.

60. Workers' struggles with Fiat are described in Giuseppe Berta, "Fiat in the Years of Major Conflict (1969–1980): Worker Mobilization and Management Policy," in *European Yearbook of Business History*, vol. 1, ed. Terry Gourvish and Wilfried Feldenkirchen (Routledge, 1998), 37–56.

61. There had been a global revival in interest in Nietzsche following Heidegger's publication of his two-volume study on the philosopher in 1961. Early reception of Nietzsche (Krummel, Faulkenberg, Brasch, etc.) most often characterized him as a literary successor to Schopenhauer. Others sought to draw out the relationship between his critique of morality and the thought of Kant (Drews, Riehl, Horneffer, Ewald, Simmel, and Vaihinger).

It was Alfred Baeumler, however, who through several influential works published in the late 1920s and the 1930s provided the unfortunate reading of Nietzsche as a precursor to National Socialism. Works by Kaufmann, Jaspers, Löwith, and (ironically) Heidegger helped to undermine this reading of Nietzsche as a proto-Nazi. In Italy, this de-Nazification can also be seen in the critical editorial work of Colli and Montinari. See Gianni Vattimo, *Nietzsche: An Introduction*, trans. Nicholas Martin (Stanford University Press, 2002), chap. 5; and Walter Kaufmann, *Nietzsche: Philosopher, Psychologist, Antichrist*, 4th ed. (Princeton University Press, 1974).

62. Gianni Vattimo, *Dialogue with Nietzsche*, trans. William McCuaig (Columbia University Press, 2006), 195; originally published in *Magazine Littéraire* 298 (April 1992).

63. Vattimo had already published *Essere, storia, e linguaggio in Heidegger* (Edizioni di "Filosofia," 1963). This work appeared the year after Vattimo received a scholarship from the Alexander von Humboldt Foundation to travel to Heidelberg. He had also previously published several other works on Heidegger, among them *Arte e verità nel pensiero di M. Heidegger: Corso di estetica dell'anno accademico 1965–1966* (Giappichelli, 1966); "Arte, sentimento, originarietà nell'estetica di Heidegger," *Rivista di estetica* 12 (1967): 267–88; and "Gli studi heideggeriani negli ultimi venti anni," *Cultura e scuola* 31 (1969): 85–99.

64. Azzarà, "Left-Wing Nietzscheanism in Italy," 275.

65. Vattimo and Paterlini, *Not Being God*, 61, 60, original emphasis.

66. Vattimo, *Dialogue with Nietzsche*, 194.

67. Vattimo, *Dialogue with Nietzsche*, 194–95.

68. Vattimo, "Towards an Ontology of Decline," in *Recoding Metaphysics*, ed. Boarradori, 66.

69. Vattimo and Paterlini, *Not Being God*, 74.

70. Vattimo and Paterlini, *Not Being God*, 50–51.

71. Santiago Zabala, "Gianni Vattimo's Life, Philosophy, and Archives," *Los Angeles Review of Books*, November 10, 2016, https://lareviewofbooks.org/article/gianni-vattimos-life-philosophy-archives/.

72. Vattimo and Paterlini, *Not Being God*, 84.

73. Drake, "Italy in the 1960s," 65, my emphasis.

74. Zabala, "Gianni Vattimo's Life, Philosophy, and Archives."

75. Vattimo and Paterlini, *Not Being God*, 84–85.

76. Gianni Vattimo, *Nihilism and Emancipation: Ethics, Politics, and Law*, ed. Santiago Zabala, trans. William McCuaig (Columbia University Press, 2004), 98.
77. Gianni Vattimo, *Belief*, trans. Luca D'Isanto and David Webb (Polity Press, 1999), 22.
78. Gianni Vattimo, *After Christianity*, trans. Luca D'Isanto (Columbia University Press, 2002), 99.
79. Fyodor Dostoevsky, "Letter XXII: to Mme. N. D. Fonvisin (March, 1854)," in *Letters of Fyodor Michailovitch Dostoevsky to His Family and Friends*, trans. Ethel Colburn Mayne (Chatto and Windus, 1914), 71. The familiar quote from Aristotle likely references the following statement: "But perhaps it is desirable that we should examine the notion of a Universal Good, and review the difficulties that it involves, although such an inquiry goes against the grain because of our friendship for the authors of the Theory of Ideas [Plato]. Still perhaps it would appear desirable, and indeed it would seem to be obligatory, especially for a philosopher, to sacrifice even one's closest personal ties in defense of the truth. Both are dear to us, yet 'tis our duty to prefer the truth" [τὸ δὲ καθόλου βέλτιον ἴσως ἐπισκέψασθαι καὶ διαπορῆσαι πῶς λέγεται, καίπερ προσάντους τῆς τοιαύτης ζητήσεως γινομένης διὰ τὸ φίλους ἄνδρας εἰσαγαγεῖν τὰ εἴδη. δόξειε δ' ἂν ἴσως βέλτιον εἶναι καὶ δεῖν ἐπὶ σωτηρίᾳ γε τῆς ἀληθείας καὶ τὰ οἰκεῖα ἀναιρεῖν, ἄλλως τε καὶ φιλοσόφους ὄντας: ἀμφοῖν γὰρ ὄντοιν φίλοιν ὅσιον προτιμᾶν τὴν ἀλήθειαν]. Aristotle, *Nicomachean Ethics*, vol. 19 of *Aristotle in 23 Volumes*, trans. H. Rackham, Loeb Classical Library (Harvard University Press/William Heinemann, 1934), bk. 1.vi, https://www.loebclassics.com/view/aristotle-nicomachean _ethics/1926/pb_LCL073.17.xml.

1. EARLY POLITICAL THOUGHT

1. "Bei der Persönlichkeit eines Philosophen hat nur das Interesse: Er war dann und dann geboren, er arbeitete und starb." Martin Heidegger, *Gesamtausgabe*, vol. 18: *Grundbegriffe der aristotelischen Philosophie* (Klostermann, 1924), 5, my translation.
2. Vattimo, "Gianni Vattimo—Philosophy as Ontology of Actuality," 311.
3. Romantic anticapitalism is not a singular worldview. Rather, it is an umbrella view representing the diverse "nonscientific" (that is, non-Marxist) responses

to modern industrial (bourgeois) society. It offers a critique of contemporary life "in the name of certain pre-capitalist social and cultural values." Given the various forms such a critique could take, it can just as well be said to encompass the worldviews of figures as diverse as Heidegger, Coleridge, London, Dickens, and Tolkien. See Michael Löwy, "The Romantic and the Marxist Critique of Modern Civilization," *Theory and Society* 16, no. 6 (November 1987): 891–904, quote on 891.

4. Matthew A. Shadle has noted, "Although shaped by the teachings of popes and priests; important efforts had been underway for several decades before the writing of Pope Leo XIII's pivotal encyclical[;] . . . and associations of Catholics continued to be the primary instigators of social Catholicism throughout the twentieth century." Shadle, *Interrupting Capitalism: Catholic Social Thought and the Economy* (Oxford University Press, 2018), 49–50.

5. Within Protestant-majority countries, such groups offered intrareligious cohesion and fellowship for Catholic minorities as a means of preserving those communities from assimilation. Secular unions, however, could criticize such attempts as undermining workers' rights in two respects: first, inclusion of bosses or employers in unions seemed to undermine the purpose and negotiating power of labor unions; and, second, by dividing the workforce, such separate organizations prevented labor from mustering a united front against the concentrated power of capital. Catholic unionism was thus suspected by some of being a form of subterfuge. The degree to which this is true, of course, depends on the individuals involved. No doubt, many in the church leadership certainly saw it as a means to another end. Even so, these attitudes can be contrasted with the surprisingly important influence of Catholic workers' movements in the predominantly Protestant United States (such as the movement led by Dorothy Day, Peter Maurin, and Ammon Hennacy). This influence owes much to the extreme governmental repression of anything resembling socialism in the United States (e.g., the Haymarket Affair, the Battle of Blair Mountain, the Coal Creek War, the Great Railroad Strike of 1877, etc.) as well as the refusal of major trade unions in the country to support the formation of a U.S. Labor Party. Thus, often strenuously antisocialist Catholic unions played a much more significant role in U.S. labor relations than they did throughout much of Europe. See Ronald W. Schatz, "American Labor and the Catholic

Church, 1919–1950," *International Labor and Working-Class History* 20 (Fall 1981): 46–53.
6. See Stephen J. C. Andes, *The Vatican and Catholic Activism in Mexico and Chile: The Politics of Transnational Catholicism, 1920–1940* (Oxford University Press, 2014), 17–21.
7. Indeed, much of integralism's program for reintegrating society into a sacred order directed in various capacities by the church leadership was finally abandoned after Vatican II's pronouncements on the autonomy of the laity (*Apostolicam actuositatem*) and the individual's right to religious freedom (*Dignitatis humanae*).
8. "The physical and ideological environment in which the growth of the [Italian Communist] [P]arty was fostered prior to its formal creation at Livorno in 1921, was principally, but, by no means exclusively, the city of Turin. The importance of this particular environment is stressed because it influenced very deeply the men who were to give *il Partito comunista italiano* its most enduring philosophical and political leadership. Above all, it worked upon the thought of Antonio Gramsci, the most subtle and profound theoretician of Italian Marxism, and [of] his colleagues Palmiro Togliatti, Umberto Terracini and Angelo Tasea, who were to collaborate with Gramsci in editing the weekly publication *L'Ordine Nuovo*." Aldo U. Marchini, "The Italian Communist Party 1921–1964: A Profile," PhD diss., University of Windsor, 1966, x–xi.
9. Antonio Gramsci, "The Turin Factory Councils Movement," in *Selections from Political Writings 1910–1920*, trans. John Mathews (Lawrence and Wishart, 1977), 313.
10. This academic dissatisfaction did not prevent Vattimo, however, from completing his thesis in 1959 on the topic of ποίησις in Aristotle (with recourse to Aquinas, along with the aesthetics of Croce and Pareyson). Where his critical view of modernity could be situated ideologically at this point is clear from a comment he once made regarding this early work on Aristotle: "I proposed a non-romantic reading of *poiesis* in Aristotle in the sense that it was considered as merely one of the many ways in which human beings 'produce' things. The central problem concerned the meaning of the idea of 'imitation': to imitate, for Aristotle, essentially signified 'to act like nature,' not simply to reproduce nature as a spectator that represents the latter. It was this twofold character in the concept of imitation that really interested

me. And, in more general terms, I think that I was particularly attracted by the idea of *going* back to the roots of a Christian mode of philosophizing, perhaps *a pre-modern mode of thinking, and one which breaks with the tradition of modern rationalism*." Vattimo, "Gianni Vattimo—Philosophy as Ontology of Actuality," 316, my emphasis.

11. Vattimo and Paterlini, *Not Being God*, 14; cf. Vattimo, *After Christianity*, 2–3.

12. Regarding one such alternative, Lukács, for example, had argued that the essence of Marxism was not reducible to some set of discrete theses that happen to have been advanced by Marx himself. Instead, the essence of Marxism, he felt, was the "method" of materialist dialectic and the need to integrate theory with praxis. See György Lukács, "What Is Orthodox Marxism?," in *History and Class Consciousness*, trans. Rodney Livingstone (MIT Press, 1971), 1–26.

13. Heidegger's rejection of the tradition of humanism had implications not only for Sartre's understanding of Dasein but also for anyone who wished to integrate Heidegger's thought with the Italian Marxist tradition. For example, Gramsci (who played an outsize role in Marxist theory in Italy) had specifically identified Marxist thought as a continuation of the humanist tradition—drawing on Italy's long philosophical engagement with Hegelianism (culminating in Croce). That is, he identified his Marxism as a "philosophy of praxis" with a kind of neohumanism birthed out of the idealist tradition. See Antonio Gramsci, *Selections from the Prison Notebooks*, ed. and trans. Quintin Hoare and Geoffrey Nowell Smith (1971; reprint, International, 1992), 417–18.

14. See John Foot, *Blood and Power: The Rise and Fall of Italian Fascism* (Bloomsbury, 2022).

15. Though not a leader in the PCI, the socialist economist Piero Sraffa—who at Cambridge would so greatly influence the course of Wittgenstein's later thought—was forced to leave Italy in 1927, shortly after the imprisonment of his close friend Gramsci, but not before supplying Gramsci with the pens and paper that he would eventually use to compose his prison notebooks. From England, Sraffa, along with Gramsci's sister-in-law Tatiana, campaigned for Gramsci's release or, at the very least, the improvement of his prison conditions. See Steve Jones, *Antonio Gramsci* (Routledge, 2006), 25.

I. EARLY POLITICAL THOUGHT   249

16. David P. Palazzo, "The 'Social Factory' in Postwar Italian Radical Thought from Operaismo to Autonomia," PhD diss., City University of New York, 2014, 14.
17. The ideological diversity of the Italian Resistance is reflected in its depiction in Roberto Rossellini's groundbreaking neorealist film *Roma città aperta* (Open city, 1945).
18. Henry A. Kissinger, "Communist Parties in Western Europe: Challenge to the West," in *Eurocommunism: The Italian Case*, ed. Austin Ranney and Giovanni Sartori (American Enterprise Institute for Public Policy Research, 1978), 183–96.
19. Kissinger, "Communist Parties in Western Europe," 191. The continuation of a robust radical unionism in Italy during these years, along with the new presence of a substantial Soviet-backed party in the Italian Parliament, proved inconvenient for the centrist DC leadership of the new republic owing to the country's recent client status in relation to the now ascendant United States.
20. See Marchini, "The Italian Communist Party 1921–1964."
21. Ronald Koven, "'Historic Compromise' Stronger in Italy," *Washington Post*, May 18, 1978, https://www.washingtonpost.com/archive/politics/1978/05/18/historic-compromise-stronger-in-italy/8798b142-49bc-44c9-a902-99a72bb94f4a/.
22. The Bretton Woods Agreement describes the international monetary system established among forty-four countries in 1944. The system attempted to prevent competitive currency devaluation by stabilizing exchange rates in the convertibility of U.S. dollars to gold. The U.S. dollar then served as the reserve currency by which other countries could peg their value. The United States under Nixon, however, unilaterally terminated the gold standard in an attempt to curb inflation. As a result, since 1973 the global monetary system has been based on a free-floating fiat-currency model.
23. James Walston, "Historic Compromise," in *Encyclopedia of Contemporary Italian Culture*, ed. Gino Moliterno (Routledge, 2000), 383.
24. Walston, "Historic Compromise," 383.
25. See David Rose, "Subject/Weak Subject," in *The Vattimo Dictionary*, ed. Simonetta Moro (Edinburgh University Press, 2023), 182–85.
26. In attendance at the meeting were several important Italian Marxist intellectuals, including Lucio Lombardo-Radice, Francesco Valentini, Cesare

Luporini, Giuseppe Semerari, Guido Piovene, Mario Alicata, Galvano Della Volpe, Bianchi Bandinelli, and Renato Gattuso.

27. See Daniel Rueda Garrido, *Forms of Life and Subjectivity: Rethinking Sartre's Philosophy* (Open Book, 2021).

28. Louis Althusser, "Reply to John Lewis" (1972), in *On Ideology* (Verso, 2008), 83.

29. Orthodox Marxism constituted the organized attempt to construct a unified body of Marxist theory—one based on a simplified and systematized version of the thought of Marx and Engels. For a further discussion of the Italian context, see Valdo Spini, "The New Left in Italy," *Journal of Contemporary History* 7, no. 1 (1972): 51–71; and Oliver Harrison, *Revolutionary Subjectivity in Post-Marx Thought: Laclau, Negri, Badiou* (Ashgate, 2014), 9–17.

30. Each of these elements had already existed in some form in prior expressions of Marxist thought, but among the New Left they began to take precedent over the traditional socialist concerns for workers' rights, class struggle, and collective ownership. This was particularly true for the works of critical theorists such as Marcuse. See Steven Gotzler, "1956—the British New Left and the 'Big Bang' Theory of Cultural Studies," *Lateral: Journal of the Cultural Studies Association* 8, no. 2 (Fall 2019), https://csalateral.org/section/years-in-cultural-studies/1956-british-new-left-gotzler/.

31. Dick Howard, *The Marxian Legacy: The Search for the New Left*, 3rd ed. (Palgrave-Macmillan, 2019), 138.

32. See Guido Starosta, *Marx's "Capital," Method, and Revolutionary Subjectivity* (Brill, 2015).

33. Michel Kail and Raoul Kirchmayr, introduction to Jean-Paul Sartre, *What Is Subjectivity?*, trans. David Broder and Trista Selous (Verso, 2016), 7–8.

34. Oliver Harrison has described Marx's position as the belief that the proletariat represented a "historically inscribed revolutionary subject." Harrison, *Revolutionary Subjectivity in Post-Marxist Thought*, 17.

35. See Paul Elias, "Revolutionary Subjectivity in the Thought of Karl Marx," PhD diss., York University, Toronto, 2019, 151–71, sections on the ethics and practice of the revolutionary subject.

36. Workerism also coincided with the maturation of the process of Italian industrialization. The movement sought to place emphasis on examining the real behavior, needs, and conditions of the working class as the only

valid starting place for any plan of revolutionary action. See Steve Wright, *Storming Heaven: Class Composition and Struggle in Italian Autonomist Marxism* (Pluto Press, 2002), 4.

37. Clay Risen, "Antonio Negri, 90, Philosopher Who Wrote a Surprise Best Seller, Dies," *New York Times*, December 22, 2023, https://www.nytimes.com/2023/12/22/world/europe/antonio-negri-dead.html.
38. See Antonio Negri, *Marx Beyond Marx: Lessons on the Grundrisse*, ed. Jim Fleming, trans. Harry Cleaver et al. (Autonomedia, 1991).
39. See Antonio Negri and Anne Dufourmantelle, *Negri on Negri*, trans. Malcolm B. DeBevoise (Routledge, 2004), 168–69.
40. There are some important differences, of course, between workerism and autonomism, but a discussion of those differences is too far outside the purview of the present study.
41. The Situationist International was a collective of avant-garde artists and left-wing political theorists who pioneered disruptive forms of political protest in the 1960s, which included situationist pranks, culture jamming, and *détournement*. After the Marxists' failures to bring about revolutionary change in the 1960s, however, the 1970s saw a "fragmentation of revolutionary subjectivity into a collection of identities and differences, or the dissolution of class politics in favor of the nomads of the 'new social movements.'" Ryan Moore, "Postmodernism and Punk Subculture: Cultures of Authenticity and Deconstruction," *Communication Review* 7 (2004): 305–6. See also Peter Marshall, *Demanding the Impossible: A History of Anarchism* (HarperCollins, 2008), 549–53.
42. In this regard, autonomism drew intellectual inspiration from figures such as Rosa Luxemburg and Anton Pannekoek. Sharing many ideological features with anarchism (left libertarianism), it gained in prominence following the death of Stalin in 1953, the de-Stalinization campaign of Khrushchev in 1956, and the left-wing reaction to the Soviet repression of the Hungarian Revolution that same year. Autonomism shared some affinities with Mao's purported vision of a so-called third-world socialism, though in practice Mao himself governed in form closer to the bureaucratized authoritarian leftism of Stalin. See Linda Martín Alcoff and José Alcoff, "Autonomism in Theory and Practice," *Science and Society* 79, no. 2 (April 2015): 221–42.
43. See Verity Burgmann, "The Multitude and the Many-Headed Hydra: Autonomist Marxist Theory and Labor History," in "Strikes and Social

Conflicts," special issue, *International Labor and Working-Class History* 83 (Spring 2013): 170–90.
44. See Teodor Shanin, "Late Marx: Gods and Craftsmen," in *Late Marx and the Russian Road: Marx and the Peripheries of Capitalism*, ed. Teodor Shanin (Monthly Review Press, 1983), 3–39.
45. Harrison, *Revolutionary Subjectivity in Post-Marxist Thought*, 70.
46. Lucio Castellano et al., "Do You Remember Revolution?," in *Radical Thought in Italy: A Potential Politics*, ed. Paolo Virno and Michael Hardt (University of Minnesota Press, 1996), 230.
47. Wright, *Storming Heaven*, 152.
48. Castellano et al., "Do You Remember Revolution?," 232.
49. Incidentally, Negri's most significant work as a theoretician did not occur until after this event. For example, today, he is perhaps most well known (at least outside of Italy) for his books, including *Marx Beyond Marx* (1979), *Revolution Retrieved* (1988), *The Politics of Subversion* (1989), *Labor of Dionysus* (1994), and *Insurgencies* (1999), as well as for his influential series *Empire* (2000, coauthored with Michael Hardt), *Multitude* (2004), and *Commonwealth* (2009). Vattimo, despite his respect for Negri, also criticized Negri's work (along with that of Giorgio Agamben) as being "guilty of too much ideological rigidity." See Gianni Vattimo and John D. Caputo, *After the Death of God*, ed. Jeffrey W. Robbins (Columbia University Press, 2007), 112.
50. Silvia Benso and Brian Schroeder, "Italian Philosophy Between 1980 and 1995," in *The History of Continental Philosophy*, vol. 7: *After Poststructuralism: Transitions and Transformations*, ed. Rosi Braidotti (Acumen, 2010), 90 n. 18.
51. Andrea Righi, *Biopolitics and Social Change in Italy: From Gramsci to Pasolini to Negri* (Palgrave Macmillan, 2011), 140, original emphasis.
52. In his book with John D. Caputo, *After the Death of God* (2007), Vattimo continued to advocate for the idea of building autonomous communities, writing, "The only possibility for democracy in our current situation is to exploit the holes, the margins, which was, by the way, the idea in the 1970s behind something Tony Negri called *autonomie* . . . not try to take the power, but try to construe peripheral powers. If people around the world protest the war in Iraq, for example, it doesn't mean taking control of Windsor Palace or the White House, but, nevertheless, it eases and slows

down the wheels of power. . . . The only possibility today is not to categorically reject the machinery of power but to slow down the process of the reproduction of capital" (112).

53. This occupation predated the more famous student protests that would occur the next year in France. For discussion of the event at Turin, see Federico Mancini, "The Italian Student Movement," *AAUP Bulletin* 54, no. 4 (December 1968): 427–32.

54. Later that same year, Parisian students would take to the streets under the slogan "the Three M's"—"Marx, Mao, and Marcuse." See Jerzy J. Wiatr, "Herbert Marcuse: Philosopher of a Lost Radicalism," *Science and Society* 34, no. 3 (Fall 1970): 319–30.

55. Pierre Viansson-Ponte, "Interview with Herbert Marcuse," *Le Monde*, June 1969, trans. Anne Fremantle, n.d., https://www.marxists.org/reference/archive/marcuse/works/1969/interview.htm, accessed May 28, 2025.

56. A Bonapartist (Nietzsche) and a Nazi (Heidegger) hardly make obvious bedfellows for Marx. Even so, given the extent to which Heidegger was almost from the beginning co-opted by the Left, his connection with Marx is perhaps less surprising than it otherwise should be. Similarly, certain elements of the Left have always been willing to overlook Nietzsche's obviously incongruous political sympathies. The reason for this arguably has less to do with what each thinker affirmed politically than what they attacked. Both Nietzsche and Heidegger were romantic anticapitalists. Thus, while both men during their lives were definitively on the political right, they could nevertheless still be viewed sympathetically by socialists. What they shared with a majority of radicals on the left, however, were their nonconformism, anticlericalism, secularism, and a hope for a "this-worldly" redemption for those willing to struggle for it. The very real differences in their worldviews could then simply be elided as deemed necessary.

57. See Giovanni Giorgio, *Il pensiero di Gianni Vattimo: L'emancipazione della metafisica tra dialettica ed ermeneutica* (Franco Angeli, 2006), 45–46.

58. See Robert T. Valgenti, "Mask," in *The Vattimo Dictionary*, ed. Moro, 126–28.

59. Gianni Vattimo, *Il soggetto e la maschera* (Fabbri-Bompiani, 1974), 348, my translation, original emphasis.

60. Azzarà, "Left-Wing Nietzscheanism in Italy," 277.

61. A more thorough critique of what Vattimo terms the "bourgeois/Christian subject" is to be found in his work *Beyond the Subject* as well as in the essay "The Decline of the Subject and the Problem of Testimony" in *The Adventure of Difference*. In this essay, Vattimo states, "Far from being able to be summed up and centered in consciousness, or in the knowledge each of us has of himself and the responsibility each conceives for himself, the individual personality is an ensemble, perhaps not even a system, of different strata or 'pulsations' as we might call them (Nietzsche calls them 'passions') that are at odds with one another and give rise to equilibria that are never more than provisional.... One does not become authentic by leaving the world of the *they* in a personal assumption of responsibility; entry into the sphere of authentic existence ... can only occur (if it can) through the modification of this world, through the transformation of one epoch of Being into another.... [B]elonging to a historical world is necessarily and unavoidably constitutive of individuality. There can be no individual authenticity in an inauthentic world; the move into authenticity depends on a comprehensive transformation of this world, on the inauguration of a different 'epoch of Being.'" Gianni Vattimo, "The Decline of the Subject and the Problem of Testimony," in *The Adventure of Difference: Philosophy After Nietzsche and Heidegger*, trans. Cyprian Blamires and Thomas Harrison (Johns Hopkins University Press, 1993), 45, 50.

62. Vattimo, *Il soggetto e la maschera*, 115–16, my translation, original emphasis.

63. Lenin had argued that without a designated contingent of specialized "professional revolutionaries" leading the way, workers could only ever achieve a trade-unionist mentality and never realize the need for social and political revolution to bring about socialism. See Vladimir Lenin, "What Is to Be Done?" (1902), in *Essential Works of Lenin*, ed. Henry M. Christman (Dover Press, 1987), 53–177.

64. The wider critique of totalizing narratives that began around this time, including those of Hegel and Marx, represent the transition toward postmodernity. Thus, reckoning with the failures and shortcomings of leftist politics during the first half of the twentieth century was a major catalyst for the development of postmodern/postmetaphysical thought.

65. Vattimo, "Gianni Vattimo—Philosophy as Ontology of Actuality," 324–25.

2. WEAK THOUGHT

1. Peter Carravetta, "What Is Weak Thought? The Original Theses and Context of *il Pensiero Debole*," in *Weak Thought*, ed. Gianni Vattimo and Pier Aldo Rovatti (SUNY Press, 2012), 3–4.
2. Vattimo, *"An-denken*: Thinking and the Foundation," in *The Adventure of Difference*, 112.
3. Regarding the Übermensch, Kaufmann argued that Nietzsche's denouncement of monotheism in *The Gay Science*, for example, is framed as a rejection of one *Normalgott*, which could serve as the basis for any *Normalmensch*—a standard that, Nietzsche felt, would militate against any real possibility of the development of heroic individuality. Instead, "it was the advantage of polytheism, Nietzsche contends, that it allowed for a *'multiplicity of norms.'*" Kaufmann, *Nietzsche*, 308, original emphasis.

    And, simply put, Adorno's concept of "negative dialectics" rejects the idea that negation and contradiction are always invariably sublated into a greater unity. For example, Adorno states, "What we differentiate will appear divergent, dissonant, negative for just as long as the structure of our consciousness obliges it to strive for unity: as long as its demand for totality will be its measure for whatever is not identical with it. This is what dialectic holds up to our consciousness as a contradiction." Theodor W. Adorno, *Negative Dialectics*, trans. E. B. Ashton (1966; reprint, Continuum, 2007), 5. Even so, Vattimo is also critical of Adorno's continued commitment to totality.
4. See Vattimo, *Il soggetto e la maschera*, 114–30, the chapter on metaphysics and violence. Cf. bell hooks, "Eating the Other: Desire and Resistance," in *Black Looks: Race and Representation* (South End Press, 1992), 21–40.
5. See Franca d'Agostini, "Weak Thought (*Pensiero Debole*)," in *The Vattimo Dictionary*, ed. Moro, 202–5.
6. It was also in this pivotal year for Vattimo that he befriended Richard Rorty. The two men met for the first time at a conference on postmodern thought held at the University of Wisconsin, Milwaukee. Rorty heard Vattimo speak and asked for a copy of his paper. In return, he gave Vattimo a copy of his newly published book, *Philosophy and the Mirror of Nature*.
7. See Nicola Abbagnano, "Verso un nuovo illuminismo: John Dewey," in *Scritti neoilluministici, 1948–1965*, ed. Bruno Maiorca (Unione Tipografico-Editrice Torinese, 2001), chap. 5.

8. See Vattimo, *The End of Modernity*, x–xi.
9. Emilio Carlo Corriero has noted, "The reason that went into *crisis* was the one that insisted on depicting itself as 'nature' that is 'on the one hand, as the nature of thought, or more precisely, as 'natural laws of thought" and, on the other, as an objective structure of the world." Corriero, *Nietzsche's Death of God and Italian Philosophy*, trans. Vanessa Di Stefano (Rowman and Littlefield, 2016), 76.
10. Carlo Augusto Viano, "La ragione, l'abbondanza e la credenza," in *Crisi della ragione: Nuovi modelli nel rapporto tra sapere e attività umane*, ed. Aldo Gargani (Einaudi, 1980), 303–66. The claim that Vattimo took the name "weak thought" from Viano's essay is repeated by Vattimo in a few places. In his biography with Paterlini, he says, "Carlo Augusto Viano had invented the expression 'weak reason' before me, which I practically copied with my 'weak thought.'" Vattimo and Paterlini, *Not Being God*, 93. Viano also wrote several responses to *Weak Thought*; the one most often cited is his book, *Va' pensiero: Il carattere della filosofia italiana contemporanea* (Einaudi, 1985).
11. See Gianni Vattimo, *Al di là del soggetto: Nietzsche, Heidegger, e l'emeneutica* (Feltrinelli, 1981); and Vattimo, *Beyond the Subject*.
12. This idea should not simply be assimilated to Kant's notion of the "conditions of the possibility of experience [Bedingungen der Möglichkeit]," however, because Heidegger's concern here is ontological, not epistemic.
13. See Martin Heidegger, *Being and Time*, trans. John MacQuarrie and Edward Robinson (1962; reprint, Harper and Rowe, 2008), 425.
14. William Faulkner, *Requiem for a Nun* (1950; reprint, Vintage, 2011), 1.3.
15. "The ancient way of interpreting the Being of entities is oriented towards the 'world' or 'Nature' in the widest sense, and that it is indeed in terms of 'time' that its understanding of Being is obtained. The outward evidence for this . . . is the treatment of the meaning of Being as παρουσία or οὐ σία, which signifies, in ontologico-temporal terms, 'presence' ['Anwesenheit']. Entities are grasped in their Being as 'presence'; this means that they are understood with regard to a definite mode of time—the '*Present*.'" Heidegger, *Being and Time*, 47.
16. Percy Bysshe Shelley, "A Defense of Poetry" (1821), in *Essays, Letters from Abroad, Translations, and Fragments* (Edward Moxon, 1840), 57.

17. The English word *ecstasy* and its German cognate *Ekstase* derive from the Greek term ἔκστασις (from ἐκ, "out," and ἵστημι, "I stand"), meaning to "stand outside" or "stand away from."
18. *Augenblick* (literally, "glance of the eye") had appeared earlier as a prominent theme in Luther, Goethe, and Kierkegaard (*Øieblikket*). Their works owe a conceptual debt to the Aristotelean and New Testament discourses on καιρός (the "right," "critical," or "opportune" time for some happening—as determined by φρόνησις, "prudence," "good sense," "sound judgment," "pragmatic understanding," or the virtue of an "astute/cultivated intuition").
19. See St. Augustine, *Conf.*, bk. 11; and Boethius, *Cons. Phil.*, bk. 5. Cf. Maimonides, *Dalālat al-ḥā'irīn*, bks. 2 and 3.
20. Aquinas, *ST, Prima Pars*, Q. 14. a. 13. For the translation, see St. Thomas Aquinas, *Summa theologica*, unabridged in a single volume (Coyote Canyon Press, 2018), 62.
21. This is essentially a rejection of the Neoplatonic notion of "beings" as *emanating from* (πρόοδος) and *returning to* (ἐπιστροφή) the superabundance of "Being," conceived as *the One* (τὸ ἕν).
22. Heidegger's position has more in common with the moderate realism of Duns Scotus—on whose work he, not coincidentally, wrote *Habilitationsschrift*. For discussion, see Philip Tonner, *Heidegger, Metaphysics, and the Univocity of Being* (Continuum, 2010).
23. "To think Being itself explicitly requires disregarding Being to the extent that it is only grounded and interpreted in terms of beings and for beings as their ground, as in all metaphysics. To think Being exactly requires us to relinquish Being as the ground of beings in favour of the giving which prevails concealed in unconcealment, that is, in favour of the es gibt (there is)." Martin Heidegger, *On Time and Being*, trans. Joan Stambaugh (Harper and Rowe, 1972), 6, quoted in Vattimo, "*An-denken*," 110.
24. Martin Heidegger, *Basic Concepts*, trans. Gary E. Aylesworth (Indiana University Press, 1993), 51–52; also quoted in Santiago Zabala, *Being at Large: Freedom in the Age of Alternative Facts* (McGill-Queen's University Press, 2020), 23–24.
25. Richard Kearney, "Heidegger and the Possible," *Philosophical Studies* 27 (1980): 177, original emphasis.
26. Vattimo, "Towards an Ontology of Decline," in *Beyond the Subject*, 18.

27. Vattimo, "Towards an Ontology of Decline," in *Beyond the Subject*, 18 .
28. Vattimo, "Gianni Vattimo—Philosophy as Ontology of Actuality," 329.
29. See Daniel Mariano Leiro, "Notas sobre ontología del decliner: La hermenéutica nihilista de Gianni Vattimo," *Anales del seminario de historia de la filosofía* 26 (2009): 208, my translation and emphasis.
30. Vattimo, "Towards an Ontology of Decline," in *Beyond the Subject*, 21–22.
31. Incidentally, it was Rovatti who suggested that the volume be called *Il pensiero debole*.
32. Gianni Vattimo, "Dialectics, Difference, Weak Thought," in *Weak Thought*, ed. Vattimo and Rovatti, 44, 45, 40, 47–48, original emphasis.
33. G. W. F. Hegel, *Elements of the Philosophy of Right*, 8th ed., ed. Allen W. Wood, trans. Hugh B. Nisbet (Cambridge University Press, 2003), 23.
34. In reflecting on this passage, the Orthodox theologian David Bentley Hart has observed that, for Hegel, "philosophy comes only at the end of an age, far too late in the day to tell us how the world ought to be; it can at most merely ponder what already has come to pass and so begun to pass away. An epoch yields its secrets to rational reflection grudgingly, only after its profoundest possibilities already have been exhausted in the actuality of history.... [It] suggests that the greatest philosopher of all would be the one who could plausibly claim to have come most belatedly of all: to have witnessed the very last crepuscular gleam of the dying day and to have learned, as no one else now can, how the story truly ends. The highest aim of philosophy, then, would be to achieve a kind of transcendent belatedness, an unsurpassable finality lying always further beyond all merely local or episodic philosophies." Hart, "A Philosopher in the Twilight: Heidegger's Philosophy as Meditation on the Mystery of Being," *First Things: A Journal of Religion and Public Life* (Institute on Religion and Public Life), February 2011, https://www.firstthings.com/article/2011/02/a-philosopher-in-the-twilight.
35. For example, Hegel argues that both subject and object find their meaning only in relation to a totality, which encompasses both. Hegel, *Elements of the Philosophy of Right*, §26.
36. According to Peter Caravetta, Vattimo argues that the "hermeneutics of suspicion" views all consciousness as potentially "'false consciousness' [which] presupposes that somewhere there is a 'true consciousness' to be sought. And this 'absent' truth is basically the reverse of a metaphysical

assumption that there exists an atemporal, transhistorical Truth" (Caravetta, "What Is 'Weak Thought'?," 17). This is also the subject of Maurizio Ferraris's essay contribution to *Weak Thought*. See Ferraris, "The Aging of the 'School of Suspicion," in *Weak Thought*, ed. Vattimo and Rovatti, 138–54.

37. For Marx, alienation is the universal condition of modern humankind. As Karl Löwith explains it, "The economic expression of this problem is the world of 'commodities,' its political expression is the contradiction between 'state' and 'society,' and its immediate social expression is the existence of the 'proletariat.'" Löwith, "Man's Self-Alienation in the Early Writings of Marx," *Social Research* 21, no. 2 (Summer 1954): 211. Cf. Hegel, *Elements of the Philosophy of Right*, §§66–67; and Karl Marx, "*From* 'The Holy Family' (1844)," in *Writings of the Young Marx on Philosophy and Society*, ed. and trans. Loyd D. Easton and Kurt H. Guddat (Hackett, 1967), 361–98.

On dialectical reappropriation, Vattimo implies that this follows the *form* of the reappropriation of surplus value by the proletariat. For Marx, "surplus value" (i.e., the value added to a product by labor) is appropriated or stolen from workers by the capitalist in the form of profit. Reappropriation, then, is the reclaiming and redistribution of labor-added value—returning added value back to those who produced it. See Marx, *Kapital* (1867), 1:8; and *Critique of the Gotha Programme* (1875), §2; cf. Slavoj Žižek, "Multitude, Surplus, and Envy," *Rethinking Marxism* 19, no. 1 (January 2007): 46–58.

38. For example, see Theodor W. Adorno, *Minima Moralia*, trans. Edmund Jephcott (New Left, 1974), 247; Ernst Bloch, *The Spirit of Utopia*, trans. Anthony A. Nassar (Stanford University Press, 2000); Bloch, *The Principle of Hope*, trans. Neville Plaice et al. (MIT Press, 1995); and Walter Benjamin, "Theological-Political Fragment," in *Reflections: Essays, Aphorisms, Autobiographical Writings*, ed. Peter Demetz, trans. Edmund Jephcott (Schocken, 1986), 312–13.

39. Vattimo, "Dialectics, Difference, Weak Thought," 43. This calls to mind Ivan's rejection of *apocatastasis* in *The Brothers Karamozov*: "I absolutely renounce all higher harmony.... And if the suffering of children goes to make up the sum of suffering needed to buy truth, then I assert beforehand that the whole of truth is not worth such a price." Fyodor Dostoevsky, *The Brothers Karamazov*, trans. Richard Pevear and Larissa Volokhonsky (Farrar, Straus and Giroux, 2002), §4, p. 245.

40. See Robert T. Valgenti, "Convalescence (*Verwindung*)," in *The Vattimo Dictionary*, ed. Moro, 52–54.
41. Vattimo, "Dialectics, Difference, Weak Thought," 46.
42. In an interview for the political newspaper *Lotta continua* in Rome on September 20, 1981, Vattimo stated: "There is no liberation beyond appearances into a supposed domain of authentic being. One the contrary, there is freedom as mobility among 'appearances.' As Nietzsche teaches, appearances no longer go by that name though, for now that 'the world has become a fable' there is no true being left to degrade them into lies and falsity. . . . I don't think philosophy should or even can teach us where we're headed. It can only teach us to live in the condition of someone not headed anywhere." Gianni Vattimo, "Author's Preface: The Bottle, the Net, the Revolution, and the Tasks of Philosophy. A Dialogue with *Lotta Continua*," in *Beyond the Subject*, xxix–xxx.
43. Vattimo, "Towards an Ontology of Decline," in *Beyond the Subject*, 17.
44. Vattimo, "Dialects, Difference, Weak Thought," 47.
45. Vattimo, "Dialects, Difference, Weak Thought," 50.
46. Immanuel Kant, *Beantwortung der Frage: Was ist Aufklärung?* (1784). According to Habermas, the enlightenment project rested on a twofold metaphysical presumption concerning the irreproachableness of human reason and the conformity of nature to comprehensible "physical laws." See Jürgen Habermas, "Modernity Versus Postmodernity," *New German Critique* 22 (Winter 1981): 3–14.
47. See Nathaniel Wolloch, *History and Nature in the Enlightenment: Praise of the Mastery of Nature in Eighteenth-Century Historical Literature* (Ashgate, 2011).
48. Vattimo, *The End of Modernity*, 2.
49. Although Vattimo appears to consider *Entmythologisierung* as both "demythization" and "demythologization" interchangeably, we can note that they are technically distinguishable from one another. *Demythization*, for example, is the attempt to eliminate myth, whereas *demythologization* questions the specific rationale of a given myth but not necessarily myth as such.
50. Max Horkheimer and Theodor Adorno, *Dialectic of Enlightenment: Philosophical Fragments*, trans. Edmund Jephcott (Stanford University Press, 2002), 7, original emphasis.

2. WEAK THOUGHT ∞ 261

51. Gianni Vattimo, *The Transparent Society*, trans. David Webb (Polity Press/ Johns Hopkins University Press, 1992), 34. Consider the similarity of this sentiment to the following quote from C. S. Lewis: "There is something which unites magic and applied science while separating both from the 'wisdom' of earlier ages. For the wise men of old, the cardinal problem had been how to conform the soul to reality, and the solution had been knowledge, self-discipline, and virtue. For magic and applied science alike, the problem is how to subdue reality to the wishes of men: the solution is a technique; and both, in the practice of this technique, are ready to do things hitherto regarded as disgusting and impious." Lewis, *The Abolition of Man* (1944; reprint, HarperCollins, 2000), 71.
52. See Friedrich Nietzsche, *Twilight of the Idols*, trans. R. J. Hollingdale (Penguin, 1968).
53. Even within an empirical model, there exist frequently overlooked constraints on the conditions and impact of the act of observation. For example, consider the so-called observer effect, in which the act of observation creates a disturbance or displacement in the object observed.
54. See James Risser, "Philosophy and Politics at the End of Metaphysics," in *Between Nihilism and Politics: The Hermeneutics of Gianni Vattimo*, ed. Silvia Benso and Brian Schroeder (SUNY Press, 2010), 167–82.
55. See Zabala, *Being at Large*, 37.
56. Vattimo, *The Transparent Society*, 25.
57. Compare the following statement: "If all theories of truth were theories about the 'real quality' or the 'real relation,' which the word 'truth' is naively supposed to stand for, they would all be nonsense. But in fact they are for the most part theories of an entirely different sort. Whatever question their authors may think they are discussing, what they are really discussing most of the time is the question, 'What makes a proposition true or false?'" A. J. Ayer, *Language, Truth, and Logic* (1946; reprint, Dover, 1952), 90.
58. Vattimo and Caputo, *After the Death of God*, 32.
59. Gianni Vattimo, *A Farewell to Truth*, trans. William McCuaig (Columbia University Press, 2011), 7–8.
60. Gadamer, *Philosophical Hermeneutics*, 14.
61. See Gianni Vattimo and Richard Rorty, *The Future of Religion*, ed. Santiago Zabala (Columbia University Press, 2005), 58–61.

62. Gaetano Chiurazzi, "The Experiment of Nihilism: Interpretation and Experience of Truth in Gianni Vattimo," in *Between Nihilism and Politics*, ed. Benso and Schroeder, 16.
63. Vattimo, *Dialogue with Nietzsche*, 139.
64. Vattimo, "The Will to Power as Art," in *The Adventure of Difference*, 99.
65. Andrzej Zawadzki, *Literature and Weak Thought*, Cross-Roads: Polish Studies in Culture, Literary Theory, and History, vol. 2, ed. Ryszard Nycz and Teresa Walas (PL Academic, 2013), 70.
66. Santiago Zabala, *Why Only Art Can Save Us: Aesthetics and the Absence of Emergency* (Columbia University Press, 2019), 123, quoting Hans-Georg Gadamer, "The Artwork in Word and Image: 'So True so Full of Being!,'" in *The Gadamer Reader: A Bouquet of the Later Writings*, ed. Richard E. Palmer (Northwestern University Press, 2007), 217.
67. See Viano, *Va' pensiero*.
68. See Paolo Rossi, *Paragone degli ingegni moderni e postmoderni* (1989; reprint, Il Mulino, 2009); and Rossi, *Speranze* (Il Mulino, 2008).
69. Eugenio Garin has pointed out that, at present at least, the works of Viano and of his collaborator and fellow torinese philosopher Pietro Rossi are remembered less for their independent contributions to contemporary thought than for their polemics against postmodernity. See Garin, *History of Italian Philosophy*, vol. 1, ed. and trans. Giorgio Pinton (Rodopi, 2008), 1108; cf. Vattimo, "Gianni Vattimo—Philosophy as Ontology of Actuality," 326.
70. See also Alberto Hernandez-Lemus, "Beyond *Pensiero Debole* in Latin America: Territories Outside State Structures," *Radical Philosophy Review* 19, no. 2 (2016): 409–27.
71. Enrique Dussel, "Un diálogo con Gianni Vattimo: De la postmodernidad a la transmodernidad," *A parte rei* 54, no. 6 (2007): 12, my translation. Cf. Eduardo Mendieta, "The End of Metaphysics, the Uses and Abuses of Philosophy, and Understanding Just a Little Better: On Gianni Vattimo and Santiago Zabala's *Hermeneutic Communism*," in *Making Communism Hermeneutical: Reading Vattimo and Zabala*, ed. Silvia Mazzini and Owen Glyn-Williams (Springer International, 2017), 3–14.
72. Dussel, "Un diálogo con Gianni Vattimo," 17.
73. Whatever the validity of Dussel's criticism at the time, Vattimo focused much more attention on Latin America in his later years. This is evidenced

particularly in *Hermeneutic Communism* (2011), in which Vattimo and Zabala took Latin American progressive governments as models for Western liberal democracy. They argue that "hermeneutics would not have been possible without the end of Eurocentrism, which has always been the sociopolitical correlation of Western metaphysics." Gianni Vattimo and Santiago Zabala, *Hermeneutic Communism: From Heidegger to Marx* (Columbia University Press, 2011), 110. Indeed, in October 2020, speaking at a conference on communications held remotely by the National University of La Plata (where Vattimo was Doctor Honoris Causa), Vattimo stated, "Today the language of the poor, of the proletariat, is Spanish. If there is a possible future health, it comes from the Spanish-speaking world." See Facultad de Periodismo y Comunicacion Social, "IV Comcis: El filósofo italiano Gianni Vattimo disertó en la facultad," 2020, Universidad Nacional de La Plata, October 9, 2020, https://perio.unlp.edu.ar/2020/10/07/iv-comcis-el-filosofo-italiano-gianni-vattimo-diserto-en-la-facultad/.

74. See William Egginton, "Realism/ New Realism," in *The Vattimo Dictionary*, ed. Moro, 163–65.
75. Graham Harman, foreword to Maurizio Ferraris, *Manifesto of New Realism*, trans. Sarah De Sanctis (SUNY Press, 2014), x.
76. See Graham Harman, *Tool-Being: Heidegger and the Metaphysics of Objects* (Open Court, 2002); Harman, *Guerilla Metaphysics: Phenomenology and the Carpentry of Things* (Open Court, 2005); and Tom Sparrow, *The End of Phenomenology: Metaphysics and the New Realism* (Edinburgh University Press, 2014).
77. Ferraris, *Manifesto of New Realism*, 8.
78. Consider the following quotes from Vattimo: "The predilection of the early twentieth-century artistic avant-garde for African masks may be taken as a sign of art's often prophetic power regarding more general movements of culture and society"; and "Art wishes to defend its own truth appeal in radical opposition to the truth of science and philosophy. Since science is subjected to the world of appearances and measurable phenomena, it is incapable of grasping the lived meaning of existence." Vattimo, *The Transparent Society*, 31; and Gianni Vattimo, *Art's Claim to Truth*, ed. Santiago Zabala, trans. Luca D'Isanto (Columbia University Press, 2010), 249.
79. Maurizio Ferraris, "Post moderni o neorealisti? L'addio al pensiero debole che divide i filosofi, dialogo tra Maurizio Ferraris e Gianni Vattimo," *La*

Repubblica, August 19, 2011, my translation, https://ricerca.repubblica.it/repubblica/archivio/repubblica/2011/08/19/post-moderni-neorealisti-addio-al-pensiero-debole.html.
80. Ferraris, *Manifesto of New Realism*, 67–68.
81. Martin Rhodes, "Tangentopoli—More Than 20 Years On," in *The Oxford Handbook of Italian Politics*, ed. Erik Jones and Gianfranco Pasquino (Oxford University Press, 2015), 312.
82. Zabala, "Gianni Vattimo's Life, Philosophy, and Archives."
83. As Vattimo and Zabala note in their introduction, *Hermeneutic Communism* builds on Vattimo's book *Ecce comu: Come si diventa cio che si era* (Ecce comu: How one becomes what one was) (Fazi, 2007) as well as on Zabala's book *The Remains of Being: Hermeneutic Ontology After Metaphysics* (Columbia University Press, 2009).
84. See Eduardo Mendieta, "Hermeneutic Communism," in *The Vattimo Dictionary*, ed. Moro, 92–95.
85. See, for example, Friedrich Engels, *Sozialismus: Utopie und Wissenschaft* (*Socialism: Utopian and Scientific*, 1880); cf. Albert Weisbord, *The Conquest of Power: Liberalism, Anarchism, Syndicalism, Socialism, Fascism, and Communism*, vol. 1 (Covici-Friede, 1937), bk. 4, §17.
86. Karl Marx, "Theses on Feuerbach," in Karl Marx and Friedrich Engels, *The Marx-Engels Reader*, 2nd ed., ed. Robert C. Tucker (Norton, 1978), §11, p. 145.
87. Vattimo and Zabala, *Hermeneutic Communism*, 4.
88. See Martin Woessner, "Hermeneutic Communism: Left Heideggerianism's Last Hope?," in *Making Communism Hermeneutical*, ed. Mazzini and Glyn-Williams, 47–48.
89. Vattimo and Zabala, *Hermeneutic Communism*, 16.
90. The present situation with regard to capitalist hegemony can be thought of in relation to two famous quotes. The first is often attributed to Fredric Jameson: "Today, it's easier to imagine the end of the world than the end of capitalism." The second comes from the novelist Ursula K. Le Guin in a speech given for the National Book Awards, where she notes (almost in direct reply to the first quote), "We live in capitalism. Its power seems inescapable—but then, *so did the divine right of kings*. Any human power can be resisted and changed by human beings. Resistance and change often begin in art, and very often in our art, the art of words." See Fredric

Jameson, "Future City," *New Left Review* 21 (May–June 2003): 65–79, quoted in Mark Fisher, *Capitalist Realism: Is There No Alternative?* (Zero Books/John Hunt, 2009), 6; and Ursula K. Le Guin, "Speech on the Occasion of the National Book Foundation Medal for Distinguished Contribution to American Letters," 2014, original emphasis, https://www.ursulakleguin.com/nbf-medal.
91. Vattimo and Zabala, *Hermeneutic Communism*, 140, original emphasis.
92. Mendieta, "The End of Metaphysics," 4.
93. The *First Declaration* was written by Subcomandante Marcos (i.e., Rafael Sebastián Guillén Vicente, then spokesperson for the Zapatista Army of National Liberation).
94. This phrase also served as the title to a collection of interviews with Rorty edited by Eduardo Mendieta for Stanford University Press. See Richard Rorty, *Take Care of Freedom and Truth Will Take Care of Itself: Interviews with Richard Rorty*, ed. Eduardo Mendieta (Stanford University Press, 2005).
95. Gianni Vattimo and Santiago Zabala, "Response to Mendieta," in *Making Communism Hermeneutical*, ed. Mazzini and Glyn-Williams, 15–18.
96. Jeff Malpas and Nick Malpas, "Politics, Hermeneutics, and Truth," in *Making Communism Hermeneutical*, ed. Mazzini and Glyn-Williams, 21.
97. Gianni Vattimo and Santiago Zabala, "Response to Jeff Malpas and Nick Malpas," in *Making Communism Hermeneutical*, ed. Mazzini and Glyn-Williams, 31–32.
98. Robert T. Valgenti, "Nietzsche the Communist? A Genealogy of Interpretation," in *Making Communism Hermeneutical*, ed. Mazzini and Glyn-Williams, 194.
99. Valgenti, "Nietzsche the Communist?," 194.
100. See Friedrich Nietzsche, *Ecce Homo: How to Become What You Are*, in *The Anti-Christ, Ecce Homo, Twilight of the Idols, and Other Writings*, ed. Aaron Ridley and Judith Norman (Cambridge University Press, 2005), 101.
101. Valgenti, "Nietzsche the Communist?," 200.
102. Valgenti, "Nietzsche the Communist?," 196, 202.
103. Valgenti, "Nietzsche the Communist?," 203.
104. Rory Carroll, "Noam Chomsky Criticises Old Friend Hugo Chávez for 'Assault' on Democracy," *The Guardian*, July 2, 2011, https://www.theguardian.com/world/2011/jul/03/noam-chomsky-hugo-chavez-democracy.

105. Valgenti, "Nietzsche the Communist," 194.
106. Gianni Vattimo and Santiago Zabala, "Response to Valgenti," in *Making Communism Hermeneutical*, ed. Mazzini and Glyn-Williams, 208.
107. Noam Chomsky, "Noam Chomsky on Revolutionary Violence, Communism, and the American Left," interview by Christopher Helali, *Pax Marxista*, March 12, 2013, https://Chomsky.info/20130312/.
108. One can usefully refer here to Vattimo's own reading of Nietzsche as found in his books *Nietzsche: An Introduction* and *Dialogue with Nietzsche*.

3. CATHOLICISM, SECULARITY, AND THE AGE OF THE SPIRIT

1. For example, Michael McGravey, "Jean-Luc Marion and Gianni Vattimo's Contributions for the Post-Modern Faith," PhD diss., Duquesne University, 2018; and Noëlle Vahanian, "Gianni Vattimo's Religion," *Los Angeles Review of Books*, November 10, 2016, https://lareviewofbooks.org/article/gianni-vattimos-religion/.
2. For example, see Peter Jonkers, "In the World, but Not of the World," *Bijdragen tijdschrift voor filosofie en theologie* 61 (2000): 370–89; and Frederiek Depoortere, *Christ in Postmodern Philosophy: Gianni Vattimo, René Girard, and Slavoj Žižek* (T&T Clark International, 2008).
3. See Vattimo, *Belief*, 41.
4. See Charles Taylor, *A Secular Age* (Belknap Press, 2007); Akeel Bilgrami, *Secularism, Identity, and Enchantment* (Harvard University Press, 2014); and José Casanova, *Public Religions in the Modern World* (University of Chicago Press, 1994). Cf. David S. Pacini, *The Cunning of Modern Religious Thought* (Fortress Press, 1987).
5. A *saeculum* is a period of time, an age, as in the present age. In Augustine, for example, all the "events of history" take place within God's time and purpose but are carried forward by individual and collective human activity. By contrast, the "story of history" narrates these events and finds those connections between them that further the sequence of human activity leading to the present. If one reads back through the events of history, those actions and connections that have led to our salvation, as in the biblical narrative, this narrative becomes a "sacred history," or history read as a *history of salvation* (*Heilsgeschichte*). All of history is not salvation history, except in the

very broadest of terms. Traditionally, there are those activities that relate to the course of human salvation and those that are merely the necessary conditions of existence in the "present age"—the latter is what is meant by the term *secular*. For example, taking the bus to work is a secular activity; prayer is not. As R. A. Markus has noted, "If 'history' is recorded, recounted and interpreted events, 'sacred history' is history to the recording, recounting and interpreting of which some special quality is attached. In calling a strand of history 'sacred,' no special claim is made on behalf of the mode of divine action in the events narrated and no special quality is attached to these events. The special quality resides in the narrative. The difference between 'sacred' and 'secular' history is therefore to be defined by distinguishing between two different kinds of narrative." Markus, *Saeculum: History and Society in the Theology of St. Augustine* (Cambridge University Press, 1970), 14.

6. Ingolf U. Dalferth, *Transcendence and the Secular World: Life in Orientation to Ultimate Presence*, 2nd rev. ed., trans. Jo Bennett (Mohr Siebeck, 2018), 12.

7. Gianni Vattimo and Carmelo Dotolo, *Dio: La possibilità buona. Un colloquio sulla soglia tra filosofia e teologia*, ed. Giovanni Giorgio (Rubbettino, 2009), §1, my translation.

8. This academic interest was preceded by the renewed social importance of religion, which reasserted itself in the mid-1970s and grew apace throughout the 1980s. This reassertion is reflected in varying ways by examples such as the spread of pan-Islamic ideologies (most notably in Iran and Afghanistan—largely in response to Western and Soviet imperialism), the importance of Catholicism to the Solidarity movement in Poland and to numerous conflicts in Latin America (especially to the Sandinistas in Nicaragua), and the growth of Protestant fundamentalism as a right-wing political force in the United States.

9. See Gregg Lambert, *Return Statements: The Return of Religion in Contemporary Philosophy* (Edinburgh University Press, 2016); and Phillip Blond, ed. *Post-Secular Philosophy: Between Philosophy and Theology* (Routledge, 1998).

10. In the opening lines of his book *The Puppet and the Dwarf*, Slavoj Žižek, referencing Benjamin, states: "Today . . . the historical materialist analysis is receding, practiced as it were under cover, rarely called by its proper name, while the theological dimension is given a new lease on life in the

guise of the 'postsecular' Messianic turn of deconstruction." Žižek, *The Puppet and the Dwarf: The Perverse Core of Christianity* (MIT Press, 2003), 3.

11. See Daniel Bell, *The End of Ideology: On the Exhaustion of Political Ideas in the Fifties*, 2nd ed. (Free Press, 1962); see also Daniel Strand, *No Alternatives: The End of Ideology in the 1950s and the Post-Political World of the 1990s* (Stockholm University Press, 2016).

12. Francis Fukuyama, *The End of History and the Last Man* (Free Press, 1992). Cf. Gianni Vattimo, "The End of (Hi)story," *Chicago Review* 35, no. 4 (1987): 20–30.

13. Nils Gilman, *Mandarins of the Future: Modernization Theory in Cold War America* (Johns Hopkins University Press, 2003), 56.

14. It should be noted that the opposite thesis advanced by Samuel Huntington—namely, that this collapse of ideological difference would merely set the stage for a so-called clash of civilizations between historically conditioned religiocultural spheres—while perhaps less naively optimistic than Fukuyama's argument, is (upon close inspection) no less monolithic, reductive, and, indeed, perniciously Eurocentric. See Samuel Huntington, "The Clash of Civilizations?," *Foreign Affairs* 72, no. 3 (Summer 1993): 22–49; and Huntington, *The Clash of Civilizations and the Remaking of World Order* (Simon and Schuster, 1996). Cf. Edward W. Said, "The Clash of Ignorance," *The Nation*, October 4, 2001; and Amartya Sen, *Identity and Violence: The Illusion of Destiny* (Norton, 2006).

15. See Friederike D. Rass, *Die Suche nach Wahrheit im Horizont fragmentarischer Existenzialität—eine Studie über den Sinn der Frage nach "Gott" in der Gegenwart in Auseinandersetzung mit Gianni Vattimo, John D. Caputo, und Jean-Luc Nancy* (Mohr Siebeck, 2017), 44–46.

16. Vattimo, *Belief*, 26.

17. Vattimo, *After Christianity*, 98.

18. Gustavo Gutiérrez, *A Theology of Liberation: History, Politics, and Salvation*, trans. and ed. Sister Caridad Inda and John Eagleson (1971; reprint, Orbis, 1973), 67–68, original emphasis.

19. Gianni Vattimo and René Girard, *Christianity, Truth, and Weakening Faith: A Dialogue*, ed. Pierpaolo Antonello, trans. William McCuaig (Columbia University Press, 2010), 35.

20. Vattimo and Caputo, *After the Death of God*, 45.

3. CATHOLICISM, SECULARITY, AND THE AGE OF THE SPIRIT ~ 269

21. See Joachim di Fiore, *Expositio in Apocalipsim* (c. 1196–1199) and *Liber concordiæ Novi ac Veteris Testamenti* (1200).
22. Both Frederiek Depoortere and Anthony C. Sciglitano Jr. have rightly pointed out the problematically supersessionistic undertones of this model. This is not changed even if we note that Vattimo does not view this division of history in "objective" terms but instead as merely a useful symbolic interpretation of his argument. Regardless of his intentions, anti-Judaism is implied in the argument. Both Depoortere and Sciglitano argue that Vattimo would therefore do better to find a model that expresses his argument without the crypto-Marcionite subtext present in Fiore. See Depoortere, *Christ in Postmodern Philosophy*, 13–17; and Anthony C. Sciglitano Jr., "Gianni Vattimo and Saint Paul: Ontological Weakening, Kenosis, and Secularity," in *Paul in the Grip of the Philosophers: The Apostle and Contemporary Continental Philosophy*, ed. Peter Frick (Fortress Press, 2013), 117–41.
23. Vattimo and Girard, *Christianity, Truth, and Weakening Faith*, 27.
24. Vattimo, *Belief*, 47.
25. See Dante Alighieri, *De Monarchia*, bk. 3; and Niccolò Machiavelli, *Discorsi sopra la prima deca di Tito Livio*, §12.
26. Chief among such forces were the members of the so-called Young Italy Movement (La Giovine Italia)—the two most notable figures of whom were Giuseppe Mazzini and Giuseppe Garibaldi. Though both men ultimately sought to establish a social-democratic government in a unified republic, they pragmatically threw their support behind the ambitious and reforming House of Savoy as the likeliest path toward achieving their short-term political goals.
27. See John Pollard, *Catholicism in Modern Italy: Religion, Society, and Politics Since 1861* (Routledge, 2008), 22–27.
28. It is telling that in July 1870 Vatican I issued *Pastor æternus*, defining, among other things, the doctrines of Petrine and papal primacy, papal supremacy, and papal infallibility. The growth of ultramontanism (and the corresponding decline of Gallicanism) in the church of this period cannot be separated from the political struggles in Italy during these decades. In particular, the events of the Revolutions of 1848 had notably soured the then young Pope Pius on the idea of liberalism. That year, the papal palace had been besieged by Italian nationalists, and the Papal State's minister of the interior, Count Pellegrino de Rossi, was assassinated by a revolutionary as he walked up the

stairs at the Palazzo della Cancelleria in Rome. These acts forced Pius to flee to Gaeta in Naples, where he spent the next year under the protection of Ferdinand II, "King Bomba" of the Two Sicilies. When he finally emerged from exile, it was as a starkly more conservative and reactionary pontiff. Indeed, Pius was so deeply affected by the events of 1848 that Italians began referring to him after this period as "Pio Nono Secondo" (Pius the Ninth, the Second). See James C. Livingston, *Modern Christian Thought*, vol. 1: *The Enlightenment and the Nineteenth Century*, 2nd ed. (Prentice Hall, 1997), 327–34.

29. The armies of the First French Republic invaded Italy in 1796 and later captured Rome, establishing the short-lived central-Italian Republic of Rome in 1798 (which, in turn, became the Kingdom of Italy when it was absorbed into the French Empire in 1805, and then the kingdom ended with the abdication of Napoleon in 1814). For a discussion of Rome in the imagination of the French during the revolutionary period, see Simon Schama, *Citizens: A Chronicle of the French Revolution* (Vintage, 1989), 169–74.

30. Such protection of papal sovereignty ultimately was likely to fail because Napoleon III supported the cause of Italian nationalization. Indeed, as John Pollard points out, in the secret Treaty of Plombières of 1858 Louis-Napoléon had agreed with the count of Cavour that in exchange for Cavour's part in the conflict with Austria, France would "acquire Lombardo-Venetia for Piedmont-Sardinia, in exchange for financial commitments and the cession of Nice and Savoy, both largely French-speaking territories but nevertheless traditional domains of the Savoyard dynasty" (Pollard, *Catholicism in Modern Italy*, 23). Even so, opposition from fervent Catholic supporters at home had caused Louis-Napoléon to capitulate over the question of Rome. This is why, for a time at least, he guaranteed the continuation of papal independence by offering military protection from the threat of Garibaldi's army. This protection is additionally ironic because Pius's predecessor in the seat of St. Peter, Pius VI, had famously died in Valence in 1799 as a prisoner of Napoleon I after the French army invaded the Papal States and demanded he relinquish his temporal authority.

31. The conflict between church and state arguably stretches back at least to the time of Constantine I (r. 306–37). Even so, canon lawyers of the medieval period reflected the distinction between ecclesiastical and secular authority primarily in the form of the Two Swords Doctrine intimated in

the letter from Pope Gelasius I to Emperor Anastasius, *Famuli vestræ pietatis* (494). Nevertheless, the formal claim concerning the primacy of church authority embodied in the papacy over the secular authority of kings was not officially promulgated until Pope Boniface VIII's bull *Unam sanctum* (1302).

32. This tendentious state of affairs was finally resolved with the ratification of the Lateran Pacts in June 1929. The agreement between the church and the king's government established Vatican City as an independent city-state under the control of the Holy See. The Italian government also agreed to retroactively compensate the church for the loss of the Papal States. After the dissolution of the monarchy and the establishment of the Italian Republic, recognition of the pacts was included in the Italian Constitution of 1948.

33. This causal relationship between capitalist exploitation and the poor's corresponding receptiveness to socialism was recognized in Pope Pius XI's anticommunist encyclical *Divini redemptoris* (promulgated in 1937).

34. Innocent III, "Ep. 401 ad Acerbum *'Sicut universitatis conditor'*" (1870), quoted in Oswald J. Reichel, *The See of Rome in the Middle Ages*, (Longmans, Green, 2017), 248 n. 3, my translation.

35. "King John Renders Homage and Fealty to Innocent III (1214)," in *Selected Letters of Pope Innocent III Concerning England*, ed. C. R. Cheney and W. H. Semple (Thomas Nelson, 1953), 177.

36. James Hennesey, "Leo XIII's Thomistic Revival: A Political and Philosophical Event," *Journal of Religion* 58, supplement (1978): S190, my emphasis.

37. Concerns among traditionalists about the growth of liberalism meant that prominent liberal Catholic figures such as Antonio Rosmini-Serbati, Vincenzo Gioberti, and Alessandro Manzoni were treated with suspicion by many in the church hierarchy. Furthermore, it is interesting to compare the Catholic Church's reaction to modernity and liberal theology with parallel developments occurring in Protestant thought (particularly in American Evangelicalism) during this same period. For example, at the same time that Vatican I was underway, Charles Hodge (a former student of the theological-liberal Friedrich Schleiermacher) was completing work on *Systematic Theology* (1871–1873), which in many ways helped to lay the groundwork for the development of conservative reform (or "Princeton") theology

and later of fundamentalism. Hodge, like Vatican I, was concerned about the influence of higher criticism and the erosion of confidence in traditional theological categories. Furthermore, just as conservative Catholics would eventually look back to the works of Aquinas for a stable Christian alternative to modernity, so too would many conservative Protestants during this time find their own antimodernist lodestar in the figure of John Calvin.

38. The groundwork for Leo XIII's letter had been established at Vatican I with the unanimous adoption of the Apostolic Constitution on Faith, *Dei Filius* (1870), which sought to clarify the church's position on the relationship between supernatural faith and natural reason. It affirmed that while God's existence and certain attributes could be inferred rationally, knowledge necessary for salvation depended on God's self-revelation and thus could not be arrived at by the light of natural reason alone. The practical effect of this program was the establishment of the Roman Academy of St. Thomas and the production of the critical *Editio Leonina* of his works. This also saw the founding of the Institut supérieur de philosophie in Louvain as a center for the study of Thomistic thought. A series of Catholic journals devoted to the promulgation of neo-Thomism also began at this time and in the following decades.

39. Livingston, *Modern Christian Thought*, 1:342.

40. Gerald A. McCool, SJ, *Nineteenth-Century Scholasticism: The Search for a Unitary Method* (Fordham University Press, 1989), 233, my emphasis.

41. Significant thinkers of the second generation of this movement included Cardinal Désiré-Joseph Mercier, Maurice de Wulf, Ambroise Gardeil, and Antonin Sertillanges. Importantly, each of these thinkers was not merely a reactionary apologist. Instead, they not only advanced the cause of the church in combating modernity but also made independent and notable contributions to the field of academic philosophy. For example, see T. E. Jessop, "The Philosophic Work of Cardinal Mercier," *Mind* 35, no. 138 (April 1926): 269–71; Fernand Van Steenberghen, "Maurice De Wulf: Historien de la philosophie médiévale," *Revue philosophique de Louvain* 46 (1948): 421–47; Camille de Belloy, "Ambroise Gardeil and the Fight to Study," *Revue des sciences philosophiques et théologiques* 92, no. 3 (2008): 423–32; and de Belloy, "A. D. Sertillanges, philosophe thomiste de la création," *Revue des sciences philosophiques et théologiques* 102, no. 3 (July-September 2018): 467–505.

3. CATHOLICISM, SECULARITY, AND THE AGE OF THE SPIRIT ⌘ 273

42. As a result, these men found their positions in the church compromised and their works restricted. Indeed, following his refusal to retract his writings, Tyrrell was even forced to leave the Jesuits, excommunicated, and ultimately denied a Catholic burial. See C. J. T. Talar, *"Pascendi dominici gregis*: The Vatican Condemnation of Modernism," in *"Pascendi dominici gregis:* 1907–2007: Centennial Essays on Responses to the Encyclical on Modernism," special issue, *U.S. Catholic Historian* 25, no. 1 (Winter 2007): 1–12.

43. Christopher M. Cullen, SJ, "Transcendental Thomism: Realism Rejected," in *The Failure of Modernism: The Cartesian Legacy and Contemporary Pluralism*, ed. Brendan Sweetman (American Maritain Association, 1999), 72.

44. Those familiar only with a certain popular image of Joseph Ratzinger (Benedict XVI) as a stalwart traditionalist might be initially surprised to find his name associated with a "progressive" Catholic movement. A common explanation for this apparent contradiction involves the assumption that Ratzinger must have been a liberal in his earlier days but that, in the words of Tracy Rowland, he became "so shocked by the student demonstrations at the University of Tübingen in 1968 that he has developed a pathological fear of 'the world' ever since." Rowland, "The World in the Theology of Joseph Ratzinger/Benedict XVI," *Journal of Moral Theology* 2, no. 2 (2013): 109. As Rowland goes on to point out, however, this is an oversimplified caricature. First, *nouvelle théologie* was more internally diverse than is sometimes acknowledged. Second, as Rahner and Ratzinger's former student Francis Schüssler Fiorenza has noted, "Whereas Rahner sought to relate concrete revelation to the more universal development of human consciousness, Ratzinger ... argued that the relation between scripture and tradition according to the Council of Trent is such that the Spirit is present when *an office holder in the hierarchy of the church* interprets tradition as clarifying the meaning of scriptures. Ratzinger's emphasis on ecclesial authority in the interpretation of scripture, his critique of the dominance of the historical critical approach, and his appeal to patristic resources for the interpretation of scriptures have remained constant features of his theological writings." Fiorenza, "From Theologian to Pope: A Personal View Back, Past the Public Portrayals," *Harvard Divinity Bulletin* 33 (2005), https://bulletin.hds.harvard.edu/from-theologian-to-pope/. Following Vatican II, the implications of Rahner's and Ratzinger's differing approaches simply became clearer. Therefore, in the years that followed, the more liberal

perspectives of the movement (e.g., Congar, Küng, Rahner, Chenu, Schillebeeckx, along with Rahner's student Johann Baptist Metz) became associated with the journal *Concilium*, while the more conservative perspective (e.g., Ratzinger, de Lubac, and von Balthasar) became connected to the journal *Communio*. See also Philip John Paul Gonzales, *Reimagining the Analogia Entis: The Future of Erich Przywara's Christian Vision* (Eerdmans, 2019), pt. 2, §5.

45. See Réginald Garrigou-Lagrange, "La nouvelle théologie, où va-t-elle?," *Angelicum* 23 (1946): 126–45.

46. Gerard Loughlin, "*Nouvelle Théologie*: A Return to Modernism?," in *Ressourcement: A Movement for Renewal in Twentieth-Century Catholic Theology*, ed. Gabriel Flynn and Paul D. Murray (Oxford University Press, 2012), 37.

47. José Míguez Bonino, *Doing Theology in a Revolutionary Situation* (Fortress Press, 1975), 9. Here Bonino is specifically referring to Spain of the same period, but this observation is arguably no less applicable to Italy. While the church, for example, opposed the regimes of Hitler, Mussolini, and Franco, it nevertheless considered the right-wing defense of traditionalism and hierarchy as preferable to either Bolshevism or Spanish anarchism. Cf. Elisa A. Carrillo, "The Italian Catholic Church and Communism, 1943–1963," *Catholic Historical Review* 77, no. 4 (October 1991): 644–57; and Giuliana Chamedes, "The Vatican, Nazi-Fascism, and the Making of Transnational Anti-Communism in the 1930s," *Journal of Contemporary History* 51, no. 2 (April 2016): 261–90.

48. Diarmaid MacCulloch, *Christianity: The First Three Thousand Years* (Penguin, 2009), 967.

49. The only previously mentioned figures associated with *nouvelle théologie* who did not play a significant role as an adviser at Vatican II were de Chardin, who had unfortunately passed away in 1955, several years before the council was convened, and von Balthasar, whose work was not yet well known enough at this point for him to have been invited.

50. Cardinal Avery Dulles, "The Sacramental Ecclesiology of 'Lumen gentium,'" *Gregorianum* 86, no. 3 (2005): 556. Cf. Joseph Ratzinger, "The Ecclesiology of the Constitution of the Church: *Lumen gentium*," and "The Local Church and the Universal Church," in *The Essential Pope Benedict XVI: His Central Writings and Speeches*, ed. John F. Thornton and Susan B. Varenne (HarperCollins, 2008), 85–102, 103–9.

51. The spirit of ecumenism had of course preceded this declaration. It had motivated the council to invite delegations of non-Catholics to be present at the sessions as observers. This intention is further felt in the declaration *Nostra aetate* (promulgated 1965), which discussed Catholics' relations with members of non-Christian religions (in particular the Jews). See Donald W. Norwood, "The Impact of Non-Roman Catholic Observers at Vatican II," *Ecclesiology* 10, no. 3 (2014): 293–312.
52. Paul VI, *Pastoral Constitution on the Church in the Modern World: Gaudium et spes*, 1965, chap. 4: "The Role of the Church in the Modern World," para. 42, my emphasis, http://www.vatican.va/archive/hist_councils/ii_vatican _council/documents/vat-ii_const_19651207_gaudium-et-spes_en.html. Cf. Joseph Xavier, "Theological Anthropology of 'Gaudium et spes' and Fundamental Theology," *Gregorianum* 91, no. 1 (2010), 124–36; and Walter Kasper, "The Theological Anthropology of *Gaudium et spes*," *Communio: International Catholic Review* 23 (1996): 129–40.
53. Both John Paul II and Benedict XVI, while obviously apprehensive or averse to certain changes, nevertheless remained in general agreement with the council's liberal or reforming spirit. This can be contrasted with various "traditionalist Catholic" movements and organizations that have subsequently emerged in reaction to Vatican II. Some traditionalists remain in good standing with the Holy See—accepting the council's legitimacy despite their own preference for the liturgical style of the Tridentine Mass or, more accurately, the Roman Missal of 1962. Indeed, Vattimo himself expressed a preference for the Latin Mass (see Vattimo, "Gianni Vattimo— Philosophy as Ontology of Actuality," 338). Others, however, have broken away from Rome—espousing Sedeprivationist or Sedevacantist positions with respect to the post–Vatican II popes. See Matthew L. Lamb and Matthew Levering, eds., *Vatican II: Renewal Within Tradition* (Oxford University Press, 2009); and Gerald O'Collins, SJ, and Mario Farrugia, SJ, *Catholicism: The Story of Catholic Christianity*, 2nd ed. (Oxford University Press, 2015), 403–15.

4. RELIGION AND THE (POST)SECULAR WORLD

1. "There had been a time when I no longer attended Mass, although I had never indulged in polemical attacks on my own religious heritage or the

Church as such." Vattimo, "Gianni Vattimo—Philosophy as Ontology of Actuality," 329.
2. Vattimo and Paterlini, *Not Being God*, 149.
3. Vattimo, "Gianni Vattimo—Philosophy as Ontology of Actuality," 335.
4. Jean-François Lyotard, *The Post-Modern Condition: A Report on Knowledge*, trans. Geoff Bennington and Brian Massumi (University of Minnesota Press, 1984), 39. See also Jean-François Lyotard and Jean-Loup Thébaud, *Just Gaming*, trans. Wlad Godzich (University of Minnesota Press, 1985); and Lyotard, "Lessons in Paganism" (1989), in *The Lyotard Reader*, ed. Andrew Benjamin (Blackwell, 1998), 122–54.
5. Vattimo, *Belief*, 28.
6. Vattimo, "Gianni Vattimo—Philosophy as Ontology of Actuality," 335.
7. Vattimo and Paterlini, *Not Being God*, 150.
8. Vattimo and Girard, *Christianity, Truth, and Weakening Faith*, 27.
9. *Things Hidden* builds on concepts introduced by Girard in his earlier works *Mensonge romantique et vérité romanesque* (1961; published in English as *Deceit, Desire, and the Novel: Self and Other in Literary Structure*, 1965) and *La violence et le sacré* (translated as *Violence and the Sacred*, 1972).
10. It's worth noting that in spite of his obvious and impressive erudition, Girard has frequently been accused of being overly simplistic and reductive, in part because he frequently published in areas outside the scope of his scholarly expertise. Girard was trained primarily as a historian and initially gained recognition as a literary critic. Even so, in addition to these areas, his work sought to drawn together such diverse fields as anthropology, sociology, psychology (including psychoanalysis), neuroscience, economics, cultural studies, evolutionary biology, theology, and philosophy. Although many of these areas obviously share significant overlaps, critics have often objected to what they perceived as his "cherry-picking" of evidence to suit his theory, while disregarding counterexamples or the potential of alternative understandings of the texts under consideration. Girard would often respond to such charges by comparing his own approach with that of Darwin, from whose writings, he (rightly) noted, thinkers often make wide-ranging claims and generalizations. The domain of applicability regarding evolutionary explanations is itself, though, a matter of some contention. Perhaps most importantly for the present discussion, however, is the criticism by folklorists, anthropologists, and scholars of religion, who point out

4. RELIGION AND THE (POST)SECULAR WORLD ⌘ 277

(among other things) the paucity of evidence supporting such claims as well as the often-apologetic nature of their presentation. With respect to its treatment of myth, at least, Girard's theory much more resembles "academic curios" like Joseph Campbell's "monomyth" and Carl Jung's "universal archetypes," each of which also makes questionable and instrumental use of comparative mythology. See, for example, François Aubral, "René Girard: *La violence et le sacré*," *Les cahiers du chemin* 17 (January 15, 1973): 192–205; David Graeber and Marshall Sahlins, *On Kings* (Hau, 2017), 71–72; as well as Michael Kirwan, *Girard and Theology* (T&T Clark, 2009).

11. See Nikolaus Wandinger, "Religion and Violence: A Girardian Overview," *Journal of Religion and Violence* 1, no. 2 (2013): 127–46.
12. Vattimo, *Belief*, 37.
13. See Jan Bremmer, "Scapegoat Rituals in Ancient Greece," *Harvard Studies in Classical Philology* 87 (1983): 299–320.
14. Girard's reading of Sophocles has been contested by classicists. See, for example, R. Drew Griffith, "Oedipus Pharmakos? Alleged Scapegoating in Sophocles' *Oedipus the King*," *Phoenix* 47, no. 2 (Summer 1993): 95–114.
15. René Girard, *Things Hidden Since the Foundation of the World*, trans. Stephen Bann and Michael Metteer (1978; reprint, Stanford University Press, 1987), 166.
16. Girard, *Things Hidden*, 167.
17. Girard, *Things Hidden*, 169–70.
18. In conversation with Girard, Pierpaolo Antonello and João Cezar de Castro Rocha raised the objection that the exclusivity of his claims regarding Christianity appear to ignore nonsacrificial religious systems such as Jainism and Buddhism. In response, Girard claimed that while Jainism and Buddhism progressively eliminated sacrifice, they did not "unmask" the anthropological mechanism of mimetic scapegoating that underpins the impulse to sacrifice in the way that the Gospels did. Needless to say, as rebuttals go, his appears to be rather facile. See René Girard, Pierpaolo Antonello, and João Cezar de Castro Rocha, *Evolution and Conversion: Dialogues on the Origin of Culture* (T&T Clark, 2007), 212–14.
19. In presenting this argument in objective metaphysical terms, Girard opens himself up to the criticism that his position ignores or "hand-waves away" the obvious counterexample of Christian violence—thereby engaging in "special pleading" or committing the "no true Scotsman" fallacy.

20. "The very concept of 'religion' is a product of Western culture, and the modern configuration of the sacred reflects a deeply Protestant view of proper religious piety. Abstracting various systems of belief and practice from diverse non-Western cultures and measuring those cultures by how closely their 'religious' systems conform to this narrow, normative Western model is a vivid example of cultural imperialism. The postcolonial critique of Western scholarly disciplines has underscored the dissonance in applying this modern Western notion of the sacred to other cultural landscapes; while it purports to produce human unity, the notion runs roughshod over meaningful cultural difference." Randall Styers, "Gianni Vattimo and the Return of the Sacred," *Annali d'italianistica* 25 (2007): 48–49. Cf. David Nirenberg, *Anti-Judaism: The Western Tradition* (Norton, 2014).

21. See G. W. F. Hegel, *Lectures on the Philosophy of Religion*, one-volume ed.: *The Lectures of 1827*, ed. Peter C. Hodgson, trans. Robert F. Brown et al. (University of California Press, 1988), pt. 3; F. D. E. Schleiermacher, *On Religion: Speeches to Its Cultured Despisers* (1799), §5; and F. Max Müller, *Lectures on the Origin and Growth of Religion* (1878).

22. See E. B. Tyler, *Primitive Culture* (1871), James George Frazer, *The Golden Bough* (1890), and Sigmund Freud, *Totem and Taboo* (1913). These perspectives tended to differ from those of writers such as Rudolf Otto, William James, and Émile Durkheim, who, while acknowledging religious development, nevertheless grounded their theories in examinations of "religious experience"—making comparisons between distinct belief systems (including science) largely irrelevant. See William James, *The Varieties of Religious Experience* (1902); Émile Durkheim, *The Elementary Forms of Religious Life* (1912); and Rudolf Otto, *The Idea of the Holy* (1917). For additional discussion of the relationship between myth and progress, see Mircea Eliade, *The Sacred and the Profane: The Nature of Religion*, trans. Williard R. Trask (Harcourt, Brace and World, 1987), 216–32; Ludwig Wittgenstein, *The Mythology in Our Language: Remarks on Frazer's "Golden Bough,"* ed. Giovanni da Col and Stephen Palmié, trans. Stephen Palmié (Hau, 2018).

23. The intellectual inheritors of this mode of scientistic Western chauvinism are without a doubt the so-called New Atheists, who attained a significant level of popular notoriety during the years of the war on terror because of their rationalized defenses of anti-Muslim sentiment and hawkish U.S. foreign policy—all supposedly in defense of "Enlightenment values." See

Luke Savage, "New Atheism, Old Empire," *Jacobin Magazine*, December 2, 2014, https://jacobin.com/2014/12/new-atheism-old-empire/.
24. Tomoko Masuzawa, *The Invention of World Religions: Or, How European Universalism Was Preserved in the Language of Pluralism* (University of Chicago Press, 2005), 12.
25. Rudyard Kipling, "The White Man's Burden," *McClure's Magazine*, February 1899.
26. Vattimo and Paterlini, *Not Being God*, 151.
27. Cf. Vattimo and Caputo, *After the Death of God*, 27–31. This difference from Girard is subtly reflected in the way Vattimo changes his authorial voice from the third person to the first person when speaking about religion.
28. I suppose one could conceivably object that by making this distinction in the first place, I am committing the selfsame conceptual move that I am criticizing; that is, by pointing out this "limitation," I am, in effect, ranking a metaphysical-objectivist model below a postmetaphysical hermeneutical model. To return to the analogy of language, though, pointing out features and distinctions of languages (or religions) is different from ranking them. For example, one could point out that standard English, unlike many other languages, lacks a formal second-person pronoun (like the German *Sie* or the Spanish *usted*). It seems rather silly, however, to think that such an observation should imply that English is thereby deficient in its ability to convey complex ideas. This manner of objection is what Wittgenstein referred to as merely "playing with words"—it is a kind of argumentative ouroboros that qualifies without either objective or end. See Ludwig Wittgenstein, *Philosophical Investigations*, 4th rev. ed., ed. and trans. G. E. M. Anscombe, P. M. S. Hacker, and Joachim Schulte (Wiley-Blackwell, 2009), §67.
29. See Jerome I. Gellman, "Religion as Language," *Religious Studies* 21, no. 2 (June 1985): 159–68. Cf. Ludwig Wittgenstein, *Culture and Value: A Selection from the Posthumous Remains*, ed. Georg Henrik von Wright (in collaboration with Heikki Nyman), trans. Peter Winch (Blackwell, 1998), 27–33; and Willard Van Orman Quine, "On Empirically Equivalent Systems of the World," *Erkenntnis* 9, no. 3 (November 1975): 313–28.
30. A *blik* (Dutch: "look," Danish: "glance") describes the unverifiable/unfalsifiable interpretation of one's own personal experience. For Hare, religious language does not represent rival data or even a distinct explanatory hypothesis from science, but rather a general disposition not subject to

empirical evidence. See R. M. Hare, "Theology and Falsification," in *New Essays in Philosophical Theology*, ed. Antony Flew and Alasdair MacIntyre (MacMillan, 1955), 99–103.

Regarding the "invisible gardener," Wisdom asks us to imagine that two people return from an extended trip and find that their long-neglected garden is thriving. One of the travelers suggests that a gardener must have been tending the garden in their absence. The second person is skeptical. They decide to resolve the matter through observation. Through a series of increasingly unlikely qualifications, the first traveler decides that the mysterious gardener must be invisible and intangible (so as to avoid their detection). The second person remains unconvinced and concludes that there is simply no gardener. A more famous construal of Wisdom's "invisible gardener" story appears in Anthony Flew's essay "Theology and Falsification," to which Hare is responding. However, in Wisdom's original argument, he utilizes the story as an example of the noncognitivist principle that people need not disagree about the facts to envision or characterize the same state of affairs differently. In such a case, it may be argued that respondents are not offering mutually exclusive informational claims but are instead describing their respective dispositions relative to the same facts. In such cases, the appropriateness of these principles is not settleable by recourse to the principle of verification advanced by logical positivists. See John Wisdom, "Gods," initially published in *Proceedings of the Aristotelian Society* (944–1945), reprinted in Wisdom, *Philosophy and Psycho-Analysis* (Blackwell, 1953), 154–55.

31. One could even say that a person's preference for their hometown team has little to do with the team itself and more to do with its being from the fan's hometown. That is, the fandom is based on the team's identity with place and the nexus of associations, relations, memories, and camaraderie that it represents for the fan. There is also the feeling of participation in a collective struggle and the pathos that it generates in both victory and loss. From such a perspective, measuring a team's "greatness" by the number of times it scores seems to misunderstand (in an almost vulgar manner) the various ways in which the game intersects the lives of its participants.

32. See Israel Scheffler, *Symbolic Worlds: Art, Science, Language, Ritual* (Cambridge University Press, 1997).

4. RELIGION AND THE (POST)SECULAR WORLD ◈ 281

33. One can see this continued "trace" in the example of France. As Craig Calhoun has noted, "France proclaims secularism, or *laïcité*, not simply as a policy choice but as part of its national identity. It is, however, a '*Catholaïcité*' shaped like French identity not just by generally Christian history but also by Catholic culture, its struggle against and ascendancy over Protestantism, and then the challenge brought by revolutionary and republican assertions of the primacy of citizenship over devotion. There remains a cross atop the Pantheon, a sign not only of its history as a church before it became a monument to the heroes of the secular state but also of the compromises between religion and *laïcité* that shape France today. These are informed by a specific history of anticlericalism, itself shaped not just by a long history of priestly involvement in politics, education, and other dimensions of social life but also by a strong reactionary effort to intensify that involvement during the nineteenth and early twentieth centuries. Thus secularism shapes the French response to Islamic immigrants, but hardly as a neutral category unrelated to its own religious history." Calhoun, "Time, World, and Secularism," in *The Post-Secular in Question: Religion in Contemporary Society*, ed. Philip S. Gorski et al. (New York University Press/Social Science Research Council, 2012), 336. Cf. Vattimo, *After Christianity*, 93–102; and Carl Schmitt, *Political Theology: Four Chapters on the Concept of Sovereignty*, trans. George Schwab (University of Chicago Press, 2005), 36–52.
34. See Vattimo, *After Christianity*, 7–9.
35. Vattimo and Caputo, *After the Death of God*, 36.
36. See Thomas Ryba, "Girard and Augustine," in *The Palgrave Handbook of Mimetic Theory and Religion*, ed. James Alison and Wolfgang Palaver (Palgrave-Macmillan, 2017), 209–16.
37. Vattimo, "Gianni Vattimo—Philosophy as Ontology of Actuality," 335.
38. See Walter Wink, *The Powers That Be: Theology for a New Millennium* (Doubleday, 1998), 42–62.
39. Vattimo and Paterlini, *Not Being God*, 150.
40. In Vattimo's view, the work of Christ is not about satisfying the wrath of God by atoning for sin, defeating the devil, or fulfilling a binding stipulation in a contract between God and humanity. Rather, it is about God's own self-identification with the suffering of humanity. It is about a self-giving love and desire for intimacy. It would perhaps be going too far to

fully associate Vattimo's position in this regard with similar positions advanced by theologians such as Robert Jenson, Jürgen Moltmann, and Eberhard Jüngel. Indeed, Vattimo does not discuss the doctrine of atonement (or nearly any other finer point of theology) in great detail. Even so, there is arguably enough affinity here to suggest that it could be fruitful grounds for a constructive dialogue. See Robert W. Jenson, *Systematic Theology*, vol. 2: *The Works of God* (Oxford University Press, 1999); Jürgen Moltmann, *The Crucified God: The Cross of Christ as the Foundation and Criticism of Christian Theology* (Fortress Press, 1993); and Eberhard Jüngel, *Death: The Riddle and the Mystery*, trans. Iain Nicol and Ute Nicol (St. Andrew Press, 1975). Cf. Jack D. Kilcrease, *The Doctrine of Atonement: From Luther to Forde* (Wipf and Stock, 2018).

41. Against the "spiritualizing" depictions of Jesus that attempt to cast him as apolitical, John Howard Yoder has instead argued, "*Because* Jesus' particular way of rejecting the sword and at the same time condemning those who wielded it *was* politically relevant, both the Sanhedrin and the Procurator had to deny him the right to live, in the name of both their forms of political responsibility. His alternative was so relevant, so much a threat, that Pilate could afford to free, in exchange for Jesus, the ordinary Guevara-type insurrectionist Barabbas. Jesus' way is not less but more relevant to the question of how society moves than is the struggle for possession of the levers of command; to this Pilate and Caiaphas testify by their judgment on him." Yoder, *The Politics of Jesus* (Eerdmans, 1972), 111–12, original emphasis.

42. Richard Rohr, *The Universal Christ: How a Forgotten Reality Can Change Everything We See, Hope For, and Believe* (Convergent, 2019), 119. Rohr attributes this argument to John Duns Scotus, but he does not provide the original citation, and I have been unable to independently verify the ascription.

43. Dietrich Bonhoeffer, *Letters and Papers from Prison*, enlarged ed. (SCM Press, 1971) 36, quoted in Moltmann, *The Crucified God*, 47.

44. Dietrich Bonhoeffer, "To Erich Seeburg, Berlin, April 21, 1933," in *Dietrich Bonhoeffer Works*, vol. 12: *Berlin: 1932–1933*, ed. Larry L. Rasmussen, trans. Isabel Best and David Higgins (Fortress Press, 2009), 104.

45. One need not stress this emphasis too much in the opposite direction. Barth, of course, saw Christ as forming a bridge to this otherwise alien and unknowable God. Likewise, Levinas and Derrida were not without their

4. RELIGION AND THE (POST)SECULAR WORLD ⌘ 283

own conceptions of mediation between humanity and radical transcendence. See Renée D. N. van Riessen, *Man as a Place of God: Levinas' Hermeneutics of Kenosis* (Springer, 2007). Vattimo also argued, "I know that in [my position on kenosis] there is a danger of pantheism, of immanentism. But the danger is only if this immanence is opposed to a transcendence always of an objectifying type. As if this immanentization meant equating God with worldly reality. In reality, immanentism and transcendentalism are two sides of the same metaphysical objectivizing position." Vattimo and Dotolo, *Dio*, §1, my translation.

46. Cf. Vattimo, *Belief*, 38–43. Kenotic Christologies, which focus on the human nature/immanence of Christ (in contrast to the traditional focus on the divinity of the second person of the Trinity) are a logical consequence of Chalcedon's proclamation of the dual natures of Christ. Even so, modern kenotic Christologies (as we currently understand them) did not become prominent until the Reformation, with figures such as Matthias Hafenreffer, Lukas Osiander, Melchior Nicolai, Balthasar Mentzer, and Justus Feuerborn advancing their own positions. In the nineteenth century, interest in kenotic Christology expanded greatly with the work of Gottfried Thomasius, Wolfgang Gess, K. T. A. Liebner, J. C. K. von Hofmann, and others. To date, however, kenotic thought has largely been restricted to the domain of Protestant discourse. Given the nature of Vattimo's appropriation of the term *kenotic* and its specific use within his thought, there seems little utility in explaining here the finer points of the concept's history (for example, the disagreement between the theologians of Tübingen and those of Giessen). For a broader discussion, see David R. Law, *Kierkegaard's Kenotic Christology* (Oxford University Press, 2013), 34–63; C. Stephen Evans, ed., *Exploring Kenotic Christology: The Self-Emptying of God* (Oxford University Press, 2006); Paul Nimmo and Keith L. Johnson, eds., *Kenosis: The Self-Emptying of Christ in Scripture and Theology* (Eerdmans, 2022); and Felice Cimatti, "Kenosis," in *The Vattimo Dictionary*, ed. Moro, 112–15.
47. Vattimo and Girard, *Christianity, Truth, and Weakening Faith*, 49; Vattimo and Dotolo, *Dio*, §1, my translation.
48. Vattimo, *Belief*, 55.
49. Vattimo, *Belief*, 77.
50. Vattimo and Caputo, *After the Death of God*, 41.

51. This principle was originally formulated by N. L. Wilson and has since gained notoriety through the work of Willard Van Orman Quine and Donald Davidson. See N. L. Wilson, "Substance Without Substrata," *Review of Metaphysics* 12 (1959): 521–39; Willard Van Orman Quine, *Word and Object* (1960; reprint, MIT Press, 2013); and Donald Davidson, "On the Very Idea of a Conceptual Scheme," *Proceedings and Addresses of the American Philosophical Association* 47 (1973–1974): 5–20.
52. Gianni Vattimo, "The Christian Message and the Dissolution of Metaphysics," in *The Blackwell Companion to Postmodern Theology*, ed. Graham Ward (Blackwell, 2001), 460.
53. Vattimo, "Gianni Vattimo—Philosophy as Ontology of Actuality," 336.
54. S. Agostino, *De magistro—De vera religione*, ed. Domenico Bassi (Edizioni Testi Cristiani, 1930), 264.
55. Gianni Vattimo, Pierangelo Sequeri, and Giovanni Ruggeri, *Interrogazioni sul cristianesimo: Cosa possiamo ancora attenderci dal Vangelo?* (Fossano, 2000), 48–49, quoted in Carmelo Dotolo, "The Hermeneutics of Christianity and Philosophical Responsibility," in *Weakening Philosophy: Essays in Honour of Gianni Vattimo*, ed. Santiago Zabala (McGill-Queen's University Press, 2007), 361. For me, at least, this calls to mind a quote from C. S. Lewis: "I believe in Christianity as I believe that the sun has risen, not only because I see it but because by it, I see everything else." Lewis, "Is Theology Poetry?," in *The Weight of Glory and Other Addresses* (1976; reprint, HarperCollins, 2001), 140.

5. AGAINST NIHILISM: VATTIMO AND HIS CRITICS

1. For a discussion of Heidegger's complicated relationship to Aristotle, see Pangiotis Thanassas, "Phronesis and Sophia: On Heidegger's Ambivalent Aristotelianism," *Review of Metaphysics* 66, no. 1 (September 2012): 31–59.
2. Richard Bernstein argues that *phrónēsis* (φρόνησις), practical philosophy, represented the "underlying common vision" of thinkers such as Gadamer, Habermas, Rorty, and Hannah Arendt. See Richard J. Bernstein, *Beyond Objectivism and Relativism: Science, Hermeneutics, and Praxis* (Blackwell, 1983); and Bernstein, *The New Constellation: The Ethical-Political Horizons of Modernity/Postmodernity* (1991; reprint, Polity Press, 2007). Cf. Manfred Riedel, ed., *Zur Rehabilitierung der praktischen Philosophie*, 2 vols.

(Rombach, 1972, 1974); Alessandro Ferrara, *Reflective Authenticity: Rethinking the Project of Modernity* (1998; reprint, Routledge, 2002); and David E. Tabachnick, "'Phronesis,' Democracy, and Technology," *Canadian Journal of Political Science/Revue canadienne de science politique* 37, no. 4 (December 2004): 997–1016.

3. The deliberative character of *phronesis* distinguishes it from mere "common sense" (αἴσθησις κοινή, *sensus communis*). This interest in practical philosophy can also be seen in the revival of *aretaic* (virtue) ethics in recent decades. For example, see the works of Elizabeth Anscombe, Philippa Foot, Alasdair MacIntyre, and Rosalind Hursthouse. For her part, Hursthouse has discussed the possible motivations for resurrecting an ethical system born in antiquity, given that the modern world has developed two major moral theories in the respective works of Immanuel Kant and Jeremy Bentham. She concludes that the system's reemergence likely stems from dissatisfaction with the overly rationalistic deontological and utilitarian systems concerning their treatment of issues such as motives, moral character, relational obligations, and wisdom. Conventionally, the distinction between aretaic ethics and modern ethical systems is that the latter are concerned with *what we ought to do*, whereas the former is concerned rather with *who we ought to be*. In this way, aretaic ethics is perceived by its proponents as providing a more holistic account of our moral concerns and practices. See Rosalind Hursthouse, *On Virtue Ethics* (Oxford University Press, 1999).

4. Despite these delineations, Aristotle's account is not systematic. More importantly, for our purposes, there is little reason to attempt to clarify the Aristotelean model any further. These categories are here presented as more suggestive than dogmatic. See Aristotle, *Nicomachean Ethics*, bk. 6, and Epictetus, *Discourses*, II. Cf. Sarah Broadie, *Ethics with Aristotle* (Oxford University Press, 1991), 179–265.

5. Hans-Georg Gadamer, "Hermeneutics and Social Science," *Cultural Hermeneutics* 2, no. 4 (1975): 312.

6. Cf. Bertrand Russell, *The Problems of Philosophy* (1912; reprint, Oxford University Press, 1997), chap. 15. Many critics would of course scoff at the very suggestion that postmodernism is in any sense "practical" or "pragmatic." Indeed, the most common characterization of postmodern works is that they represent the apex of academic self-indulgence—obscure, pedantic, self-referential, and ultimately vapid. No doubt when applied to certain

(usually minor) figures, such criticism is sometimes warranted. In most instances, however, as in the case of Derrida, it fails to properly account for what these authors are actually doing and the context in which they are doing it. In that respect, they are no less *practical* than a paper written in a field such as theoretical physics that is laden with its own jargon and thus incomprehensible to the average reader outside the field of specialization. As with physics, though, while the language is often dense (sometimes needlessly so), the concepts contained within do indeed have practical and pragmatic value.

7. Vattimo once said, "I always try to reduce ethics to the problem of charity, to the problem of relationship with others. Kant would agree with this: 'Always consider your neighbor never as a simple means but always as an end.'" Gianni Vattimo et al., "*Fratelli tutti*: Dialogo con Gianni Vattimo," in *Fratelli tutti? Credenti e non credenti in dialogo con Papa Francesco*, ed. Debora Tonelli (Castelvecchi, 2022), 149, my translation.

8. Richard Rorty, "Introduction: Metaphilosophical Difficulties of Linguistic Philosophy," in *The Linguistic Turn: Essays in Philosophical Method, with Two Retrospective Essays*, ed. Richard Rorty (1967; reprint, University of Chicago Press, 1992), 2.

9. In some sense, there will always be a limit to such a procedure. That is, one can never fully escape the potential for misjudging a worldview by unfairly measuring it against the standards of one's own position. This is why a truly pluralistic and democratic exchange of ideas relies upon charity.

10. Sparrow, *The End of Phenomenology*, 12.

11. Quoted in Pol Vandevelde, "Edmund Husserl," in *The Blackwell Companion to Hermeneutics*, ed. Niall Keane and Chris Lawn (Wiley Blackwell, 2016), §46.

12. Russell, *The Problems of Philosophy*, 97–98, original emphasis.

13. Ferraris, *Manifesto of New Realism*, 39.

14. This is why Wittgenstein once remarked, "If a lion could talk, we wouldn't be able to understand it." That is, either the lion or we would have to become quite different creatures in order to bridge the ultimately insurmountable divide between our different modes of consciousness and respective experiences of the world. Wittgenstein, *Philosophical Investigations*, 327.

15. On this question, see Thomas Nagel, "What Is It Like to Be a Bat?," *Philosophical Review* 83, no. 4 (1974): 435–50.

16. John Locke, *An Essay Concerning Human Understanding* (1690), bk. 2, chap. 1, §19.
17. In a comment as bizarrely hyperbolic as it is amusing, Ferraris claims that the use of quotation marks around objects, such as "real," began as a Husserlian gesture to indicate *epoché*, or the suspension of judgment. Now, he claims, it is performed reflexively as "a protocol of *political correctness* by which one proclaims that whoever [dares to] remove the inverted commas would be performing an act of inacceptable violence." Ferraris, *Manifesto of New Realism*, 5. This comment, I must admit, seems to reflect the general overdefensive and polemical tone of his book. To be quite frank concerning this point, though, the idea that a practice—especially one as seemingly innocuous as the use of quotation marks—has shifted into common practice not because of its persuasiveness but rather because its users secretly fear reprisals or recriminations from an imagined "thought police" seems, not to put too fine a point on it, *unrealistic*.
18. Gianni Vattimo, *Of Reality: The Purposes of Philosophy*, trans. Robert T. Valgenti (Columbia University Press, 2016), 102.
19. It bears repeating that the critique of the Enlightenment that one finds in thinkers such as Horkheimer and Adorno is not a pyrrhonistic recoiling from any and all claims of ascertainable knowledge. Instead, it is an intellectual excavation of the remnants of a world then only recently torn apart by the actions of men who claimed to lead the most technologically and culturally advanced countries that humanity had ever known. What these thinkers concluded is that, in retrospect, "Enlightenment philosophers were blind to the limitations and dangers of their own project. . . . In the conflict between nature and the human species reason becomes the tool with which nature is brought under our control. . . . Reason, in its efforts to subdue the world, is itself overwhelmed by computation and technique; instead of referring to our critical capacity to orient ourselves in a reality that is always not wholly of our choosing, reason becomes identified with natural science. In the modern, enlightened world what 'men want to learn from nature is how to use it in order wholly to dominate it and other men. Ruthlessly, in spite of itself, the Enlightenment has extinguished any trace of its own self-consciousness.'" Howard Williams, "An Enlightenment Critique of *The Dialectic of Enlightenment*," in *The Enlightenment World*, ed. Martin Fitzpatrick et al. (Routledge, 2004), 640, quoting Horkheimer and Adorno, *Dialectic of Enlightenment*, 4.

20. For example, the so-called radical orthodoxy of John Milbank has come under fire for seeming to use postmodern criticism in this way—namely, as a shield with which to retreat back to a more naive and insular theological discourse. Unlike the postliberal narrative theology of the Yale School, which under Wittgenstein's influence viewed Christian theology as a distinct religious language among others and attempted to address how one could live constructively in a pluralistic society while affirming the particularity of one's own faith, radical orthodoxy essentially hits the same argumentative beats as Barth's critique of Bultmann. Likewise, it has opened itself up to the same criticism of advancing a fideism whose claims of revelation are seemingly immune from all potential criticism. As with Barth, the fairness of this critique is a matter of some debate. See John Milbank, *Theology and Social Theory: Beyond Secular Reason*, 2nd ed. (Blackwell, 2006); and John Milbank et al., eds., *Radical Orthodoxy: A New Theology* (Routledge, 1999).

21. In this regard, Ferrari provocatively claims that postmodernity has its very origin and natural home in the reactionary irrationalism and traditionalism of the Counter-Enlightenment (with figures such as Joseph de Maistre and Juan Donoso Cortés). Given the very tenuous nature of this link between postmodern thinkers and arch-Catholic reactionary figures such as de Maistre and Donoso Cortés, Ferrari's decision to make this connection can only be seen as a deliberate rhetorical choice or an instance of apophenia. Surely, a greater connection to postmodernity could be drawn, for example, from a figure such as Giambattista Vico. Other right-wing figures to which Ferraris points are Nietzsche, Heidegger, and Schmitt (though, curiously, not Paul De Man). These connections can arguably be explained better by the notion of romantic anticapitalism. Regardless, the notion that postmodernity is somehow essentially "right-wing" because of these early conservative connections ignores far too much contextual information and subsequent history to be taken seriously.

22. It is also perhaps worth pointing out that Ferraris's characterization of "political correctness" (or what has more recently been referred to in the United States as "wokeness") is indistinguishable from a common right-wing talking point to this effect. It does not have the marks of a real substantive criticism.

23. As a specific extreme example, Ferraris refers to the work of Paul Feyerabend, whose commitment to a "methodological anarchism" in the sciences

has led him to defend even such universally disparaged ideas as astrology and creationism. See Feyerabend's books *Against Method* (1975), *Science in a Free Society* (1978), and *Farewell to Reason* (1987). In more general terms, the problem of how far a society should tolerate ideologies that potentially undermine the very existence of a social order that aims at a maximally free and democratic system of governance was famously treated by Karl Popper in *The Open Society and Its Enemies* (1945). There, Popper concludes that the paradox of tolerance is that an unlimited tolerance of "intolerant" ideologies will lead to the destruction of a tolerant society. In other words, exclusivism is inimical to an open society. As a matter of discernment regarding disparaged ideas, here also the notion of phronesis can play an important role in social discourse regarding the limits of acceptability and what to do about it.

24. Lee McIntyre, *Post-Truth* (MIT Press, 2018), 126, my emphasis.
25. Conway's comments were made in an interview with host Chuck Todd on the NBC show *Meet the Press*, January 22, 2017, https://www.nbcnews.com/meet-the-press/video/conway-press-secretary-gave-alternative-facts-860142147643. She was defending the false statements made by Spicer at his first press conference. See "Statement by Press Secretary Sean Spicer," January 21, 2017, https://trumpwhitehouse.archives.gov/briefings-statements/statement-press-secretary-sean-spicer/; and "User Clip: Sean Spice January 21, 2017," https://www.c-span.org/video/?c4892491/user-clip-sean-spice-january-21-2017.
26. Giuliani's comments were also made in a separate interview with Chuck Todd. See "Giuliani: 'Truth Isn't Truth,'" *Meet the Press*, August 19, 2018, https://www.nbcnews.com/meet-the-press/video/giuliani-truth-isn-t-truth-1302113347986.
27. Blaming leftists and progressives for society's supposed state of "cultural decline" is hardly new. Consider, for example, the long-standing far-right (and frequently antisemitic) conspiracy theories concerning so-called degenerate art (*Entartete Kunst*) and "cultural Bolshevism" (*Kulturbolschewismus*), the latter almost indistinguishable from more recent right-wing criticisms of so-called postmodern neo-Marxism. This more recent iteration of the idea, which blames a host of societal problems on the academic prevalence of Derridean deconstruction and the critical theory of the Frankfurt School, has appeared in the manifestos of white-supremacist

terrorists such as Anders Breivik and John T. Earnest. Of course, it is more than incidental for the shaping of the conspiracy that Marx, Derrida, and most of the members of the Frankfurt School were Jewish. More recently, this conspiracy has also been mainstreamed on the political right in the English-speaking world by right-wing public figures such as Jordan Peterson. See, for example, Tanner Mirrlees, "The Alt-Right's Discourse of 'Cultural Marxism': A Political Instrument of Intersectional Hate," *Atlantis Journal* 31, no. 1 (2018): 49–69; cf. Dennis Dworkin, *Cultural Marxism in Postwar Britain: History, the New Left, and the Origins of Cultural Studies* (Duke University Press, 1997).

28. Alessia Ricciardi, *After "La dolce vita": A Cultural Prehistory of Berlusconi's Italy* (Stanford University Press, 2012), 148–49.

29. In spite of the popular tendency to assume that standards of living rise in proportion to technological innovation (à la Steven Pinker), there are plenty of reasons to assume that conditions are not actually improving greatly for the average person throughout much of the world. For example, economists such as Jason Hickel have argued that the manner in which data on rates of global poverty are gathered (and utilized by the likes of Pinker and others) often obscure the reality. In response to high-profile publications by the economist Branko Milanović and the World Bank claiming that inter-country inequality has been on the decline since 1960, Hinkel has said, "A key shortcoming of [Milanović and the World Bank's] approach (namely, representing inequality as between anonymous countries) is that it implicitly regards the disparate fortunes of poor countries and rich countries as separate and unrelated phenomena, which has the effect of depoliticizing the analysis of global inequality. This is in keeping with the World Bank's ideology, which generally seeks to explain and redress underdevelopment by focusing on the internal policies and institutions of poor countries." Hickel, "Is Global Inequality Getting Better or Worse? A Critique of the World Bank's Convergence Narrative," *Third World Quarterly* 38, no. 10 (2017): 3. This assessment is unsurprising if one understands the degree to which the World Bank and the International Monetary Fund have historically viewed the causes and solutions to global poverty more generally through the framework of neoliberalism. Given these institutions' political structure and financial policies (e.g., structural adjustment, the so-called Washington Consensus for reform, etc.), their data, which form the standard

for most measures of global development and poverty, cannot reasonably be seen as disinterested. Thus, studies as well as works written for popular audiences that uncritically utilize data that implicitly or explicitly attempt to positively characterize developments as reflective of the merits of neoliberal policies fail to account for the value-laden nature of the methodologies that render those results. This example further illustrates that facts are rarely collected disinterestedly and that data do not interpret themselves. See, for example, David Lewis, "Anthropology and Development: The Uneasy Relationship," in *A Handbook of Economic Anthropology*, ed. James G. Carrier (Edward Elgar, 2005), 472–88; and Saskia Sassen, *Globalization and Its Discontents: Essays on the New Mobility of People and Money* (New Press, 1998), 111–31.

30. Michael Hardt and Antonio Negri, *Empire* (Harvard University Press, 2001), 291.
31. Marshall McLuhan, *Understanding Media: The Extensions of Man* (1964; reprint, MIT Press, 1994), 9.
32. See Tina Besley et al., "Afterword—Viral Modernity: From Postmodernism to Post-Truth?," in *Post-Truth, Fake News: Viral Modernity and Higher Education*, ed. Michael A. Peters et al. (Springer International, 2018), 217–24.
33. Furthermore, just in the first few decades of the twenty-first century, the world has faced a number of global crises and revelations, each of which has affected to varying degrees the popular confidence and perceptions of social stability in the West. They include but are certainly not limited to: the terrorist attacks on the United States on September 11, 2001, the post-9/11 U.S.-led global war on terror (including the invasions of Afghanistan and Iraq, the latter of which was justified by lies made by Bush administration officials before the United Nations concerning Saddam Hussein's supposed possession of weapons of mass destruction), the European migrant crisis, the global financial crisis of 2008, the Great Recession, the European debt crisis, the events of the so-called Arab Spring and the subsequent Syrian Civil War, the disclosures by Edward Snowden of governmental privacy violations and global surveillance, the Wikileaks release of classified government information by the U.S. Army intelligence analyst Chelsea Manning (which detailed government lies and misconduct in the wars in Iraq and Afghanistan), the release of the Panama

Papers, social unrest over police brutality and continued racial injustice in the United States, the COVID-19 pandemic, the Russian invasion of Ukraine, as well as the ever-looming specters of manmade ecological collapse and nuclear disaster. If there is a crisis of confidence in the transparency and trustworthiness of institutions, it stands to reason that these events are greater factors in this crisis than are colleges teaching critical theory.

34. Ferraris, *Manifesto of New Realism*, 14. The comment about Benedict is a reference to Joseph Ratzinger, *A Turning Point for Europe?* (Ignatius Press, 2010), 101–5.
35. See David Hume, *A Treatise of Human Nature*, bk. 1, pt. 3, §6; cf. Nelson Goodman, *Fact, Fiction, and Forecast* (Harvard University Press, 1955).
36. See Gianni Vattimo, *Being and Its Surroundings*, ed. Giuseppe Iannantuono et al., trans. Corrado Federici (McGill-Queen's University Press, 2021), 51–55; cf. Zabala, *Being at Large*, 7–9, 70–72.
37. The appeal to "reason" or "reality" as concepts *functions* in roughly the same manner as the appeal to "transcendence"—namely, as an abstract foundation, existing outside the human activity of interpretation, that correspondingly possesses the power by which one can suspend the interpretive process. But because human beings have no unmediated access to pure reason, reality (as such), or divine transcendence, the sovereign that ends up wielding this power *in the name of* reason, the real, or the transcendent—that is, the one who declares or establishes the authority of a particular interpretation over all others—is always necessarily a human being or an institution composed of human beings.
38. James Traub, "It's Time for the Elites to Rise Up Against the Ignorant Masses," *Foreign Policy*, June 28, 2016, my emphasis, https://foreignpolicy.com/2016/06/28/its-time-for-the-elites-to-rise-up-against-ignorant-masses-trump-2016-brexit/.
39. Mikhail Bakunin, *God and the State* (New York: Dover, 1970), 32, my emphasis of "all."
40. Bakunin, *God and the State*, 33.
41. Gianni Vattimo, "After Onto-Theology: Philosophy Between Science and Religion," in *Religion After Metaphysics*, ed. Mark A. Wrathall (Cambridge University Press, 2003), 29–36.
42. Vattimo and Girard, *Christianity, Truth, and Weakening Faith*, 50–51.

43. One can see potential parallels here between this conception of bolstering democratic values and Habermas's views on participatory democracy and the notion of the "public sphere" (*Öffentlichkeit*). Where they differ, I would say, centers primarily on their respective understandings of the role of reason. Unfortunately, there is no space here to recount debates between Habermas and, say, Lyotard on postmodernity's (in)ability to critique the prevalent order of things without implicit appeal to a transhistorical rational basis for doing so. For a more extended discussion, see Vattimo, "The End of (His)story." Cf. Jürgen Habermas, *The Structural Transformation of the Public Sphere: An Inquiry Into a Category of Bourgeois Society*, trans. Thomas Burger with the assistance of Frederick Lawrence (MIT Press, 1991).
44. See, in contrast, Clayton Crockett, "Violence," in *The Vattimo Dictionary*, ed. Moro, 199–200.
45. Gianni Vattimo and Santiago Zabala, "'Weak Thought' and the Reduction of Violence: A Dialogue with Gianni Vattimo," trans. Yaakov Mascetti, *Common Knowledge* 25, nos. 1–3 (2019): 455.
46. One can compare this construal with similar statements made by Paulo Freire. For example, "Any situation in which some individuals prevent others from engaging in the process of inquiry is one of violence. The means used are not important; to alienate human beings from their own decision-making is to change them into objects." Paulo Freire, *Pedagogy of the Oppressed*, trans. Myra Bergman Ramos (Continuum, 2005), 85.
47. Ferraris, "Post moderni o neorealisti?," my emphasis.
48. Cf. Stanley Feldman and Christopher Johnston, "Understanding the Determinants of Political Ideology: Implications of Structural Complexity," *Political Psychology* 35, no. 3 (June 2014): 337–58; and Benjamin A. Valentino, "Why We Kill: The Political Science of Political Violence Against Civilians," *Annual Review of Political Science* 17 (2014): 89–103.
49. James K. A. Smith, *Introducing Radical Orthodoxy: Mapping a Post-Secular Theology* (Baker Academic, 2004), 31.
50. Depoortere, *Christ in Postmodern Philosophy*, 19; cf. Frederiek Depoortere, "Gianni Vattimo's Concept of Truth and Its Consequences for Christianity," in *Theology and the Quest for Truth: Historical- and Systematic-Theological Studies*, ed. Mathijs Lamberigts et al., Bibliotheca Ephemeridum Theologicarum Lovaniensium no. 202 (Leuven University Press, 2006), 241–58.

51. Depoortere continues by referring to *Verwindung* as "problematic" and without further elaboration of this point proceeds to ask a series of rhetorical questions meant to illustrate its apparent absurdity. He asks, for example, "What does it mean to weaken Plato?" He questions how charity can function as a categorical imperative when weak thought has supposedly particularized and rendered provisional all strong claims. He even takes time to draw into question the orthodoxy of Vattimo's conception of the Trinity. Again, whether one agrees with Vattimo in such regards is quite beside the point. Depoortere doesn't seem to realize that these problems are not insurmountable difficulties or internal contradictions if one bothers to take Vattimo seriously on his own terms.
52. Rass, *Die Suche nach Wahrheit im Horizont fragmentarischer Existenzialität*, 61, my translation.
53. Depoortere, *Christ in Postmodern Philosophy*, 19, my emphasis.
54. Depoortere, *Christ in Postmodern Philosophy*, 20. See also Jonkers, "In the World, but Not of the World."
55. In *On Liberty* (1859), Mill famously argued that "the only purpose for which power can be rightfully exercised over any member of a civilized community, against his will, is to prevent harm to others." That is, the only justified use of coercive force over another person is to prevent harm to others. *Harm* can be a nebulous term, but it is meant here in its common everyday use. More colloquially, then, we might say, "Your free right to swing your fist as you like ends where my nose begins." See John Stuart Mill, *On Liberty* (1859; reprint, P. F. Collier, 1909), 212.
56. Vattimo and Dotolo, *Dio*, §1, my translation.
57. "Despoiling the Egyptians" is a reference to Exodus 12:36, which tells how the Israelites plundered the Egyptians on the way to the promised land as a form of reparation or recompense for hundreds of years of forced enslavement. Origen later used this image as a metaphor for the use of earlier philosophical concepts to elucidate Christian theology—that is, taking what was best from pagan thought and placing it in service of the Gospels. In his work *Against Celsus*, Origen says: "We are careful not to raise objections to any good teachings, even if their authors are outside the faith, nor to seek an occasion for a dispute with them, nor to find a way of overthrowing statements which are sound." *Contra Celsum*, 7:46, quoted in Thomas G. Guarino, *Vattimo and Theology* (T&T Clark, 2009), 53.

58. Literally, the phrase in Latin reads, "Let him understand that he is his master, wherever he finds the truth." It is sometimes more colloquially rendered as "All truth is God's truth." See St. Augustine, *De doctrina christiana*, bk. 2, §18; cf. C. S. Lewis, *Mere Christianity* (1952; reprint, HarperCollins, 2001), 35.
59. Though Vattimo doesn't say so, I suspect that the reference to the quote from Augustine was, for Vattimo, preferable even over the comments from Jesus insofar as it omits reference to the requirement for one to love (a) God, which would thereby accommodate the affirmations of nontheists as well.
60. G. K. Chesterton, *Saint Francis of Assisi* (1957; reprint, Doubleday, 2001), 145.
61. Depoortere, *Christ in Postmodern Philosophy*, 22.
62. St. Augustine, *In epistulam Johannis as Parthos*, 10.7.8; see also Vattimo, *Belief*, 64.
63. A similar conflict would also later play itself out in Islamic philosophy. On the one hand, you had philosophers such as al-Kindī, al-Fārābī, ibn Sīnā (Avicenna), and ibn Rušd (Averröes) advocating for the use of Greek thought in the explication of Kalām. On the other, you had figures such as ibn Hanbal, al-Ash'ari, and al-Ghazali arguing against the "corruptive" mingling of Greek philosophy and Islamic theology. Interestingly, this debate over the proper role of philosophy vis-à-vis religion has been much less pronounced in Jewish thought. On the whole, classical Jewish thinkers from Philo on through most of the medieval commentators expressed comparatively little concern regarding the use of systems borrowed from philosophy. One notable exception, however, was the Sephardi writer Judah Halevi, whose work *Sefer ha-Kuzari* (1140) presented an antiphilosophical polemic.
64. Tertullian, *De prasecriptione hæreticorum*, 7.9; for the translation, see Tertullian, *On the Proscription of Heretics*, trans. T. Herbert Bindley, (SPCK, 1914), excerpt at https://sourcebooks.fordham.edu/source/200Tertullian-pagan.asp. For a broader context in which to understand Tertullian's position, see Justo L. González, "Athens and Jerusalem Revisited: Reason and Authority in Tertullian," *Church History* 43, no. 1 (March 1974): 17–25.

If we consider Luther's work of September 1517, *Disputatio contra scholasticism theologiam*, there he says that "it is an error to say that no man can become a theologian without Aristotle....Indeed, no one can become a theologian unless he becomes one without Aristotle....No syllogistic form is valid when applied to divine terms....If a syllogistic form of reasoning holds in divine matters, then the doctrine of the Trinity is demonstrable and not the object of faith. Briefly, the whole [of] Aristotle is to theology as darkness is to light." Martin Luther, "Disputation Against Scholastic Theology," in *Martin Luther's Basic Theological Writings*, ed. Timothy F. Lull (Fortress Press, 1989), 16. The Scholastics—sophists and papists to Luther—are, in his opinion, ceding too much to a human faculty. He feels that in our corruptible state, reason is dangerous because it gives us the pretention that it is possible to have knowledge of God apart from an act of God. Despite his rhetoric, however, Luther is less concerned with reason and philosophy as such. Instead, he pours out this invective against what he views as the excessive confidence placed in human capacities as a means of obtaining truth, in particular truth about God.

65. See Justin Martyr, *Dialogue with Trypho*, 8.1; Clement of Alexandria, *Stromata*, 1.28.3, 1.28.4, 1.80.5, 1.80.6.

66. Augustine, *Against Julian*, 4.14.72; Aquinas, *ST*, 1.1.1–8, and *Summa contra Gentiles* 1.1.1–9. Cf. Stephen Jay Gould, "Nonoverlapping Magisteria," *Natural History* 106 (March 1997): 16–22.

6. FINAL REFLECTIONS: NEW PATHWAYS IN VATTIMIAN THOUGHT

1. See Norman Doe, ed., *Christianity and Natural Law: An Introduction* (Cambridge University Press, 2017).

2. See John Witte Jr., *The Reformation of Rights: Law, Religion, and Human Rights in Early Modern Calvinism* (Cambridge University Press, 2007).

3. See Stuart Banner, *The Decline of Natural Law: How American Lawyers Once Used Natural Law and Why They Stopped* (Oxford University Press, 2021); J. M. Kelly, *A Short History of Western Legal Theory* (1992; reprint, Clarendon Press, 2013); and Sionaidh Douglas-Scott, *Law After Modernity* (Hart, 2013).

4. See James E. Herget and Stephen Wallace, "The German Free Law Movement as the Source of American Legal Realism," *Virginia Law Review* 73, no. 2 (March 1987): 399–455; Horst Klaus Lücke, "The European Natural Law Codes: The Age of Reason and the Powers of Government," *University*

6. FINAL REFLECTIONS ◌ 297

of Queensland Law Journal 31, no. 1 (2012): 7–38; and Wencelas J. Wagner, "Codification of Law in Europe and the Codification Movement in the Middle of the Nineteenth Century in the United States," *Saint Louis University Law Journal* 1953:335–59.

5. More precisely, Holmes can be considered a "legal realist," but making this distinction would take us too far afield for our present purposes.
6. Ana Messuti, "Justice/Law," in *The Vattimo Dictionary*, ed. Moro, 112.
7. Vattimo, *Nihilism and Emancipation*, 136.
8. Vattimo, *Nihilism and Emancipation*, 143.
9. See Ian Ward, *Kantianism, Postmodernism, and Critical Legal Thought* (Kluwer Academic, 1997); Douglas E. Litowitz, *Postmodern Philosophy and Law* (University Press of Kansas, 1997); and Allan C. Hutchinson, *It's All in the Game: A Nonfoundationalist Account of Law and Adjudication* (Duke University Press, 2000).
10. The 1960s saw what Joseph S. O'Leary has referred to as "a meltdown in talk of God." Joseph O'Leary, "Questions to and from a Tradition in Disarray," in *After God: Richard Kearney and the Religious Turn in Continental Philosophy*, ed. John Panteleimon Manoussakis (Fordham University Press, 2006), 185. This meltdown, he thought, was exemplified by the thought of Thomas J. J. Altizer and Don Cupitt, but the trend was wider than merely these two figures. A few titles that can be broadly categorized under the umbrella of early "death of God" theology include Gabriel Vahanian's *The Death of God: The Culture of Our Post-Christian Era* (1961), J. A. T. Robinson's *Honest to God* (1963), Paul Van Buren's *The Secular Meaning of the Gospel* (1963), Harvey Cox's *The Secular City* (1965), Thomas J. J. Altizer's *The Gospel of Christian Atheism* (1965), Richard L. Rubenstein's *After Auschwitz: Radical Theology and Contemporary Judaism* (1966), and William Hamilton's *Radical Theology and the Death of God* (1968, coauthored with Altizer). The culmination of this movement was undoubtedly the appearance of the headline "Is God Dead?" on the cover of *Time* magazine on April 8, 1966. By this point, however, the movement had already begun to lose steam. Don Cupitt's *Taking Leave of God* would appear much later—in 1980.
11. On the shared beliefs with postliberal narrative theology, as Gary Dorrien has pointed out, "American theology . . . was predominantly liberal from 1900 to 1935, predominantly neoorthodox/neoliberal from 1935 to 1965, and

predominantly pluralistic and postmodern from 1965 to 2000." The postliberal theology that took root in the 1960s (most famously at Yale) was philosophically influenced by figures such as Derrida, Kuhn, and Wittgenstein and by the anthropology of Clifford Geertz. Despite being influenced also by Catholic figures such as de Lubac and by Jewish thinkers such as Heschel, postliberalism has for the most part continued the post-Barthian tradition in Protestant thought (associated with thinkers such as Jürgen Moltmann). Postliberalism's major figures are arguably George Lindbeck, Hans Frei, and Stanely Hauerwas but can also include Brevard Childs, Langdon Gilkey, Ian McFarland, Kathryn Tanner, and (in the United Kingdom) Rowan Williams. See Gary Dorrien, "Modernism as a Theological Problem: The Theological Legacy of Langdon Gilkey," *American Journal of Theology and Philosophy* 28, no. 1 (January 2007): 64–94; and R. R. Reno, "Postliberal Theology," *First Things*, February 2018, https://www.firstthings.com/article/2018/02/postliberal-theology.

On the differentiation of radical theology, see Jeffrey W. Robbins and Clayton Crockett, "A Radical Theology for the Future: Five Theses," *Palgrave Communications* 1 (October 13, 2015): art. 15028, https://www.nature.com/articles/palcomms201528.

12. Other figures sometimes linked to radical theology include Alain Badiou, Slavoj Žižek, Richard Kearney, Merold Westphal, Jean-Luc Marion, and Jean-Luc Nancy, although these thinkers do not self-identify as "radical theologians."

13. See Dietrich Bonhoeffer, *Akt und Sein: Transzendentalphilosophie und Ontologie in der systematischen Theologie* (Chr. Kaiser, 1956), 94. In context, Bonhoeffer was arguing that "God talk" is always embedded in a concrete context. "The church is not allowed to preach principles that are always true; only commandments that are true today. Because what 'always' is true, is not true 'today': God is 'always' God to us today [Gott ist uns 'immer' gerade 'heute' Gott]." Dietrich Bonhoeffer, "14. Lecture in Ciernohorské Kúpele: One the Theological Foundation of the Work of the World Alliance" (1932), in *Dietrich Bonhoeffer Works*, vol. 11: *Ecumenical, Academic, and Pastoral Work, 1931–1932*, ed. Victoria J. Barnett et al., trans. Anne Schmidt-Lange et al. (Fortress Press, 2012), 359–60. Compare this with his later, more famous phrase: "Any god whose existence we could prove would be an idol." Dietrich Bonhoeffer, "Draft for

a Catechism: As You Believe, so You Receive," in *Dietrich Bonhoeffer Works*, 11:260.

14. Vattimo, *Being and Its Surroundings*, 144.
15. Vattimo, *Being and Its Surroundings*, 144, 145.
16. See John D. Caputo, *The Weakness of God: A Theology of the Event* (Indiana University Press, 2006); Clayton Crockett et al., eds., *The Future of Continental Philosophy of Religion* (University of Indiana Press, 2014); and Katharine Sarah Moody, *Radical Theology and Emerging Christianity: Deconstruction, Materialism and Religious Practices* (Ashgate, 2015).
17. Unlike postliberalism, the Emergent Church movement was less an intellectual movement in the academy than a social movement within the church. It became prominent among progressive post-Evangelicals during the 1990s and into the early 2000s—gaining notoriety in large part through the popular writings of figures such as Brian McLaren, Rob Bell, Doug Pagitt, Rachel Held Evans, Scot McKnight, Shane Claiborne, Diana Butler Bass, and Tony Jones. Some of these figures have since then, however, sought to distance themselves from the label.
18. By contrast, if one were to look for an example of a religious thinker who has constructively engaged Vattimo's work from outside this framework of radical theology, then one needs to consider the work of the Italian theologian Carmelo Dotolo. See, for example, Dotolo, *La teologia fondamentale—davanti alle sfide del "pensiero debole" di G. Vattimo* (LAS, 1999); and Dotolo, *The Christian Revelation: Word, Event, and Mystery*, trans. Cavallo Domenica (Davies Group, 2006).
19. With the institutional suppression of liberation theology by the Catholic Church during the pontificates of John Paul II and Benedict XVI as well as the collapse of Soviet-style communism, many have simply assumed that liberation theology has progressively lost all theological currency since the late 1980s. The social conditions that gave a sense of urgency to liberation thought, however, have not gone away in recent decades. If anything, they have been exacerbated. Since the early 2000s, therefore, liberation theology has reemerged as a force in contemporary dialogues on issues such as the effects of globalization, forced immigration, late-stage capitalism, environmental degradation, and health and wealth disparities, particularly as they affect the Global South. See Thia Cooper, ed., *The Reemergence of Liberation Theologies: Models for the Twenty-First Century* (Palgrave-Macmillan,

2013); and Joerg Rieger, ed., *Opting for the Margins: Postmodernity and Liberation in Christian Theology* (Oxford University Press, 2003).

20. Vattimo said, "I would never go against the Church as a Catholic, as, for example, I would never go on strike against a trade union. Because they are the historical truth of this thing and, therefore, I have no tendency [even] to become Protestant." Vattimo et al., *"Fratelli tutti,"* 154–55.

21. See Gerd-Rainer Horn, *Western European Liberation Theology: The First Wave, 1924–1959* (Oxford University Press, 2008); and Horn, *The Spirit of Vatican II: Western European Progressive Catholicism in the Long Sixties* (Oxford University Press, 2015).

22. The church's first official statement concerning communism was Pius IX's encyclical *Qui pluribus* (1846). Later, he also attacked communism and socialism in *Nostis et nobiscum* (1849) and, of course, *Quanta cura* (1864). Likewise, Pope Leo XIII issued *Quod apostolici muneris* (1878) and *Rerum novarum* (1891), the latter of which, in spite of supporting workers, did so in opposition to (not solidarity with) communism. Pius XI issued *Quadragesimo anno* in 1931—on the fortieth anniversary of *Rerum novarum*. Arguably, no pope was more paranoid about communism than Pius XII, who issued *Decree Against Communism* in 1949—excommunicating for apostasy any Catholics who held communist political beliefs.

23. See John Francis Charles, seventh count de Salis-Soglio, British Minister at the Vatican Foreign Office, *Vatican Relations with Italy, Annual Report* (n.p., October 25, 1922), quoted in Paul Higginson, "The Vatican and Communism from 'Divini Redemptoris' to Pope Paul VI, Part 1," *New Blackfriars* 61, no. 719 (April 1980): 160.

24. Kenneth S. Zagacki, "Pope John Paul II and the Crusade Against Communism: A Case Study in Secular and Sacred Time," *Rhetoric and Public Affairs* 4, no. 4 (Winter 2001): 689–710.

25. See Peter Hebblethwaite, "Liberation Theology and the Roman Catholic Church," in *The Cambridge Companion to Liberation Theology*, ed. Christopher Rowland (Cambridge University Press, 1999), 179–98; and Leonardo Boff, *Ecclesiogenesis: The Base Communities Reinvent the Church*, trans. Robert R. Barr (Orbis, 1986).

26. Deane William Ferm, *Third World Liberation Theologies* (Orbis, 1988), 7. The quote from Gutiérrez originally appeared in *National Catholic Reporter*, December 17, 1982, 10–11.

27. For a more complete picture, see Gustavo Gutiérrez, *A Theology of Liberation* (1971); Enrique Dussel, *A History of the Church in Latin America: Colonialism to Liberation* (1974); Juan Luis Segundo, *A Theology for Artisans of a New Humanity*, 5 vols. (1973–1974), and *The Liberation of Theology* (1976); Leonardo Boff, *Jesus Christ Liberator: A Critical Christology for Our Time* (1978); José Porfirio Miranda, *Communism in the Bible* (1981); and Jon Sobrino, *Christology at the Crossroads: A Latin American Approach* (1978).
28. See Ole Jakob Løland, "The Solved Conflict: Pope Francis and Liberation Theology," *International Journal of Latin American Religions* 5 (July 2021): 287–314.
29. Francis himself commented on this. In 2019, the pope was in Panama for World Youth Day. In speaking with a group of thirty Jesuit representatives from Latin America, he said, "Today, we old people laugh about how worried we were about liberation theology." He went on to say, "Let me tell you a funny story, the one most persecuted, (Dominican Father) Gustavo Gutiérrez, a Peruvian, concelebrated Mass with me and the then-prefect of the Congregation for the Doctrine of the Faith, Cardinal (Gerhard) Müller. And it happened because Müller himself brought him to me as his friend. If anybody had said back then that the prefect of the CDF [Congregation for the Doctrine of the Faith] would have brought Gutiérrez to concelebrate with the pope, they would have taken him for a drunk." Quoted in Cindy Wooden, "Pope Reflects on Changed Attitudes Toward Liberation Theology," Catholic News Service, February 14, 2019, https://cruxnow.com/vatican/2019/02/pope-reflects-on-changed-attitudes-toward-liberation-theology.
30. Associated Press, "Pope Francis Says He Wasn't Offended by 'Communist Crucifix' Gift," *The Guardian*, July 13, 2015, https://www.theguardian.com/world/2015/jul/13/pope-francis-communist-crucifix-gift-bolivia.
31. Løland, "The Solved Conflict," 301.
32. Indeed, Bergoglio had originally been scheduled to speak at a conference in Argentina on the same panel as Vattimo in March 2013 when he was called to the conclave in Rome and ultimately declared pope.
33. Quoted in Fernando Ciberira, "Entrevista al filósofo italiano y eurodiputado de la izquierda Gianni Vattimo," *Página 12*, November 10, 2013, https://www.pagina12.com.ar/diario/elpais/1-233272-2013-11-10.html.

34. Vattimo et al., "*Fratelli tutti.*"
35. Pope Francis issued a joint statement with the grand imam of al-Azhar, Ahmad al-Tayyeb, in Abu Dhabi, United Arab Emirates, on February 4, 2019. Entitled *A Document on Human Fraternity for World Peace and Living Together*, the statement is referred to as the Abu Dhabi Document.
36. Vattimo et al., "*Fratelli tutti*, 148–49, original emphasis.
37. Cf. Vattimo and Rorty, *The Future of Religion*, 16–18. See Jorge Mario Bergoglio, *Open Mind, Faithful Heart: Reflections on Following Jesus*, trans. Joseph V. Owens, SJ (Crossroads, 2013).
38. Vattimo et al., "*Fratelli tutti*," 152. Cf. Vattimo, *Being and Its Surroundings*, 149–54. Some would no doubt suggest that Vattimo's enthusiasm for Francis should perhaps have been tempered. It is worth considering to what extent his feelings were a matter of conjecture or projection. For a nuanced view, see Keith Edward Lemna, "Pope Francis's Strong Thought," *Theological Librarianship* 7, no. 2 (July 2014): 45–53.
39. Vattimo, *Being and Its Surroundings*, 149, 150.
40. The most famous example of the "Christ Pantocrator" trope is from the sixth century and appears in the Orthodox Monastery of St. Catherine in Sinai, Egypt. It is among the earliest surviving artistic depictions of Christ and perhaps the most famous example of Byzantine art in the world. The most famous example of the "Christ Militant" trope appears in the sixth-century vault mosaic *Ego sum via, veritas, et vita* in the Oratory of Sant' Andrea, Archiepiscopal Chapel, Ravenna, Italy. At the time, Ravenna served as capital of the empire, and the image depicts Christ as a Roman legionnaire. For a discussion of the various depictions of Christ in art and literature, see Jaroslav Pelikan, *Jesus Through the Centuries: His Place in the History of Culture* (Harper and Rowe, 1985).
41. A brief representative cross-section of the literature on this struggle between Rome and Christianity includes Luke Timothy Johnson, *Among the Gentiles: Greco-Roman Religion and Christianity* (Yale University Press, 2009); John Dominic Crossan, *Jesus: A Revolutionary Biography* (HarperCollins, 1994); John Dominic Crossan, *God and Empire: Jesus Against Rome, Then and Now* (HarperCollins, 2007); Wes Howard-Brook and Anthony Gwyther, *Unveiling Empire: Reading Revelation, Then and Now* (Orbis, 1999); Reza Aslan, *Zealot: The Life and Times of Jesus of Nazareth*

(Random House, 2013); Yoder, *The Politics of Jesus*; N. T. Wright and Michael F. Bird, *Jesus and the Powers* (Zondervan, 2024); and Jaques Ellul, *The Subversion of Christianity*, trans. Geoffrey W. Bromiley (Eerdmans, 1986).

42. Vattimo, *Being and Its Surroundings*, 151.
43. Vattimo, *Being and Its Surroundings*, 154.
44. Vattimo et al., *"Fratelli tutti,"* 157.
45. Marta Frascati-Lochhead, *Kenosis and Feminist Theology: The Challenge of Gianni Vattimo* (SUNY Press, 1998), 21.
46. Frascati-Lochhead, *Kenosis and Feminist Theology*, 214–15.
47. James H. Cone, *A Black Theology of Liberation*, 20th Anniversary Ed. (Orbis, 1990), 51.
48. Dorothee Sölle, *Suffering* (Augsburg Fortress Press, 1984), 32.
49. Cone, *A Black Theology of Liberation*, 6.
50. "Become Black" is here obviously not meant in some literal *transracial* sense.
51. Cone, *A Black Theology of Liberation*, 63.
52. Kimberlé Crenshaw, "Demarginalizing the Intersection of Race and Sex: A Black Feminist Critique of Antidiscrimination Doctrine, Feminist Theory, and Antiracist Politics," *University of Chicago Legal Forum*, no. 1 (1989): 149.
53. In this regard, I think that some degree of discernment and prudence (*phronesis*) is required with respect to transgressive behavior. This may seem contradictory at first, but let me explain what I mean. For anything that we recognize as progress to occur, unjust norms must from time to time necessarily be contravened, but transgression itself is a blade that cuts both ways and does not always serve liberative ends. Take, for example, the neo-Nazi Skinheads' appropriation of the transgressive aesthetic of the underground Punk scene. The unqualified valorization of "transgression" as such means there could be no meaningful distinction between the Swastika and the flag of Antifaschistische Aktion, a militant Communist organization formed in 1932.
54. See Ish Ruiz, "Queer Theology and the Synodal Catholic Church," *Feminist Theology* 32, no. 3 (2024): 283–304.
55. Indeed, Simonetta Moro and the contributors to the recently published and wide-ranging *Vattimo Dictionary* considered Vattimo's homosexuality so

peripheral to his thought that a dedicated entry to it was not considered necessary. See Simonetta Moro, introduction to *The Vattimo Dictionary*, ed. Moro, 8.

56. On this connection, cf. Jin Wang and Keebom Nahm, "From Confucianism to Communism and Back: Understanding the Cultural Roots of Chinese Politics," *Journal of Asian Sociology* 48, no. 1 (March 2019): 91–114.
57. See Venu Mehta, "Anekāntavāda: The Jaina Epistemology," in *Constructing the Pluriverse: The Geopolitics of Knowledge*, ed. Bernd Reiter (Duke University Press, 2018), 259–75.
58. John Berger, *G: A Novel* (1972; reprint, Vintage, 1991), 129.

EPILOGUE

1. Sarah Martinenghi, "Gianni Vattimo è morto: Il filosofo aveva 87 anni," *La Repubblica*, September 19, 2023, https://torino.repubblica.it/cronaca/2023/09/19/news/e_morto_il_filosofo_gianni_vattimo-415090320/.
2. See Antonio Carioti, "È morto Gianni Vattimo, il filosofo aveva 87 anni," *Corriere della sera*, September 19, 2023, https://www.corriere.it/cultura/23_settembre_19/gianni-vattimo-morto-8d9e08e4-52db-11ee-9c68-5070f213fc3b.shtml; Roberta Damiata, "È morto Gianni Vattimo: Il filosofo del 'pensiero debole' aveva 87 anni," *Il Giornale*, September 19, 2023, https://www.ilgiornale.it/news/letteratura/morto-filosofo-gianni-vattimo-aveva-87-anni-2213251.html; Maurizio Ferraris, "Vattimo, nemico dei dogmi," *Corriere della sera*, September 19, 2023, https://www.corriere.it/cultura/23_settembre_19/vattimo-nemico-dogmi-82884018-53c7-11ee-8884-717525326594.shtml; Roberto Esposito, "Gianni Vattimo è morto: È stato il filosofo pensiero debole e del postmoderno," *La Repubblica*, September 20, 2023, https://www.repubblica.it/cultura/2023/09/20/news/gianni_vattimo_morto_filosofo-415094684/.
3. See Lorena Pacho, "At the End of His Life, Was the Great Philosopher Gianni Vattimo a Victim of the Courts or of a Predatory Assistant?," *El País*, October 1, 2023, https://english.elpais.com/culture/2023-10-02/at-the-end-of-his-life-was-the-great-philosopher-gianni-vattimo-a-victim-of-the-courts-or-of-a-predatory-assistant.html.
4. Jacopo Ricca, "Caso Vattimo, 2 anni di carcere a Simone Caminada," *Rai News*, June 2, 2023, https://www.rainews.it/tgr/piemonte/articoli/2023/02

/caso-vattimo-il-giorno-del-giudizio-per-lassistente-caminada-27bc10cc
-b56f-42c7-ac76-a6ec21c701aa.html; Sarah Martinenghi, "Gianni Vattimo
vuole sposare Caminada ma la procura di Torino blocca l'unione civile," *La
Repubblica*, December 14, 2022, https://torino.repubblica.it/cronaca/2022/12
/14/news/gianni_vattimo_vuole_sposare_caminada_ma_la_procura_di
_torino_blocca_lunione_civile-379048608/; Redazione Milano, "Gianni
Vattimo e Simone Caminada, una storia d'amore in tribunale," *Gay.it*,
July 2, 2023, https://www.gay.it/gianni-vattimo-simone-caminada-storia
-amore-tribunale.

5. Quoted in Martinenghi, "Gianni Vattimo vuole sposare Caminada."
6. Vattimo and Paterlini, *Not Being God*, 166, 168.
7. Irene Famà, "Sul patrimonio di Vattimo scoppia la battaglia legale: Ora i conti sono bloccati," *La Stampa*, September 21, 2023, https://www.lastampa.it/torino/2023/09/21/news/patrimonio_vattimo_battaglia_legale_conti_bloccati-13395253/.
8. See Aldo Cazzullo, "Gianni Vattimo: Il '68, le scorrettezze politiche e la rivalità con Eco: 'Sono più intelligente di lui,'" *Corriere della sera*, September 20, 2023, https://www.corriere.it/cultura/23_settembre_20/gianni-vattimo-68-quella-rivalita-eco-scorrettezze-politiche-f7b0e1a2-5740-11ee-a17f-69493a54d671.shtml.
9. Vattimo and Paterlini, *Not Being God*, 116.
10. Vattimo and Paterlini, *Not Being God*, 134, 135.
11. See Pacho, "At the End of His Life."
12. Candida Morvillo, "Martine Tedeschi, l'ex moglie di Vattimo (sposata solo per poterle lasciare i suoi beni): 'Uno choc quando chiese il divorzio,'" *Corriere della sera*, February 12, 2023, https://www.corriere.it/cronache/23_febbraio_12/martine-tedeschi-vattimo-ex-moglie-c66c530a-aa4e-11ed-9a4b-673945879bc9.shtml.
13. Sarah Martinenghi, "Caso Vattimo, Caminada condannato a 2 anni: 'Ha approfittato del filosofo,'" *La Repubblica*, February 6, 2023, https://torino.repubblica.it/cronaca/2023/02/06/news/caso_vattimo_condanna_caminada-386718947/#:~:text=Home-,Caso%20Vattimo%2C%20Caminada%20condannato%20a%202,%3A%20%22Ha%20approfittato%20del%20filosofo%22&text=Due%20anni%20di%20carcere%20per,%C3%A8%20al%20fianco%20del%20filosofo.
14. Pacho, "At the End of His Life."

15. *Giornale la voca*, "Torino dà l'ultimo saluto a Gianni Vattimo," September 23, 2023, https://www.giornalelavoce.it/news/attualita/536729/torino-da-l-ultimo-saluto-a-gianni-vattimo.html.
16. Sarah Martinenghi, "L'eredità di Vattimo va a due cugine, i giudici: 'Caminada indegno,'" *La Repubblica*, July 31, 2024, https://torino.repubblica.it/cronaca/2024/07/31/news/gianni_vattimo_eredita_due_cugine_caminada_indegno-423422499/#google_vignette.

ACKNOWLEDGMENTS

First and foremost, I thank my wife and children, whose unwavering love and support serve as constant sources of strength and inspiration. In addition, I have been blessed to have had the help and encouragement of my parents, Ray and Susan Farmer; my in-laws, Keith and Faye Dixon; as well as a wider network of wonderful family and friends. To each and every one I am grateful.

This project would not have been possible without the incomparable guidance of Ingolf U. Dalferth, who oversaw it from its inception through to its completion at the University of Münster. Similarly, I would here also like to offer my sincere appreciation to the Faculty of Protestant Theology at Münster, including Arnulf von Scheliha, Eve-Marie Becker, Holger Strutwolf, and especially Hans-Peter Großhans. I thank many other teachers, colleagues, and friends who provided assistance, inspiration, and support throughout my work on this book, including Michael Granado, Summer Granado, Raymond Perrier, James Thomas, José Francisco Morales Torres, Philip Clayton, the late Anselm K. Min, and countless others. In addition, I am grateful to Alice Cameron, Ish Ruiz, Friederike D. Rass, Santiago Zabala, Massimilano Lacertosa, Debora Tonelli, Michael Haskell, Annie Barva, and Wendy Lochner for their help in various aspects of thinking, writing, and publication. Thanks to Phil and Tammey Bohlen for their kind hospitality. Thanks to John Witte Jr., Whittney Barth, Amy Wheeler, Alexa Windsor, Silas W. Allard, and the other members of Emory's Center for the Study of Law and Religion. Finally, I would especially like to thank my former professor Luke Timothy Johnson, who served as an unofficial reader, editor, and veritable midwife to this project. I quite simply could not have completed it without Luke. For many years of friendship, kindness, wisdom, and encouragement, I will be forever grateful.

WORKS BY VATTIMO

A complete list of publications is available at the website of the Universitat Pompeu Fabra Center for Vattimo's Philosophy and Archives: https://www.upf.edu/en/web/gianni-vattimo/arxius.

PRIMARY WORKS BY VATTIMO

* Identifies works for which there is at present no official English translation.

"Imitazione e catarsi in alcuni recenti studi aristotelici." 1960. In *Opere complete*, vol. 1.1: *Ermeneutica*, ed. Mario Cedrini, Alberto Martinengo, and Santiago Zabala. Meltemi, 2007.*

"Opera d'arte e organismo in Aristotele." 1960. In *Opere complete*, vol. 1.1: *Ermeneutica*, ed. Mario Cedrini, Alberto Martinengo, and Santiago Zabala. Meltemi, 2007.*

"Il concetto di fare in Aristotele." 1961. In *Opere complete*, vol. 1.1: *Ermeneutica*, ed. Mario Cedrini, Alberto Martinengo, and Santiago Zabala. Meltemi, 2007.*

Essere, storia, e linguaggio in Heidegger. Edizioni di "Filosofia," 1963.*

Ipotesi su Nietzsche. Giappichelli, 1967.*

Poesia e ontologia. Mursia, 1967.*

Schleiermacher, filosofo dell'interpretazione. Mursia, 1968.*

Introduzione ad Heidegger. Laterza, 1971.*

Arte e utopia. Litografia Artigiana M & S, 1972.*

"L'ontoloia ermeneutica nella filosofia contemporanea." In Hans-Georg Gadamer, *Verità e metodo*. Bompiani, 1972.*

Il soggetto e la maschera. Fabbri-Bompiani, 1974.*
Introduzione a *Estetica moderna*, ed. Gianni Vattimo. Il Mulino, 1977.*
Introduction to Gilles Deleuze, Nietzsche e la filosofia. Colportage, 1978.*
"Introduction to Friedrich Nietzsche." In Friedrich Nietzsche, *La gaia scienza*, ed. Ferrucio Masini, trans. Gianni Vattimo, vii–xxviii. Einaudi, 1979.
Le avventure della differenza: Che cosa significa pensare dopo Nietzsche e Heidegger. Aldo Garzanti Editore, 1980. English: *The Adventure of Difference: Philosophy After Nietzsche and Heidegger*. Trans. Cyprian Blamires and Thomas Harrison. Johns Hopkins University Press, 1993.
Al di là del soggetto: Nietzsche, Heidegger, e l'emeneutica. Feltrinelli, 1981. English: *Beyond the Subject: Nietzsche, Heidegger, and Hermeneutics*. Trans. Peter Carravetta. SUNY Press, 2019. The essay "Verso un'ontologia del decline" is translated into English as "Towards an Ontology of Decline" and published in both *Beyond the Subject*, 17–34, and *Recoding Metaphysics: The New Italian Philosophy*, ed. Giovanna Borradori, trans. Barbara Spackman, 63–76. Northwestern University Press, 1988.
(Ed. with Pier Aldo Rovatti) *Il pensiero debole*. Feltrinelli, 1983. English: *Weak Thought*. Trans. Peter Carravetta. State University of New York, 2012.
Prefazione a *Il soggetto e la maschera: Nietzsche e il problema della liberazione*, 2nd ed. Bompiani, 1983.*
La fine della modernità: Nichilismo ed ermeneutica nella cultura post-moderna. Girzanti, 1985. English: *The End of Modernity: Nihilism and Hermeneutics in Postmodern Culture*. Trans. Jon R. Snyder. Polity/Johns Hopkins University Press, 1988.
Introduzione a Nietzsche. Laterza, 1985. English: *Nietzsche: An Introduction*. Trans. Nicholas Martin. Stanford University Press, 2002.
"Myth and the Destiny of Secularization." In "Myth in Contemporary Life." Special issue, *Social Research* 52, no. 2 (Summer 1985): 347–62.
Poesia e ontologia. 2nd expanded ed. Mursia, 1985. Includes "Prefazione alla seconda edizione" and the additional chapter "Estetica ed ermeneutica" (1979), 185–202. English: *Art's Claim to Truth*. Ed. Santiago Zabala. Trans. Luca. D'Isanto. Columbia University Press, 2010.
"The Crisis of Subjectivity from Nietzsche to Heidegger." *Differentia: Review of Italian Thought* 1 (Autumn 1986): art. 5.
"Metafisica, violenza, secolarizzazione." In *Filosofia '86*, ed. Gianni Vattimo. Laterza, 1986. English: "Metaphysics, Violence, and Secularization." In

Recoding Metaphysics: The New Italian Philosophy, ed. Giovanna Borradori, trans. Barbara Spackman, 45–62. Northwestern University Press, 1988.

"Nietzsche and Heidegger." *Stanford Italian Review* 6, nos. 1–2 (1986): 19–29.

"The End of (Hi)story." *Chicago Review* 35, no. 4 (1987): 20–30.

"Hermeneutics as Koine." *AUT AUT* 217–18 (1987): 3–11.

"'Verwindung': Nihilism and the Postmodern in Philosophy." In "Contemporary Italian Thought." Special issue, *SubStance* 16, no. 2 (1987): 7–17.

"Au-delà de la matière et du texte: La dissolution de la matière dans la pensée contemporaine." In *Matière et philosophie: Architecture, science, théorie*, trans. Federico Benedetti and Paolo Antonelli. Éditions du Centre Pompidou, 1988.*

Etica dell'interpretazione. Rosenberg e Sellier, 1989.*

La società trasparente. Gerzanti, 1989. English: *The Transparent Society*. Trans. David Webb. Polity/Johns Hopkins University Press, 1992.

Filosofia al presente: Conversazioni di Gianni Vattimo con Francesco Barone, Remo Bodei, Italo Mancini, Vittorio Mathieu, Mario Perniola, Pier Aldo Rovatti, Emanuele Severino, Carlo Sini. Ed. Gianni Vattimo. Garzanti, 1990.*

"La realtà consumata." In *Che cos'è la conoscenza*, ed. Mauro Ceruti and Lorena Preta. Laterza, 1990.*

"Optimistic Nihilism." *Common Dreams* 1 (1992): 37–44.

Oltre l'interpretazione. Laterza & Figli, 1994. English: *Beyond Interpretation: The Meaning of Hermeneutics for Philosophy*. Trans. David Webb. Polity/Stanford University Press, 1997.

Credere di credere. Garzanti, 1996. English: *Belief*. Trans. Luca D'Isanto and David Webb. Polity, 1999.

(Ed. with Jacques Derrida.) *La religion: Seminaire de Capri*. Éditions du Seuil et Éditions Laterza, 1996. English: *Religion*. Stanford University Press, 1998.

Tecnica ed esistenza: Una mappa filosofica del Novecento. Mondadori, 1997.*

(With Jacques Derrida.) *Diritto, giustizia e interpretazione: Annuario filosofico europeo*. Laterza, 1998.*

"Democracy, Reality, and the Media: Educating the Übermensch." In *Democracy and the Arts*, ed. Arthur M. Melzer, Jerry Weinberger, and M. Richard Zinman, 146–58. Cornell University Press, 1999.

Dialogo con Nietzsche: Saggi 1961–2000. Garzanti Libri, 2000. English: *Dialogue with Nietzsche*. Trans. William McCuaig. Columbia University Press, 2006.

"The Story of a Comma: Gadamer and the Sense of Being." *Revue internationale de philosophie* 54 (2000): 499–513.

Vocazione e responsabilità del filosofo. Il Melangolo, 2000. English: *The Responsibility of the Philosopher.* Ed. Franca D'Agostini. Trans. William McCuaig. Columbia University Press, 2010.

"The Christian Message and the Dissolution of Metaphysics." In *The Blackwell Companion to Postmodern Theology*, ed. Graham Ward, 458–66. Blackwell, 2001.

Dopo la cristianità: Per un cristianesimo non religioso. Garzanti, 2002. English: *After Christianity.* Trans. Luca D'Isanto. Columbia University Press, 2002.

"Gadamer and the Problem of Ontology." In *Gadamer's Century*, ed. Jeff Malpas, Ulrich Arnswald, and Jens Kertscher, 299–306. MIT Press, 2002.

(With Enrique Dussel and Guillermo Hoyos.) *La postmodernidad a debite.* Ed. L. Tovar. Universidad Santo Tomàs, 2002.*

Vero e falso universalismo cristiano. Educam-Editora Universitária Candido Mendes and Academia da Latinidade, 2002.*

"'Weak Thought' and the Reduction of Violence: A Dialogue with Gianni Vattimo." Interview by Santiago Zabala. *Common Knowledge* 8, no. 3 (2002): 425–63.

"After Onto-Theology: Philosophy Between Science and Religion." In *Religion After Metaphysics*, ed. Mark A. Wrathall, 29–36. Cambridge University Press, 2003.

"Ethics Without Transcendence." *Common Knowledge* 9, no. 3 (2003): 399–405.

Nichilismo ed emancipazione: Etica, politica, diritto. Garzanti, 2003. English: *Nihilism and Emancipation: Ethics, Politics, and Law.* Foreword by Richard Rorty. Ed. Santiago Zabala. Trans. William McCuaig. Columbia University Press, 2004.

Prefazione a Santiago Zabala, *Filosofare con Ernst Tugendhat: Il carattere ermeneutico della filosofia analitica.* Franco Angeli Ediotore, 2004. English: Foreword to Santiago Zabala, *The Hermeneutic Nature of Analytic Philosophy: A Study of Ernst Tugendhat*, trans. Santiago Zabala and Michael Haskell, xi–xlix. Columbia University Press, 2008.

Il socialismo ossia l'Europa. Ed. Giuseppe Iannantuono and Mario Cedrini. Trauben, 2004.*

(With Richard Rorty.) *The Future of Religion.* Ed. Santiago Zabala. Columbia University Press, 2005. Italian: *Il futuro della religione: Solidarietà, ironia, carità.* Garzanti, 2005.

(With Piergiorgio Paterlini.) *Non essere Dio: Un'autobiografia a quattro mani.* Ponte Alle Grazie, 2006. English: *Not Being God: A Collaborative Autobiography.* Trans. William McCuaig. Columbia University Press, 2009.

(With René Girard.) *Verità o fede debole? Dialogo su cristianesimo e relativismo.* Giangiacomo Feltrinelli Editore Milano, 2006. English: *Christianity, Truth, and Weakening Faith: A Dialogue.* Ed. Pierpaolo Antonello. Trans. William McCuaig. Columbia University Press, 2010.

La vita dell'altro: Bioetica senza metafisica. Marco, 2006.*

(With John D. Caputo.) *After the Death of God.* Ed. Jeffrey W. Robbins. Columbia University Press, 2007.

(With Paolo Flores D'Arcais and Michel Onfray.) *Atei o credenti?* Fazi, 2007.*

"Conclusion: Metaphysics and Violence." In *Weakening Philosophy: Essays in Honour of Gianni Vattimo*, ed. Santiago Zabala, 400–421. McGill-Queen's University Press, 2007.

"A 'Dictatorship of Relativism'?" Trans. Robert Valgenti. *Common Knowledge* 13, nos. 2–3 (2007): 214–18.

Ecce comu: Come si diventa cio che si era. Fazi, 2007.*

Opere complete. Volume introduttivo. Ed. Mario Cedrini, Alberto Martinengo, and Santiago Zabala. Meltemi, 2007.*

"Postmodernity and (the End of) Metaphysics." In *Postmodernism: What Moment?*, ed. Pelagia Goulimari, trans. David Rose, 32–38. Manchester University Press, 2007.

Introduction to Richard Rorty, *Un'etica per i laici*, 7–13. Bollati, 2008.

Preface to Alberto Martinengo, *Introduzione a Reiner Schürmann*, 7–11. Meltemi, 2008.*

(With Dario Antiseri.) *Ragione filosofica e fede religiosa nell'era postmoderna.* Rubbettino, 2008.*

Addio alla verità. Meltemi, 2009. English: *A Farewell to Truth.* Trans. William McCuaig. Foreword by Robert T. Valgenti. Columbia University Press, 2011.

(With Carmelo Dotolo.) *Dio: La possibilità buona. Un colloquio sulla soglia tra filosofia e teologia.* Ed. Giovanni Giorgio. Rubbettino, 2009.*

"Gianni Vattimo—Philosophy as Ontology of Actuality: A Biographical-Theoretical Interview with Luca Savarino and Federico Vercellone." *Iris: European Journal of Philosophy and Public Debate* 1, no. 2 (October 2009): 311–50.

"Nihilism as Emancipation." *Cosmos and History* 5, no. 1 (2009): 20–23.

"The End of Reality." Glasgow Gifford Lectures, June 2010. https://www.gla.ac.uk/events/lectures/gifford/recentlectures/giannivattimo/.

Introduction to Richard Rorty, *An Ethics for Today: Finding Common Ground Between Philosophy and Religion*, 1–5. Columbia University Press, 2010.

Introduzione all'estetica. Ed. Leonardo Amoroso. ETS, 2010.*

"Truth, Solidarity, History." In *The Philosophy of Richard Rorty*, ed. Randall E. Auxier and Lewis Edwin Hahn, 575–83. Open Court, 2010.

(With Santiago Zabala.) *Hermeneutic Communism: From Heidegger to Marx*. Columbia University Press, 2011.

Magnificat: Un'idea di montagna. Vivalda, 2011.*

Della realtà. Garzanti, 2012. English: *Of Reality: The Purposes of Philosophy*. Trans. Robert T. Valgenti. Columbia University Press, 2016.

(With Giovanni Ruggeri and Pierangelo Sequeri.) *Interrogazioni sul cristianesimo: Cosa possiamo ancora attenderci dal Vangelo?* Castelvecchi Lit Edizioni, 2013.*

(Ed. with Michael Marder.) *Deconstructing Zionism: A Critique of Political Metaphysics*. Bloomsbury Academic, 2014.

Dios es comunista: Conversaciones con Manuel Gonzalez Magnasco y Adriana Farias. Editoria FEDUN, Azcuènaga 770, 2014.*

"Insuperable Contradictions and Events." In *Being Shaken: Ontology and the Event*, ed. Michael Marder and Santiago Zabala, 70–76. Palgrave Macmillan, 2014.

"Luigi Pareyson." In *Dizionario biografico degli Italiani*, vol. 81. Instituto della Enciclopedia Italiana Fondata da Giovanni Treccni, 2014. https://www.treccani.it/enciclopedia/luigi-pareyson_(Dizionario-Biografico)/.

"What Need, What Metaphysics?" *Parrhesia: A Journal of Critical Philosophy*, no. 21 (2014): 51–57.

"Emergency and Event: Technique, Politics, and the Work of Art." *Philosophy Today* 59, no. 4 (2015): 583–86.

"Kenotic Sacrifice and Philosophy: Paolo Diego Bubbio." *Research in Phenomenology* 45, no. 3 (2015): 431–35.

"Anatheism, Nihilism, and Weak Thought." In *Reimagining the Sacred: Richard Kearney Debates God with James Wood, Catherine Keller, Charles Taylor, Julia Kristeva, Gianni Vattimo, Simon Critchley, Jean-Luc Marion, John Caputo, David Tracy, Jens Zimmermann, and Merold Westphal*, ed. Richard Kearney and Jens Zimmerman, 128–48. Columbia University Press, 2016.

Preface to E. C. Corriero, *Nietzsche's Death of God and Italian Philosophy*, ix–xi. Rowman and Littlefield, 2016.

(With Claudio Gallo and Armando Torno.) *A proposito dell'amore*. Book Time, 2017.*

"Towards (Back to?) a Philosophical Education: An Interview with Gianni Vattimo." Interview by Gabriel Serbu. *Philosophy Today* 61, no. 2 (2017): 281–90.

(With Santiago Zabala.) "'Weak Thought' and the Reduction of Violence: A Dialogue with Gianni Vattimo." Trans. Yaakov Mascetti. *Common Knowledge* 25, nos. 1–3 (2019): 92–103.

Essere e dintorni. La Nave di Teseo, 2018. English: *Being and Its Surroundings*. Ed. Giuseppe Iannantuono, Alberto Martinengo, and Santiago Zabala. Trans. Corrado Federici. McGill-Queen's University Press, 2021.

Scritti filosofici e politici. Ed. Gaetano Chiurazzi. La Nave di Teseo, 2021.*

SECONDARY VATTIMO LITERATURE

Azzarà, Stefano Giuseppe. "Left-Wing Nietzscheanism in Italy: Gianni Vattimo." *Rethinking Marxism* 30, no. 2 (2018): 275–90.

———. *Un Nietzsche italiano: Gianni Vattimo e le avventure dell'oltreuomo rivoluzionario*. Manifesto Libri, 2011.*

Benso, Silvia, and Brian Schroeder, eds. *Between Nihilism and Politics: The Hermeneutics of Gianni Vattimo*. SUNY Press, 2010.

Borradori, Giovanna, ed. *Recoding Metaphysics: The New Italian Philosophy*. Trans. Barbara Spackman. Northwestern University Press, 1998.

Bosteels, B. "Gianni Vattimo: A Bibliography 1956–1993." *Differentia: Review of Italian Thought* 8 (1999): 233–52.

Carchia, Gianni, and Maurizio Ferrarise, eds. *Interpretazione ed emancipazione: Studi in onore di Gianni Vattimo*. Raffaello Cortina, 1996.*

Chiurazzi, Gaetano, ed. *Pensare l'attualità, cambiare il mondo: Riflessioni sul pensiero di Gianni Vattimo*. Mondadori, 2008.*

Coralluzzo, Francesco. *Oltre il relativismo: Comprendere e superare le ragioni di Nietzsche, Heidegger e Vattimo*. Leonardo da Vinci, 2013.*

Depoortere, Frederiek. *Christ in Postmodern Philosophy: Gianni Vattimo, René Girard, and Slavoj Žižek*. T&T Clark, 2008.

———. "Weak Faith." In *The Palgrave Handbook of Mimetic Theory and Religion*, ed. James Alison and Wolfgang Palaver, 387–93. Palgrave Macmillan, 2017.

Dotolo, Carmelo. *La teologia fondamentale davanti alle sfide del "Pensiero debole" di G. Vattimo*. Religione e Spiritualità, 1999.*

Franci, Tommaso. *Vattimo o del nichilismo: Provocazione alla filosofia*. Armando, 2011.*

Frascati-Lochhead, Marta. *Kenosis and Feminist Theology: The Challenge of Gianni Vattimo*. SUNY Press, 1998.

Giorgio, Giovanni. *Il pensiero di Gianni Vattimo: L'emancipazione della metafisica tra dialettica ed ermeneutica*. Franco Angeli, 2006.*

———. "La portata politica del 'pensiero debole' di Gianni Vattimo." *Trópos* 2, no. 1 (2009): 113–25.*

Gnoli, Antonio. "La debole forza di essere stati." Introduction to Gianni Vattimo, *Scritti filosofici e politici*, 11–32. La Nave di Teseo, 2021.*

Guarino, Thomas G. *Vattimo and Theology*. T&T Clark, 2009.

Harris, Matthew Edward. *Essays on Gianni Vattimo: Religion, Ethics, and the History of Ideas*. Cambridge Scholars, 2016.

———. "Gianni Vattimo (1936-)." In *Internet Encyclopedia of Philosophy*, 2013. https://www.iep.utm.edu/vattimo.

———. "Nietzsche's 'Death of God,' Modernism, and Postmodernism in the Twentieth Century: Insights from Altizer and Vattimo." *Heythrop Journal* 62, no. 1 (2021): 53–64.

Irrgang, Ulrike. *"Das Wiederauftauchen einer verwehten Spur": Das religiöse Erbe im Werk Gianni Vattimos und Hans Magnus Enzensbergers*. Matthias-Grünewald, 2019.*

Marzano, Silvia. *Lévinas, Jaspers e il pensiero della differenza: Confronti con Derrida, Vattimo, Lyotard*. Zamorani, 2019.*

Mazzini, Silvia. *Für eine mannigfaltige mögliche Welt: Kunst und Politik bei Ernst Bloch und Gianni Vattimo*. Peter Lang, 2010.*

Mazzini, Sylvia, and Owen Glyn-Williams, eds. *Making Communism Hermeneutical: Reading Vattimo and Zabala*. Contributions to Hermeneutics, vol. 6. Springer International, 2017.

McGravey, Michael. "Jean-Luc Marion and Gianni Vattimo's Contributions for the Postmodern Faith." PhD diss. Duquesne University, 2018.

Meganck, Erik, "'*Nulla in mundo pax sincera . . .*': Secularisation and Violence in Vattimo and Girard." *International Journal of Philosophy and Theology* 74, no. 5 (2013): 410–31.

Migone, Paolo, ed. *Psicoanalisi ed ermeneutica: Dibattito tra Robert R. Holt, Horst Kächele, e Gianni Vattimo*. Métis, 1995.*

Monaco, Davide, *Gianni Vattimo: Ontologia ermeneutica, cristianesimo e modernità*. ETS, 2006.*

Moro, Simonetta, ed. *The Vattimo Dictionary*. Edinburgh University Press, 2023.
Rass, Friederike D. *Die Suche nach Wahrheit im Horizont fragmentarischer Existenzialität—eine Studie über den Sinn der Frage nach "Gott" in der Gegenwart in Auseinandersetzung mit Gianni Vattimo, John D. Caputo und Jean-Luc Nancy*. Mohr Siebeck, 2019.*
Schönherr-Mann, Hans-Martin. *Die Technik und die Schwäche: Ökologie nach Nietzsche, Heidegger und dem "schwachen" Denken*. Passagen, 1989.*
Sciglitano, Anthony C., Jr. "Contesting the World and the Divine: Balthasar's Trinitarian 'Response' to Gianni Vattimo's Secular Christianity." *Modern Theology* 23, no. 4 (2013): 525–59.
———. "Gianni Vattimo and Saint Paul: Ontological Weakening, Kenosis, and Secularity." In *Paul in the Grip of the Philosophers*, ed. Peter Frick, 117–41. Fortress Press, 2013.
Snyder, Jon R. "Translator's Introduction." In Gianni Vattimo, *The End of Modernity: Nihilism and Hermeneutics in Postmodern Culture*, vi–lviii. Johns Hopkins University Press, 1988.
Styers, Randall. "Gianni Vattimo and the Return of the Sacred." In "Literature, Religion, and the Sacred." Special issue, *Annali d'italianistica* 25 (2007): 47–75.
Sützl, Wolfgang. "Gianni Vattimo's Media Philosophy and Its Relevance to Digital Media." *Philosophy Today* 60, no. 3 (2016): 743–59.
Valgenti, Robert. "Vattimo's Nietzsche." In *Interpreting Nietzsche: Reception and Influence*, ed. Ashley Woodward, 149–62. Continuum, 2011.
Vattimo, Gianni, Antonio Cecere, and Debora Tonelli. "*Fratelli tutti*: Dialogo con Gianni Vattimo." In *Fratelli tutti? Credenti e non credenti in dialogo con Papa Francesco*, ed. Debora Tonelli, 143–69. Castelvecchi, 2022.*
Weiss, Martin G. *Gianni Vattimo: Einführung*. 3rd ed. Passagen, 2012.*
Woodward, Ashley. "Being and Information: On the Meaning of Vattimo." *Philosophy Today* 60, no. 3 (2016): 723–41.
———. *Nihilism in Postmodernity: Lyotard, Baudrillard, Vattimo*. Davies Group, 2010.
———. "The Verwindung of Capital: On the Philosophy and Politics of Gianni Vattimo." *Symposium: Canadian Journal of Continental Philosophy/Revue canadienne de philosophie continentale* 13, no. 1 (2009): 73–99.
Zabala, Santiago. "Being Is Conversation: Remains, Weak Thought, and Hermeneutics." In *Consequences of Hermeneutics: Fifty Years After Gadamer's*

Truth and Method, ed. Jeff Malpas and Santiago Zabala, 161–76. Northwestern University Press, 2010.

———. "Gianni Vattimo (1936–)." In *The Cambridge Habermas Lexicon*, ed. Amy Allen and Eduardo Mendieta, 700–701. Cambridge University Press, 2019.

———, ed. *Weakening Philosophy: Essays in Honour of Gianni Vattimo*. McGill-Queen's University Press, 2007.

———. "Weakening Philosophy: A Forum on Gianni Vattimo." *Los Angeles Review of Books*, November 10, 2016. https://lareviewofbooks.org/feature/weakening-philosophy-forum-gianni-vattimo/.

Zawadzki, Andrzej, ed. *Literature and Weak Thought*. Peter Lang, 2013.

BIBLIOGRAPHY

Abbagnano, Nicola. *Historia del la filosofía*. Vol. 4, book 2: *La filosofía contemporánea*. HORA, S.A., 1996.

——. "Verso un nuovo illuminismo: John Dewey." In *Scritti neoilluministici, 1948–1965*, ed. Bruno Maiorca, chap. 5. Unione Tipografico-Editrice Torinese, 2001.

Adorno, Theodor W. *Minima Moralia*. Trans. Edmund Jephcott. New Left, 1974.

——. *Negative Dialectics*. Trans. E. B. Ashton. 1966. Reprint. Continuum, 2007.

Alcoff, Linda Martín, and José Alcoff. "Autonomism in Theory and Practice." *Science and Society* 79, no. 2 (April 2015): 221–42.

Ali, Tariq. *Uprising in Pakistan: How to Bring Down a Dictatorship*. Verso, 2018.

Althusser, Louis. *On Ideology*. Verso, 2008.

Álvarez, Andrés Beltramo. "El Papa llama a Vattimo, el filósofo del pensamiento débil." *La Stampa*, July 9, 2018. https://www.lastampa.it/vatican-insider/es/2018/07/09/news/el-papa-llama-a-vattimo-el-filosofo-del-pensamiento-debil-1.34030484/.

Andes, Stephen J. C. *The Vatican and Catholic Activism in Mexico and Chile: The Politics of Transnational Catholicism, 1920–1940*. Oxford University Press, 2014.

Aristotle. *Nicomachean Ethics*. Vol. 19 of *Aristotle in 23 Volumes*. Trans. H. Rackham. Loeb Classical Library. Harvard University Press/William Heinemann, 1934. https://www.loebclassics.com/view/aristotle-nicomachean_ethics/1926/pb_LCL073.17.xml.

Aslan, Reza. *Zealot: The Life and Times of Jesus of Nazareth*. Random House, 2013.

Associated Press. "Pope Francis Says He Wasn't Offended by 'Communist Crucifix' Gift." *The Guardian*, July 13, 2015. https://www.theguardian.com/world/2015/jul/13/pope-francis-communist-crucifix-gift-bolivia.

Aubral, François. "René Girard: *La violence et le sacré*." *Les cahiers du chemin* 17 (January 15, 1973): 192–205.

Ayer, A. J. *Language, Truth, and Logic*. 1946. Reprint. Dover, 1952.

Azzarà, Stefano G. "Left-Wing Nietzscheanism in Italy: Gianni Vattimo." *Rethinking Marxism* 30, no. 2 (2018): 275–90.

Backman, Jussi. "Radical Contextuality in Heidegger's Postmetaphysics: The Singularity of Being and the Fourfold." In *Paths in Heidegger's Later Thought*, ed. Günter Figal, Diego D'Angelo, Tobias Keiling, and Guang Yang, 190–211. University of Indiana Press, 2012.

Bakunin, Mikhail. *God and the State*. Dover, 1970.

Banner, Stuart. *The Decline of Natural Law: How American Lawyers Once Used Natural Law and Why They Stopped*. Oxford University Press, 2021.

Beardsley, Eleanor. "In France, the Protests of May 1968 Reverberate Today—and Still Divide the French." NPR, May 29, 2018. https://www.npr.org/sections/parallels/2018/05/29/613671633/in-france-the-protests-of-may-1968-reverberate-today-and-still-divide-the-french.

Bell, Daniel. *The End of Ideology: On the Exhaustion of Political Ideas in the Fifties*. 2nd ed. Free Press, 1962.

Benjamin, Walter. "Theological-Political Fragment." In *Reflections: Essays, Aphorisms, Autobiographical Writings*, ed. Peter Demetz, trans. Edmund Jephcott, 312–13. Schocken, 1986.

Benso, Silvia. "Luigi Pareyson's Ontology of Freedom: Encounters with Martin Heidegger and F. W. J. Schelling." In *Open Borders: Encounters Between Italian Philosophy and Continental Thought*, ed. Sylvia Benso and Antonio Calcagno, 21–43. SUNY Press, 2021.

———. "On Luigi Pareyson: A Master in Italian Hermeneutics." *Philosophy Today* 49, no. 4 (Winter 2005): 381–90.

Benso, Silvia, and Brian Schroeder, eds. 2010. *Between Nihilism and Politics: The Hermeneutics of Gianni Vattimo*. SUNY Press.

———. "Italian Philosophy Between 1980 and 1995." In *The History of Continental Philosophy*, vol. 7: *After Poststructuralism: Transitions and Transformations*, ed. Rosi Braidotti, 83–110. Acumen, 2010.

Berger, John. *G: A Novel*. 1972. Reprint. Vintage, 1991.

Berghahn, Klaus L. "From Classicist to Classical Literary Criticism, 1730–1806." In *A History of German Literary Criticism, 1730–1980*, ed. Peter Uwe Hohendahl, 13–98. University of Nebraska Press, 1988.

Bergoglio, Jorge Mario. *Open Mind, Faithful Heart: Reflections on Following Jesus*. Trans. Joseph V. Owens, SJ. Crossroads, 2013.

Bernstein, Richard J. *Beyond Objectivism and Relativism: Science, Hermeneutics, and Praxis*. Blackwell, 1983.

———. "The Constellation of Hermeneutics, Critical Theory, and Deconstruction." In *The Cambridge Companion to Gadamer*, ed. Robert J. Dostal, 267–82. Cambridge University Press, 2002.

———. "The Conversation That Never Happened (Gadamer/Derrida)." *Review of Metaphysics* 61, no. 3 (March 2008): 577–603.

———. *The New Constellation: The Ethical-Political Horizons of Modernity/Postmodernity*. 1991. Reprint. Polity, 2007.

Berta, Giuseppe. "Fiat in the Years of Major Conflict (1969–1980): Worker Mobilization and Management Policy." In *European Yearbook of Business History*, vol. 1, ed. Terry Gourvish and Wilfried Feldenkirchen, 37–56. Routledge, 1998.

Besley, Tina, Michael Peters, and Sharon Rider. "Afterword—Viral Modernity: From Postmodernism to Post-Truth?" In *Post-Truth, Fake News: Viral Modernity and Higher Education*, ed. Michael A. Peters, Sharon Rider, Mats Hyvönen, and Tina Besley, 217–24. Springer International, 2018.

Bethge, Eberhard. *Dietrich Bonhoeffer: A Biography*. Rev. ed. Fortress Press, 2000.

Bianchi, Nicola, and Michela Giorcelli. "Reconstruction Aid, Public Infrastructure, and Economic Development: The Case of the Marshall Plan in Italy." *Journal of Economic History*, working paper, n.d.

Bilgrami, Akeel. *Secularism, Identity, and Enchantment*. Harvard University Press, 2014.

Billings, Joshua. "Nietzsche's Philology of the Present." *New Literary History* 15, no. 3 (2020): 549–65.

Bleicher, Josef. *Contemporary Hermeneutics: Hermeneutics as Method, Philosophy, and Critique*. Routledge and Kegan Paul, 1980.

Bloch, Ernst. *The Principle of Hope*. Trans. Neville Plaice, Stephen Plaice, and Paul Knight. MIT Press, 1995.

———. *The Spirit of Utopia*. Trans. Anthony A. Nassar. Stanford University Press, 2000.

Blond, Phillip, ed. *Post-Secular Philosophy: Between Philosophy and Theology*. Routledge, 1998.

Boff, Leonardo. *Ecclesiogenesis: The Base Communities Reinvent the Church*. Trans. Robert R. Barr. Orbis, 1986.

Bonhoeffer, Dietrich. *Akt und Sein: Transzendentalphilosophie und Ontologie in der systematischen Theologie*. Chr. Kaiser, 1956.

——. 2012. *Dietrich Bonhoeffer Works*. Vol. 11: *Ecumenical, Academic, and Pastoral Work, 1931–1932*. Ed. Victoria J. Barnett, Mark S. Brocker, and Michael B. Lukens. Trans. Anne Schmidt-Lange, with Isabel Best, Nicolas Humphrey, and Marion Pauck. Fortress Press, 2012.

——. "Draft for a Catechism: As You Believe, so You Receive." In *Dietrich Bonhoeffer Works*, 11:258–66.

——. "14. Lecture in Ciernohorské Kúpele: One the Theological Foundation of the Work of the World Alliance" (1932). In *Dietrich Bonhoeffer Works*, 11:359–60.

——. *Letters and Papers from Prison*. Enlarged ed. SCM Press, 1971.

——. "To Erich Seeburg, Berlin, April 21, 1933." In *Dietrich Bonhoeffer Works*, vol. 12: *Berlin: 1932–1933*, ed. Larry L. Rasmussen, trans. Isabel Best and David Higgins, 104. Fortress Press, 2009.

Bonino, José Míguez. *Doing Theology in a Revolutionary Situation*. Fortress Press, 1975.

Borradori, Giovanna, ed. *Recoding Metaphysics: The New Italian Philosophy*. Trans. B. Spackman. Northwestern University Press, 1988.

Bosteels, Bruno. "Gianni Vattimo: A Bibliography 1956–1993." *Differentia: Review of Italian Thought* 8, no. 20 (1999): 233–52.

Botbol, Michel, and Adeline Gourbil. "The Place of Psychoanalysis in French Psychiatry." *British Journal of Psychiatry International* 15, no. 1 (2018): 3–5.

Bremmer, Jan. "Scapegoat Rituals in Ancient Greece." *Harvard Studies in Classical Philology* 87 (1983): 299–320.

Broadie, Sarah. *Ethics with Aristotle*. Oxford University Press, 1991.

Brommage, Thomas J., Jr. "Wittgenstein: Interpreting the *Tractatus Logico-Philosophicus*." PhD diss., University of South Florida, 2008.

Bruns, Gerald L. *Heidegger's Estrangements: Language, Truth, and Poetry in the Later Writings*. Yale University Press, 1989.

Burgmann, Verity. "The Multitude and the Many-Headed Hydra: Autonomist Marxist Theory and Labor History." In "Strikes and Social Conflicts."

Special issue, *International Labor and Working-Class History* 83 (Spring 2013): 170–90.

Calhoun, Craig. "Time, World, and Secularism." In *The Post-Secular in Question: Religion in Contemporary Society*, ed. Philip S. Gorski, David Kyuman Kim, John Torpey, and Jonathan VanAntwerpen, 335–64. New York University Press/Social Science Research Council, 2012.

Caputo, John D. *Radical Hermeneutics: Repetition, Deconstruction, and the Hermeneutic Project*. Indiana University Press, 1987.

——. *The Weakness of God: A Theology of the Event*. Indiana University Press, 2006.

Carey, Elaine. "Mexico's 1968 Olympic Dream." In *Protests in the Streets: 1968 Across the Globe*, ed. Elaine Carey, 91–119. Hackett, 2016.

Carioti, Antonio. "È morto Gianni Vattimo, il filosofo aveva 87 anni." *Corriere della sera*, September 19, 2023. https://www.corriere.it/cultura/23_settembre_19/gianni-vattimo-morto-8d9e08e4-52db-11ee-9c68-5070f213fc3b.shtml.

Carravetta, Peter. "An Introduction to the Hermeneutics of Luigi Pareyson." *Differentia: Review of Italian Thought* 3–4, no. 22 (Spring–Autumn 1989): 217–41.

——. "What Is Weak Thought? The Original Theses and Context of *il Pensiero Debole*." In Vattimo and Rovatti, eds., *Weak Thought*, 3–4.

Carrillo, Elisa A. "The Italian Catholic Church and Communism, 1943–1963." *Catholic Historical Review* 77, no. 4 (October 1991): 644–57.

Carroll, Rory. "Noam Chomsky Criticises Old Friend Hugo Chávez for 'Assault' on Democracy." *The Guardian*, July 2, 2011. https://www.theguardian.com/world/2011/jul/03/noam-chomsky-hugo-chavez-democracy.

Casanova, José. *Public Religions in the Modern World*. University of Chicago Press, 1994.

Cassirer, Ernst. *The Philosophy of the Enlightenment*. Trans. Fritz C. A. Koelln and James P. Pettegrove. Beacon Press, 1964.

Castellano, Lucio, Arigo Cavallina, Giustino Cortiana, Mario Dalmaviva, Luciano Ferrari Bravo, Chicco Funaro, et al. "Do You Remember Revolution?" In *Radical Thought in Italy: A Potential Politics*, ed. Paolo Virno and Michael Hardt, 225–40. University of Minnesota Press, 1996.

Cazzullo, Aldo. "Gianni Vattimo: Il '68, le scorrettezze politiche e la rivalità con Eco: 'Sono più intelligente di lui.'" *Corriere della sera*, September 20, 2023. https://www.corriere.it/cultura/23_settembre_20/gianni-vattimo-68-quella

-rivalita-eco-scorrettezze-politiche-f7b0e1a2-5740-11ee-a17f-69493a54d671 .shtml.

Chamedes, Giuliana. "The Vatican, Nazi-Fascism, and the Making of Transnational Anti-Communism in the 1930s." *Journal of Contemporary History* 51, no. 2 (April 2016): 261–90.

Chesterton, G. K. *Saint Francis of Assisi*. 1957. Reprint. Doubleday, 2001.

Chiurazzi, Gaetano. "The Experiment of Nihilism: Interpretation and Experience of Truth in Gianni Vattimo." In Benso and Schroeder, eds., *Between Nihilism and Politics*, 15–32.

Chomsky, Noam. "Noam Chomsky on Revolutionary Violence, Communism, and the American Left." Interview by Christopher Helali. *Pax Marxista*, March 12, 2013. https://Chomsky.info/20130312/.

Ciberira, Fernando. "Entrevista al filósofo italiano y eurodiputado de la izquierda Gianni Vattimo." *Página 12*, November 10, 2013. https://www.pagina12 .com.ar/diario/elpais/1-233272-2013-11-10.html.

Cimatti, Felice. "Kenosis." In Moro, ed., *The Vattimo Dictionary*, 112–15.

Comas, James. "The Presence of Theory/Theorizing the Present." *Research in African Literatures/Critical Theory and African Literature* 21, no. 1 (1990): 5–31.

Cone, James H. *A Black Theology of Liberation*. 20th Anniversary Ed. Orbis, 1990.

Cooper, Thia, ed. *The Reemergence of Liberation Theologies: Models for the Twenty-First Century*. Palgrave-Macmillan, 2013.

Copleston, Frederick, SJ. *A History of Philosophy*. Vol. 8: *Bentham to Russell*. Newman Press, 1966.

Corriero, Emilio Carlo. *Nietzsche's Death of God and Italian Philosophy*. Trans. Vanessa Di Stefano. Rowman and Littlefield, 2016.

Crenshaw, Kimberlé. "Demarginalizing the Intersection of Race and Sex: A Black Feminist Critique of Antidiscrimination Doctrine, Feminist Theory, and Antiracist Politics." *University of Chicago Legal Forum*, no. 1 (1989): 139–67.

Crockett, Clayton. "Violence." In Moro, ed., *The Vattimo Dictionary*, 199–200.

Crockett, Clayton, B. Keith Putt, and Jeffrey W. Robbins, eds. *The Future of Continental Philosophy of Religion*. University of Indiana Press, 2014.

Crossan, John Dominic. *God and Empire: Jesus Against Rome, Then and Now*. HarperCollins, 2007.

——. *Jesus: A Revolutionary Biography*. HarperCollins, 1994.

Cullen, Christopher M., SJ. "Transcendental Thomism: Realism Rejected." In *The Failure of Modernism: The Cartesian Legacy and Contemporary Pluralism*, ed. Brendan Sweetman, 72–86. American Maritain Association, 1999.

d'Agostini, Franca. "Weak Thought (*Pensiero Debole*)." In Moro, ed. *The Vattimo Dictionary*, 202–5.

Dalferth, Ingolf U. *Transcendence and the Secular World: Life in Orientation to Ultimate Presence*. 2nd rev. ed. Trans. Jo Bennett. Mohr Siebeck, 2018.

Damiata, Roberta. "È morto Gianni Vattimo: Il filosofo del 'pensiero debole' aveva 87 anni." *Il Giornale*, September 19, 2023. https://www.ilgiornale.it/news/letteratura/morto-filosofo-gianni-vattimo-aveva-87-anni-2213251.html.

Davidson, Donald. "On the Very Idea of a Conceptual Scheme." *Proceedings and Addresses of the American Philosophical Association* 47 (1973–1974): 5–20.

de Belloy, Camille. "A. D. Sertillanges, philosophe thomiste de la création." *Revue des sciences philosophiques et théologiques* 102, no. 3 (July–September 2018): 467–505.

———. "Ambroise Gardeil and the Fight to Study." *Revue des sciences philosophiques et théologiques* 92, no. 3 (2008): 423–32.

Depoortere, Frederiek. *Christ in Postmodern Philosophy: Gianni Vattimo, René Girard, and Slavoj Žižek*. T&T Clark International, 2008.

———. "Gianni Vattimo's Concept of Truth and Its Consequences for Christianity." In *Theology and the Quest for Truth: Historical- and Systematic-Theological Studies*, ed. Mathijs Lamberigts, Lieven Boeve, and Terrence Merrigan, 241–58. Bibliotheca Ephemeridum Theologicarum Lovaniensium no. 202. Leuven University Press, 2006.

Derrida, Jacques. "*Fichus*: Frankfurt Address." In *Paper Machine*, trans. Rachel Bowlby, 164–82. Stanford University Press, 2005.

———. "Wie recht er hatte! Mein Cicerone Hans-Georg Gadamer." *Frankfurter Allgemeine Zeitung*, March 28, 2002.

de Saussure, Ferdinand. *Course in General Linguistics*. Trans. Roy Harris. Open Court, 1986.

Dewey, John. "Propositions, Warranted Assertibility, and Truth." *Journal of Philosophy* 38, no. 7 (1941): 169–86.

Doe, Norman, ed. *Christianity and Natural Law: An Introduction*. Cambridge University Press, 2017.

Donovan, Mark. "Democrazia Cristiana: Party of Government." In *Christian Democracy in Europe: A Comparative Perspective*, ed. David Hanley, 71–86. Pinter, 1996.

Dorrien, Gary. "Modernism as a Theological Problem: The Theological Legacy of Langdon Gilkey." *American Journal of Theology and Philosophy* 28, no. 1 (January 2007): 64–94.

Dostoevsky, Fyodor. *The Brothers Karamazov*. Trans. Richard Pevear and Larissa Volokhonsky. Farrar, Straus and Giroux, 2002.

———. *Letters of Fyodor Michailovitch Dostoevsky to His Family and Friends*. Trans. Ethel Colburn Mayne. Chatto and Windus, 1914.

Dotolo, Carmelo. *The Christian Revelation: Word, Event, and Mystery*. Trans. Cavallo Domenica. Davies Group, 2006.

———. "The Hermeneutics of Christianity and Philosophical Responsibility." In Zabala, ed., *Weakening Philosophy*, 348–68.

———. *La teologia fondamentale—davanti alle sfide del "pensiero debole" di G. Vattimo*. LAS, 1999.

Douglas-Scott, Sionaidh. *Law After Modernity*. Hart, 2013.

Drake, Richard. "Italy in the 1960s: A Legacy of Terrorism and Liberation." In "Rethinking 1968: The United States and Western Europe." Special issue, *South Central Review* 16, no. 4–17, no. 1 (Winter 1999–Spring 2000): 62–76.

Draper, Susana. *1968 Mexico: Constellations of Freedom and Democracy*. Duke University Press, 2018.

Drèze, Jean, and Amartya Sen, eds. *The Political Economy of Hunger: Selected Essays*. 3 vols. Clarendon Press, 1991.

Dulles, Cardinal Avery. "The Sacramental Ecclesiology of 'Lumen gentium.'" *Gregorianum* 86, no. 3 (2005): 550–62.

Dussel, Enrique. "Un diálogo con Gianni Vattimo: De la postmodernidad a la transmodernidad." *A parte rei* 54, no. 6 (2007): 1–32.

Dworkin, Dennis. *Cultural Marxism in Postwar Britain: History, the New Left, and the Origins of Cultural Studies*. Duke University Press, 1997.

Eco, Umberto. *The Limits of Interpretation*. Indiana University Press, 1990.

Egginton, William. "Realism/ New Realism." In Moro, ed., *The Vattimo Dictionary*, 163–65.

Eliade, Mircea. *The Sacred and the Profane: The Nature of Religion*. Trans. Williard R. Trask. Harcourt, Brace and World, 1987.

Elias, Paul. "Revolutionary Subjectivity in the Thought of Karl Marx." PhD diss., York University, Toronto, 2019.

Ellul, Jaques. *The Subversion of Christianity*. Trans. Geoffrey W. Bromiley. Eerdmans, 1986.

Esposito, Roberto. "Gianni Vattimo è morto: È stato il filosofo pensiero debole e del postmoderno." *La Repubblica*, September 20, 2023. https://www.repubblica.it/cultura/2023/09/20/news/gianni_vattimo_morto_filosofo-415094684/.

Evans, C. Stephen, ed. *Exploring Kenotic Christology: The Self-Emptying of God*. Oxford University Press, 2006.

Facultad de Periodismo y Comunicacion Social. "IV Comcis: El filósofo italiano Gianni Vattimo disertó en la facultad, 2020." Universidad Nacional de La Plata, October 9, 2020. https://perio.unlp.edu.ar/2020/10/07/iv-comcis-el-filosofo-italiano-gianni-vattimo-diserto-en-la-facultad/.

Famà, Irene. "Sul patrimonio di Vattimo scoppia la battaglia legale: Ora i conti sono bloccati." *La Stampa*, September 21, 2023. https://www.lastampa.it/torino/2023/09/21/news/patrimonio_vattimo_battaglia_legale_conti_bloccati-13395253/.

Faulkner, William. *Requiem for a Nun*. 1950. Reprint. Vintage, 2011.

Feldman, Stanley, and Christopher Johnston. "Understanding the Determinants of Political Ideology: Implications of Structural Complexity." *Political Psychology* 35, no. 3 (June 2014): 337–58.

Ferm, Deane William. *Third World Liberation Theologies*. Orbis, 1988.

Ferrara, Alessandro. *Reflective Authenticity: Rethinking the Project of Modernity*. 1998. Reprint. Routledge, 2002.

Ferraris, Maurizio. "The Aging of the 'School of Suspicion." In Vattimo and Rovatti, eds., *Weak Thought*, 138–54.

———. *Manifesto of New Realism*. Trans. Sarah De Sanctis. SUNY Press, 2014.

———. "Post moderni o neorealisti? L'addio al pensiero debole che divide i filosofi, dialogo tra Maurizio Ferraris e Gianni Vattimo." *La Repubblica*, August 19, 2011. https://ricerca.repubblica.it/repubblica/archivio/repubblica/2011/08/19/post-moderni-neorealisti-addio-al-pensiero-debole.html.

———. "Vattimo, nemico dei dogmi." *Corriere della sera*, September 19, 2023. https://www.corriere.it/cultura/23_settembre_19/vattimo-nemico-dogmi-82884018-53c7-11ee-8884-717525326594.shtml.

Fiorenza, Francis Schüssler. 2005. "From Theologian to Pope: A Personal View Back, Past the Public Portrayals." *Harvard Divinity Bulletin* 33 (2005). https://bulletin.hds.harvard.edu/from-theologian-to-pope/.

Fisher, Mark. *Capitalist Realism: Is There No Alternative?* Zero Books/John Hunt, 2009.

Foot, John. *Blood and Power: The Rise and Fall of Italian Fascism*. Bloomsbury, 2022.

Frascati-Lochhead, Marta. *Kenosis and Feminist Theology: The Challenge of Gianni Vattimo*. SUNY Press, 1998.

Frederico, Giovanni, and Paolo Malanima. "Progress, Decline, Growth: Product and Productivity in Italian Agriculture, 1000–2000." *Economic History Review* 57, no. 3 (2004): 437–64.

Freire, Paulo. *Pedagogy of the Oppressed*. Trans. Myra Bergman Ramos. Continuum, 2005.

Fröhlich, Grit. "Culture and Invention—Umberto Eco and the Aesthetics of Luigi Pareyson." In *Umberto Eco in His Own Words*, ed. Torkild Thellefsen and Bent Sørensen, 34–40. De Gruyter Mouton, 2017.

Fukuyama, Francis. *The End of History and the Last Man*. Free Press, 1992.

Gadamer, Hans-Georg. "The Artwork in Word and Image: 'So True so Full of Being!'" In *The Gadamer Reader: A Bouquet of the Later Writings*, ed. Richard E. Palmer, 192–226. Northwestern University Press, 2007.

———. "Hermeneutics and Social Science." *Cultural Hermeneutics* 2, no. 4 (1975): 307–16.

———. "The Phenomenological Movement" (1963). In Gadamer, *Philosophical Hermeneutics*, 130–81.

———. *Philosophical Hermeneutics*. Trans. David E. Linge. Paperback ed. University of California Press, 1977.

———. "The Science of the Life-World." In Gadamer, *Philosophical Hermeneutics*, 182–97.

———. *Truth and Method*. Trans. rev. Joel Weinsheimer and Donald G. Marshall. 2nd ed. Continuum, 2004.

Garin, Eugino. *History of Italian Philosophy*. 2 vols. Ed. and trans. Giorgio Pinton. Rodopi, 2008.

Garrido, Daniel Rueda. *Forms of Life and Subjectivity: Rethinking Sartre's Philosophy*. Open Book, 2021.

Garrigou-Lagrange, Réginald. "La nouvelle théologie, où va-t-elle?" *Angelicum* 23 (1946): 126–45.

Gellman, Jerome I. "Religion as Language." *Religious Studies* 21, no. 2 (June 1985): 159–68.

Gilman, Nils. *Mandarins of the Future: Modernization Theory in Cold War America*. Johns Hopkins University Press, 2003.

Ginsborg, Paul. *A History of Contemporary Italy: Society and Politics, 1943–1988*. Palgrave Macmillan, 2003.

Giorgio, Giovanni. *Il pensiero di Gianni Vattimo: L'emancipazione della metafisica tra dialettica ed ermeneutica*. Franco Angeli, 2006.

Giornale la voca. "Torino dà l'ultimo saluto a Gianni Vattimo." September 23, 2023. https://www.giornalelavoce.it/news/attualita/536729/torino-da-l-ultimo-saluto-a-gianni-vattimo.html.

Girard, René. *Things Hidden Since the Foundation of the World*. Trans. Stephen Bann and Michael Metteer. 1978. Reprint. Stanford University Press, 1987.

Girard, René, Pierpaolo Antonello, and João Cezar de Castro Rocha. *Evolution and Conversion: Dialogues on the Origin of Culture*. T&T Clark, 2007.

Gonzales, Philip John Paul. *Reimagining the Analogia Entis: The Future of Erich Przywara's Christian Vision*. Eerdmans, 2019.

González, Justo L. "Athens and Jerusalem Revisited: Reason and Authority in Tertullian." *Church History* 43, no. 1 (March 1974): 17–25.

Goodman, Nelson. *Fact, Fiction, and Forecast*. Harvard University Press, 1955.

Gotzler, Steven. "1956—the British New Left and the 'Big Bang' Theory of Cultural Studies." *Lateral: Journal of the Cultural Studies Association* 8, no. 2 (Fall 2019). https://csalateral.org/section/years-in-cultural-studies/1956-british-new-left-gotzler/.

Gould, Stephen Jay. "Nonoverlapping Magisteria." *Natural History* 106 (March 1997): 16–22.

Graeber, David, and Marshall Sahlins. *On Kings*. Hau, 1997.

Gramsci, Antonio. *Selections from the Prison Notebooks*. Trans. Quintin Hoare and Geoffrey Nowell Smith. 1971. Reprint. International, 1992.

———. "The Turin Factory Councils Movement." In *Selections from Political Writings 1910–1920*, trans. John Mathews, 310–20. Lawrence and Wishart, 1977.

Griffith, R. Drew. "Oedipus Pharmakos? Alleged Scapegoating in Sophocles' Oedipus the King." *Phoenix* 47, no. 2 (Summer 1993): 95–114.

Grondin, Jean. *Hans-Georg Gadamer: A Biography*. Trans. Joel Weinsheimer. Yale University Press, 2011.

Guarino, Thomas G. *Vattimo and Theology*. T&T Clark, 2009.

Gutiérrez, Gustavo. *A Theology of Liberation: History, Politics, and Salvation*. Trans. and ed. Sister Caridad Inda and John Eagleson. 1971. Reprint. Orbis, 1973.

Habermas, Jürgen. "Modernity Versus Postmodernity." *New German Critique* 22 (Winter 1981): 3–14.

———. *Philosophical-Political Profiles*. Trans. Frederick G. Lawrence. MIT Press, 1983.

———. *The Structural Transformation of the Public Sphere: An Inquiry Into a Category of Bourgeois Society*. Trans. Thomas Burger with the assistance of Frederick Lawrence. MIT Press, 1991.

Hardt, Michael, and Antonio Negri. *Empire*. Harvard University Press, 2001.

Hare, R. M. "Theology and Falsification." In *New Essays in Philosophical Theology*, ed. Antony Flew and Alasdair MacIntyre, 99–103. MacMillan, 1955.

Harman, Graham. Foreword to Maurizio Ferraris, *Manifesto of New Realism*, trans. Sarah De Sanctis, ix–xii. SUNY Press, 2014.

———. *Guerilla Metaphysics: Phenomenology and the Carpentry of Things*. Open Court, 2005.

———. *Tool-Being: Heidegger and the Metaphysics of Objects*. Open Court, 2002.

Harrison, Oliver. *Revolutionary Subjectivity in Post-Marx Thought: Laclau, Negri, Badiou*. Ashgate, 2014.

Hart, David Bentley. "A Philosopher in the Twilight: Heidegger's Philosophy as Meditation on the Mystery of Being." *First Things: A Journal of Religion and Public Life* (Institute on Religion and Public Life), February 2011. https://www.firstthings.com/article/2011/02/a-philosopher-in-the-twilight.

Hartley, L. P. *The Go-Between*. 1953. Reprint. New York Review of Books, 2002.

Hebblethwaite, Peter. "Liberation Theology and the Roman Catholic Church." In *The Cambridge Companion to Liberation Theology*, ed. Christopher Rowland, 179–98. Cambridge University Press, 1999.

Hegel, G. W. F. *Elements of the Philosophy of Right*. 8th ed.Ed. Allen W. Wood. Trans. Hugh B. Nisbet. Cambridge University Press, 2002.

———. *Lectures on the Philosophy of Religion*. One-volume ed.: *The Lectures of 1827*. Ed. Peter C. Hodgson. Trans. Robert F. Brown, Peter C. Hodgson, and J. M. Stewart, with the assistance of H. S. Harris. University of California Press, 1988.

Heidegger, Martin. *Basic Concepts*. Trans. Gary E. Aylesworth. Indiana University Press, 1993.

———. *Being and Time*. Trans. John MacQuarrie and Edward Robinson. 1962. Reprint. Harper and Rowe, 2008.

———. *Gesamtausgabe*. Vol. 18: *Grundbegriffe der aristotelischen Philosophie*. Vittorio Klostermann, 1924.

———. *On Time and Being*. Trans. Joan Stambaugh. Harper and Rowe, 1972.

Hennesey, James. "Leo XIII's Thomistic Revival: A Political and Philosophical Event." *Journal of Religion* 58, supplement (1978): S185–S197.

Herget, James E., and Stephen Wallace. "The German Free Law Movement as the Source of American Legal Realism" *Virginia Law Review* 73, no. 2 (March 1987): 399–455.

Hernandez-Lemus, Alberto. "Beyond *Pensiero Debole* in Latin America: Territories Outside State Structures." *Radical Philosophy Review* 19, no. 2 (2016): 409–27.

Hickel, Jason. "Is Global Inequality Getting Better or Worse? A Critique of the World Bank's Convergence Narrative." *Third World Quarterly* 38, no. 10 (2017): 2208–22.

Higginson, Paul. "The Vatican and Communism from 'Divini Redemptoris' to Pope Paul VI, Part 1." *New Blackfriars* 61, no. 719 (April 1980): 158–71.

hooks, bell. "Eating the Other: Desire and Resistance." In *Black Looks: Race and Representation*, 21–40. South End Press, 1992.

Horkheimer, Max, and Theodor Adorno. *Dialectic of Enlightenment: Philosophical Fragments*. Trans. Edmund Jephcott. Stanford University Press, 2002.

Horn, Gerd-Rainer. *The Spirit of Vatican II: Western European Progressive Catholicism in the Long Sixties*. Oxford University Press, 2015.

———. *Western European Liberation Theology: The First Wave, 1924–1959*. Oxford University Press, 2008.

Howard, Dick. *The Marxian Legacy: The Search for the New Left*. 3rd ed. Palgrave-Macmillan, 2019.

Howard-Brook, Wes, and Anthony Gwyther. *Unveiling Empire: Reading Revelation, Then and Now*. Orbis, 1999.

Huntington, Samuel P. "The Clash of Civilizations?" *Foreign Affairs* 72, no. 3 (Summer 1993): 22–49.

———. *The Clash of Civilizations and the Remaking of World Order*. Simon and Schuster, 1996.

Hurst, Andrea. *Derrida Vis-à-Vis Lacan: Interweaving Deconstruction and Psychoanalysis*. Fordham University Press, 2008.

Hursthouse, Rosalind. *On Virtue Ethics*. Oxford University Press, 1999.

Hutchinson, Allan C. *It's All in the Game: A Nonfoundationalist Account of Law and Adjudication.* Duke University Press, 2000.

Istituto della Enciclopedia Italiana. "Umberto Eco." In *Lessico del XXI secolo.* Istituto della Enciclopedia Italiana fondata da Giovanni Treccani, 2012. https://www.treccani.it/enciclopedia/umberto-eco_(Lessico-del-XXI -Secolo)/.

James, Harold, and Kevin H. O'Rourke. "Italy and the First Age of Globalization, 1861–1940." In Toniolo, ed., *The Oxford Handbook of the Italian Economy Since Unification,* 37–68.

Jameson, Fredric. "Future City." *New Left Review* 21 (May–June 2003): 65–79.

Jenson, Robert W. *Systematic Theology.* Vol. 2: *The Works of God.* Oxford University Press, 1999.

Jessop, T. E. "The Philosophic Work of Cardinal Mercier." *Mind* 35, no. 138 (April 1926): 269–71.

Jian, Chen, Martin Klimke, Masha Kirasirova, Mary Nolan, Marilyn Young, and Joanna Waley-Cohen, eds. *The Routledge Handbook of the Global Sixties: Between Protest and Nation Building.* Routledge, 2018.

Johnson, Luke Timothy. *Among the Gentiles: Greco-Roman Religion and Christianity.* Yale University Press, 2009.

Jones, Steve. *Antonio Gramsci.* Routledge, 2006.

Jonkers, Peter. "In the World, but Not of the World." *Bijdragen tijdschrift voor filosofie en theologie* 61 (2000): 370–89.

Jüngel, Eberhard. *Death: The Riddle and the Mystery.* Trans. Iain Nicol and Ute Nicol. St. Andrew Press, 1975.

Kail, Michel, and Raoul Kirchmayr. Introduction to Jean-Paul Sartre, *What Is Subjectivity?,* trans. David Broder and Trista Selous, 5–20. Verso, 2016.

Kasper, Walter. "The Theological Anthropology of *Gaudium et spes.*" *Communio: International Catholic Review* 23 (1996): 129–40.

Katsiaficas, George. *The Global Imagination of 1968: Revolution and Counterrevolution.* PM Press, 2018.

Kaufmann, Walter. *Nietzsche: Philosopher, Psychologist, Antichrist.* 4th ed. Princeton University Press, 1974.

Kearney, Richard. "Heidegger and the Possible." *Philosophical Studies* 27 (1980): 176–95.

Kelly, J. M. *A Short History of Western Legal Theory.* 1992. Reprint. Clarendon Press, 2013.

Kilcrease, Jack D. *The Doctrine of Atonement: From Luther to Forde.* Wipf and Stock, 2018.

"King John Renders Homage and Fealty to Innocent III (1214)." In *Selected Letters of Pope Innocent III Concerning England*, ed. C. R. Cheney and W. H. Semple, 177–82. Thomas Nelson, 1953.

Kipling, Rudyard. "The White Man's Burden." *McClure's Magazine*, February 1899.

Kirwan, Michael. *Girard and Theology.* T&T Clark, 2009.

Kissinger, Henry A. "Communist Parties in Western Europe: Challenge to the West." In *Eurocommunism: The Italian Case*, ed. Austin Ranney and Giovanni Sartori, 183–96. American Enterprise Institute for Public Policy Research, 1978.

Koven, Ronald. "'Historic Compromise' Stronger in Italy." *Washington Post*, May 18, 1978. https://www.washingtonpost.com/archive/politics/1978/05/18/historic-compromise-stronger-in-italy/8798b142-49bc-44c9-a902-99a72bb94f4a/.

Lamb, Matthew L., and Matthew Levering, eds. *Vatican II: Renewal Within Tradition.* Oxford University Press, 2009.

Lambert, Gregg. *Return Statements: The Return of Religion in Contemporary Philosophy.* Ediburgh University Press, 2016.

Lammi, Walter. "Hans-Georg Gadamer's 'Correction' of Heidegger." *Journal of the History of Ideas* 52, no. 3 (July–September 1991): 487–507.

Langland, Victoria. *Speaking of Flowers: Student Movements and the Making and Remembering of 1968 in Military Brazil.* Duke University Press, 2013.

Law, David R. *Kierkegaard's Kenotic Christology.* Oxford University Press, 2013.

Le Guin, Ursula K. "Speech on the Occasion of the National Book Foundation Medal for Distinguished Contribution to American Letters." 2014. https://www.ursulakleguin.com/nbf-medal.

Leiro, Daniel Mariano. "Notas sobre ontología del decliner: La hermenéutica nihilista de Gianni Vattimo." *Anales del seminario de historia de la filosofía* 26 (2009): 207–16.

Lemna, Keith Edward. "Pope Francis's Strong Thought." *Theological Librarianship* 7, no. 2 (July 2014): 45–53.

Lenin, Vladimir. "What Is to Be Done? (1902)." In *Essential Works of Lenin*, ed. Henry M. Christman, 53–177. Dover, 1987.

Lewis, C. S. *The Abolition of Man.* 1944. Reprint. HarperCollins, 2000.

———. *Mere Christianity*. 1952. Reprint. HarperCollins, 2001.

———. *The Weight of Glory and Other Addresses*. 1976. Reprint. HarperCollins, 2001.

Lewis, David. "Anthropology and Development: The Uneasy Relationship." In *A Handbook of Economic Anthropology*, ed. James G. Carrier, 472–88. Edward Elgar, 2005.

Liceo Classico e Linguistico Vincenzo Gioberti. "In memoria di Gianni Vattimo." Ministero dell'Istruzione e del Merito, Italy, n.d. https://www.liceogioberti.edu.it/pagine/in-memoria-di-gianni-vattimo. Accessed March 12, 2024.

Litowitz, Douglas E. *Postmodern Philosophy and Law*. University Press of Kansas, 1997.

Livingston, James C. *Modern Christian Thought*. Vol. 1: *The Enlightenment and the Nineteenth Century*. 2nd ed. Prentice Hall, 1997.

Løland, Ole Jakob. "The Solved Conflict: Pope Francis and Liberation Theology." *International Journal of Latin American Religions* 5 (July 2021): 287–314.

Loughlin, Gerard. *"Nouvelle Théologie*: A Return to Modernism?" In *Ressourcement: A Movement for Renewal in Twentieth-Century Catholic Theology*, ed. Gabriel Flynn and Paul D. Murray, 36–50. Oxford: Oxford University Press, 2012.

Lovell, Julia. *Maoism: A Global History*. Penguin Random House, 2019.

Löwith, Karl. "Man's Self-Alienation in the Early Writings of Marx." *Social Research* 21, no. 2 (Summer 1954): 204–30.

Löwy, Michael. "The Romantic and the Marxist Critique of Modern Civilization." *Theory and Society* 16, no. 6 (November 1987): 891–904.

Lücke, Horst Klaus. "The European Natural Law Codes: The Age of Reason and the Powers of Government." *University of Queensland Law Journal* 31, no. 1 (2012): 7–38.

Lukács, György. "What Is Orthodox Marxism?" In *History and Class Consciousness: Studies in Marxist Dialectics*, trans. Rodney Livingstone, 1–26. MIT Press, 1971.

Luther, Martin. "Disputation Against Scholastic Theology," In *Martin Luther's Basic Theological Writings*, ed. Timothy F. Lull, 13–20. Fortress Press, 1989.

Lyotard, Jean-François. "Lessons in Paganism" (1989). In *The Lyotard Reader*, ed. Andrew Benjamin, 122–54. Blackwell, 1998.

———. *The Post-Modern Condition: A Report on Knowledge*. Trans. Geoff Bennington and Brian Massumi. University of Minnesota Press, 1984.
Lyotard, Jean-François, and Jean-Loup Thébaud. *Just Gaming*. Trans. Wlad Godzich. University of Minnesota Press, 1985.
MacCulloch, Diarmaid. *Christianity: The First Three Thousand Years*. Penguin, 2009.
Malpas, Jeff, and Nick Malpas. "Politics, Hermeneutics, and Truth." In Mazzini and Glyn-Williams, eds., *Making Communism Hermeneutical*, 19–30.
Mancini, Federico. "The Italian Student Movement." *AAUP Bulletin* 54, no. 4 (December 1968): 427–32.
Marchini, Aldo U. "The Italian Communist Party 1921–1964: A Profile." PhD diss., University of Windsor, 1966.
Markus, R. A. *Saeculum: History and Society in the Theology of St. Augustine*. Cambridge University Press, 1970.
Marshall, Peter. *Demanding the Impossible: A History of Anarchism*. HarperCollins, 2008.
Martinenghi, Sarah. "Caso Vattimo, Caminada condannato a 2 anni: 'Ha approfittato del filosofo.'" *La Repubblica*, February 6, 2023. https://torino.repubblica.it/cronaca/2023/02/06/news/caso_vattimo_condanna_caminada-386718947/#:~:text=Home-,Caso%20Vattimo%2C%20Caminada%20condannato%20a%202,%3A%20%22Ha%20approfittato%20del%20filosofo%22&text=Due%20anni%20di%20carcere%20per,%C3%A8%20al%20fianco%20del%20filosofo.
———. "L'eredità di Vattimo va a due cugine, i giudici: 'Caminada indegno.'" *La Repubblica*, July 31, 2024. https://torino.repubblica.it/cronaca/2024/07/31/news/gianni_vattimo_eredita_due_cugine_caminada_indegno-423422499/#google_vignette.
———. "Gianni Vattimo è morto: Il filosofo aveva 87 anni." *La Repubblica*, September 19, 2023. https://torino.repubblica.it/cronaca/2023/09/19/news/e_morto_il_filosofo_gianni_vattimo-415090320/.
———. 2022. "Gianni Vattimo vuole sposare Caminada ma la Procura di Torino blocca l'unione civile." *La Repubblica*, December 14, 2022. https://torino.repubblica.it/cronaca/2022/12/14/news/gianni_vattimo_vuole_sposare_caminada_ma_la_procura_di_torino_blocca_lunione_civile-379048608/.
Marwick, Arthur. *The Sixties: Cultural Revolution in Britain, France, Italy, and the United States, c. 1958–c. 1974*. Bloomsbury Reader, 2012.

Marx, Karl. "*From* 'The Holy Family' (1844)." In *Writings of the Young Marx on Philosophy and Society*, trans. Loyd D. Easton and Kurt H. Guddat, 361–98. Hackett, 1967.

———. "Theses on Feuerbach." In Karl Marx and Friedrich Engels, *The Marx-Engels Reader*, 2nd ed., ed. Robert C. Tucker, 143–45. Norton, 1978.

Masuzawa, Tomoko. *The Invention of World Religions: Or, How European Universalism Was Preserved in the Language of Pluralism*. University of Chicago Press, 2005.

Mazzini, Silvia, and Owen Glyn-Williams. 2017. *Making Communism Hermeneutical: Reading Vattimo and Zabala*. Springer International.

McCool, Gerald A., SJ. *Nineteenth-Century Scholasticism: The Search for a Unitary Method*. Fordham University Press, 1989.

McGravey, Michael. 2018. "Jean-Luc Marion and Gianni Vattimo's Contributions for the Post-Modern Faith." PhD diss., Duquesne University, 2018.

McIntyre, Lee. *Post-Truth*. MIT Press, 2018.

McLuhan, Marshall. *Understanding Media: The Extensions of Man*. 1964. Reprint. MIT Press, 1994.

Mehta, Venu. "Anekāntavāda: The Jaina Epistemology." In *Constructing the Pluriverse: The Geopolitics of Knowledge*, ed. Bernd Reiter, 259–75. Duke University Press, 2018.

Mendieta, Eduardo. "The End of Metaphysics, the Uses and Abuses of Philosophy, and Understanding Just a Little Better: On Gianni Vattimo and Santiago Zabala's *Hermeneutic Communism*." In Mazzini and Glyn-Williams, eds., *Making Communism Hermeneutical*, 3–14.

———. "Hermeneutic Communism." In Moro, ed., *The Vattimo Dictionary*, 92–95.

Messuti, Ana. "Justice/Law." In Moro, ed., *The Vattimo Dictionary*, 110–12.

Milano, Redazione. "Gianni Vattimo e Simone Caminada, una storia d'amore in tribunale." *Gay.it*, July 2, 2023. https://www.gay.it/gianni-vattimo-simone-caminada-storia-amore-tribunale.

Milbank, John. *Theology and Social Theory: Beyond Secular Reason*. 2nd ed. Blackwell, 2006.

Milbank, John, Catherine Pickstock, and Graham Ward, eds. *Radical Orthodoxy: A New Theology*. Routledge, 1999.

Mill, John Stuart. *On Liberty*. 1859. Reprint. P. F. Collier, 1909.

Mirrlees, Tanner. "The Alt-Right's Discourse of 'Cultural Marxism': A Political Instrument of Intersectional Hate." *Atlantis Journal* 31, no. 1 (2018): 49–69.

Moltmann, Jürgen. *The Crucified God: The Cross of Christ as the Foundation and Criticism of Christian Theology*. Fortress Press, 1993.

Moody, Katharine Sarah. *Radical Theology and Emerging Christianity: Deconstruction, Materialism, and Religious Practices*. Ashgate, 2015.

Moore, Ryan. "Postmodernism and Punk Subculture: Cultures of Authenticity and Deconstruction." *Communication Review* 7 (2004): 305–27.

Moro, Simonetta. Introduction to Moro, ed., *The Vattimo Dictionary*, 1–20.

———, ed. *The Vattimo Dictionary*. Edinburgh University Press, 2023.

Morvillo, Candida. "Martine Tedeschi, l'ex moglie di Vattimo (sposata solo per poterle lasciare i suoi beni): 'Uno choc quando chiese il divorzio.'" *Corriere della sera*, February 12, 2023. https://www.corriere.it/cronache/23_febbraio_12/martine-tedeschi-vattimo-ex-moglie-c66c530a-aa4e-11ed-9a4b-673945879bc9.shtml.

Nagel, Thomas. *The View from Nowhere*. Oxford University Press, 1986.

———. "What Is It Like to Be a Bat?" *Philosophical Review* 83, no. 4 (1974): 435–50.

Negri, Antonio. *Marx Beyond Marx: Lessons on the Grundrisse*. Ed. Jim Fleming. Trans. Harry Cleaver, Michael Ryan, and Maurizio Viano. Autonomedia, 1991.

Negri, Antonio, and Anne Dufourmantelle. *Negri on Negri*. Trans. Malcolm B. DeBevoise. Routledge, 2004.

Nietzsche, Friedrich. *Ecce Homo: How to Become What You Are*. In *The Anti-Christ, Ecce Homo, Twilight of the Idols, and Other Writings*, ed. Aaron Ridley, trans. Judith Norman, 69–152. Cambridge University Press, 2005.

———. *Twilight of the Idols*. Trans. R. J. Hollingdale. Penguin, 1968.

Nimmo, Paul, and Keith L. Johnson, eds. *Kenosis: The Self-Emptying of Christ in Scripture and Theology*. Eerdmans, 2022.

Nirenberg, David. *Anti-Judaism: The Western Tradition*. Norton, 2014.

Norwood, Donald W. "The Impact of Non–Roman Catholic Observers at Vatican II." *Ecclesiology* 10, no. 3 (2014): 293–312.

O'Collins, Gerald, SJ, and Mario Farrugia, SJ. *Catholicism: The Story of Catholic Christianity*. 2nd ed. Oxford University Press, 2015.

O'Leary, Joseph. "Questions to and from a Tradition in Disarray." In *After God: Richard Kearney and the Religious Turn in Continental Philosophy*, ed. John Panteleimon Manoussakis, 185–207. Fordham University Press, 2006.

Pacho, Lorena. "At the End of His Life, Was the Great Philosopher Gianni Vattimo a Victim of the Courts or of a Predatory Assistant?" *El País*, October 1,

2023. https://english.elpais.com/culture/2023-10-02/at-the-end-of-his-life-was-the-great-philosopher-gianni-vattimo-a-victim-of-the-courts-or-of-a-predatory-assistant.html.

Pacini, David S. *The Cunning of Modern Religious Thought*. Fortress Press, 1987.

Palazzo, David P. "The 'Social Factory' in Postwar Italian Radical Thought from Operaismo to Autonomia." PhD diss., City University of New York, 2014.

Paul VI. *Pastoral Constitution on the Church in the Modern World: Gaudium et spes*. 1965. http://www.vatican.va/archive/hist_councils/ii_vatican_council/documents/vat-ii_const_19651207_gaudium-et-spes_en.html.

Pelikan, Jaroslav. *Jesus Through the Centuries: His Place in the History of Culture*. Harper and Rowe, 1985.

Pinotti, Ferruccio. "Vattimo: 'Papa Francesco? È un amico. Oggi mi manca un figlio, adesso mi starebbe vicino.'" *Corriere della sera*, June 6, 2022. https://www.corriere.it/cronache/22_giugno_06/vattimo-papa-francesco-amico-oggi-mi-manca-figlio-adesso-mi-starebbe-vicino-d6270966-e271-11ec-9f19-f9603cda965c.shtml.

Pizzolato, Nicola. "'I Terroni in Città': Revisiting Southern Migrants' Militancy in Turin's 'Hot Autumn.'" *Contemporary European History* 21, no. 4 (November 2012): 619–34.

Pollard, John. *Catholicism in Modern Italy: Religion, Society, and Politics Since 1861*. Routledge, 2008.

Prince, Simon. *Northern Ireland's '68: Civil Rights, Global Revolt, and the Origins of the Troubles*. Irish Academic Press, 2018.

Quine, Willard Van Orman. "On Empirically Equivalent Systems of the World." *Erkenntnis* 9, no. 3 (November 1975): 313–28.

———. *Word and Object*. 1960. Reprint. MIT Press, 2013.

Rass, Friederike D. *Die Suche nach Wahrheit im Horizont fragmentarischer Existenzialität—eine Studie über den Sinn der Frage nach "Gott" in der Gegenwart in Auseinandersetzung mit Gianni Vattimo, John D. Caputo und Jean-Luc Nancy*. Mohr Siebeck, 2017.

Ratzinger, Joseph. "The Ecclesiology of the Constitution of the Church: *Lumen gentium*." In Ratzinger, *The Essential Pope Benedict XVI*, 85–102.

———. *The Essential Pope Benedict XVI: His Central Writings and Speeches*. Ed. John F. Thornton and Susan B. Varenne. HarperCollins, 2008.

———. "The Local Church and the Universal Church." In Ratzinger, *The Essential Pope Benedict XVI*, 103–9.

———. *A Turning Point for Europe?* Ignatius Press, 2010.
Reichel, Oswald J. *The See of Rome in the Middle Ages.* Longmans, Green, 2017.
Reno, R. R. "Postliberal Theology." *First Things*, February 2018. https://www.firstthings.com/article/2018/02/postliberal-theology.
Rhodes, Martin. "Tangentopoli—More Than 20 Years On." In *The Oxford Handbook of Italian Politics*, ed. Erik Jones and Gianfranco Pasquino, 309–24. Oxford University Press, 2015.
Ricca, Jacopo. "Caso Vattimo, 2 anni di carcere a Simone Caminada." *Rai News*, June 2, 2023. https://www.rainews.it/tgr/piemonte/articoli/2023/02/caso-vattimo-il-giorno-del-giudizio-per-lassistente-caminada-27bc10cc-b56f-42c7-ac76-a6ec21c701aa.html.
Ricciardi, Alessia. *After "La dolce vita": A Cultural Prehistory of Berlusconi's Italy.* Stanford University Press, 2012.
Riedel, Manfred, ed. *Zur Rehabilitierung der praktischen Philosophie.* 2 vols. Rombach, 1972, 1974.
Rieger, Joerg, ed. *Opting for the Margins: Postmodernity and Liberation in Christian Theology.* Oxford University Press, 2003.
Righi, Andrea. *Biopolitics and Social Change in Italy: From Gramsci to Pasolini to Negri.* Palgrave Macmillan, 2011.
Risen, Clay. "Antonio Negri, 90, Philosopher Who Wrote a Surprise Best Seller, Dies." *New York Times*, December 22, 2023. https://www.nytimes.com/2023/12/22/world/europe/antonio-negri-dead.html.
Risser, James. "Philosophy and Politics at the End of Metaphysics." In Benso and Schroeder, eds., *Between Nihilism and Politics*, 167–82.
Robbins, Jeffrey W., and Clayton Crockett. "A Radical Theology for the Future: Five Theses." *Palgrave Communications* 1 (October 13, 2015): art. 15028. https://www.nature.com/articles/palcomms201528.
Rohr, Richard. *The Universal Christ: How a Forgotten Reality Can Change Everything We See, Hope For, and Believe.* Convergent, 2019.
Rorty, Richard. "Introduction: Metaphilosophical Difficulties of Linguistic Philosophy." In *The Linguistic Turn: Essays in Philosophical Method, with Two Retrospective Essays*, ed. Richard Rorty, 1–39. 1967. Reprint. University of Chicago Press, 1992.
———. *Philosophy and the Mirror of Nature.* 1979. Reprint. Princeton University Press, 2009.

———. *Take Care of Freedom and Truth Will Take Care of Itself: Interviews with Richard Rorty*. Ed. Eduardo Mendieta. Stanford University Press, 2005.
Rose, David. "Subject/Weak Subject." In Moro, ed., *The Vattimo Dictionary*, 182–85.
Rossi, Paolo. *Paragone degli ingegni moderni e postmoderni*. 1989. Reprint. Il Mulino, 2009.
———. *Speranze*. Il Mulino, 2008.
Rowland, Tracey. "The World in the Theology of Joseph Ratzinger/Benedict XVI." *Journal of Moral Theology* 2, no. 2 (2013): 109–32.
Ruiz, Ish. 2024. "Queer Theology and the Synodal Catholic Church." *Feminist Theology* 32, no. 3 (2024): 283–304.
Russell, Bertrand. *The Problems of Philosophy*. 1912. Reprint. Oxford University Press, 1997.
Ryba, Thomas. "Girard and Augustine." In *The Palgrave Handbook of Mimetic Theory and Religion*, ed. James Alison and Wolfgang Palaver, 209–16. Palgrave-Macmillan, 2017.
Said, Edward W. "The Clash of Ignorance." *The Nation*, October 4, 2001.
Sassen, Saskia. *Globalization and Its Discontents: Essays on the New Mobility of People and Money*. New Press, 1998.
Savage, Luke. "New Atheism, Old Empire." *Jacobin Magazine*, December 2014. https://jacobin.com/2014/12/new-atheism-old-empire/.
Schama, Simon. *Citizens: A Chronicle of the French Revolution*. Vintage, 1989.
Schatz, Ronald W. "American Labor and the Catholic Church, 1919–1950." *International Labor and Working-Class History* 20 (Fall 1981): 46–53.
Scheffler, Israel. *Symbolic Worlds: Art, Science, Language, Ritual*. Cambridge University Press, 1997.
Schmitt, Carl. *Political Theology: Four Chapters on the Concept of Sovereignty*. Trans. George Schwab. University of Chicago Press, 2005.
Sciglitano, Anthony C., Jr. "Gianni Vattimo and Saint Paul: Ontological Weakening, Kenosis, and Secularity." In *Paul in the Grip of the Philosophers: The Apostle and Contemporary Continental Philosophy*, ed. Peter Frick, 117–41. Fortress Press, 2013.
Sen, Amartya. *Identity and Violence: The Illusion of Destiny*. Norton, 2006.
Shadle, Matthew A. *Interrupting Capitalism: Catholic Social Thought and the Economy*. Oxford University Press, 2018.
Shanin, Teodo. "Late Marx: Gods and Craftsmen." In *Late Marx and the Russian Road: Marx and the Peripheries of Capitalism*, ed. Teodor Shanin, 3–39. Monthly Review Press, 1983.

Shelley, Percy Bysshe. "A Defense of Poetry (1821)." In *Essays, Letters from Abroad, Translations, and Fragments*, 1–57. Edward Moxon, 1840.

Slobodian, Quinn. "The Meanings of Western Maoism in the Global 1960s." In *The Routledge Handbook of the Global Sixties: Between Protest and Nation-Building*, ed. Chen Jian, Martin Klimke, Masha Kirasirova, Mary Nolan, Marilyn Young, and Joanna Waley-Cohen, 67–78. Routledge, 2018.

Smith, James K. A. *Introducing Radical Orthodoxy: Mapping a Post-Secular Theology*. Baker Academic, 2004.

Snyder, Jon R. "Translator's Introduction." In Vattimo, *The End of Modernity*, vi–lviii.

Sölle, Dorothee. *Suffering*. Augsburg Fortress Press, 1984.

Sparrow, Tom. *The End of Phenomenology: Metaphysics and the New Realism*. Edinburgh University Press, 2014.

Spini, Valdo. "The New Left in Italy." *Journal of Contemporary History* 7, no. 1 (1972): 51–71.

S. Agostino. *De magistro—De vera religione*. Ed. Domenico Bassi. Edizioni Testi Cristiani, 1930.

Starosta, Guido. *Marx's "Capital," Method, and Revolutionary Subjectivity*. Brill, 2015.

Strand, Daniel. *No Alternatives: The End of Ideology in the 1950s and the Post-Political World of the 1990s*. Stockholm University Press, 2016.

Styers, Randall. "Gianni Vattimo and the Return of the Sacred." *Annali d'italianistica* 25 (2007): 47–75.

Tabachnick, David E. "'Phronesis,' Democracy, and Technology." *Canadian Journal of Political Science/Revue canadienne de science politique* 37, no. 4 (December 2004): 997–1016.

Talar, C. J. T. "*Pascendi dominici gregis*: The Vatican Condemnation of Modernism." In "*Pascendi dominici gregis:* 1907–2007: Centennial Essays on Responses to the Encyclical on Modernism." Special issue, *U.S. Catholic Historian* 25, no. 1 (Winter 2007): 1–12.

Taylor, Charles. *A Secular Age*. Belknap Press, 2007.

Tertullian. *On the Proscription of Heretics*. trans. T. Herbert Bindley. SPCK, 1914. Excerpt at https://sourcebooks.fordham.edu/source/200Tertullian-pagan.asp.

Thanassas, Pangiotis. "Phronesis and Sophia: On Heidegger's Ambivalent Aristotelianism." *Review of Metaphysics* 66, no. 1 (September 2012): 31–59.

Toniolo, Gianni. "An Overview of Italy's Economic Growth." In Toniolo, ed., *The Oxford Handbook of the Italian Economy Since Unification*, 3–36.

———, ed. *The Oxford Handbook of the Italian Economy Since Unification*. Oxford University Press, 2013.

Tonner, Philip. *Heidegger, Metaphysics, and the Univocity of Being*. Continuum, 2010.

Tracy, David. *Selected Essays. Vol. 1: Fragments: The Existential Situation of Our Time*. University of Chicago Press, 2020.

Traub, James. "It's Time for the Elites to Rise Up Against the Ignorant Masses." *Foreign Policy*, June 28, 2016. https://foreignpolicy.com/2016/06/28/its-time-for-the-elites-to-rise-up-against-ignorant-masses-trump-2016-brexit/.

Vahanian, Noëlle. "Gianni Vattimo's Religion." *Los Angeles Review of Books*, November 10, 2016. https://lareviewofbooks.org/article/gianni-vattimos-religion/.

Valentino, Benjamin A. "Why We Kill: The Political Science of Political Violence Against Civilians." *Annual Review of Political Science* 17 (2014): 89–103.

Valgenti, Robert T. "Convalescence (*Verwindung*)." In Moro, ed. *The Vattimo Dictionary*, 52–54.

———. "Mask." In Moro, ed., *The Vattimo Dictionary*, 126–28.

———. "Nietzsche the Communist? A Genealogy of Interpretation." In Mazzini and Glyn-Williams, eds., *Making Communism Hermeneutical*, 193–206.

Vandevelde, Pol. "Edmund Husserl." In Keane and Lawn, eds., *The Blackwell Companion to Hermeneutics*, 383–88.

van Riessen, Renée D. N. *Man as a Place of God: Levinas' Hermeneutics of Kenosis*. Springer International, 2007.

Van Steenberghen, Fernand. "Maurice De Wulf: Historien de la philosophie médiévale." *Revue philosophique de Louvain* 46 (1948): 421–47.

Vattimo, Gianni. *The Adventure of Difference: Philosophy After Nietzsche and Heidegger*. Trans. Cyprian P. Blamires and Thomas Harrison. Johns Hopkins University Press, 1993.

———. *After Christianity*. Trans. Luca D'Isanto. Columbia University Press, 2002.

———. "After Onto-Theology: Philosophy Between Science and Religion." In *Religion After Metaphysics*, ed. Mark A. Wrathall, 29–36. Cambridge University Press, 2003.

———. "*An-denken*: Thinking and the Foundation." in Vattimo, *The Adventure of Difference*, 110–36.

——. *Arte e verità nel pensiero di M. Heidegger: Corso di estetica dell'anno accademico 1965–1966*. Giappichelli, 1966.

——. "Arte, sentimento, originarietà nell'estetica di Heidegger." *Rivista di estetica* 12 (1967): 267–88.

——. *Art's Claim to Truth*. Ed. Santiago Zabala. Trans. Luca D'Isanto. Columbia University Press, 2010.

——. "Author's Preface: The Bottle, The Net, the Revolution, and the Tasks of Philosophy. A Dialogue with *Lotta Continua*." In Vattimo, *Beyond the Subject*, xxix–xl.

——. *Being and Its Surroundings*. Ed. Giuseppe Iannantuono, Alberto Martinengo, and Santiago Zabala. Trans. Corrado Federici. McGill-Queen's University Press, 2021.

——. *Belief*. Trans. Luca D'Isanto and David Webb. Polity Press, 1999.

——. *Beyond Interpretation: The Meaning of Hermeneutics for Philosophy*. Trans. David Webb. Polity Press/Stanford University Press, 1997.

——. *Beyond the Subject: Nietzsche, Heidegger, and Hermeneutics*. Ed. and trans. Peter Carravetta. SUNY Press, 2019.

——. "The Christian Message and the Dissolution of Metaphysics." In *The Blackwell Companion to Postmodern Theology*, ed. Graham Ward, 458–66. Blackwell, 2001.

——. *Dialogue with Nietzsche*. Trans. William McCuaig. Columbia University Press, 2006.

——. "Dialectics, Difference, Weak Thought." In Vattimo and Rovatti, eds., *Weak Thought*, 39–52.

——. *Ecce comu: Come si diventa cio che si era*. Fazi, 2007.

——. "The End of (Hi)story." *Chicago Review* 35, no. 4 (1987): 20–30.

——. *The End of Modernity: Nihilism and Hermeneutics in Postmodern Culture*. Trans. Jon R. Snyder. Polity Press/Johns Hopkins University Press, 1988.

——. *Essere, storia, e linguaggio in Heidegger*. Edizioni di "Filosofia," 1963.

——. *A Farewell to Truth*. Trans. William McCuaig. Columbia University Press, 2011.

——. "Gianni Vattimo—Philosophy as Ontology of Actuality: A Biographical-Theoretical Interview with Luca Savarino and Federico Vercellone." *Iris: European Journal of Philosophy and Public Debate* 1, no. 2 (October 2009): 311–50.

——. "Gli studi heidegerriani negli ultimi venti anni." *Cultura e scuola* 31 (1969): 85–99.

——. "Luigi Pareyson." In *Dizionario biografico degli italiani*, vol. 81. Instituto della Enciclopedia Italiana Fondata da Giovanni Treccni, 2014. https://www.treccani.it/enciclopedia/luigi-pareyson_(Dizionario-Biografico)/.
——. *Nietzsche: An Introduction*. Trans. Nicholas Martin. Stanford University Press, 2002.
——. *Nihilism and Emancipation: Ethics, Politics, and Law*. Ed. Santiago Zabala. Trans. William McCuaig. Columbia University Press, 2004.
——. *Of Reality: The Purposes of Philosophy*. Trans. Robert T. Valgenti. Columbia University Press, 2016.
——. *Il soggetto e la maschera*. Fabbri-Bompiani, 1974.
——. "Towards an Ontology of Decline." In Vattimo, *Beyond the Subject*, 17–34. Also in Borradori, ed., *Recoding Metaphysics*, 63–76.
——. *The Transparent Society*. Trans. David Webb. Polity Press/Johns Hopkins University Press, 1992.
——. "The Will to Power as Art." In Vattimo, *The Adventure of Difference*, 85–109.
Vattimo, Gianni, and John D. Caputo. *After the Death of God*. Ed. Jeffrey W. Robbins. Columbia University Press, 2007.
Vattimo, Gianni, Antonio Cecere, and Debora Tonelli. "*Fratelli tutti*: Dialogo con Gianni Vattimo." In *Fratelli tutti? Credenti e non credenti in dialogo con Papa Francesco*, ed. Debora Tonelli, 143–69. Castelvecchi, 2022.
Vattimo, Gianni, and Carmelo Dotolo. *Dio: La possibilità buona. Un colloquio sulla soglia tra filosofia e teologia*. Ed. Giovanni Giorgio. Rubbettino, 2009.
Vattimo, Gianni, and René Girard. *Christianity, Truth, and Weakening Faith: A Dialogue*. Ed. Pierpaolo Antonello. Trans. William McCuaig. Columbia University Press, 2010.
Vattimo, Gianni, and Piergiorgio Paterlini. *Not Being God: A Collaborative Autobiography*. Trans. William McCuaig. Columbia University Press, 2009.
Vattimo, Gianni, and Richard Rorty. *The Future of Religion*. Ed. Santiago Zabala. Columbia University Press, 2005.
Vattimo, Gianni, and Pier Aldo Rovatti, eds. *Weak Thought*. Trans. Peter Carravetta. SUNY Press, 2012.
Vattimo, Gianni, Pierangelo Sequeri, and Giovanni Ruggeri. *Interrogazioni sul cristianesimo: Cosa possiamo ancora attenderci dal Vangelo?* Fossano, 2000.
Vattimo, Gianni, and Santiago Zabala. *Hermeneutic Communism: From Heidegger to Marx*. Columbia University Press, 2011.

———. "Response to Jeff Malpas and Nick Malpas." In Mazzini and Glyn-Williams, eds., *Making Communism Hermeneutical*, 31–34.

———. "Response to Mendieta." In Mazzini and Glyn-Williams, eds., *Making Communism Hermeneutical*, 15–18.

———. "Response to Valgenti." In Mazzini and Glyn-Williams, eds., *Making Communism Hermeneutical*, 207–10.

———. "'Weak Thought' and the Reduction of Violence: A Dialogue with Gianni Vattimo." Trans. Yaakov Mascetti. *Common Knowledge* 25, nos. 1–3 (2019): 92–103.

Viano, Carlo Augusto. "La ragione, l'abbondanza e la credenza." In *Crisi della ragione: Nuovi modelli nel rapporto tra sapere e attività umane*, ed. Aldo Gargani, 303–66. Einaudi, 1980.

———. *Va' pensiero: Il carattere della filosofia italiana contemporanea.* Einaudi, 1985.

Viansson-Ponte, Pierre. "Interview with Herbert Marcuse." *Le Monde*, June 1969. Trans. Anne Fremantle, n.d. https://www.marxists.org/reference/archive/marcuse/works/1969/interview.htm. Accessed May 28, 2025.

Wagner, Wencelas J. "Codification of Law in Europe and the Codification Movement in the Middle of the Nineteenth Century in the United States." *Saint Louis University Law Journal* 1953:335–59.

Walston, James. "Historic Compromise." In *Encyclopedia of Contemporary Italian Culture*, ed. Gino Moliterno, 383. Routledge, 2000.

Wandinger, Nikolaus. "Religion and Violence: A Girardian Overview." *Journal of Religion and Violence* 1, no. 2 (2013): 127–46.

Wang, Jin, and Keebom Nahm. "From Confucianism to Communism and Back: Understanding the Cultural Roots of Chinese Politics." *Journal of Asian Sociology* 48, no. 1 (March 2019): 91–114.

Ward, Ian. *Kantianism, Postmodernism, and Critical Legal Thought.* Kluwer Academic, 1997.

Weisbord, Albert. *The Conquest of Power: Liberalism, Anarchism, Syndicalism, Socialism, Fascism, and Communism.* Vol. 1. Covici-Friede, 1937.

Wiatr, Jerzy J. "Herbert Marcuse: Philosopher of a Lost Radicalism." *Science and Society* 31, no. 3 (Fall 1970): 319–30.

Williams, Howard. "An Enlightenment Critique of *The Dialectic of Enlightenment*." In *The Enlightenment World*, ed. Martin Fitzpatrick, Peter Jones, Christa Knellwolf, and Ian McCalman, 635–47. Routledge, 2004.

Wilson, N. L. "Substance Without Substrata." *Review of Metaphysics* 12 (1959): 521–39.
Wink, Walter. *The Powers That Be: Theology for a New Millennium*. Doubleday, 1998.
Wisdom, John. *Philosophy and Psycho-Analysis*. Blackwell, 1953.
Witte, John, Jr. *The Reformation of Rights: Law, Religion, and Human Rights in Early Modern Calvinism*. Cambridge University Press, 2007.
Wittgenstein, Ludwig. *Culture and Value: A Selection from the Posthumous Remains*. Ed. Georg Henrik von Wright (in collaboration with Heikki Nyman). Trans. Peter Winch. Blackwell, 1998.
———. *The Mythology in Our Language: Remarks on Frazer's "Golden Bough."* Ed. Giovanni da Col and Stephen Palmié. Trans. Stephen Palmié. Hau, 2018.
———. *Philosophical Investigations*. 4th rev. ed. Ed. and trans. G. E. M. Anscombe, P. M. S. Hacker, and Joachim Schulte. Wiley-Blackwell, 2009.
Woessner, Martin. "Hermeneutic Communism: Left Heideggerianism's Last Hope?" In Mazzi and Glyn-Williams, eds., *Making Communism Hermeneutical*, 35–48.
Wolloch, Nathaniel. *History and Nature in the Enlightenment: Praise of the Mastery of Nature in Eighteenth-Century Historical Literature*. Ashgate, 2011.
Wooden, Cindy. "Pope Reflects on Changed Attitudes Toward Liberation Theology." Catholic News Service, February 14, 2019. https://cruxnow.com/vatican/2019/02/pope-reflects-on-changed-attitudes-toward-liberation-theology.
Wright, N. T., and Michael F. Bird. *Jesus and the Powers*. Zondervan, 2024.
Wright, Steve. *Storming Heaven: Class Composition and Struggle in Italian Autonomist Marxism*. Pluto Press, 2002.
Xavier, Joseph. "Theological Anthropology of 'Gaudium et spes' and Fundamental Theology." *Gregorianum* 91, no. 1 (2010): 124–36.
Yoder, John Howard. *The Politics of Jesus*. Eerdmans, 1972.
Zabala, Santiago. *Being at Large: Freedom in the Age of Alternative Facts*. McGill-Queens University Press, 2020.
———. "Gianni Vattimo's Life, Philosophy, and Archives." *Los Angeles Review of Books*, November 10, 2016. https://lareviewofbooks.org/article/gianni-vattimos-life-philosophy-archives/.
———. *The Remains of Being: Hermeneutic Ontology After Metaphysics*. Columbia University Press, 2009.

———, ed. *Weakening Philosophy: Essays in Honour of Gianni Vattimo*. McGill-Queen's University Press, 2007.

———. "Why Did the Pope Phone the Philosopher?" *Aeon*, October 1, 2018. https://aeon.co/ideas/why-did-the-pope-phone-the-philosopher.

———. *Why Only Art Can Save Us: Aesthetics and the Absence of Emergency*. Columbia University Press, 2019.

Zagacki, Kenneth. "Pope John Paul II and the Crusade Against Communism: A Case Study in Secular and Sacred Time." *Rhetoric and Public Affairs* 4, no. 4 (Winter 2001): 689–710.

Zawadzki, Andrzej. *Literature and Weak Thought*. Cross-roads: Polish Studies in Culture, Literary Theory, and History, vol. 2. Edited by Ryszard Nycz and Teresa Walas. PL Academic, 2013.

Žižek, Slavoj. "Multitude, Surplus, and Envy." *Rethinking Marxism* 19, no. 1 (January 2007): 46–58.

———. *The Puppet and the Dwarf: The Perverse Core of Christianity*. MIT Press, 2003.

INDEX

Abbagnano, Nicola, 66, 164
Abel (biblical character), 140
Abendland ("Land of Twilight"), 78.
  See also West, the
absolutism, 10, 118
Abu Dhabi Document (*Document on Human Fraternity for World Peace and Living Together*), 199, 302n35
academia, 116, 194, 232, 272n38, 299n17
Academy (Plato's), 184;
Acerbus (prefect), 123
adaequatio intellectus et rei, 83. See also veritas qua adaequatio rei et intellectus
adiaphora (ἀδιάφορα), 151
Addio alla verità (Vattimo), 33, 234, 313
Adorno, Theodor, 43, 64, 77, 81, 100, 226, 240n35, 255n3, 287n19
Adorno Prize, 240n35
Adventure of Difference, The (Vattimo). See *Avventure della differenza*
Aeschylus, 60
aesthetic(s), 8–11, 17, 86, 228–229, 235, 247n10, 303n53

Aesthetics: Theory of Formativity (Pareyson). see *Estetica: Teoria della formatività*
Æterni Patris (Pope Leo XIII), 124–125, 223
Afghanistan, 96, 267n8, 291n33
Afiuni, María Lourdes, 107
Africa, 4, 21, 196; African, 263n78.
  See also Egypt; Morocco; Tunisia; Ethiopia; Tanzania; Congo; South Africa; and Sub-Sahara
After Christianity (Vattimo). See *Dopo la cristianità*
After the Death of God (Vattimo and Caputo), 35, 234, 252n49, 252n52, 261n58
Agamben, Giorgio, 98, 252n49
Age; of the Father 118; of the Son, 118; of the Spirit, 113, 118–119
aggiornamento, 129–130
Agnelli, Gianni, 25
ahiṃsā, 211
AIDS, 92, 231–232

Al di là del soggetto: Nietzsche, Heidegger, e l'emeneutica [*Beyond the Subject*] (Vattimo), 18, 33, 65, 67, 230, 254n61
Alexander von Humboldt Foundation, 10, 228, 244n63
Alfa Romero, 54
alienation (*Entfremdung/Entäußerung*), 27, 59, 64, 77, 259n37. *See also* Marx, Karl
Alleanza Nazionale (National Alliance), 95
Allende, Salvador, 49
Alliance of Liberals and Democrats for Europe, 235
Allies (WWII), 4, 46, 226, 242
Alps (mountain range), 26, 59, 229
alterity, 35, 77, 151
alternative facts. *See* truth
Althaus-Reid, Marcella, 207–208
Althusser, Louis, 51, 57
Altissimo, Renato, 94
Altizer, Thomas J. J., 192, 297n10
Amazon (rainforest), 148
America, 22, 142, 232, 271n37, 297–298n11; Americas, 235; Italian Americans, 224; Latin Americans, 49, 88, 97–98, 107, 196, 198, 262–263n73, 267n8, 301n29; South Americans, 97, 107–108. *See also* United States
American Enterprise Institute for Public Policy Research, 249n18
Amoris lætitia (Pope Francis), 199. *See also* encyclicals
Amsterdam, 233

anarchy, 30, 54, 97, 105, 172, 251nn41–42, 264n85; methodological anarchism, 288n23; Spanish anarchism, 274n47; anarchic, 202, 209, 224; anarchists, 44, 106, 172; anarchistic, 64; libertarian-anarchist, 26
An-Denken, 65, 78
"*An-denken*: Il pensare e il fondamento" [An-denken: Thinking and Foundation] (Vattimo), 17, 64, 230
anekāntavāda, 211
Angelelli, Enrique, 198
Anglicans, 48
Anni di Piombo, 19, 30
atheism, 297n10; atheists, 137, 148, 278n23
anthropology, 168, 275n52, 276n10, 291n29, 298n11; anthropological, 140, 142, 277n18
anticapitalist, 41. *See also* capital; romantic anticapitalism
anticommunist. *See* communism
antifascists, 46; Anti-Fascist Resistance, 8, 46; Antifaschistische Aktion, 303n53. *See also* fascism; Resistenza
antimetaphysician. *See* metaphysics
antimodernist, 9, 41, 43, 126, 272n37. *See also* modern
antiquity (Western), 14, 80, 188, 285n3; late, 201
antisemitic, 189, 289n27
Aparecida Document, 198
aparigraha, 211

Apel, Karl-Otto, 2
Apollonian, 60, 82; Apollonianism, 60. *See also* Dionysian
Aquinas, St. Thomas, 6, 10, 32, 69, 125, 152, 185, 188, 247n10, 272n37, 296n66; Thomism, 126–127; Thomistic, 76, 124–125, 127, 271n36, 272n38; neo-Thomism, 272n38, 273n43; neo-Thomists, 5, 125, 128; neo-Thomistic, 9; non-Thomistic, 43. *See also* neo-Scholastic
archmetaphysician, 15. *See also* metaphysics
Argentina, 8, 99, 301n32; Argentinian, 129, 198, 202, 207
Aristotle, 9, 32, 34, 39–40, 157–159, 188, 220, 245n79, 247n10, 284n1, 285n4, 295–296n64; Aristotelian/Aristotelean, 73, 76, 79, 125, 184, 257n18, 280n30, 285n4; Aristotelianism, 284n1
Asclepius, 169
Asia, 196
Asnieres-sur-Oise, 228
Athens, 184, 295n64
Aufhebung (sublation/sublimation), 14, 33, 77, 86, 116, 165, 209
Aufklärung. *See* Enlightenment
Augenblick (moment of vision), 68, 257n18
Augustine of Hippo St., 32, 68, 154, 181, 183, 185, 257n19, 266–267n5, 281n36, 295nn58–59, 62, 296n66
Austin, John, 189
Australia, 99
Austro-Hungarian, 224

authority, xii, 53, 120–123, 125–126, 129–130, 135, 158, 171–174, 202, 270nn30–31, 271n31, 273n44, 292n37, 295n64; authorities, 141; authoritarian, xii; authoritarian leadership, 54; authoritarian leftism, 251n42
Autonomia, 30, 249n16; Autonomia Operaia (Autonomous Workers), 53–54
autonomy, 50, 54–55, 247n7
autoreduction, 56
Autunno Caldo, 25
avant-garde, 26, 99, 251n41, 263n78
Avicenna (Ibn Sīnā), 76, 295n63
Avventure della differenza (*The Adventure of Difference*) (Vattimo), 17, 33, 63, 230, 254n61
Azione Cattolica (Catholic Action), 6, 28, 41–42, 227
Azzarà, Stefano G., 60, 243n55, 244n64, 253n60

bad infinity ("endlessness"), 14, 64, 209
Badiou, Alain, 98, 250n29, 298n12
Badoglio, Pietro, 225–226, 242n43
Bakunin, Mikhail, 172, 292nn39–40
Barth, Karl, 77, 127, 150, 184, 209, 282n45, 288n20; post-Barthian, 298n11
base communities, 196, 198, 300n25. *See also* comunidades eclesiales de base (CEBs)
Battle of the Milvian Bridge, 201
Beardsley, Eleanor, 22, 242n52

beatification, 198. *See also* saints
Being: beings, 1, 13, 17, 27–28, 59, 64, 67–76, 78–79, 81, 98, 105, 115, 150–151, 163–164, 254n61, 256n15, 257n21, 257n23, 260n42; decline of, 65; being-for-itself (Sartre), 51; beings-in-themselves, 50. *See also* Dasein
Being and Its Surroundings (Vattimo). *See Essere e dintorni*
Being and Time (Heidegger). *See Sein und Zeit*
Being, History, and Language in Heidegger (Vattimo). *See Essere, storia, e linguaggio in Heidegger*
Belgium, 177, 195
belief, xii, 66, 74, 81, 101, 143, 152, 179–180, 250n34, 278n20, 278n22; in God, 11; religious, 11; structures, xiii, 13, 32
Belief (Vattimo). *See Credere di credere*
Benedetto Croce Istituto Italiano per Gli Studi Storici (Benedetto Croce Institute for Historical Studies), 54. *See also* Croce, Benedetto
Benjamin, Walter, 77, 98, 116, 225, 259n38, 267n10
Bentham, Jeremy, 189, 285n3
Berger, John, 211
Bergoglio, Jorge Mario (Pope Francis). *See* popes
Bergson, Henri, 106
Berlinguer, Enrico, 49–50
Berlusconi, Silvio, 92, 95–96, 167, 290n28

Bernstein, Richard J., 14, 239n27, 240–241n35, 284n2
Betti, Emilio, 191
Beyond Interpretation (Vattimo). *See Oltre l'nterpretazione*
Beyond the Subject: Nietzsche, Heidegger, and Hermeneutics (Vattimo). *See Al di là del soggetto: Nietzsche, Heidegger, e l'emeneutica*
Bible, 127–128, 139, 148, 192–193, 273n44, 283n46, 301n27; Hebrew, 140; criticism, 121, 126; exegesis, 126; hermeneutics, 192; imagery, xii, 140; narrative, 139, 266n5; New Testament, 141, 257n18
Biblioteca Filosofica (Turin), 228
Biennio Rosso, 44, 224
Bildung (self-cultivation), 14, 203
Bilgrami, Akeel, 114
Birault, Henri, 228
Birth of Tragedy, The (Nietzsche), 60
Black, 194, 204–208, 303n50; Blackness, 206; Black Panther Party, 204; Black Power (movement), 204
Black liberation theology. *See* theology
Blackshirts, 3, 44, 224. *See also* Squadrismo militias
Black Theology of Liberation, A (Cone), 205
Blair, Tony, 93
blank slate (tabla rasa), 18
bliks (Hare), 147
Bloch, Ernst, 11, 43, 77
Blondel, Maurice, 126
Bobbio, Norberto, 29, 66, 164

Body of the Dead Christ in the Tomb (Holbein), 201. *See also* Christ
Boethius, 68, 257n19
Bolivia, 96, 198
Bologna: 54; University of, 7
Bonaparte, Louis-Napoléon, 121, 270n30;
Bonaparte, Napoleon, 270nn29–30; Bonapartist, 253n56; Napoleonic Wars, 121; French Civil Code (or Code Napoléon), 189
Bonaventure, St., 126
Bonhoeffer, Dietrich, 150–151, 298n13
Bonino, José Míguez, 128, 274n47
Bonomi, Ivanoe, 226
Bordiga, Amadeo, 45
Borgia, Cesare, 106
Borgo San Paolo, 3, 225
Borradori, Giovanna, 231
Bouillard, Henri, 128
bourgeois, 22–23, 60, 123, 246, 254n61
Bozzola, Annibale, 5
Brazil, 21, 96, 198, 202, 214
Bresci, Gaetano, 224
Bretton Woods (system), 48, 249n22
Brexit, 171
Bribesville (political scandal). *See* Tangentopoli
Bricherasio, 4
Brigate Rosse (Red Brigade), 29–30, 50, 56, 205, 230
Britain. *See* England
Brockmann, Father Miguel d'Escoto, 198
Brown, John, 206
Budapest, 229

Buddhism, 203, 277n18
Buenos Aires, 198
Bultmann, Rudolf, 127–128, 288n20
Bush, George W., 97, 291

Cacciari, Massimo, 232, 241
Cajetan, Thomas Cardinal, 126
Calabria, 3–4; Calabrese dialect, 5
California, 21, 234
Calvin, John, 272n37
Câmara, Helder, 198
Caminada, Simone, 214–215, 217–220
Canada, 99
Canon Law. *See* law
canonization. *See* saints
capital, 42, 200, 223; capitalism, 22, 24, 42–43, 200, 231; capitalist, 25, 41, 202. *See also* romantic anticapitalism
Caputo, John D., 2, 15–16, 35, 192–194, 234, 240n35, 252n52
Capri, 35, 232
Caramello, Monsignor Pietro, 5–6, 42, 227
Cardenal, Father Ernesto, 198
Cardijn, Joseph-Léon Cardinal, 195
Cardinal Mercier Chair Lectures (Leuven), 2, 235
caritas, xiii, 34, 152, 197. *See also* charity
Carmichael, Stokely. *See* Ture, Kwame
Carravetta, Peter, 9, 64
Casa di Carità Arti e Mestieri (House of Charity—Art and Tradecraft), 7, 227
Casanova, José, 114
Castellano, Lucio, 55–56

Catholics, xii, 2, 5–11, 20, 28, 41–43, 48, 90, 113–114, 117, 123–127, 130–132, 135, 149, 188, 193, 195–197, 200–201, 208, 219, 228, 246nn4–5, 270n30, 271–272nn37–38, 273n42, 273n44, 275n51, 275n53, 281n33, 288n21, 298n11, 299n19, 300n20, 300n22; Catholicism, x, 10, 41–43, 48, 59, 119–120, 122, 129–130, 195–196, 228, 246n4, 267n8; Catholic Mass, 10; Catholic social thought, 41; Catholic integralism, 41–42; Catholic trade-unions, 41, 42, 246n5. *See also* Azione Cattolica
Cavaglià, Gianpiero, 28, 92–93, 216, 219, 229
Casalegno, Carlo, 29
Castro, Fidel, 108
Cavour, Camillo Benso, Count of, 121, 270n30
Cecere, Antonio, 199
Center for Vattimo's Philosophy and Archives, 3, 236, 309
Central Intelligence Agency (CIA), 49, 198
Centro Cristiano Democratico (Christian Democratic Center), 95
Cetraro, 3–5
Cézanne, Paul, 138
Chabod, Federico, 54
charity, xiii, 7, 33–34, 114, 117–118, 132, 151–153, 173, 178–179, 182–183, 187, 200, 209, 211, 219, 221, 286n7, 286n9, 294n51; principle of, 152. *See also* caritas
Charles, John Francis, 195

chauvinism, xii, 278n23
Chávez, Hugo, 96, 107–108
Cheng, Patrick S., 208
Chenu, Marie-Dominique, 128, 130, 196, 274n44
Chesterton, G. K., 182
Chicago, 21
Chiesa, Mario, 93–94
Chile, 49, 99
China, 24, 88, 97, 200, 209–210, 243n56; Mandarin (language), 146; Mandarins, 116
Chiurazzi, Gaetano, 85
Chomsky, Noam, 109
Chopp, Rebecca S., 203
Christ, xii–xiii, 32, 35, 106, 118, 124, 129, 131–132, 140, 149–151, 153–154, 177, 184, 188, 207–208, 281n40, 282n45, 283n46; anti-Christ, 105; Militant, 201, 302n40; Pantocrator, 201, 302n40; *Body of the Dead Christ in the Tomb* (Holbein), 201; *Piss Christ* (Serrano), 208; Christocentric, 145; Christology, 283n46
Christendom, xii–xiii, 33, 125
Christianity, x–xii, 15, 32–35, 43, 79, 105–107, 113–114, 117, 131, 136, 138, 140, 142–143, 145–149, 154, 181–184, 192, 194, 200–202, 204, 221, 232, 277n18, 284n55, 302n41; Christians, xiii, 34–35; literature, 7; society, 34; spirituality, 8; theology, 33
Christianity, Truth, and Weakening Faith (Vattimo and Girard). *See Verità o fede debole?*

INDEX ∞ 355

Christ in Postmodern Philosophy (Depoortere), 177, 269n22
church, xii–xiii, 5–7, 10, 41, 48, 113, 117–120, 122–126, 128–133, 135, 169, 171, 182, 184, 187–188, 193–195, 197–202, 208–209, 219, 221, 238n9, 239n15, 246n5, 247n7, 269n28, 270–271nn31–32, 271n37, 272n38, 272n41, 273n42, 273n44, 274n47, 281n33, 298n13, 299n17, 299n19, 300n20, 300n22; ecclesiastical hierarchy, 41, 119–120, 128; Emergent Church movement, 193, 299n17; parachurch, 41, 122
Church of the Holy Spirit, 10, 239n15
CIA. *See* Central Intelligence Agency
Cicero, 188
Cimitero Monumentale (Turin), 219
civil rights, 21. *See also* race; rights
Civiltà Cattolica, 199
class, 3, 6–7, 23, 41, 48, 52–53, 55, 57–60, 93, 108, 120, 129, 174, 195, 200, 207, 243n53, 250n36, 251n41; classism, 215; struggle, 55, 250n30
Clement of Alexandria, 184
Clinton, Bill, 93
Code Napoléon. *See* laws
Codex Iuris Canonici. See laws
codification (law). *See* laws
colonialism, 34, 61, 89, 132
Colombia, 99, 196
Columbia University, 206, 232–233; Columbia Law, 206
commodities, 55, 57, 259n37; commodification, 57
Comintern, 45, 200

comunidades eclesiales de base (CEBs), 196
communism, 43–44, 102, 105, 107, 123, 195–196, 200, 202, 210, 299n19, 300n22; anticommunist, 50, 95, 274n47; hermeneutic, x, 31, 33, 40, 89, 92, 96–99, 105, 107–108, 110, 159, 206, 210, 235; communists, 2, 21, 41, 45–49, 52–53, 55, 59, 61, 95, 97, 99, 105, 200, 226, 247n8, 300n22, 303n53; crypto-communist prophet, 26; Third Communist International (Comintern), 45, 200. *See also* France; Lenin, Vladimir; Mao Zedong; Partito Comunista Italiano (PCI)
Communist Manifesto, The (Marx and Engels), 99
compromesso storico (historic compromise), 49–50, 92–93
Concept of Poiesis in Aristotle (Vattimo). *See Il concetto di fare in Aristotele*
Cone, James H., 204–205, 207
Conference of Latin American Bishops, 198
confirmation bias, 168
Confucianism, 210
Congar, Yves, 128, 130, 196, 274n44
Congregation for the Doctrine of the Faith (CDF), 126, 197, 301n29
Congo, Republic of the, 21
consciousness, 13–15, 52, 100, 161, 254n61, 255n3, 258n36, 273n44, 286n14; class, 52; collective, 32, 81; conscious will, 52; self-, 52, 287n19

conservatives, 15–16, 20–22, 42, 95, 122, 129, 132, 166, 193, 240n32, 270n28, 271–272n37, 274n44, 288n21
Consiglio dei Ministri, 44
conspiracy theories, 211, 289–290n27
Constantine, xiii, 201, 270n31
consumerism, 22; consumer culture, 95
conventio ad excludendum, 49
Conway, Kellyanne, 166–167, 169, 289n25
Copernicus, Nicolaus, 74, 169
Council of Ministers (Italy). *See* Consiglio dei Ministri
Count de Salis. *See* Charles, John Francis
Corinthians I, 152. *See also* Bible
Cornoldi, Giovanni Maria, 124
coup d'état, 49
Craxi, Bettino, 93–95
Credere di credere (*Belief*) (Vattimo), x, 35, 232
Crenshaw, Kimberlé, 206–207
Crisi della ragione (*The Crisis of Reason*) (Gargani, ed.), 66, 256n2
crisis, 48, 55–56, 66, 102, 137, 187, 256n9, 291–292n33; of meaning, 212; of Reason, ix
Critchley, Simon, 15
Critique de la raison dialectique (*Critique of Dialectical Reason*) (Sartre), 50
Croce, Benedetto, xii, 8, 34, 54, 247n10, 248n13. *See also* Benedetto Croce Istituto Italiano per Gli Studi Storici
Crockett, Clayton, 193

crucifix, 198. *See also* Christ
Culte de la Raison, 81
Cultural Revolution (China), 24
culture, xii, 7, 10, 33, 51, 57, 81, 89, 95, 128–129, 158, 168, 177, 199–200, 212, 228, 231, 263n78, 278n20, 281n33; cultural inheritance, 34; jamming, 98, 251n41
Curia, Roman, 129–130
Cuyo, National University of, 8
cyberspace, 168

Dalferth, Ingolf U., 115, 117
Daly, Mary, 203
Damocles, 70
Dante, 120, 213
Daoism; Daoist, 210
D'Aquino, Tommaso. *See* Aquinas, St. Thomas
Dasein, 13, 67–69, 71, 74, 90, 248n13
da Silva, Luiz Inácio "Lula," 96
das Nichts ("nothingness"), 69–70
Das Testament des Dr. Mabuse (film), 81
Da Vinci, Leonardo, 138
DC. *See* Democrazia Cristiana
death of God. *See* God; theology
debolist thinking. *See pensiero debole*
Debord, Guy, 228
Declaration of the Occupation of New York City, The, 100
decolonization, 21
deconstruction, 16, 91, 289n27
de Gaulle, Charles, 22
De Gesperi, Alcide, 47, 49, 226–227

degrounding ("*sfondante*"), 65, 74. See also ungrounding
Dei Filius (Pope Pius IX), 223, 272n38
Deleuze, Gilles, 26, 167, 228
della Chiesa, Giacomo (Pope Benedict XV). See popes
Della realtà (*Of Reality*) (Vattimo), 33, 235
de Lubac, Henri, 127–128, 130, 196, 274n44, 298n11
de Maistre, Joseph comte, 90, 240n32, 288n20
democracy, 21, 30, 34, 46, 94–95, 100, 105, 107–108, 226, 120–121, 132, 171, 174, 190–191, 252n52, 263n73, 286n9, 293n43; antidemocracy, 171; democratic order, 32; social democrats, 44; democratically, 49, 97, 108
Democratic Party (US): 21–22; Democratic National Convention, 21
Democratic Party of the Left (Italy). See Partito Democratico della Sinistra
Democrazia Cristiana (DC, "Christian Democrats"), 20–21, 29, 47–50
De Nicola, Enrico, 226
Depoortere, Frederiek, 177–179, 181–183, 185, 269n22, 294n51
demythologization, 61, 80, 81, 143, 260n49. See also *Entmythologisierung*; myth
DePaul University, 99
Derrida, Jacques, 2, 35, 64, 80, 92, 98, 116, 150, 167, 191, 228, 232, 240n35, 282n45, 286n6, 298n11; Derridean, 16, 148, 179, 194, 289–290n27
Derry, 21. See also Ireland
Der Spiegel, 229
Des choses cachées depuis la fondation du monde (*Things Hidden Since the Foundation of the World*) (Girard), 136, 138–139, 276n9
de Vitoria, Francisco, 188
Dewey, John, 1, 173
dialectic, 27, 64, 74, 81, 226, 248n12, 255n3; dialectical, 27, 33, 39, 50, 64, 73, 77, 88, 106, 165, 259n37; dialectical materialism (Marx), 27
Dialectic of Enlightenment (Horkheimer and Adorno), 81, 226
Dicastery for the Doctrine of the Faith. See Congregation for the Doctrine of the Faith
différance (Derrida), 228; and difference, 17, 63–64, 74, 230, 254n61
di Fiore, Joachim, 118
Dilthey, Wilhelm, 13, 86
Dionysian, 60–61, 86. See also Apollonian
direct action, 45, 56; wildcat action, 23; sabotage, 23, 45
divorce, 28, 219
Document on Human Fraternity for World Peace and Living Together. See Abu Dhabi Document
dogma, 43, 130, 180, 285n4; dogmatism, 23, 90, 164; nondogmatic, 117
dollar gap, 20

Dominicans, 196, 301n29
Dopo la cristianità (*After Christianity*) (Vattimo), x, 35, 118, 232–233
Dostoyevsky, Fyodor, 35
Dotolo, Carmelo, 179, 299n18
doublespeak (Orwell), 167
Drake, Richard, 30
duce. *See* Mussolini, Benito
Duchamp, Marcel, 91
Duchesne, Louis, 126
Duke Kunshan Humanities Research Center, 209
Dulles, Avery Cardinal, 131
Dussel, Enrique, 88–89
Dworkin, Ronald, 191

East, the, 60, 97; Eastern philosophy, 209–210. *See also* West
East China Normal University, 209
Ecce Homo (Nietzsche), 224
Ecclesia semper reformanda est, 209
ecclesiastical hierarchy. *See* church
Eco, Umberto, 6–7, 9, 227, 232, 237, 238n7
École normale supérieure Paris, 57
economy, 20, 48, 51, 125, 138, 168; economics, 4, 19, 22, 44, 56, 58, 107, 123, 125, 131, 259n37; political, 51; global, 48, 168. *See also* il boom economico
Editions du Seuil, 232
Ekstases, 68, 257n17
Egypt, 21, 302n40; Alexandria, 226
Einaudi, Luigi, 227
Einaudi Press, 136
elites, 171, 174

El Salvador, 197–198
emancipation, 52, 59, 77, 82, 86, 88, 91, 97–98, 105–106, 164, 169, 176, 190, 201–202, 233. *See also* liberation
Emergent Church movement. *See* church
empire, xiii, 89, 270n29, 302n40. *See also* imperialism
empirical, 18, 84, 97, 102, 246–147, 158, 193, 261n53, 280n30
Enciclopedia filosofica, 11
Encolpius (fictional character), 140
encyclicals, 41, 121, 124, 126, 128–129, 131, 199, 223–224, 246n4, 271n33, 300n22
end of history. *See* Fukuyama, Francis
End of Modernity, The (Vattimo). *See La fine della modernità*
Engels, Friedrich, 54, 97, 250n29
England, 21, 123, 248n15; Britain, 4, 195, 300n23; English language, 28, 68, 96, 224, 257n17, 279n28; English-speaking, ix, 2, 7, 192, 290n27. *See also* United Kingdom
Enlightenment, 66, 80–81, 90, 164–165, 188, 201, 226, 260n46, 278n23, 287n19; Aufklärung, 80; Counter-Enlightenment, 288n21. *See also* neo-Enlightenment
ens et verum convertuntur, 83
epistēmē, 158; epistemic, 159, 167, 256n12; epistemology, x, 80, 83, 161, 211
epoché, 76, 287n17
environmentalism, 21, 132, 200, 299n19

Entmythologisierung ("disenchantment/ demythologization"), 80, 81, 260n49
Entschlossenheit ("resoluteness"), 68
Entzauberung ("disenchantment"), 82
Ereignis ("event"), 73, 76
Eros and Civilization (Marcuse), 58
equality, 34, 208
es gibt, 69, 98, 192, 257n23
eschatology, 15, 77, 118
Essere e dintorni (*Being and Its Surroundings*) (Vattimo), 33, 200, 236
Essere, storia, e linguaggio in Heidegger (*Being, History, and Language in Heidegger*) (Vattimo), 11, 228, 244n63
Estetica: Teoria della formatività (*Aesthetics: Theory of Formativity*) (Pareyson), 8
ethics, x, 30, 34, 62, 125, 159, 175, 190, 200, 220, 231, 233–234, 250n35, 285n3, 286n7. *See also* moral
Ethiopia, 4, 21
Euripides, 60
Europe, 88–89, 120, 125–126, 142, 144, 195–196, 200, 234, 246n5; European Economic Community, 19; European Parliament, x, 2, 19, 96, 191–192, 217, 235; European Philosophical Yearbook, 92; European Union, 19, 96; Eurocentrism, 88, 205, 263n73, 268n14
Evangelii gaudium (Pope Francis), 199. *See also* encyclicals
exchange-value (Marx), 57

excommunication, 48, 119, 122, 273n42, 300n22
existentialism, ix, 7, 8, 9, 18, 73, 127, 138, 179, 227
exploitation, 41, 57, 271n33

Fabro, Cornelio, 126
Facebook, 168
Facta, Luigi, 44, 224, 226
fallibilism, xi, xii, 77, 173
Famà, Irene, 216
Fanfani, Amintore, 227
Fanon, Frantz, 98
Farewell to Truth, A (Vattimo). *See Addio alla verità*
fascism, 7–8, 23, 44–46, 54, 66, 166, 224–226, 232; Fascist regime, 3, 20, 45–46, 224; neofascists, 20, 29, 95; post-Fascist Italy, 20. *See also* Partito Nazionale Fascista
fatalism, 68
Faulkner, William, 68
feminist, 194, 203, 204, 207. *See also* theology
Ferdinand, Archduke Franz, 224
Ferm, Deane William, 196
Ferraris, Maurizio, 89–92, 160, 162, 164–166, 169–172, 174–176, 181, 287n17, 288nn21–23
Ferretti, Giovanni (philosopher), 219
Ferretti, Giovanni (Pope Pius IX). *See* popes
Fiat, 25, 29
Filosofia in Movimento, 199
financialization, 168
Finnis, John, 190

Fiorenza, Elizabeth Schüssler, 203
First Declaration of the Lacandon Jungle, The, 99
first principles, 32, 35, 75, 152
First Republic (Italian), 19, 46
First Vatican Council, 121, 223
Florence, 122; University of, 87
foreign policy, 22, 278n23
Foreign Policy (magazine), 171
forma, 9
Forza Italia! (Forward Italy Party), 95
Foucault, Michel, 26, 167, 191, 228
Foucault's Pendulum (Eco). *See Il pendolo di Foucault*
Fourier, Charles, 97
France, 4, 6, 8, 47, 57, 66, 99, 121–122, 124, 197, 218, 225, 232, 253n53, 270nn29–30, 281n33; Franco-Prussian War, 121; French Civil Code, 189; French Communist Party, 22; French interpretations of Nietzsche, 26; French language, 146, 202, 232, 270n30; French Revolution, 30; French Riviera, 139; foreign policy, 22; workers in, 22
Frascati-Lochhead, Marta, 203–204
Fratelli delle Scuole Cristiane (Fratres Scholarum Christianarum), 28, 238n8
Fratelli d'Italia (Brothers of Italy Party), 96
Fratelli tutti (Pope Francis), 187, 199–200. *See also* encyclicals
Fratelli tutti? Credenti e non credenti in dialogo con Papa Francesco (Tonelli, ed.), 199

Frazer, James George, 143
freedom, xii, 52, 60, 100, 118, 120–121, 132, 179, 197, 205, 215, 247n7, 260n42
Frege, Gottlob, 225
Freiburg, University of, 70, 225
Freud, Sigmund, 143, 278n22
From Sin to Amazing Grace (Cheng), 208
Front Line (group). *See* Prima Linea
Fronte Unitario Omosessuale Rivoluzionario Italiano (FUORI!), 28
Fukuyama, Francis, 116, 268n14
FUORI!. *See* Fronte Unitario Omosessuale Rivoluzionario Italiano (FUORI!)
Future of Religion, The (Vattimo and Rorty), x, 35, 234

Gadamer, Hans-Georg, ix, 2, 10–17, 31, 64, 85, 87, 157–158, 203, 209, 223, 227–229, 232, 240n35, 284n2; Gadamerian, 16–17
games, 64, 83, 180, 280n31; language, of Wittgenstein, 18, 103, 146, 173
Gargani, Aldo, 66
Garibaldi, Giuseppe, 269n26; Garibaldi Brigades, 46
Garrigou-Lagrange, Réginald, 126, 128
Gaudium et spes, the Pastoral Constitution on the Church in the Modern World, 131. *See also* Vatican II
gay rights movement. *See* LGBTQ+
gender, 207–208

Genealogy of Morals (Nietzsche), 106
Geneva, University of, 224
Genoa, 20, 44
Gentile, Giovanni, 8, 225
George, Robert P., 190
Georgetown University, 199
Germany, 4, 5, 8, 10–12, 21, 43, 99, 124, 197, 224–226
Geschick/Ge-schick ("fate/destiny"), 68, 71, 75, 78
Gewesenheit ("having-been"), 68
Geworfenheit ("thrownness"), 82
Giammarinaro, Corrada, 215
Gifford Lectures, 2, 235
Gilman, Nils, 116
Gilson, Étienne, 126
Girard, René, 2, 35, 136–137, 142, 144–147, 149, 177, 234, 276n9, 276–277n10, 277nn18–19, 279n27
Giuliani, Rudy, 167, 169, 289n26
Giulino di Mezzegra, 226
Glasgow, University of, 2, 235
globalization, 168, 233, 299n19
Global South, 88, 96, 108, 196, 299n19
Glyn-Williams, Owen, 99
Go-Between, The (Hartley), 14
God, xi, 11–12, 31–32, 35, 43, 68–69, 73, 78, 80, 113, 117–119, 123–124, 128, 132, 137, 140–142, 145, 148–152, 154, 181–183, 188, 192, 199, 205–209, 229, 266n5, 272n38, 281n40, 282–283n45, 295nn58–59, 296n64, 297n10, 298n13; death of, 31, 35, 78, 80, 117, 192, 234, 297n10; Eternal Father, 199; of the philosophers, 31
Google, 168

Gospel, 139–141, 149–150, 184, 208, 277n18, 294n57; Matthew, 183. *See also* Bible
Gramsci, Antonio, 39, 42, 45, 50, 247n8, 248n13, 248n15; Gramsci Institute of Rome, 50
Grande, Father Rutilio, 198
Grand Officer of Merit of the Italian Republic, 233
Great Britain, 4, 195. *See also* Derry; England
Great Leap Forward (China), 25
Grisez, Germain, 190
Gronchi, Giovanni, 227–228
Grotius, Hugo, 188
Grundlinien der Philosophie des Rechts (Hegel), 76
Grundrisse (Marx), 57
Grünewald, Matthias, 201
Guarino, Thomas G., 181–183, 185
Guatemala, 197
guerilla group, 29. *See also* militants
Guglielminetti, Marziano, 7
Gutenberg's printing press, 168
Gutiérrez, Gustavo, 117, 196–197, 301n29

Habermas, Jürgen, 12, 15–16, 135, 234, 260n46, 284n2, 293n43
Hacer lío, 202
Hamilton, William, 192
Hannah Arendt Prize for Political Thinking, 2, 233
Hardt, Michael, 168
Hare, R. M., 147, 279n30, 280n30
Harman, Graham, 89–90, 160

harm principle (Mill), 179
Hart, H. L. A., 189
Hartley, Leslie Poles (L. P.), 14
Havana, 2
Hebrew Bible. *See* Bible
Hegel, G. W. F., 32, 60, 76–77, 82, 106, 143, 254n64, 258nn34–35; Hegelianism, 14, 52, 64, 137, 209, 248n13
Heidegger, Martin, ix, 1, 2, 8, 10–13, 15–18, 26–28, 30–31, 33, 39–40, 43, 50, 59–60, 63–65, 67–74, 78, 80, 83, 86–87, 89, 96, 105, 128, 136–138, 160, 220, 225, 227–230, 235, 243–244n61, 244n63, 246n3, 248n13, 253n56, 256n12, 257n22, 284n1, 288n21; Heideggerians, 12–13, 16–17, 26–27, 60, 73, 113, 157, 210
Heidelberg, 11–12; University, 10–11, 34, 135, 228, 244n63
Hennesey, James, 124
heresy, 48, 182
Hermeneutic Communism (Vattimo and Zabala), x, 33, 40, 89, 92, 96, 98–99, 105, 107–108, 235, 262–263n71, 264n83
hermeneutics, xi, xii, 1–2, 12–13, 15–18, 31–32, 36, 65, 75, 82, 86, 96–97, 100, 103, 108, 117, 127, 137, 140, 145–147, 157, 160–162, 164, 173, 182, 190–192, 209–211, 238n7, 263n73, 279n28; Gadamerian, 13, 15–17; of retrieval, 15–16; of suspicion, 16, 258n36; *hermeneia*, 79
heteronormativity, 217

historical materialism (Marx), 39, 43, 97; historical materialist, 267n10
historic compromise. *See compromesso storico*
historicism, 16, 153
History of Religions School. *See* Religionsgeschichtliche Schule
Hitler, Adolf, 4, 274n47
Hobbes, Thomas, 189
Holbein the Younger, Hans, 201
Holmes, Oliver Wendell, Jr., 189, 297n5
holy, 10, 131–132, 141
Homo sacer (Agamben), 98
homosexual. *See* LGBTQ+
Hong Kong, 99. *See also* China
horizons, 12, 14, 31–32, 67, 71–72, 75; fusion of horizons, 14, 16, 31, 203
Horizontverschmelzung ("fusion of horizons"), 14, 16, 31, 203
Horkheimer, Max, 81, 100, 226, 287n19
Horn, Gerd-Rainer, 195
hospitality, 34, 183
Hot Autumn. *See* Autunno Caldo
House of Charity—Art and Tradecraft. *See* Casa di Carità Arti e Mestieri
House of Savoy, 6, 120, 269n26; Savoyard dynasty, 223, 270n30; King Umberto I, 223–224; King Umberto II, 226; Victor Emmanuel II, 44, 46, 121, 223; King Victor Emmanuel III, 44, 224–226, 241n43
Humani generis (Pius XII), 128–129. *See also* encyclicals

humanism, 43, 248n13; Christian, 6; Renaissance, 188
human rights, 107, 131–132, 189, 200
Hume, David, 189
Humphrey, Hubert, 22
Hungary, 99; Hungarian Revolution, 251n42; Austro-Hungarian, 224
Husserl, Edmund, 10, 12, 161, 225, 287n17
Hypothesis on Nietzsche (Vattimo). See *Ipotesi su Nietzsche*

idealism, 84, 72, 90, 160–161, 248n13; German, 127
identitarians, xii
ignoratio elenchi, 178
il boom economico, 20
Il concetto di fare in Aristotele (*The concept of poiesis in Aristotle*) (Vattimo), 9
Il nome della rosa (*The Name of the Rose*) (Eco), 7
Il pendolo di Foucault (*Foucault's Pendulum*) (Eco), 7
Il pensiero debole (Weak Thought) (Vattimo and Rovatti, eds.), ix, 18, 33, 63, 74, 80, 231, 237, 256n10; 259n36
Il soggetto e la Maschera (*The Subject and the Mask*) (Vattimo), 17, 26–27, 29, 40, 52, 58–59, 61, 63–64, 66, 106, 229
imperialism, 4, 34, 51, 124, 132, 143, 200, 201, 267n8, 278n20; anti-imperialism, 96. See also empire
Incarnation of Christ, 35, 150–151, 153, 193

incorrigible knowledge, 35
Indecent Theology (Althaus-Reid), 207–208
India, 200; Indian philosophy, 211
indigenous, 144, 196
Indochina. See Vietnam
Inquisition. See Congregation for the Doctrine of the Faith
Institute for Doctoral Studies in the Visual Arts, 99
Instruction on Christian Freedom and Liberation, 197
integralist. See Catholic
Interiore homine habitat veritas (St. Augustine), 154. See also truth
intersectional theology, 194, 206–207
Introduction to Heidegger (Vattimo). See *Introduzione ad Heidegger*
Introduzione ad Heidegger (Vattimo), 26, 229
Invention of World Religions, The (Masuzawa), 143
invisible gardener (Wisdom), 147, 280n30
Ipotesi su Nietzsche (*Hypothesis on Nietzsche*) (Vattimo), 11, 228
Ireland, 21, 99; Irish Republican Army (IRA), 28
Isaiah (biblical book), 140
Isenheim Altarpiece (Grünewald), 201
Islam, 203, 267n8, 278n23, 281n33, 295n63
Istanbul, 234
Italia dei Valori (Italy of Values) Party, 235

Italian Academy Lectureship (Columbia University), 232
Italian Communist Party (PCI). See Partito Comunista Italiano (PCI)
Italian Democratic-Socialist Party. See Partito Socialista Democratico Italiano
Italian Liberal Party. See Partito Liberale Italiano
Italian Philosophical Yearbooks, 92, 231–232
Italian Republican Party. See Partito Repubblicano Italiano
Italian Socialist Party (PSI). See Partito Socialista Italiano (PSI)

Jainism, 211, 277n18
Jameson, Fredric, 231, 264n90
Japan, 21
Jaspers, Karl, 8, 244n61
Jerusalem, 184
Jesus. See Christ
Jesuits, 235, 238n9, 301n29
Jews, 116, 120, 139, 201, 275n51, 290n27, 295n63, 298n11; Jewish law, 118; Judaism, 201, 269n22
Job (biblical character), 140
Johnson, Lyndon B., 21
Jonkers, Peter, 178
Joseph (biblical character), 140
Joy, Morny, 203
judges, 107, 189–191, 217, 220. See also laws
justice, 189–191, 205–206, 209–210, 221. See also law(s)
Justin Martyr, 184

Kail, Michel, 52
Kant, Immanuel, 76, 80, 243n61, 256n12, 285n3, 286n7; Kantianism, 161; post-Kantian, 161
Karenga, Ron, 204
Kautsky, Karl, 54
Kearney, Richard, 72, 235
Kelsen, Hans, 189
Kennedy, John F., 21
Kennedy, Sr., Robert F., 21
kenosis ("self-emptying"), xii, 33, 114, 150–151, 153, 203, 283n45; kenotic, 35, 151, 208, 283n46
Kenosis and Feminist Theology: The Challenge of Gianni Vattimo (Frascati-Lochhead), 203
King, Dr. Martin Luther, Jr., 21, 204
Kingdom of Italy, 121, 223, 270n29
kings, 44–46, 121–122, 124, 164, 264n90, 270n28, 271nn31–32; John of England, 123. See also House of Savoy; monarchy
Kipling, Rudyard, 144
Kirchmayr, Raoul, 52
Kissinger, Henry, 47
Klossowski, Pierre, 228
Koven, Ronald, 48
Kuhn, Thomas, 85, 170, 298n11
Küng, Hans, 128, 130, 274n44

labor, 28, 44, 53, 55, 57, 59, 93, 123, 172, 195, 246n5, 259n37; laborism, 51. See also workers
Lacertosa, Massimiliano, 209–210

INDEX ❧ 365

"La dottrina del fascismo" ("The Doctrine of Fascism") (Mussolini and Gentile), 225
La filosofia dell'esistenza e C. Jaspers (Pareyson), 8
La fine della modernità (*The End of Modernity*) (Vattimo), 33, 231
La Malfa, Giorgio, 94
Lamentabili sane exitu (Pope Pius X), 126, 224
language-game(s) (*Sprachspiel*). *See* games
La Plata, Universidad Nacional de, 2, 263n73
"La ragione, l'abbondanza e la credenza" ("Reason, Abundance, and Belief") (Viano), 66
La religion (Vattimo and Derrida, eds.), x, 35, 79, 232
La Repubblica (newspaper), 91
La società trasparente (*The Transparent Society*) (Vattimo), 33, 153, 231, 263n78
La Stampa (newspaper), 19, 216
Lateran Pacts, 225, 271
Laterza, Giuseppe, 231–232
Laterza (publisher), 92
Latin America. *See* America
Laudato si' (Pope Francis), 199. *See also* encyclicals
laurea, 9, 227
Lavelle, Louis, 8
laws, 23, 41, 57–58, 118, 126, 131, 170, 175, 183, 187–192, 208–209, 212, 233; canon, 126, 188, 270n31; civil, 41; *Codex Iuris Canonici*, 126;
codification, 126–127, 189; French Civil Code (or Code Napoléon), 189; Jewish law, 118; jurisprudence, 188; juridical, 191–192; legal despotism, 189; legal experts, 190; lawyers, 189–190, 215, 270; legal philosophy, 188; legal positivism, 188–189; natural, 188–190, 208, 256n9; prosecutors, 190, 215, 218–219; public policy, 41; Zeroth law of thermodynamics, 175
Lazio region, 121, 223
Lebanon Valley College, 105
Lefort, Guy, 138
Left, *the* (politics), x, 6, 44–46, 49, 51, 53–54, 61, 93, 97, 165–167, 251nn41–42, 253n56; center left, 20, 29, 47; far left, 20, 47–48; extreme left, 26, 30; Italian democratic left, 30; leftist agitation, 25; leftists, 23–25, 41–42, 44, 47, 53, 95, 254n64, 289n27; left wing, 28, 43, 56, 95–96, 105, 195–197, 224, 251n41; militant leftists, 24; New Left, 50–51, 53, 58–59, 250n30; partisans on, 46; radical left, 47, 50; Western leftists, 24–25
Lega Nord (Northern League), 95
legitimist, 8
Lenin, Vladimir, 54, 254n63; Leninist, 22, 24, 29–30, 62
Leopardi, Giacomo, 63
Le Roy, Édouard, 126
Le Senne, René, 8

"Letter on Humanism," (Heidegger). See "Über den Humanismus"
Leuven, Katholieke Universiteit, 2, 253
Levinas, Emmanuel, 116, 150, 282n45
Lewis, John, 202
LGBTQ+, 2, 218; gay rights, 21, 132, 208; homosexuality, 6, 28, 217, 228–229, 303; marriage equality, 208; queer, 208, 217; queering, 208; queer theory, 209; queer theology, 194, 207, 209; same-sex marriage, 218
li, 210
liberalism, 34, 121, 269n28, 271n37; liberal, 21, 41–43, 93–95, 116, 120, 122, 124, 128, 205, 224, 235, 263n73, 271n37, 273n44, 275n53, 297n11; liberalization, 91, 93; neoliberalism, 98, 107, 290–291n29; postliberalism, 192, 288n20, 297–298n11, 299n17
liberation, xiii, 51, 60, 88, 91, 106–107, 109, 119, 197–198, 200, 209, 211, 260n42; theology, 98, 117, 194–198, 205, 299n19, 301n29; Black, theology, 204–206; sexual, 21
libertarian-anarchist, 26. See also anarchism
Libertatis nuntius. See *Instructions on Certain Aspects of the Theology of Liberation*
Liceo Classico e Linguistico Vincenzo Gioberti (Vincenzo Gioberti State Classical and Linguistic High School), 5
life-project (*le project fondamental*), 51–52

life-world (*Lebenswelt*), 12
linguistic, 5, 75; philosophy, 18; turn, 31, 117, 228
Liu, Liangjian, 209–210
Locke, John, 163
Loisy, Alfred, 126
Lombardy, 8
Lonergan, Bernard, 127
Lo Russo, Stefano, 219
Louis-Napoléon. See Bonaparte
Löwith, Karl, 10, 34, 228, 244n61, 259n37
Loyola Marymount University, 209
Loyola University Andalusia, 210
Luciani, Albino (Pope John Paul I). See popes
Lukács, György, 52, 229, 248n12
Lumen fidei (Pope Francis), 199. See also encyclicals
Lumen gentium, 130. See also Vatican II
Lumières, 188
L'Unità (newspaper), 19, 29
Luther, Martin, 184, 257n18, 295–296n64; Lutheran, 150
Lyotard, Jean-François, xi, 2, 137, 168, 191, 230, 293n43

Machiavelli, 106, 120
Madrid, Universidad Nacional de Educación a Distancia (UNED), 2
maestros, 7, 219
Making Communism Hermeneutical (Mazzini and Glyn-Williams, eds.), 99
Malcolm X, 204
Malpas, Jeff, 100, 103–105

Malpas, Nick, 100, 103–105
Malvezzi, Aldina, 53
Mamino, Sergio, 216, 219, 230, 233
Mandarin (language), 146
Mandarins of the Future (Gilman), 116
Manifesto of New Realism (Ferraris), 92, 287n17
Mani Pulite ("Clean Hands") Affair, 93
Mao Zedong, 22–25, 29, 108, 243n56, 251n42; Maoism, 24, 29; Maoist, 22–24, 59, 229
Marburg, 223, 225
Marcel, Gabriel, 8, 228
March on Rome (Fascists), 3, 44
Marcuse, Herbert, 39, 58–59, 229, 250n30
Marder, Michael, 235
Maréchal, Joseph, 127
Marion, Jean-Luc, 113, 187, 298n12
Maritain, Jacques, 6, 43, 126
Marshall Plan, 20, 47
Marwick, Arthur, 23
Marx, Karl, 26–27, 43, 51–52, 54, 57, 59, 61, 97, 105, 250n34, 253n56, 254n64, 259n37, 290n27; heterodox Marxism, 43; Marxism, ix, 24, 27, 51, 54, 58–60, 97, 240, 247n8, 248n12, 289n27; Marxist alienation, 27, 59, 64, 77, 259n37; Marxist literature, 23; Marxists, 23, 41–44, 49, 51, 54, 57, 59, 76, 96, 98, 137, 197–198, 245, 248n13, 249n26, 250n30, 251n41; orthodox Marxism, 24, 51–52, 250n29
Marx oltre Marx (*Marx Beyond Marx*) (Negri), 57, 252n49

Mass. *See* Catholics
Masuzawa, Tomoko, 143
materialism: historical materialism, 39, 43, 97, 267n10; materialist dialectic, 248n12; vulgar materialists, 52
Max Planck-Humboldt Award for Humanities and Social Sciences, 2, 232
Mazzini, Silvia, 99
McCool, Gerald A., SJ, 125
McIntyre, Lee, 166–167
McLuhan, Marshall, 168
Medellín, 196
Medellín Conference. *See* Second Episcopal Conference of Latin America
Meillassoux, Quentin, 89
Meloni, Giorgia, 96
Memphis, 21
Mendieta, Eduardo, 99–100, 262n71, 265n94
Messuti, Ana, 190
metaphysics, 15, 27–28, 31, 35, 59–62, 67, 69–73, 76–79, 83–84, 98–100, 109, 113, 136–137, 153, 175, 177–178, 190, 257n23; antimetaphysics, 106; metaphysical, xii, 18, 26–27, 29–30, 32, 35–36, 60–62, 64, 71, 74–76, 78–79, 85–86, 100, 104, 106, 117, 125, 144, 146, 151–152, 160, 176, 178–180, 190, 203–204, 211, 258n36, 260n46, 263n73, 277n19, 279n28, 283n45; metaphysical letters, 30. *See also* postmetaphysics
Metz, Johann Baptist, 196, 274n44

Mexico, 21, 88; Mexico City, 21
Milan, 20, 22, 54, 93, 226
Miles, Jack, 2, 234
militants, 23, 40, 48, 54, 98, 201, 205, 302n40, 303n53; militant leftists, 24; militant unionism, 42; militant workers, 23, 56. *See also* Blackshirts; guerilla group; Squadrismo militias
Milizia Volontaria per la Sicurezza Nazionale (MVSN). *See* Blackshirts
Mill, John Stuart, 179, 294n55
Miller, James, 209
Min, Anselm K., 135
Minerva, 76
MMR (measles, mumps, rubella) vaccine, 102
modern, 13, 30, 41–42, 61, 80–81, 89, 115–116, 124–125, 128–129, 131–132, 144, 158–159, 169, 188, 246n3, 259n37, 278n20, 283n46, 285n3, 287n19; antimodernists, 9, 41, 43, 126, 272n37; modernism, 42, 121, 126, 128; modernists, xi, 26, 43, 60, 65, 80, 82, 86, 97, 108, 125–126, 137; modernity, x–xi, 34, 43, 60, 66, 79–82, 87–88, 117, 121, 123–124, 126, 136–137, 147–148, 164–165, 202, 204, 247n10, 271–272nn37, 41; premodern, 42, 248n10; transmodernity, 88
mokṣa, 211
monarchy, 46, 226, 271n32; monarchists, 8, 47. *See also* kings
Monateri, Pier Giuseppe, 190
Montini, Giovanni Battista (Pope Paul VI). *See* Popes

Monza, 218
Moore, G. E., 224
morals, 1, 56, 62, 85, 99–100, 122, 125, 152, 158, 189, 192, 205, 240n32, 285n3; morality, 106, 189, 209, 243; revolutionary moralism, 30, 205
Morales, Evo, 96, 198
Moro, Aldo, 29, 50, 56
Morrocco, 21, 217
Moscow, 45
mos maiorum (Roman), 201
motivated reasoning, 168
Mounier, Emmanuel, 6, 43, 227
Movimento Sociale Italiano, 29. *See also* fascism
Müller, F. Max, 143
Muslims. *See* Islam
Mussolini, Benito, 3, 20, 44–46, 224–226, 241–242n43, 274n47
mystery, 35, 258n34; *mysterium tremendum et fascinans*, 118
Mystici corporis Christi (Pope Pius XII), 131. *See also* encyclicals
mysticism, 190
myths, 81–82, 88, 91, 139, 151, 176, 260n49, 277n10, 278n22; monomyth (Campbell), 277n10; mythization, 80; myth of transparency, 85; myth of victimization, 138, 145; myth of redemptive violence, 149. *See also* demythologization

Name of the Rose, The (Eco). *See Il nome della rosa*
Nancy, Jean-Luc, 2, 234, 298n12
Naples, 23, 54, 270n28

Napoleon. *See* Bonaparte
National Assembly (France), 22
National Fascist Party. *See* Partito
  Nazionale Fascista
NATO (North Atlantic Treaty
  Organization), 19
natural law. *See* laws
Nazis, 46, 86, 150, 189, 225–226, 242,
  253n56; de-Nazification, 244n61;
  Germany, 4–5; German forces,
  46; invasion of Poland, 4;
  neo-Nazi, 303n53. *See also*
  Germany
negative dialectics (Adorno), 64, 255n3
Negri, Antonio, 53–58, 98, 168,
  252n49, 252n52
Negri, Nerio, 53–54
neo-Enlightenment, ix; new
  Enlightenment, 66
neofascists. *See* fascism
neoliberalism. *See* liberalism
neopositivism. *See* positivism
neorealism, 89–91, 160–161. *See also*
  phenomena; realism
neo-Scholastics, 42, 125; neo-
  Scholasticism, 123, 126–127. *See also*
  Aquinas, St. Thomas
neo-Thomism. *See* Aquinas,
  St. Thomas
nephrology, 213
New Left. *See* Left, the
New Testament. *See* Bible
Newton's gravitational constant, 175
New York, 100, 233; mayor of, 167
Nezahualcóyotl, 88
Nicaragua, 197–198, 267n8

Nichilismo ed emancipazione (*Nihilism
  and Emancipation*) (Vattimo), 33,
  190, 233
Nicomachean Ethics (Aristotle), 34,
  245n79
Nietzsche, Friedrich, ix, 2, 10–11, 18,
  26–28, 33, 43, 59–61, 63–65, 74, 78,
  80, 82, 86–87, 89, 91, 105–106,
  109–110, 157, 191, 223–224, 228,
  230–231, 233, 243–244n61, 253n56,
  254n61, 255n3, 260n42, 288n21;
  Nietzschean, 25, 27, 29–30, 60, 62,
  107, 109, 113
"Nietzsche and Difference,"
  (Vattimo), 64. *See Avventure della
  differenza*
Nietzsche (Heidegger), 43
Nietzschean-Heideggerian. *See*
  Heidegger and Nietzsche
nihilism, xi, 2, 27–28, 30–31, 65, 74,
  79–80, 83, 86, 88, 91, 104, 117, 145,
  157, 173, 178, 190–191, 204, 231, 233,
  235; anti-nihilist, 105
Nihilism and Emancipation (Vattimo).
  See Nichilismo ed emancipazione
Nixon, Richard M., 22, 249n22;
  anti-Nixon, 229; Nixon Shock, 48
nominalism, 70
nonabsolutism, xi, 211
Non essere Dio (*Not Being God*)
  (Vattimo), 30, 213, 215, 220,
  232, 234
non-Thomistic. *See* Aquinas,
  St. Thomas
nonviolence, 30, 142, 210
North Vietnam. *See* Vietnam

Not Being God (Vattimo). *See Non essere Dio*
Nouvelle théologie, 127–128, 130, 273n44, 274n49
nuclear disarmament movement, 21
Nuova Corrente (journal), 17

Oath Against Modernism, 126
Obama, Barak, 96
Oedipus, 140
Of Reality (Vattimo). *See Della realtà*
Ogden, C. K., 224
Old Testament. *See* Bible
Oltre l'nterpretazione (Beyond Interpretation) (Vattimo), 33, 232
Onnis, Erica, 209–210
On the Doctrine of the Modernists. See Pascendi Dominici gregis
ontology, 1, 17–18, 28, 64, 67, 70, 72, 74, 163–164, 230, 235, 238n10; ontological difference (Heidegger), 30; ontos on, 79; ontotheology, 32, 113; weak, 33, 35, 113, 117
operaismo, 53
Order of Merit of the Italian Republic, 2
Orwellian, 166
Oughourlian, Jean-Michel, 138
Our Lady of Guadalupe, 208
overman. *See Übermensch*

Pacelli, Eugenio (Pope Pius XII). *See* popes
Pact of Steel (Patto d'Acciaio), 4
Padua, 29, 53; University of, 54
Pakistan, 21

Palazzo, David P., 45
Palazzo Campana, 58
Palermo, Universidad de, 2
Palestine, Roman, 201
Palo Alto, 234
Panzieri, Raniero, 55
parachurch organizations. *See* church
paradox of tolerance (Popper), 179, 289n23
paramilitary groups, 23, 46. *See also* Blackshirts; Garibaldi, Giuseppe
Pareyson, Luigi, 7–11, 17, 26, 42–43, 73, 227, 229, 231, 247n10
Paris, 22–23, 57, 228; University of Paris at Nanterre, 22
Parkes, Graham, 209–210
Parkinson's disease, 217
Parliament (Italy), 44–46, 48, 249n19
Parri, Ferruccio, 226
Parsifal, 106
Partito Comunista Italiano (PCI), 20, 23, 43–47, 49–50, 53–54, 93–94, 243n53, 247n8, 248n15
Partito Democratico della Sinistra, x, 94, 233
Partito Liberale Italiano, 93–94
Partito Nazionale Fascista, 44–46. *See also* fascism
Partito Radicale, 28, 229
Partito Repubblicano Italiano, 47, 94
Partito Socialista Democratico Italiano, 47, 94
Partito Socialista Italiano (PSI), 44, 47, 49, 93–94
Party of European Socialists, 233
Party of Italian Communists, x

Pascendi Dominici gregis (Pope Pius X), 126. *See also* encyclicals
Passion of Christ, 141
Pasteur, Louis, 169
Paterlini, Piergiorgio, 215, 234
paternalistic, 215
patriarcha, 122, 129, 203
patristic, 125, 273n44; Patristic Period, 128, 184
Paul, St.. *See* saints
Peter, St.. *See* saints
Pavia, University of, 8
PCI. *See* Partito Comunista Italiano (PCI)
peace movement, 21. *See also* Abu Dhabi Document
Pecci, Giuseppe, 124
Pecci, Vincenzo (Pope Leo XIII). *See* popes
Peirce, C. S., 173
Pella, Giuseppe, 227
Pellegrino, Michele, 7, 238n9
Pennsylvania, University of, 99
pensiero debole ("weak thought"), 2, 17–19, 29–32, 40, 63, 65–67, 74, 78, 80, 87–91, 97–98, 106, 109, 113–114, 117, 138, 144–145, 157, 159, 164, 167, 174, 176, 180–181, 183–185, 187–188, 194, 199, 203–211, 230, 235, 237n7, 256n10, 294n51; debolist thinking, 40, 87, 89. *See also Il pensiero debole*
pensiero rammemorante ("recalling thinking"), 73
Pentapartito, 92–93
people of color, 206

"Perchè non passiamo non dirci cristiani" ("Why We Cannot but Call Ourselves Christians") (Croce), 34, 148
periti, 130
Peru, 117, 196–197, 301n29
Petrograd (St. Petersburg), 42
Petronius, Gaius, 140
Phaedo (Plato), 34
pharmakós, 140
phenomena, 31, 84, 161, 263n78, 290n29; phenomenology, 72, 89–90, 101, 160–161, 163–164; phenomenologists, 90, 161, 163
philology, 16
philosophy, ix, xi, 1–2, 8, 12, 15–16, 18, 26, 30, 32, 36, 40, 42–43, 50, 52, 54, 59, 63–64, 66, 72, 74, 76, 78, 80, 82, 90, 92, 98–100, 114, 124–126, 152, 157, 159, 174–175, 177, 183–185, 188, 190, 192, 203, 209–212, 214, 248n13, 258n34, 260n42, 263n78, 272n41, 276n10, 285n3, 295n63, 296n64; linguistic, 18, 238n7; Greek, 32, 157; philosophers, ix, x, xiii, 2, 5, 7, 11, 15, 19, 26, 29, 31, 39–40, 84, 86–88, 91, 97, 115, 145, 166, 169–170, 176, 196, 212, 215, 219–220, 227, 241n40, 243n61, 245n79, 248n13, 258n34, 262n69, 287n19, 295n63; of religion, 36
Philosophy of Existence and Karl Jaspers, The (Pareyson). *See La filosofia dell'esistenza e C. Jaspers*
phronesis, 157–159, 284n2, 285n3, 289n23, 303n53

Piazza Castello (Turin), 219
Piedmont, 4, 8, 225, 242; Piedmont-Sardinia, 120–121, 223, 270n30
pink tide, 107
Pinochet, Augusto, 49
Piss Christ (Serrano). *See also* Christ
Plato, 15, 34, 106, 245n79, 294n51; Neoplatonic, 257n21; Platonists, 16
play, in Derrida, 64, 82, 179–181, 210
Plekhanov, Georgi, 54
Pleroma, 70
pluralism, 34, 124, 135
poiesis ("making/doing"), 9, 247n10
police, 3, 22–23, 50, 56, 242–243n53, 292n33; thought police, 287n17
politics, x, 2, 5, 11, 30, 43, 55, 92–93, 98, 100–101, 104, 116, 120, 122, 147, 167, 169, 177, 197, 207, 212, 251n41; geopolitics, 24, 116, 167; Italian, 11, 47, 93, 95–96, 99; political economy, 51; political leaflets, 25; political opposition, 45; political practice, 34; political tensions, 29
Polo del Buon Governo (Pole of Good Government), 95
Polo delle Libertà (Pole of Freedoms), 95
Polo Liberal Democratico (Liberal Democratic Pole), 95
Pompeu Fabra University, Barcelona, 3, 209, 236, 309
pontiff. *See* Pope
poor, 88, 98, 122–123, 196, 198, 206, 263n73, 271n33, 290n29
popes, 119; Benedict XV; Benedict XVI, 128; as bishop of Rome, 123; Francis, 2, 132; Gregory XVI; Holy See, 121; Innocent III, 123; John XXIII, 129; John Paul I; John Paul II, 132; Leo XIII, 41, 124; Leo XIV, 133; Papal States, 120; Paul VI, 130; Pius IX, 120; Pius X, 42; Pius XI, 41; Pius XII, 128; seat of St. Peter, 124; Sixtus V, 126; as vicar of Christ, 124
Popper, Karl, 179, 289n23
Portugal, 99
positivism, 54, 72, 84; legal positivism, 188–189; neopositivist, 18
post-Evangelicals, 194, 299n17
post-Fascist. *See* fascism
postmodernism, ix, xi, 2, 32, 81, 91, 136, 165–170, 172, 176–177, 191–193, 203, 230–231, 233, 255, 288nn20–21, 289n27, 298n11; postmodernists, xi, 161–162, 164, 166–167; postmodernity, ix–x, 2, 34, 66, 88–91, 117, 137, 159, 164–165, 167, 204, 254, 262n69, 288n21, 293n43. *See also* modern
postmetaphysical, ix, 2, 16, 26–27, 36, 40, 43, 78–79, 85, 100, 105, 117, 193, 254n64, 279n28; postmetaphysics, xi. *See also* metaphysics
postsecular, 193
post-truth. *See* truth
Post-Truth (McIntyre), 166
Potere Operaio, 53
pragmatics, xi, 47, 83, 132, 147, 170, 179, 257n18, 269n26, 285n6, 286n6; pragmatism, 100, 159
praxis, x, 9, 88, 157–159, 211, 248nn12–13

preferential option for the poor, 98, 196, 198
premodern. *See* modern
presence, in philosophy, 28, 64, 67–69, 71–73, 77–78, 256n15
Prevost, Robert Francis (Pope Leo XIV). *See* popes
priest, 5, 196, 208, 238n9
Prima Linea, 56
prisoners, 29, 39, 50, 56, 94, 122, 150, 219–220, 225–226, 270n30; imprisonment, 45, 54, 107, 248n15
Prodi, Romano, 96
prohairesis, 157
proletariat, 11, 52, 58, 250n34, 259n37, 263n73; proletarian revolution, 53
prosecutors. *See* laws
proselytize, xii
Protestants, 90, 120, 127, 239n15, 246n5, 267n8, 271n37, 272n37, 278n20, 283n46, 298n11; Protestantism, 128, 281n33, 300n20; Protestant Reformation, 201; Protestant reformers, 188
PSI. *See* Partito Socialista Italiano (PSI)
psychoanalysis, 60, 276n10
Ptolemy, 169
public policy. *See* American Enterprise Institute for Public Policy Research; laws
Puebla, 198
Punctum Archimedis, 31

Quaderni rossi (journal), 55
Quadragesimo anno (Pope Pius XI), 41, 300n22. *See also* encyclicals

Quanta cura (Pope Pius IX), 121, 223, 300n22. *See also* encyclicals
queering. *See* LGBTQ+

race, 207; racial equity (movement), 21; racism, 206. *See also* Black: Black Power (movement); civil rights
Radbruch, Gustav, 189
Radical Hermeneutics (Caputo), 16
Radical Love (Cheng), 208
Radical Party (Italy). *See* Partito Radicale
radical theology, 192–194, 298nn11–12, 299n18
Rahner, Karl, 127–128, 130, 196, 273–274n44
RAI (Radiotelevisione Italiana), 6–7, 227
Rainbow Theology (Cheng), 208
Ramsey, Frank P., 224
Rass, Friederike, 178, 307
Raz, Joseph, 189
rationality, 34, 60, 66, 81, 83, 86, 97, 115, 164, 210; irrationalism, 60, 66, 87, 288n21; rational order, 35. *See also Wertrational*; *Zweckrationalität*
Ratti, Achille (Pope Pius XI). *See* popes
Ratzinger, Joseph (Pope Benedict XVI). *See* popes
Rawls, John, 191
Real Chiesa di San Lorenzo, 219
realism, 90, 92, 160–161, 163, 171, 202, 257n22. *See also* idealism and phenomena

Red Brigades. *See* Brigate Rosse
Red Notebooks. *See Quaderni rossi*
Red Star Over China (Snow), 24
Reformation, 125, 201, 283n46;
    pre-Reformation, 125. *See also*
    Protestants
relativism, x–xi, 91, 104, 165, 169,
    173, 204
religions, ix–xii, 2, 7, 32–36, 79, 82,
    114–117, 120–121, 135, 137, 140,
    142–147, 171, 184, 192, 201, 203, 207,
    211–212, 232, 234, 267n8, 275n51,
    276n10, 278n20, 279nn27–28,
    281n33, 295n63; religiosity, 5, 34, 117
Religion (Vattimo and Derrida, eds.).
    See La religion
Religionsgeschichtliche Schule, 143
ren, 210
Renaissance, 188
reproductive rights, 28. *See also*
    liberation
Republican Party (U.S.), 22
Republic of Salò, 46, 226, 242n43. *See
    also* fascism; Mussolini, Benito
Rerum Novarum (Pope Leo XIII), 41,
    300n22. *See also* encyclicals
Resistenza ("Resistance"), 45. *See also*
    Anti-Fascist Resistance Movement
return to religion, ix, 32, 114, 135, 137;
    recovery of religion, 34
revisionism (Soviet), 24
revolutions, 22, 25–27, 29–30, 44, 46,
    51, 53, 59, 61–62, 98–99, 106, 108,
    122, 168, 202, 251n42, 269n28;
    Cultural Revolution, 24; February
    Revolution (Russia), 24; French

Revolution, 30; October
    Revolution (Russia), 24;
    revolutionaries, 120, 188, 254n63;
    revolutionary subjectvity, 30, 50,
    52, 58–59, 61, 250n34; revolutionary
    vanguardism, 54
rhetoric, 61, 79, 83, 104, 205, 296n64
Rhodes, Martin, 94
Ricciardi, Alessia, 167
Richiero, Rosa, 3
Ricoeur, Paul, 77
Righi, Andrea, 57
Right, the (politics), 6, 17, 49, 93,
    95–96, 165, 167, 290n27; right-wing,
    xii, 23, 44, 96, 166–167, 198, 267n8,
    274n47, 288nn21–22; center right,
    20; far right, 20, 23, 48, 95, 289n27
rights, 21, 25, 28, 41, 102, 107–109, 120,
    131–132, 151, 167, 172, 189, 191, 197,
    200, 208, 218, 246n5, 247n7, 250n30,
    253n56, 264n90, 282n41, 288n21
rimettersi ("recovery"), 78
Rio de Janeiro (Brazilian city), 202
Risorgimento, 121
Rivoli Hospital (Turin), ix, 213, 236
Rizzo, Giulia, 215
Robbins, Jeffrey, 193, 298n11
Rohr, Richard, 150, 282n42
Rollins, Peter, 193–194
Roman Catholic Church. *See* Catholic
romantic anticapitalism, 25, 41, 245n3,
    288n21; romantic anticapitalists,
    253n56
Rome, 3, 19, 44, 50, 120–123, 223–224,
    242n53, 260n42, 270nn28–30,
    301n32; Roman Empire, 201

Romero, Archbishop Óscar, 198
Roncalli, Angelo Giuseppe (Pope John XXIII). *See* popes
Roquebrune-Cap-Martin, 218
Rorty, Richard, x, 2, 15, 35, 91, 100, 160, 168, 176, 191, 228, 230, 233–234, 255, 265n94, 284n2
Rosatelli, Jacopo, 219
Rosmini High School, 7, 11
Rossi, Paolo, 87, 89
Rousselot, Pierre, 127
Rovatti, Pier Aldo, ix, 18, 33, 231, 237n7, 258n31
Royal Ulster Constabulary, 21. *See also* Ireland
Royaumont Abbey, 228
Ruether, Rosemary Radford, 203
Russell, Bertrand, 162, 225
Russia, 24, 172, 195, 292. *See also* Soviet Union
RWTH Aachen University, 209–210

sabotage. *See* direct action
Said, Edward, 232
saints: St. Augustine of Hippo, 32, 68, 154, 181, 183, 185, 266n5, 295n59; St. Bonaventure, 126; St. Óscar Romero, 198; St. Paul, 32, 152; St. Peter, 122, 124, 129, 195, 270n30; St. Thomas Aquinas, 6, 10, 32, 69, 125, 152, 185, 188, 247n10, 272n37
Saint-Simon, Henri de, 97
Salerno Turn. *See* Svolta di Salerno
Salò. *See* Republic of Salò
salvation, 115, 118, 141, 145, 188, 197, 266–267n5, 272n38; salvation history (*Heilsgeschichte*), 33–34, 114, 118, 153
Sandinistas, 198, 267n8
San Marcos of Lima, Universidad Nacional Mayor de, 2
Santo Domingo, 198
Sanseverino, Gaetano, 124
Santiago, 49
Sarajevo, 224
Sarto, Giuseppe (Pope Pius X). *See* popes
Sartre, Jean-Paul, 50–52, 59, 108, 248n13
satyagraha, 211
Satyricon (Petronius), 140
Savoy, Royal House of. *See* House of Savoy
scapegoating, 139–140, 277n18
Scelba, Mario, 227
Scheffler, Israel, 148
Schicksal ("fate/destiny"), 68
Schillebeeckx, Edward, 128, 130, 196, 274n44
Schleiermacher, Friedrich, 11, 13, 143, 271n37
Schleiermacher, filosofo dell'interpretazione (Vattimo), 11, 229
Schleiermacher: Philosopher of interpretation (Vattimo). *See Schleiermacher, filosofo dell'interpretazione*
sciences, xi, 2, 15, 80, 82, 84–85, 87, 90, 102, 115–116, 125, 137, 158, 160, 166, 169–172, 180, 202, 232–233, 261n51, 263n78, 278n22, 279n30, 281n33, 287n19, 288n23; neuroscience, 276n10; technoscience, 72

Scoccimarro, Mauro, 45
Scriptures. *See* Bible
Second Episcopal Conference of Latin America, 196, 198
Second Italo-Ethiopian War, 4. *See also* Ethiopia
Second Vatican Council. *See* Vatican II
secularism, 121, 125, 253n56, 281n33; postsecular, 193; secularization, xii, 33–34, 114, 117, 119, 133, 136, 138, 148, 152–153, 178, 182, 201, 219; secularity, 113–115
sedition, 56
Segni, Antonio, 227–228
Sein. *See* being
Sein und Zeit (Heidegger), 12, 28, 67, 73–74, 225
semiotics, 7, 10, 66, 238n7
Serrano, Andres, 208
sex, 132, 200, 208, 215; sexual identity, 207; sexuality, 28
Shanin, Teodor, 54
Shelley, Percy Bysshe, 68
Shroud of Turin. *See* Turin
Sisters in the Wilderness (Williams), 207
situationism, 54, 97–98; Situationist International, 251n41
Smith, James K. A., 176
Snow, Edgar, 24
Snyder, John R., 19
socialism, 24, 59–60, 97, 105, 107, 121, 195, 221, 233, 243n54, 246n5, 271n33, 300n22; socialists, 41, 50, 61, 93, 97, 105, 110, 198, 233, 248n15, 250n30,

253n56, 254n63; utopian socialists, 97; scientific socialism, 97; third world socialism, 97, 251n42. *See also* communism and Marx, Karl
Socrates, 60, 106
Sölle, Dorothee, 205
sophía, 158; sophists, 158, 296n64
Sophocles, 60, 140, 277n14
Sorbonne, Université de Paris, 22, 240n35
South African, 21
Soviet Marxism: A Critical Analysis (Marcuse), 39, 59
Soviet Union, 24, 43, 45, 94, 97, 116, 195, 200, 243n56, 249n19, 251n42, 267n8, 299n19; Soviet-backed dogmatism, 23; Soviet bloc, 59; Soviet Marxism, 39, 59
Spain, 225–226, 236, 274n47
Sparrow, Tom, 89, 160–162
Spicer, Sean, 166–167, 169, 289n25
Spinoza, Baruch, 225
Sprachlichkeit ("linguistics"), 17
Squadrismo militias, 44. *See also* Blackshirts; militants
Stalin, Joseph, 243n56, 251n42; Stalinist regime, 24, 243n56. *See also* Soviet Union
State University of New York (SUNY), 229
Stati della Chiesa. *See* popes
Stoic, 184
strikes, 25, 28, 44–46, 54, 56, 98, 246n5, 300n20; general, 22–23
structuralism, ix, 51, 66; poststructuralism, 66

student movement, 22, 25–26, 58; student protests of 1968, 19, 23, 253n53. *See also* strikes
Suárez, Francisco, 188
subject (philosophy), 17–18, 27, 29–30, 40, 50–52, 58, 62, 65–66, 72, 100, 191, 254n61; revolutionary subject(ivity), 30, 50, 59, 61, 251n41; subjectivity, 29, 34, 51–52, 55–58, 62, 65
Subject and the Mask, The (Vattimo). *See Il soggetto e la maschera*
sublation. *See Aufhebung*
suffering, 150
summus pontifex. See popes
superman. *See Übermensch*
Sub-Sahara, 88. *See also* Africa
Svolta di Salerno ("Salerno Turn"), 46
Sweden, 21
Switzerland, 226
Sydney, University of, 100
Syllabus of Errors. *See Quanta cura*
symbols, xiii, 32, 35, 147–148; symbolic systems, 31, 142, 146; symbolic world, 148; symbolism, 149

Tamil (language), 146
Tangentopoli ("Bribesville"), 94
Tanzania, 21
Tarkovsky, Andrei, 63
Tasmania, University of, 100
Taylor, Charles, 2, 114, 234
téchnē, 158
technology, 87, 90, 168–169, 202, 210; information technologies, 168; technoscience, 72

Tedeschi, Martine, 218
Teilhard de Chardin, Pierre, 128, 196, 274n49
teleology, 27; teleological, 77
Terracini, Umberto, 45, 247
terrone, 5
terrorism, 23, 29–30; terrorists, 29–30, 56, 62, 290, 291n33; war on terror, 97; 278n23; 291n33
Tertullian, 184, 295n64
theology, 6, 33, 36, 68, 113, 124–125, 128, 130, 151, 184–185, 192–194, 200, 205, 207, 271n37, 276n10, 282n40, 288n20, 294n57, 295n63, 296n64, 297–298nn11–12, 299n18; Black liberation theology, 204–206; death of God theology, 297n10; feminist theology, 203; intersectional theology, 206–207; queer theology, 207–209. *See also* liberation
theōría, 158; theory, x, 16, 39, 51, 54, 57, 75, 86, 88, 90–91, 139, 142, 160, 173, 177, 188–190, 208–209, 245n79, 248nn12–13, 250nn29–30, 276–277n10, 289n27, 292n33; theory of everything, 176
Things Hidden Since the Foundation of the World (Girard). *See Des choses cachées depuis la fondation du monde*
Third Communist International (Comintern), 45. *See also* Comintern
Thistlethwaite, Susan Brooks, 203
Tibone, Dionigi, 215
Tlalnepantla, 88

Tlatelolco massacre (Mexico), 21
Togliatti, Palmiro, 45–46, 247n8
Tonelli, Debora, 199
topos ("place"), 13–14
Toronto, University of, 210
Towards a New Manifesto (Horkheimer and Adorno), 100
"Towards an Ontology of Decline," (Vattimo). *See* "Verso un'ontologia del declino"
trace (Derrida), 148, 182, 213, 281n33, 287n19
Tracy, David, 16
traditionalists, 16, 41, 271n37, 273n44, 275n53, 292n37
transcendence, 115, 151, 169, 283n45; transcendentalism, 70, 86, 127, 283n45; transcendental signified (Derrida), 148
Transparent Society, The (Vattimo). *See La società trasparente*
Traub, James, 171
Treaty of Rome, 19
Treaty of Versailles, 224
Trias, Eugenio, 232
Trinity, 118, 283n46, 294n51, 296n64
Tronti, Mario, 55
Tronzano, Andrea, 219
Troubles, the (Ireland), 21
Truman Doctrine, 47
Trump, Donald, 171
truths, xi, xiii, 9, 12–13, 15–16, 18, 31–35, 55, 63, 65, 73, 75–76, 78–81, 83–87, 91–92, 100–106, 117, 128, 137, 152–154, 162, 165–167, 169–170, 173–176, 180–182, 191–193, 204, 211–212, 240n32, 245n79, 258n36, 259n36, 259n39, 261n57, 263n78, 295n58, 296n64, 300n20; alternative facts, 166; post-truth, xi, 166–167, 169, 211; truth claims, 32, 101–102
Truth and Method (Gadamer). *See Wahrheit und Methode*
Turner, Nat, 206
Tuscany, 123
Tunisia, 21, 94
Ture, Kwame, 204
Turin, ix, 3–5, 7, 11, 20, 29, 42, 88, 213, 218–219, 223, 225, 236, 238n9, 247n8, 253n53; Shroud of Turin, 5; University of Turin, 6–11, 17, 25, 43, 58, 210, 227–231, 234
turn, of Heidegger, 12
Twentieth General Assembly of Caritas Internationalis, 197
Twilight of the Idols (Nietzsche), 82
Twitter, 168
Two Red Years. *See* Biennio Rosso
Tyler, E. B., 143, 278n22
Tyrrell, George, 126, 273n42

"Über den Humanismus" (Heidegger), 43
Überlieferung ("inherited tradition"), 65, 75
Übermensch ("Overman"), 27, 29–30, 64, 105–106, 255n3
Überwindung ("overcoming"), 77, 81, 105
Überwunden ("defeating, forgetting or removing"), 105
ulcer surgery, 11, 23, 229
Ulpian, 188

understanding (*nous*), 157. *See also* Verstehen

"Un diálogo con Gianni Vattimo: De la postmodernidad a la transmodernidad" (Dussell), 88

ungrounding, 64. *See* degrounding

Unione di Centro (Union of the Center), 95

unions, 22–23, 25, 28, 41, 53–54, 159, 246n5, 300n20; unionism, 6, 42, 249n19; unionists, 44, 254n63

universalism, 34, 182; universality, 34; universal singular (Sartre), 50

University of Wisconsin–Milwaukee, 230, 255n6

United Kingdom, 99, 171, 298n11. *See also* England

United Nations, 19, 291n33

United States, 20–22, 24, 47, 49, 88, 96, 99, 171, 193, 205–206, 229, 246n5, 249n19, 249n22, 267n8, 288n22, 291–292n33, 297n4; U.S. government, 47. *See also* America

urbanization, 17, 20

Urdu (language), 146

"Ur-Fascism," (Eco), 7, 232

use-value/utility (Marx), 57. *See also* exchange-value

utopia, 15, 77; utopian socialists, 97

Valgenti, Robert T., 105–107

Vallora, Marco, 136

van Buren, Paul, 192, 297n10

vanguardism, 24, 54, 144. *See also* revolution

Vatican. *See* popes

Vatican II, 48, 126, 128–133, 195–196, 247n7, 273n44, 274n49, 275n53

Vattimo, Liliana, 3, 216, 231

Vattimo, Raffaele, 3

Vattimo and Theology (Guarino), 181

Veneto, 53

Venezuela, 96, 107–108

Venice, 54; patriarch of, 129

Verità e metodo (Gadamer; Vattimo's Italian translation). *See Wahrheit und Methode*

Verità o fede debole? (Vattimo and Girard), 35, 234

veritas qua adaequatio rei et intellectus, 152–153. *See also* truth

"Verso un'ontologia del declino" (Vattimo), 18, 67

Verstehen ("understanding"), 13

Verwindung ("declination/ distortion," "twisting"), 31, 78–79, 81, 105, 178, 294n51

Viano, Carlo Augusto, ix, 66, 87, 164, 256n10, 262n69

Victor Emmanuel II; Victor Emmanuel III. *See* House of Savoy

Vienna: University of, 209; Vienna Circle, 225

Vietnam, 21, 25; Vietnam War, 21–22, 24

violence, xi, xiii, 21, 23– 24, 29–30, 32, 35, 44–45, 56, 61–62, 65, 88–89, 91–92, 106, 108–109, 138–142, 144, 146, 149, 174–176, 181, 200, 203–204, 211, 277n19, 287n17, 293n46; nonviolence, 30, 142, 210

Virgin Mary, 193

Vizzini, Carlo, 94
Vogliamo tutto! ("We want everything!"), workers' slogan, 25
von Balthasar, Hans Urs, 128, 274n44, 274n49
voting, 44, 130, 190

Wahrheit und Methode (Gadamer), 12–13, 227, 229
Wang, Robin R., 209
Ward, Graham, 233
warranted assertability (Dewey), 103, 173
Warwick, University of, 209
Washington, DC, 229, 290n29
Washington Post (newspaper), 48
weakness, 35, 63, 74, 98, 101, 103, 106, 137, 146, 150, 178, 210, 214; weakening, 30, 32–33, 66, 89, 105–106, 114, 119, 138, 145, 153, 202, 211; weak ontology, 33, 35; weak thinking, xi, 18, 64. *See also pensiero debole*
Weak Thought (Vattimo and Rovatti, eds.). *See Il pensiero debole*
Weimar (city), 223
Wenning, Mario, 210
Wertrational ("value-rational action"), 35. *See also* rationality
West, the, x, xii, 20, 25, 32–33, 46, 61, 78–79, 88, 95–97, 116–117, 147–148, 184, 201, 291n33. *See also* Abendland
White House, 166, 252n52
whiteness, 204–206
"Why We Cannot but Call Ourselves Christians" (Croce). *See Perchè non passiamo non dirci cristiani*

"wildcat" actions. *See* direct action
Williams, Delores S., 207
"Will to Power as Art, The" (Vattimo), 64; see *Avventure della differenza*
Wink, Walter, 149
Winter Palace, 27
Wirkungsgeschichtliches Bewußtsein ("historically effected consciousness"), 14, 16
Wisdom, John, 147, 280n30
Wittgenstein, Ludwig, 18, 64, 224–225, 227, 248n15, 279n28, 286n14, 288n20, 298n11
Wizard of Oz, The, 81
Wojtyła, Karol Józef (Pope John Paul II). *See* popes
"Womanist Theology: Black Women's Voices" (Williams), 207
women's liberation movement. *See* liberation
workers, 20, 22–23, 25, 41, 44–46, 48, 53–59, 129, 195, 197, 227, 243n60, 246n5, 250n30, 254n63, 259n37, 300n22; working-class, 3, 6–7, 23, 52–53, 55, 58, 195, 243n53, 250n36; workerism. *See* Autonomous Workers. *See also* operaismo; Autonomia Operaia; Potere Operaio; unions
World Conference of Philosophy, 234
world-viewing, 136
World War I, 44, 224
World War II, 4, 20, 46–47, 95, 189
Wright, Steve, 55
wuwei, 210

X. *See* Twitter
Xie, Ming, 210
xin, 210

Years of Lead, 19, 30. *See also* Anni di Piombo
yi, 210
Young Christian Workers (Kristene Arbeidersjeugd/Jeunesse ouvrière chrétienne), 195

Zabala, Santiago, x, 29–30, 33, 35, 40, 87, 95–101, 104–110, 210, 234–235, 263n73
Zawadzki, Andrzej, 86
Zeroth law of thermodynamics, 175
zhi, 210
Zimmerman, Jens, 235
Žižek, Slavoj, 2, 177
Zweckrationalität ("instrumental reason"), 83, 210. *See also* rationality

GPSR Authorized Representative: Easy Access System Europe, Mustamäe tee 50, 10621 Tallinn, Estonia, gpsr.requests@easproject.com

www.ingramcontent.com/pod-product-compliance
Lightning Source LLC
Chambersburg PA
CBHW022025290426
44109CB00014B/753